W9-CFL-529

GENERAL MOTORS | TRAILBLAZER
2002-09 REPAIR MANUAL

CHILTON'S

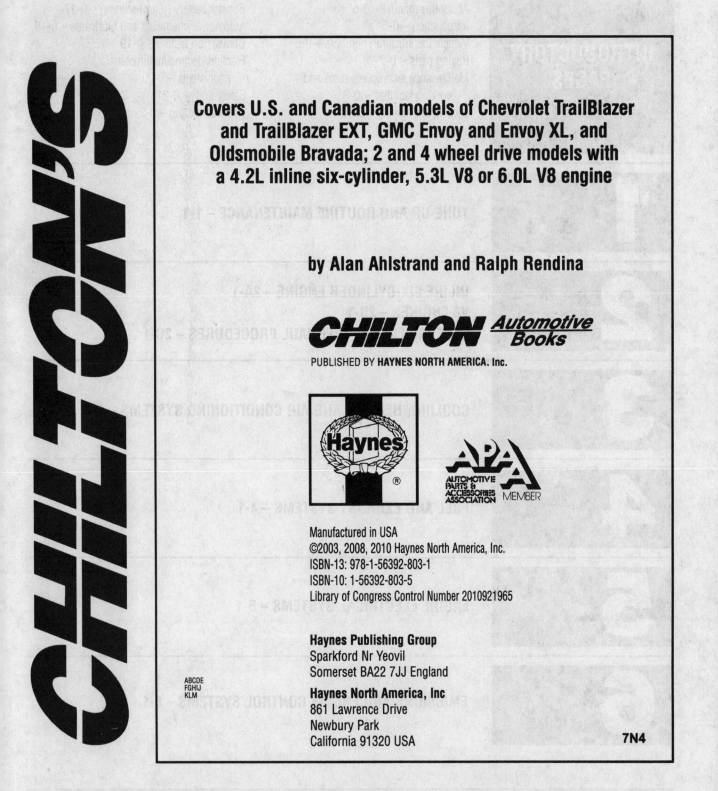

Covers U.S. and Canadian models of Chevrolet TrailBlazer and TrailBlazer EXT, GMC Envoy and Envoy XL, and Oldsmobile Bravada; 2 and 4 wheel drive models with a 4.2L inline six-cylinder, 5.3L V8 or 6.0L V8 engine

by Alan Ahlstrand and Ralph Rendina

CHILTON Automotive Books

PUBLISHED BY **HAYNES NORTH AMERICA. Inc.**

Haynes®

AUTOMOTIVE PARTS & ACCESSORIES ASSOCIATION MEMBER

Manufactured in USA
©2003, 2008, 2010 Haynes North America, Inc.
ISBN-13: 978-1-56392-803-1
ISBN-10: 1-56392-803-5
Library of Congress Control Number 2010921965

Haynes Publishing Group
Sparkford Nr Yeovil
Somerset BA22 7JJ England

Haynes North America, Inc
861 Lawrence Drive
Newbury Park
California 91320 USA

ABCDE
FGHIJ
KLM

7N4

Contents

INTRODUCTORY PAGES

1 TUNE-UP AND ROUTINE MAINTENANCE – 1-1

2 INLINE SIX-CYLINDER ENGINE – 2A-1
V8 ENGINES – 2B-1
GENERAL ENGINE OVERHAUL PROCEDURES – 2C-1

3 COOLING, HEATING AND AIR CONDITIONING SYSTEMS – 3-1

4 FUEL AND EXHAUST SYSTEMS – 4-1

5 ENGINE ELECTRICAL SYSTEMS – 5-1

6 EMISSIONS AND ENGINE CONTROL SYSTEMS – 6-1

2002 Chevrolet TrailBlazer

ACKNOWLEDGEMENTS

Wiring diagrams provided by Valley Forge Technical Information Services.

About this manual

ITS PURPOSE

The purpose of this manual is to help you get the best value from your vehicle. It can do so in several ways. It can help you decide what work must be done, even if you choose to have it done by a dealer service department or a repair shop; it provides information and procedures for routine maintenance and servicing; and it offers diagnostic and repair procedures to follow when trouble occurs.

We hope you use the manual to tackle the work yourself. For many simpler jobs, doing it yourself may be quicker than arranging an appointment to get the vehicle into a shop and making the trips to leave it and pick it up. More importantly, a lot of money can be saved by avoiding the expense the shop must pass on to you to cover its labor and overhead costs. An added benefit is the sense of satisfaction and accomplishment that you feel after doing the job yourself.

USING THE MANUAL

The manual is divided into Chapters. Each Chapter is divided into numbered Sections, which are headed in bold type between horizontal lines. Each Section consists of consecutively numbered paragraphs.

At the beginning of each numbered Section you will be referred to any illustrations which apply to the procedures in that Section. The reference numbers used in illustration captions pinpoint the pertinent Section and the Step within that Section. That is, illustration 3.2 means the illustration refers to Section 3 and Step (or paragraph) 2 within that Section.

Procedures, once described in the text, are not normally repeated. When it's necessary to refer to another Chapter, the reference will be given as Chapter and Section number. Cross references given without use of the word "Chapter" apply to Sections and/or paragraphs in the same Chapter. For example, "see Section 8" means in the same Chapter.

References to the left or right side of the vehicle assume you are sitting in the driver's seat, facing forward.

Even though we have prepared this manual with extreme care, neither the publisher nor the author can accept responsibility for any errors in, or omissions from, the information given.

➥**NOTE**

A *Note* provides information necessary to properly complete a procedure or information which will make the procedure easier to understand.

✳✳ **CAUTION**

A *Caution* provides a special procedure or special steps which must be taken while completing the procedure where the Caution is found. Not heeding a Caution can result in damage to the assembly being worked on.

✳✳ **WARNING**

A *Warning* provides a special procedure or special steps which must be taken while completing the procedure where the Warning is found. Not heeding a Warning can result in personal injury.

Introduction

Introduced in 2002, the Chevrolet Trailblazer, Oldsmobile Bravada and the GMC Envoy are the newest additions to GM's offering of SUVs. These vehicles are available in a number of configurations that include 2WD, 4WD, standard five passenger and extended-chassis seven passenger models. The vehicles covered in this manual are equipped with either a 4.2L in-line six cylinder, a 5.3L V8 or a 6.0L V8 engine, and a 4-speed automatic transmission with overdrive.

The chassis layout is conventional with a front-mounted engine transmitting power to the rear axle and wheels. On 4WD models, a transfer case transmits power to the front differential, then to the wheels through independent driveaxles.

These models feature independent front suspension with coil spring/shock absorber units. At the rear, all models have a solid rear axle supported by four trailing arms, a track bar, coil springs and shock absorbers.

The power-assisted steering is rack-and-pinion. The steering unit is mounted to the frame aft of the front wheels. All models have power assisted disc-type front and rear brakes system with Anti-lock Brake System (ABS) standard.

Vehicle identification numbers

VEHICLE IDENTIFICATION NUMBERS

Modifications are a continuing and unpublicized process in vehicle manufacturing. Since spare parts manuals and lists are compiled on a numerical basis, the individual vehicle numbers are essential to correctly identify the component required.

VEHICLE IDENTIFICATION NUMBER (VIN)

The Vehicle Identification Number (VIN), which appears on the Vehicle Certificate of Title and Registration, is also embossed on a gray plate located on the left (driver's side) corner of the dashboard, near the windshield (see illustration). The VIN tells you when and where a vehicle was manufactured, its country of origin, make, type, passenger safety system, line, series, body style, engine and assembly plant.

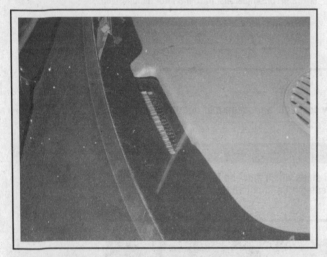

The VIN plate is visible from the outside of the vehicle, through the driver's side of the windshield

VIN ENGINE AND MODEL YEAR CODES

Two particularly important pieces of information found in the VIN are the engine code and the model year code. Counting from the left, the engine code letter designation is the 8th character and the model year code is the 10th character.

On the models covered in this manual the engine codes are:

S.....................4.4L inline six cylinder (LL8)
P.....................5.3L V8 (LM4)
M....................5.3L V8 (LH6)
H 6.0L V8 (LS2)

On the models covered in this manual the model year codes are:

2...............................2002
3...............................2003
4...............................2004
5...............................2005
6...............................2006
7...............................2007

VEHICLE SAFETY CERTIFICATION LABEL

The Vehicle Safety Certification label is attached to the rear edge of the driver's door (see illustration). The label contains the name of the manufacturer, the month and year of production, the Gross Vehicle Weight Rating (GVWR), the Gross Axle Weight Rating (GAWR) and the certification statement. On most models, the label also includes the OEM tire sizes and pressures.

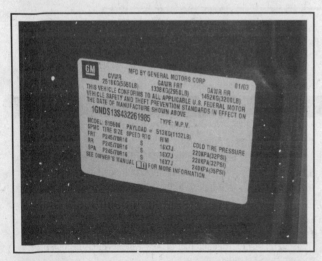

The Vehicle Safety Certification label is affixed to the driver's side door end or post.

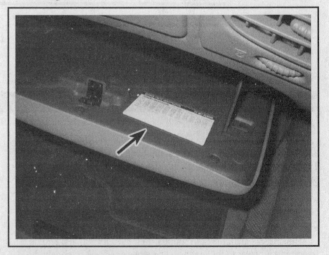

The Service Parts Identification label contains information on options and trim/paint codes

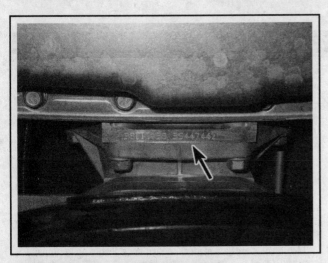

Typical automatic transmission identification number location

Location of the transfer case identification tag

SERVICE PARTS IDENTIFICATION LABEL

Located on the inside of the glove compartment door, this label contains information about the options on your vehicle and the paint and trim codes (see illustration). This information is important when ordering parts or when bodywork and repainting is done.

ENGINE IDENTIFICATION NUMBER (EIN)

The inline six cylinder Engine Identification Number (EIN) is stamped into the lower left front of the engine block just above the oil pan sealing surface. Additionally, an engine I.D. label is affixed to the left rear of the valve cover.

TRANSMISSION IDENTIFICATION NUMBER (TIN)

The Transmission Identification Number (TIN) is stamped or etched into the bottom of the transmission case, to the rear of the fluid pan (see illustration).

TRANSFER CASE IDENTIFICATION LABEL

The transfer case identification information is on a tag affixed to the rear side of the case (see illustration).

Buying parts

Replacement parts are available from many sources, which generally fall into one of two categories - authorized dealer parts departments and independent retail auto parts stores. Our advice concerning these parts is as follows:

Retail auto parts stores: Good auto parts stores will stock frequently needed components which wear out relatively fast, such as clutch components, exhaust systems, brake parts, tune-up parts, etc. These stores often supply new or reconditioned parts on an exchange basis, which can save a considerable amount of money. Discount auto parts stores are often very good places to buy materials and parts needed for general vehicle maintenance such as oil, grease, filters, spark plugs, belts, touch-up paint, bulbs, etc. They also usually sell tools and general accessories, have convenient hours, charge lower prices and can often be found not far from home.

Authorized dealer parts department: This is the best source for parts which are unique to the vehicle and not generally available elsewhere (such as major engine parts, transmission parts, trim pieces, etc.).

Warranty information: If the vehicle is still covered under warranty, be sure that any replacement parts purchased - regardless of the source - do not invalidate the warranty!

To be sure of obtaining the correct parts, have engine and chassis numbers available and, if possible, take the old parts along for positive identification.

MAINTENANCE TECHNIQUES

There are a number of techniques involved in maintenance and repair that will be referred to throughout this manual. Application of these techniques will enable the home mechanic to be more efficient, better organized and capable of performing the various tasks properly, which will ensure that the repair job is thorough and complete.

Fasteners

Fasteners are nuts, bolts, studs and screws used to hold two or more parts together. There are a few things to keep in mind when working with fasteners. Almost all of them use a locking device of some type, either a lockwasher, locknut, locking tab or thread adhesive. All threaded fasteners should be clean and straight, with undamaged threads and undamaged corners on the hex head where the wrench fits. Develop the habit of replacing all damaged nuts and bolts with new ones. Special locknuts with nylon or fiber inserts can only be used once. If they are removed, they lose their locking ability and must be replaced with new ones.

Rusted nuts and bolts should be treated with a penetrating fluid to ease removal and prevent breakage. Some mechanics use turpentine in a spout-type oil can, which works quite well. After applying the rust penetrant, let it work for a few minutes before trying to loosen the nut or bolt. Badly rusted fasteners may have to be chiseled or sawed off or removed with a special nut breaker, available at tool stores.

If a bolt or stud breaks off in an assembly, it can be drilled and removed with a special tool commonly available for this purpose. Most automotive machine shops can perform this task, as well as other repair procedures, such as the repair of threaded holes that have been stripped out.

Flat washers and lockwashers, when removed from an assembly, should always be replaced exactly as removed. Replace any damaged washers with new ones. Never use a lockwasher on any soft metal surface (such as aluminum), thin sheet metal or plastic.

Fastener sizes

For a number of reasons, automobile manufacturers are making wider and wider use of metric fasteners. Therefore, it is important to be able to tell the difference between standard (sometimes called U.S. or SAE) and metric hardware, since they cannot be interchanged.

All bolts, whether standard or metric, are sized according to diameter, thread pitch and length. For example, a standard 1/2 - 13 x 1 bolt is 1/2 inch in diameter, has 13 threads per inch and is 1 inch long. An M12 - 1.75 x 25 metric bolt is 12 mm in diameter, has a thread pitch of 1.75 mm (the distance between threads) and is 25 mm long. The two bolts are nearly identical, and easily confused, but they are not interchangeable.

In addition to the differences in diameter, thread pitch and length, metric and standard bolts can also be distinguished by examining the bolt heads. To begin with, the distance across the flats on a standard bolt head is measured in inches, while the same dimension on a metric bolt is sized in millimeters (the same is true for nuts). As a result, a standard wrench should not be used on a metric bolt and a metric wrench should not be used on a standard bolt. Also, most standard bolts have slashes

radiating out from the center of the head to denote the grade or strength of the bolt, which is an indication of the amount of torque that can be applied to it. The greater the number of slashes, the greater the strength of the bolt. Grades 0 through 5 are commonly used on automobiles. Metric bolts have a property class (grade) number, rather than a slash, molded into their heads to indicate bolt strength. In this case, the higher the number, the stronger the bolt. Property class numbers 8.8, 9.8 and 10.9 are commonly used on automobiles.

Strength markings can also be used to distinguish standard hex nuts from metric hex nuts. Many standard nuts have dots stamped into one side, while metric nuts are marked with a number. The greater the number of dots, or the higher the number, the greater the strength of the nut.

Metric studs are also marked on their ends according to property class (grade). Larger studs are numbered (the same as metric bolts), while smaller studs carry a geometric code to denote grade.

It should be noted that many fasteners, especially Grades 0 through 2, have no distinguishing marks on them. When such is the case, the only way to determine whether it is standard or metric is to measure the thread pitch or compare it to a known fastener of the same size.

Standard fasteners are often referred to as SAE, as opposed to metric. However, it should be noted that SAE technically refers to a non-metric fine thread fastener only. Coarse thread non-metric fasteners are referred to as USS sizes.

Since fasteners of the same size (both standard and metric) may have different strength ratings, be sure to reinstall any bolts, studs or nuts removed from your vehicle in their original locations. Also, when replacing a fastener with a new one, make sure that the new one has a strength rating equal to or greater than the original.

Tightening sequences and procedures

Most threaded fasteners should be tightened to a specific torque value (torque is the twisting force applied to a threaded component such as a nut or bolt). Overtightening the fastener can weaken it and cause it to break, while undertightening can cause it to eventually come loose. Bolts, screws and studs, depending on the material they are made of and their thread diameters, have specific torque values, many of which are noted in the Specifications at the end of each Chapter. Be sure to follow the torque recommendations closely. For fasteners not assigned a specific torque, a general torque value chart is presented here as a guide. These torque values are for dry (unlubricated) fasteners threaded into steel or cast iron (not aluminum). As was previously mentioned, the size and grade of a fastener determine the amount of torque that can safely be applied to it. The figures listed here are approximate for Grade 2 and Grade 3 fasteners. Higher grades can tolerate higher torque values.

Fasteners laid out in a pattern, such as cylinder head bolts, oil pan bolts, differential cover bolts, etc., must be loosened or tightened in sequence to avoid warping the component. This sequence will normally be shown in the appropriate Chapter. If a specific pattern is not given, the following procedures can be used to prevent warping.

Initially, the bolts or nuts should be assembled finger-tight only. Next, they should be tightened one full turn each, in a criss-cross or diagonal pattern. After each one has been tightened one full turn, return to the first one and tighten them all one-half turn, following the same

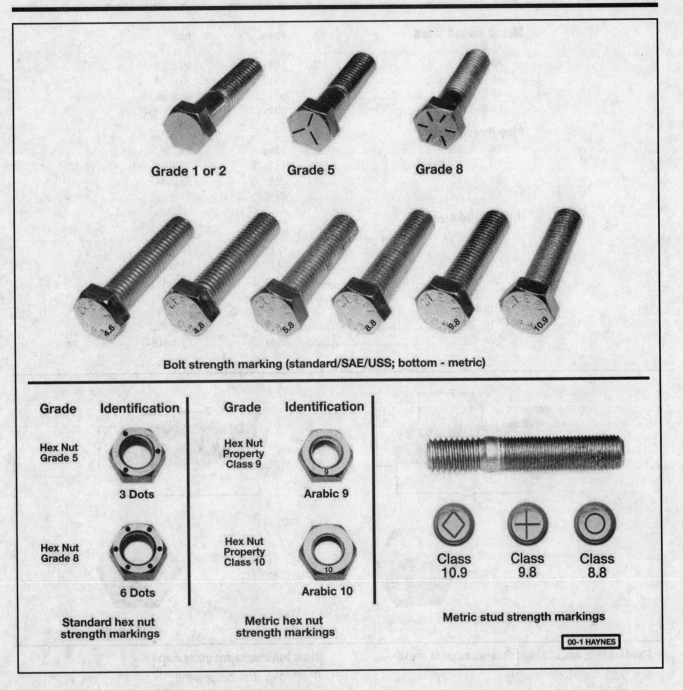

Grade 1 or 2 Grade 5 Grade 8

Bolt strength marking (standard/SAE/USS; bottom - metric)

Grade	Identification	Grade	Identification
Hex Nut Grade 5	3 Dots	Hex Nut Property Class 9	Arabic 9
Hex Nut Grade 8	6 Dots	Hex Nut Property Class 10	Arabic 10

Standard hex nut strength markings

Metric hex nut strength markings

Class 10.9   Class 9.8   Class 8.8

Metric stud strength markings

00-1 HAYNES

pattern. Finally, tighten each of them one-quarter turn at a time until each fastener has been tightened to the proper torque. To loosen and remove the fasteners, the procedure would be reversed.

Component disassembly

Component disassembly should be done with care and purpose to help ensure that the parts go back together properly. Always keep track of the sequence in which parts are removed. Make note of special characteristics or marks on parts that can be installed more than one way, such as a grooved thrust washer on a shaft. It is a good idea to lay the disassembled parts out on a clean surface in the order that they were removed. It may also be helpful to make sketches or take instant photos of components before removal.

When removing fasteners from a component, keep track of their locations. Sometimes threading a bolt back in a part, or putting the washers and nut back on a stud, can prevent mix-ups later. If nuts and bolts cannot be returned to their original locations, they should be kept in a compartmented box or a series of small boxes. A cupcake or muffin tin is ideal for this purpose, since each cavity can hold the bolts and nuts from a particular area (i.e. oil pan bolts, valve cover bolts, engine

Metric thread sizes	Ft-lbs	Nm
M-6	6 to 9	9 to 12
M-8	14 to 21	19 to 28
M-10	28 to 40	38 to 54
M-12	50 to 71	68 to 96
M-14	80 to 140	109 to 154

Pipe thread sizes		
1/8	5 to 8	7 to 10
1/4	12 to 18	17 to 24
3/8	22 to 33	30 to 44
1/2	25 to 35	34 to 47

U.S. thread sizes		
1/4 - 20	6 to 9	9 to 12
5/16 - 18	12 to 18	17 to 24
5/16 - 24	14 to 20	19 to 27
3/8 - 16	22 to 32	30 to 43
3/8 - 24	27 to 38	37 to 51
7/16 - 14	40 to 55	55 to 74
7/16 - 20	40 to 60	55 to 81
1/2 - 13	55 to 80	75 to 108

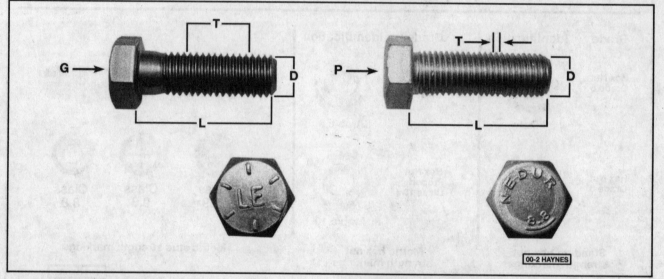

Standard (SAE and USS) bolt dimensions/grade marks

G   Grade marks (bolt strength)
L   Length (in inches)
T   Thread pitch (number of threads per inch)
D   Nominal diameter (in inches)

Metric bolt dimensions/grade marks

P   Property class (bolt strength)
L   Length (in millimeters)
T   Thread pitch (distance between threads in millimeters)
D   Diameter

mount bolts, etc.). A pan of this type is especially helpful when working on assemblies with very small parts, such as the carburetor, alternator, valve train or interior dash and trim pieces. The cavities can be marked with paint or tape to identify the contents.

Whenever wiring looms, harnesses or connectors are separated, it is a good idea to identify the two halves with numbered pieces of masking tape so they can be easily reconnected.

Gasket sealing surfaces

Throughout any vehicle, gaskets are used to seal the mating surfaces between two parts and keep lubricants, fluids, vacuum or pressure contained in an assembly.

Many times these gaskets are coated with a liquid or paste-type gasket sealing compound before assembly. Age, heat and pressure can sometimes cause the two parts to stick together so tightly that they are very difficult to separate. Often, the assembly can be loosened by striking it with a soft-face hammer near the mating surfaces. A regular hammer can be used if a block of wood is placed between the hammer and the part. Do not hammer on cast parts or parts that could be easily damaged. With any particularly stubborn part, always recheck to make sure that every fastener has been removed.

Avoid using a screwdriver or bar to pry apart an assembly, as they

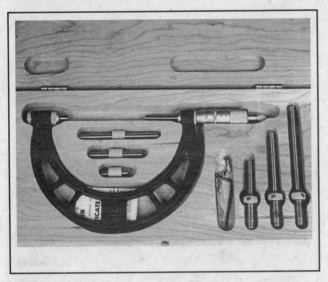

Micrometer set

Dial indicator set

can easily mar the gasket sealing surfaces of the parts, which must remain smooth. If prying is absolutely necessary, use an old broom handle, but keep in mind that extra clean up will be necessary if the wood splinters.

After the parts are separated, the old gasket must be carefully scraped off and the gasket surfaces cleaned. Stubborn gasket material can be soaked with rust penetrant or treated with a special chemical to soften it so it can be easily scraped off.

❊❊ CAUTION:

Never use gasket removal solutions or caustic chemicals on plastic or other composite components.

A scraper can be fashioned from a piece of copper tubing by flattening and sharpening one end. Copper is recommended because it is usually softer than the surfaces to be scraped, which reduces the chance of gouging the part. Some gaskets can be removed with a wire brush, but regardless of the method used, the mating surfaces must be left clean and smooth. If for some reason the gasket surface is gouged, then a gasket sealer thick enough to fill scratches will have to be used during reassembly of the components. For most applications, a non-drying (or semi-drying) gasket sealer should be used.

Hose removal tips

❊❊ WARNING:

If the vehicle is equipped with air conditioning, do not disconnect any of the A/C hoses without first having the system depressurized by a dealer service department or a service station.

Hose removal precautions closely parallel gasket removal precautions. Avoid scratching or gouging the surface that the hose mates against or the connection may leak. This is especially true for radiator hoses. Because of various chemical reactions, the rubber in hoses can bond itself to the metal spigot that the hose fits over. To remove a hose, first loosen the hose clamps that secure it to the spigot. Then, with slip-joint pliers, grab the hose at the clamp and rotate it around the spigot. Work it back and forth until it is completely free, then pull it off. Silicone or other lubricants will ease removal if they can be applied between the hose and the outside of the spigot. Apply the same lubricant to the inside of the hose and the outside of the spigot to simplify installation.

As a last resort (and if the hose is to be replaced with a new one anyway), the rubber can be slit with a knife and the hose peeled from the spigot. If this must be done, be careful that the metal connection is not damaged.

If a hose clamp is broken or damaged, do not reuse it. Wire-type clamps usually weaken with age, so it is a good idea to replace them with screw-type clamps whenever a hose is removed.

TOOLS

A selection of good tools is a basic requirement for anyone who plans to maintain and repair his or her own vehicle. For the owner who has few tools, the initial investment might seem high, but when compared to the spiraling costs of professional auto maintenance and repair, it is a wise one.

To help the owner decide which tools are needed to perform the tasks detailed in this manual, the following tool lists are offered: *Maintenance and minor repair, Repair/overhaul and Special.*

The newcomer to practical mechanics should start off with the *maintenance and minor repair* tool kit, which is adequate for the simpler jobs performed on a vehicle. Then, as confidence and experience grow, the owner can tackle more difficult tasks, buying additional tools as they are needed. Eventually the basic kit will be expanded into the *repair and overhaul* tool set. Over a period of time, the experienced do-it-yourselfer will assemble a tool set complete enough for most repair and overhaul procedures and will add tools from the special category when it is felt that the expense is justified by the frequency of use.

Maintenance and minor repair tool kit

The tools in this list should be considered the minimum required for performance of routine maintenance, servicing and minor repair work. We recommend the purchase of combination wrenches (box-end and open-end combined in one wrench). While more expensive than open end wrenches, they offer the advantages of both types of wrench.

Combination wrench set (1/4-inch to 1 inch or 6 mm to 19 mm)
Adjustable wrench, 8 inch
Spark plug wrench with rubber insert

Spark plug gap adjusting tool
Feeler gauge set
Brake bleeder wrench
Standard screwdriver (5/16-inch x 6 inch)
Phillips screwdriver (No. 2 x 6 inch)
Combination pliers - 6 inch
Hacksaw and assortment of blades
Tire pressure gauge
Grease gun

Oil can
Fine emery cloth
Wire brush
Battery post and cable cleaning tool
Oil filter wrench
Funnel (medium size)
Safety goggles
Jackstands (2)
Drain pan

Dial caliper

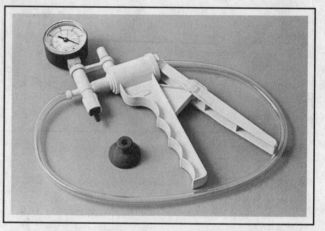

Hand-operated vacuum pump

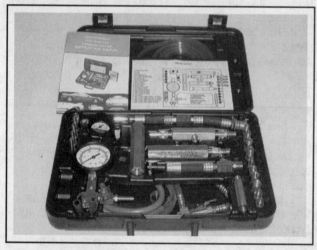

Fuel pressure gauge set

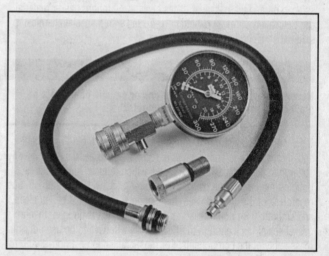

Compression gauge with spark plug hole adapter

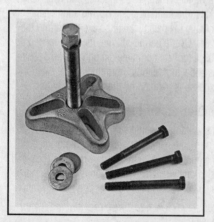

Damper/steering wheel puller

General purpose puller

Hydraulic lifter removal tool

➡Note: If basic tune-ups are going to be part of routine maintenance, it will be necessary to purchase a good quality stroboscopic timing light and combination tachometer/dwell meter. Although they are included in the list of special tools, it is mentioned here because they are absolutely necessary for tuning most vehicles properly.

Repair and overhaul tool set

These tools are essential for anyone who plans to perform major repairs and are in addition to those in the maintenance and minor repair tool kit. Included is a comprehensive set of sockets which, though expensive, are invaluable because of their versatility, especially when various extensions and drives are available. We recommend the 1/2-inch drive over the 3/8-inch drive. Although the larger drive is bulky and more expensive, it has the capacity of accepting a very wide range of large sockets. Ideally, however, the mechanic should have a 3/8-inch drive set and a 1/2-inch drive set.

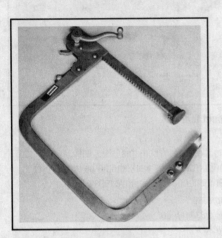
Valve spring compressor

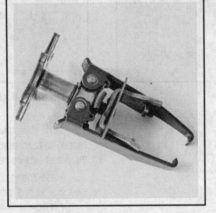
Valve spring compressor

Ridge reamer

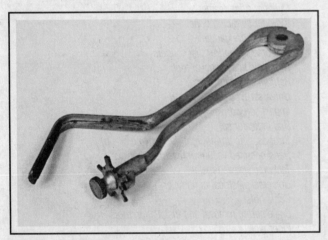
Piston ring groove cleaning tool

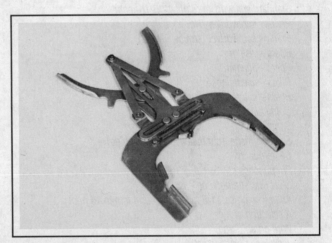
Ring removal/installation tool

Ring compressor

Cylinder hone

Brake hold-down spring tool

Torque angle gauge

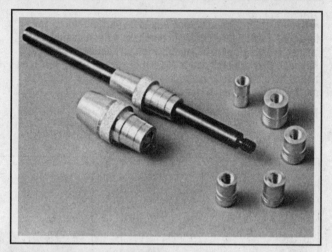

Clutch plate alignment tool

Socket set(s)
Reversible ratchet
Extension - 10 inch
Universal joint
Torque wrench (same size drive as sockets)
Ball peen hammer - 8 ounce
Soft-face hammer (plastic/rubber)
Standard screwdriver (1/4-inch x 6 inch)
Standard screwdriver (stubby - 5/16-inch)
Phillips screwdriver (No. 3 x 8 inch)
Phillips screwdriver (stubby - No. 2)
Pliers - vise grip
Pliers - lineman's
Pliers - needle nose
Pliers - snap-ring (internal and external)
Cold chisel - 1/2-inch
Scribe
Scraper (made from flattened copper tubing)
Centerpunch
Pin punches (1/16, 1/8, 3/16-inch)
Steel rule/straightedge - 12 inch
Allen wrench set (1/8 to 3/8-inch or 4 mm to 10 mm)
A selection of files
Wire brush (large)
Jackstands (second set)
Jack (scissor or hydraulic type)

➡**Note: Another tool which is often useful is an electric drill with a chuck capacity of 3/8-inch and a set of good quality drill bits.**

Special tools

The tools in this list include those which are not used regularly, are expensive to buy, or which need to be used in accordance with their manufacturer's instructions. Unless these tools will be used frequently, it is not very economical to purchase many of them. A consideration would be to split the cost and use between yourself and a friend or friends. In addition, most of these tools can be obtained from a tool rental shop on a temporary basis.

This list primarily contains only those tools and instruments widely available to the public, and not those special tools produced by the vehicle manufacturer for distribution to dealer service departments. Occasionally, references to the manufacturer's special tools are included in the text of this manual. Generally, an alternative method of doing the job without the special tool is offered. However, sometimes there is no alternative to their use. Where this is the case, and the tool cannot be purchased or borrowed, the work should be turned over to the dealer service department or an automotive repair shop.

Valve spring compressor
Piston ring groove cleaning tool
Piston ring compressor
Piston ring installation tool
Cylinder compression gauge
Cylinder ridge reamer
Cylinder surfacing hone
Cylinder bore gauge
Micrometers and/or dial calipers
Hydraulic lifter removal tool
Balljoint separator
Universal-type puller
Impact screwdriver
Dial indicator set
Stroboscopic timing light (inductive pick-up)
Hand operated vacuum/pressure pump
Tachometer/dwell meter
Universal electrical multimeter
Cable hoist
Brake spring removal and installation tools
Floor jack

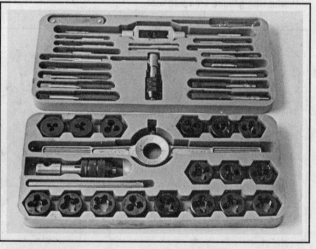

Tap and die set

Buying tools

For the do-it-yourselfer who is just starting to get involved in vehicle maintenance and repair, there are a number of options available when purchasing tools. If maintenance and minor repair is the extent of the work to be done, the purchase of individual tools is satisfactory. If, on the other hand, extensive work is planned, it would be a good idea to purchase a modest tool set from one of the large retail chain stores. A set can usually be bought at a substantial savings over the individual tool prices, and they often come with a tool box. As additional tools are needed, add-on sets, individual tools and a larger tool box can be purchased to expand the tool selection. Building a tool set gradually allows the cost of the tools to be spread over a longer period of time and gives the mechanic the freedom to choose only those tools that will actually be used.

Tool stores will often be the only source of some of the special tools that are needed, but regardless of where tools are bought, try to avoid cheap ones, especially when buying screwdrivers and sockets, because they won't last very long. The expense involved in replacing cheap tools will eventually be greater than the initial cost of quality tools.

Care and maintenance of tools

Good tools are expensive, so it makes sense to treat them with respect. Keep them clean and in usable condition and store them properly when not in use. Always wipe off any dirt, grease or metal chips before putting them away. Never leave tools lying around in the work area. Upon completion of a job, always check closely under the hood for tools that may have been left there so they won't get lost during a test drive.

Some tools, such as screwdrivers, pliers, wrenches and sockets, can be hung on a panel mounted on the garage or workshop wall, while others should be kept in a tool box or tray. Measuring instruments, gauges, meters, etc. must be carefully stored where they cannot be damaged by weather or impact from other tools.

When tools are used with care and stored properly, they will last a very long time. Even with the best of care, though, tools will wear out if used frequently. When a tool is damaged or worn out, replace it. Subsequent jobs will be safer and more enjoyable if you do.

HOW TO REPAIR DAMAGED THREADS

Sometimes, the internal threads of a nut or bolt hole can become stripped, usually from overtightening. Stripping threads is an all-too-common occurrence, especially when working with aluminum parts, because aluminum is so soft that it easily strips out.

Usually, external or internal threads are only partially stripped. After they've been cleaned up with a tap or die, they'll still work. Sometimes, however, threads are badly damaged. When this happens, you've got three choices:

1) *Drill and tap the hole to the next suitable oversize and install a larger diameter bolt, screw or stud.*

2) *Drill and tap the hole to accept a threaded plug, then drill and tap the plug to the original screw size. You can also buy a plug already threaded to the original size. Then you simply drill a hole to the specified size, then run the threaded plug into the hole with a bolt and jam nut. Once the plug is fully seated, remove the jam nut and bolt.*

3) *The third method uses a patented thread repair kit like Heli-Coil or Slimsert. These easy-to-use kits are designed to repair damaged threads in straight-through holes and blind holes. Both are available as kits which can handle a variety of sizes and thread patterns. Drill the hole, then tap it with the special included tap. Install the Heli-Coil and the hole is back to its original diameter and thread pitch.*

Regardless of which method you use, be sure to proceed calmly and carefully. A little impatience or carelessness during one of these relatively simple procedures can ruin your whole day's work and cost you a bundle if you wreck an expensive part.

WORKING FACILITIES

Not to be overlooked when discussing tools is the workshop. If anything more than routine maintenance is to be carried out, some sort of suitable work area is essential.

It is understood, and appreciated, that many home mechanics do not have a good workshop or garage available, and end up removing an engine or doing major repairs outside. It is recommended, however, that the overhaul or repair be completed under the cover of a roof.

A clean, flat workbench or table of comfortable working height is an absolute necessity. The workbench should be equipped with a vise that has a jaw opening of at least four inches.

As mentioned previously, some clean, dry storage space is also required for tools, as well as the lubricants, fluids, cleaning solvents, etc. which soon become necessary.

Sometimes waste oil and fluids, drained from the engine or cooling system during normal maintenance or repairs, present a disposal problem. To avoid pouring them on the ground or into a sewage system, pour the used fluids into large containers, seal them with caps and take them to an authorized disposal site or recycling center. Plastic jugs, such as old antifreeze containers, are ideal for this purpose.

Always keep a supply of old newspapers and clean rags available. Old towels are excellent for mopping up spills. Many mechanics use rolls of paper towels for most work because they are readily available and disposable. To help keep the area under the vehicle clean, a large cardboard box can be cut open and flattened to protect the garage or shop floor.

Whenever working over a painted surface, such as when leaning over a fender to service something under the hood, always cover it with an old blanket or bedspread to protect the finish. Vinyl covered pads, made especially for this purpose, are available at auto parts stores.

Jacking and towing

JACKING

The jack supplied with the vehicle should only be used for raising the vehicle when changing a tire or placing jackstands under the frame. NEVER work under the vehicle or start the engine when the vehicle supported only by a jack.

The vehicle should be parked on level ground with the wheels blocked, the parking brake applied and the transmission in Park. If the vehicle is parked alongside the roadway, or in any other hazardous situation, turn on the emergency hazard flashers. If a tire is to be changed, loosen the lug nuts one-half turn before raising off the ground.

Place the jack under the vehicle in the indicated position (see illustrations). Operate the jack with a slow, smooth motion until the wheel is raised off the ground. Remove the lug nuts, pull off the wheel, install the spare and thread the lug nuts back on with the beveled side facing in. Tighten the lug nuts snugly, lower the vehicle until some weight is on the wheel, then tighten them completely in a criss-cross pattern and remove the jack.

TOWING

Equipment specifically designed for towing should be used and attached to the main structural members of the vehicle. Optional tow hooks may be attached to the frame at both ends of the vehicle; they are intended for emergency use only, for rescuing a stranded vehicle. Do not use the tow hooks for highway towing. Stand clear when using tow straps or chains (they may break, causing serious injury.)

The manufacturer recommends that these vehicles be towed only by wheel-lift equipment or a flatbed car-carrier.

Safety is a major consideration when towing and all applicable state and local laws must be obeyed. In addition to a tow bar, a safety chain must be used for all towing.

Two-wheel drive vehicles may be towed with the rear wheels on a towing dolly with no mileage restriction (at posted highway speeds). If the front wheels are on the dolly, speed should be no more than 35 mph for no more than 50 miles, or damage may be done to the transmission.

Four-wheel drive vehicles with a transfer case selector switch on the instrument panel should be towed with the transfer case in Neutral. With the front end lifted, towing is not limited, but if the rear end is lifted and the front is on the ground, towing is restricted to a maximum of 50 miles distance.

Four-wheel drive vehicles without a transfer case selector switch on the instrument panel should only be towed from the front, with the front wheels raised or, preferably, on a flat-bed carrier.

If any vehicle is to be towed with the front wheels on the ground and the rear wheels raised, the ignition key must be turned to the OFF position to unlock the steering column and a steering wheel clamping device designed for towing must be used or damage to the steering column lock may occur.

Front jacking location - make sure the jack head securely engages the cutout in the frame

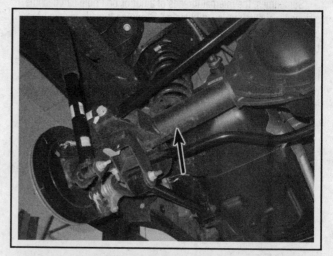

Rear jacking location - the jack must be positioned directly under the axle tube (do NOT place the jack under the trailing arm or stabilizer bar)

Booster battery (jump) starting

Observe these precautions when using a booster battery to start a vehicle:

a) *Before connecting the booster battery, make sure the ignition switch is in the Off position.*

b) *Turn off the lights, heater and other electrical loads.*

c) *Your eyes should be shielded. Safety goggles are a good idea.*

d) *Make sure the booster battery is the same voltage as the dead one in the vehicle.*

e) *The two vehicles MUST NOT TOUCH each other!*

f) *Make sure the transmission in each vehicle is in Neutral (manual) or Park (automatic).*

g) *If the booster battery is not a maintenance-free type, remove the vent caps and lay a cloth over the vent holes.*

The battery on these vehicles is located in the left front corner of the engine compartment.

Connect the red jumper cable to the positive (+) terminals of each battery (see illustration).

Connect one end of the black cable to the negative (-) terminal of the booster battery. The other end of this cable should be connected to a good ground, such as a bracket or bolt on the engine block. If your vehicle is the one with the dead battery, connect the negative cable to the engine lifting bracket at the left front of the engine. Make sure the cable will not come into contact with the fan, drivebelts or other moving parts of the engine.

Start the engine using the booster battery, then run the booster vehicle at a fast idle for a few minutes to instill some charge in the dead battery. Let the engine idle, then disconnect the jumper cables in the reverse order of connection. The vehicle with the dead battery may have to be driven for 20 minutes or more to sufficiently recharge the battery for independent starting.

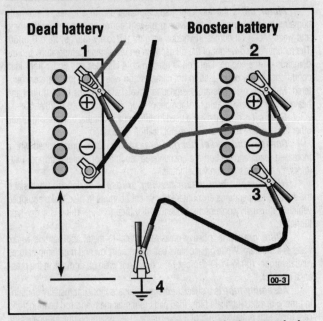

Make the booster battery cable connections in the numerical order shown (note that the negative cable of the booster battery is NOT attached to the negative terminal of the dead battery)

Automotive chemicals and lubricants

A number of automotive chemicals and lubricants are available for use during vehicle maintenance and repair. They include a wide variety of products ranging from cleaning solvents and degreasers to lubricants and protective sprays for rubber, plastic and vinyl.

CLEANERS

Carburetor cleaner and choke cleaner is a strong solvent for gum, varnish and carbon. Most carburetor cleaners leave a dry-type lubricant film which will not harden or gum up. Because of this film it is not recommended for use on electrical components.

Brake system cleaner is used to remove brake dust, grease and brake fluid from the brake system, where clean surfaces are absolutely necessary. It leaves no residue and often eliminates brake squeal caused by contaminants.

Electrical cleaner removes oxidation, corrosion and carbon deposits from electrical contacts, restoring full current flow. It can also be used to clean spark plugs, carburetor jets, voltage regulators and other parts where an oil-free surface is desired.

Demoisturants remove water and moisture from electrical components such as alternators, voltage regulators, electrical connectors and fuse blocks. They are non-conductive and non-corrosive.

Degreasers are heavy-duty solvents used to remove grease from the outside of the engine and from chassis components. They can be sprayed or brushed on and, depending on the type, are rinsed off either with water or solvent.

LUBRICANTS

Motor oil is the lubricant formulated for use in engines. It normally contains a wide variety of additives to prevent corrosion and reduce foaming and wear. Motor oil comes in various weights (viscosity ratings) from 0 to 50. The recommended weight of the oil depends on the season, temperature and the demands on the engine. Light oil is used in cold climates and under light load conditions. Heavy oil is used in hot climates and where high loads are encountered. Multi-viscosity oils are designed to have characteristics of both light and heavy oils and are available in a number of weights from 0W-20 to 20W-50.

Gear oil is designed to be used in differentials, manual transmissions and other areas where high-temperature lubrication is required.

Chassis and wheel bearing grease is a heavy grease used where increased loads and friction are encountered, such as for wheel bearings, ball-joints, tie-rod ends and universal joints.

High-temperature wheel bearing grease is designed to withstand the extreme temperatures encountered by wheel bearings in disc brake equipped vehicles. It usually contains molybdenum disulfide (moly), which is a dry-type lubricant.

White grease is a heavy grease for metal-to-metal applications where water is a problem. White grease stays soft under both low and high temperatures (usually from -100 to +190-degrees F), and will not wash off or dilute in the presence of water.

Assembly lube is a special extreme pressure lubricant, usually containing moly, used to lubricate high-load parts (such as main and rod bearings and cam lobes) for initial start-up of a new engine. The assembly lube lubricates the parts without being squeezed out or washed away until the engine oiling system begins to function.

Silicone lubricants are used to protect rubber, plastic, vinyl and nylon parts.

Graphite lubricants are used where oils cannot be used due to contamination problems, such as in locks. The dry graphite will lubricate metal parts while remaining uncontaminated by dirt, water, oil or acids. It is electrically conductive and will not foul electrical contacts in locks such as the ignition switch.

Moly penetrants loosen and lubricate frozen, rusted and corroded fasteners and prevent future rusting or freezing.

Heat-sink grease is a special electrically non-conductive grease that is used for mounting electronic ignition modules where it is essential that heat is transferred away from the module.

SEALANTS

RTV sealant is one of the most widely used gasket compounds. Made from silicone, RTV is air curing, it seals, bonds, waterproofs, fills surface irregularities, remains flexible, doesn't shrink, is relatively easy to remove, and is used as a supplementary sealer with almost all low and medium temperature gaskets.

Anaerobic sealant is much like RTV in that it can be used either to seal gaskets or to form gaskets by itself. It remains flexible, is solvent resistant and fills surface imperfections. The difference between an anaerobic sealant and an RTV-type sealant is in the curing. RTV cures when exposed to air, while an anaerobic sealant cures only in the absence of air. This means that an anaerobic sealant cures only after the assembly of parts, sealing them together.

Thread and pipe sealant is used for sealing hydraulic and pneumatic fittings and vacuum lines. It is usually made from a Teflon compound, and comes in a spray, a paint-on liquid and as a wrap-around tape.

CHEMICALS

Anti-seize compound prevents seizing, galling, cold welding, rust and corrosion in fasteners. High-temperature anti-seize, usually made with copper and graphite lubricants, is used for exhaust system and exhaust manifold bolts.

Anaerobic locking compounds are used to keep fasteners from vibrating or working loose and cure only after installation, in the absence of air. Medium strength locking compound is used for small nuts, bolts and screws that may be removed later. High-strength locking compound is for large nuts, bolts and studs which aren't removed on a regular basis.

Oil additives range from viscosity index improvers to chemical treatments that claim to reduce internal engine friction. It should be noted that most oil manufacturers caution against using additives with their oils.

Gas additives perform several functions, depending on their chemical makeup. They usually contain solvents that help dissolve gum and varnish that build up on carburetor, fuel injection and intake parts. They also serve to break down carbon deposits that form on the inside surfaces of the combustion chambers. Some additives contain upper cylinder lubricants for valves and piston rings, and others contain chemicals to remove condensation from the gas tank.

MISCELLANEOUS

Brake fluid is specially formulated hydraulic fluid that can withstand the heat and pressure encountered in brake systems. Care must be taken so this fluid does not come in contact with painted surfaces or plastics. An opened container should always be resealed to prevent contamination by water or dirt.

Weatherstrip adhesive is used to bond weatherstripping around doors, windows and trunk lids. It is sometimes used to attach trim pieces.

Undercoating is a petroleum-based, tar-like substance that is designed to protect metal surfaces on the underside of the vehicle from corrosion. It also acts as a sound-deadening agent by insulating the bottom of the vehicle.

Waxes and polishes are used to help protect painted and plated surfaces from the weather. Different types of paint may require the use of different types of wax and polish. Some polishes utilize a chemical or abrasive cleaner to help remove the top layer of oxidized (dull) paint on older vehicles. In recent years many non-wax polishes that contain a wide variety of chemicals such as polymers and silicones have been introduced. These non-wax polishes are usually easier to apply and last longer than conventional waxes and polishes.

CONVERSION FACTORS

LENGTH (distance)

Inches (in)	X	25.4	= Millimeters (mm)	X 0.0394	= Inches (in)
Feet (ft)	X	0.305	= Meters (m)	X 3.281	= Feet (ft)
Miles	X	1.609	= Kilometers (km)	X 0.621	= Miles

VOLUME (capacity)

Cubic inches (cu in; in³)	X	16.387	= Cubic centimeters (cc; cm³)	X 0.061	= Cubic inches (cu in; in³)
Imperial pints (Imp pt)	X	0.568	= Liters (l)	X 1.76	= Imperial pints (Imp pt)
Imperial quarts (Imp qt)	X	1.137	= Liters (l)	X 0.88	= Imperial quarts (Imp qt)
Imperial quarts (Imp qt)	X	1.201	= US quarts (US qt)	X 0.833	= Imperial quarts (Imp qt)
US quarts (US qt)	X	0.946	= Liters (l)	X 1.057	= US quarts (US qt)
Imperial gallons (Imp gal)	X	4.546	= Liters (l)	X 0.22	= Imperial gallons (Imp gal)
Imperial gallons (Imp gal)	X	1.201	= US gallons (US gal)	X 0.833	= Imperial gallons (Imp gal)
US gallons (US gal)	X	3.785	= Liters (l)	X 0.264	= US gallons (US gal)

MASS (weight)

Ounces (oz)	X	28.35	= Grams (g)	X 0.035	= Ounces (oz)
Pounds (lb)	X	0.454	= Kilograms (kg)	X 2.205	= Pounds (lb)

FORCE

Ounces-force (ozf; oz)	X	0.278	= Newtons (N)	X 3.6	= Ounces-force (ozf; oz)
Pounds-force (lbf; lb)	X	4.448	= Newtons (N)	X 0.225	= Pounds-force (lbf; lb)
Newtons (N)	X	0.1	= Kilograms-force (kgf; kg)	X 9.81	= Newtons (N)

PRESSURE

Pounds-force per square inch (psi; lbf/in²; lb/in²)	X	0.070	= Kilograms-force per square centimeter (kgf/cm²; kg/cm²)	X 14.223	= Pounds-force per square inch (psi; lbf/in²; lb/in²)
Pounds-force per square inch (psi; lbf/in²; lb/in²)	X	0.068	= Atmospheres (atm)	X 14.696	= Pounds-force per square inch (psi; lbf/in²; lb/in²)
Pounds-force per square inch (psi; lbf/in²; lb/in²)	X	0.069	= Bars	X 14.5	= Pounds-force per square inch (psi; lbf/in²; lb/in²)
Pounds-force per square inch (psi; lbf/in²; lb/in²)	X	6.895	= Kilopascals (kPa)	X 0.145	= Pounds-force per square inch (psi; lbf/in²; lb/in²)
Kilopascals (kPa)	X	0.01	= Kilograms-force per square centimeter (kgf/cm²; kg/cm²)	X 98.1	= Kilopascals (kPa)

TORQUE (moment of force)

Pounds-force inches (lbf in; lb in)	X	1.152	= Kilograms-force centimeter (kgf cm; kg cm)	X 0.868	= Pounds-force inches (lbf in; lb in)
Pounds-force inches (lbf in; lb in)	X	0.113	= Newton meters (Nm)	X 8.85	= Pounds-force inches (lbf in; lb in)
Pounds-force inches (lbf in; lb in)	X	0.083	= Pounds-force feet (lbf ft; lb ft)	X 12	= Pounds-force inches (lbf in; lb in)
Pounds-force feet (lbf ft; lb ft)	X	0.138	= Kilograms-force meters (kgf m; kg m)	X 7.233	= Pounds-force feet (lbf ft; lb ft)
Pounds-force feet (lbf ft; lb ft)	X	1.356	= Newton meters (Nm)	X 0.738	= Pounds-force feet (lbf ft; lb ft)
Newton meters (Nm)	X	0.102	= Kilograms-force meters (kgf m; kg m)	X 9.804	= Newton meters (Nm)

VACUUM

Inches mercury (in. Hg)	X	3.377	= Kilopascals (kPa)	X 0.2961	= Inches mercury
Inches mercury (in. Hg)	X	25.4	= Millimeters mercury (mm Hg)	X 0.0394	= Inches mercury

POWER

Horsepower (hp)	X	745.7	= Watts (W)	X 0.0013	= Horsepower (hp)

VELOCITY (speed)

Miles per hour (miles/hr; mph)	X	1.609	= Kilometers per hour (km/hr; kph)	X 0.621	= Miles per hour (miles/hr; mph)

FUEL CONSUMPTION *

Miles per gallon, Imperial (mpg)	X	0.354	= Kilometers per liter (km/l)	X 2.825	= Miles per gallon, Imperial (mpg)
Miles per gallon, US (mpg)	X	0.425	= Kilometers per liter (km/l)	X 2.352	= Miles per gallon, US (mpg)

TEMPERATURE

Degrees Fahrenheit = (°C x 1.8) + 32   Degrees Celsius (Degrees Centigrade; °C) = (°F - 32) x 0.56

*It is common practice to convert from miles per gallon (mpg) to liters/100 kilometers (l/100km), where mpg (Imperial) x l/100 km = 282 and mpg (US) x l/100 km = 235

FRACTION/DECIMAL/MILLIMETER EQUIVALENTS

DECIMALS TO MILLIMETERS

Decimal	mm	Decimal	mm
0.001	0.0254	0.500	12.7000
0.002	0.0508	0.510	12.9540
0.003	0.0762	0.520	13.2080
0.004	0.1016	0.530	13.4620
0.005	0.1270	0.540	13.7160
0.006	0.1524	0.550	13.9700
0.007	0.1778	0.560	14.2240
0.008	0.2032	0.570	14.4780
0.009	0.2286	0.580	14.7320
		0.590	14.9860
0.010	0.2540		
0.020	0.5080		
0.030	0.7620		
0.040	1.0160	0.600	15.2400
0.050	1.2700	0.610	15.4940
0.060	1.5240	0.620	15.7480
0.070	1.7780	0.630	16.0020
0.080	2.0320	0.640	16.2560
0.090	2.2860	0.650	16.5100
		0.660	16.7640
0.100	2.5400	0.670	17.0180
0.110	2.7940	0.680	17.2720
0.120	3.0480	0.690	17.5260
0.130	3.3020		
0.140	3.5560		
0.150	3.8100		
0.160	4.0640	0.700	17.7800
0.170	4.3180	0.710	18.0340
0.180	4.5720	0.720	18.2880
0.190	4.8260	0.730	18.5420
		0.740	18.7960
0.200	5.0800	0.750	19.0500
0.210	5.3340	0.760	19.3040
0.220	5.5880	0.770	19.5580
0.230	5.8420	0.780	19.8120
0.240	6.0960	0.790	20.0660
0.250	6.3500		
0.260	6.6040		
0.270	6.8580	0.800	20.3200
0.280	7.1120	0.810	20.5740
0.290	7.3660	0.820	20.8280
		0.830	21.0820
0.300	7.6200	0.840	21.3360
0.310	7.8740	0.850	21.5900
0.320	8.1280	0.860	21.8440
0.330	8.3820	0.870	22.0980
0.340	8.6360	0.880	22.3520
0.350	8.8900	0.890	22.6060
0.360	9.1440		
0.370	9.3980		
0.380	9.6520		
0.390	9.9060	0.900	22.8600
0.400	10.1600	0.910	23.1140
0.410	10.4140	0.920	23.3680
0.420	10.6680	0.930	23.6220
0.430	10.9220	0.940	23.8760
0.440	11.1760	0.950	24.1300
0.450	11.4300	0.960	24.3840
0.460	11.6840	0.970	24.6380
0.470	11.9380	0.980	24.8920
0.480	12.1920	0.990	25.1460
0.490	12.4460	1.000	25.4000

FRACTIONS TO DECIMALS TO MILLIMETERS

Fraction	Decimal	mm	Fraction	Decimal	mm
1/64	0.0156	0.3969	33/64	0.5156	13.0969
1/32	0.0312	0.7938	17/32	0.5312	13.4938
3/64	0.0469	1.1906	35/64	0.5469	13.8906
1/16	0.0625	1.5875	9/16	0.5625	14.2875
5/64	0.0781	1.9844	37/64	0.5781	14.6844
3/32	0.0938	2.3812	19/32	0.5938	15.0812
7/64	0.1094	2.7781	39/64	0.6094	15.4781
1/8	0.1250	3.1750	5/8	0.6250	15.8750
9/64	0.1406	3.5719	41/64	0.6406	16.2719
5/32	0.1562	3.9688	21/32	0.6562	16.6688
11/64	0.1719	4.3656	43/64	0.6719	17.0656
3/16	0.1875	4.7625	11/16	0.6875	17.4625
13/64	0.2031	5.1594	45/64	0.7031	17.8594
7/32	0.2188	5.5562	23/32	0.7188	18.2562
15/64	0.2344	5.9531	47/64	0.7344	18.6531
1/4	0.2500	6.3500	3/4	0.7500	19.0500
17/64	0.2656	6.7469	49/64	0.7656	19.4469
9/32	0.2812	7.1438	25/32	0.7812	19.8438
19/64	0.2969	7.5406	51/64	0.7969	20.2406
5/16	0.3125	7.9375	13/16	0.8125	20.6375
21/64	0.3281	8.3344	53/64	0.8281	21.0344
11/32	0.3438	8.7312	27/32	0.8438	21.4312
23/64	0.3594	9.1281	55/64	0.8594	21.8281
3/8	0.3750	9.5250	7/8	0.8750	22.2250
25/64	0.3906	9.9219	57/64	0.8906	22.6219
13/32	0.4062	10.3188	29/32	0.9062	23.0188
27/64	0.4219	10.7156	59/64	0.9219	23.4156
7/16	0.4375	11.1125	15/16	0.9375	23.8125
29/64	0.4531	11.5094	61/64	0.9531	24.2094
15/32	0.4688	11.9062	31/32	0.9688	24.6062
31/64	0.4844	12.3031	63/64	0.9844	25.0031
1/2	0.5000	12.7000	1	1.0000	25.4000

Safety first!

Regardless of how enthusiastic you may be about getting on with the job at hand, take the time to ensure that your safety is not jeopardized. A moment's lack of attention can result in an accident, as can failure to observe certain simple safety precautions. The possibility of an accident will always exist, and the following points should not be considered a comprehensive list of all dangers. Rather, they are intended to make you aware of the risks and to encourage a safety conscious approach to all work you carry out on your vehicle.

ESSENTIAL DOS AND DON'TS

DON'T rely on a jack when working under the vehicle. Always use approved jackstands to support the weight of the vehicle and place them under the recommended lift or support points.

DON'T attempt to loosen extremely tight fasteners (i.e. wheel lug nuts) while the vehicle is on a jack - it may fall.

DON'T start the engine without first making sure that the transmission is in Neutral (or Park where applicable) and the parking brake is set.

DON'T remove the radiator cap from a hot cooling system - let it cool or cover it with a cloth and release the pressure gradually.

DON'T attempt to drain the engine oil until you are sure it has cooled to the point that it will not burn you.

DON'T touch any part of the engine or exhaust system until it has cooled sufficiently to avoid burns.

DON'T siphon toxic liquids such as gasoline, antifreeze and brake fluid by mouth, or allow them to remain on your skin.

DON'T inhale brake lining dust - it is potentially hazardous (see Asbestos below).

DON'T allow spilled oil or grease to remain on the floor - wipe it up before someone slips on it.

DON'T use loose fitting wrenches or other tools which may slip and cause injury.

DON'T push on wrenches when loosening or tightening nuts or bolts. Always try to pull the wrench toward you. If the situation calls for pushing the wrench away, push with an open hand to avoid scraped knuckles if the wrench should slip.

DON'T attempt to lift a heavy component alone - get someone to help you.

DON'T rush or take unsafe shortcuts to finish a job.

DON'T allow children or animals in or around the vehicle while you are working on it.

DO wear eye protection when using power tools such as a drill, sander, bench grinder, etc. and when working under a vehicle.

DO keep loose clothing and long hair well out of the way of moving parts.

DO make sure that any hoist used has a safe working load rating adequate for the job.

DO get someone to check on you periodically when working alone on a vehicle.

DO carry out work in a logical sequence and make sure that everything is correctly assembled and tightened.

DO keep chemicals and fluids tightly capped and out of the reach of children and pets.

DO remember that your vehicle's safety affects that of yourself and others. If in doubt on any point, get professional advice.

STEERING, SUSPENSION AND BRAKES

These systems are essential to driving safety, so make sure you have a qualified shop or individual check your work. Also, compressed suspension springs can cause injury if released suddenly - be sure to use a spring compressor.

AIRBAGS

Airbags are explosive devices that can CAUSE injury if they deploy while you're working on the vehicle. Follow the manufacturer's instructions to disable the airbag whenever you're working in the vicinity of airbag components.

ASBESTOS

Certain friction, insulating, sealing, and other products - such as brake linings, brake bands, clutch linings, torque converters, gaskets, etc. - may contain asbestos or other hazardous friction material. Extreme care must be taken to avoid inhalation of dust from such products, since it is hazardous to health. If in doubt, assume that they do contain asbestos.

FIRE

Remember at all times that gasoline is highly flammable. Never smoke or have any kind of open flame around when working on a vehicle. But the risk does not end there. A spark caused by an electrical short circuit, by two metal surfaces contacting each other, or even by static electricity built up in your body under certain conditions, can ignite gasoline vapors, which in a confined space are highly explosive. Do not, under any circumstances, use gasoline for cleaning parts. Use an approved safety solvent.

Always disconnect the battery ground (-) cable at the battery before working on any part of the fuel system or electrical system. Never risk spilling fuel on a hot engine or exhaust component. It is strongly recommended that a fire extinguisher suitable for use on fuel and electrical fires be kept handy in the garage or workshop at all times. Never try to extinguish a fuel or electrical fire with water.

FUMES

Certain fumes are highly toxic and can quickly cause unconsciousness and even death if inhaled to any extent. Gasoline vapor falls into this category, as do the vapors from some cleaning solvents. Any draining or pouring of such volatile fluids should be done in a well ventilated area.

When using cleaning fluids and solvents, read the instructions on the container carefully. Never use materials from unmarked containers.

Never run the engine in an enclosed space, such as a garage. Exhaust fumes contain carbon monoxide, which is extremely poisonous. If you need to run the engine, always do so in the open air, or at least have the rear of the vehicle outside the work area.

THE BATTERY

Never create a spark or allow a bare light bulb near a battery. They normally give off a certain amount of hydrogen gas, which is highly explosive.

Always disconnect the battery ground (-) cable at the battery before working on the fuel or electrical systems.

If possible, loosen the filler caps or cover when charging the battery from an external source (this does not apply to sealed or maintenance-free batteries). Do not charge at an excessive rate or the battery may burst.

Take care when adding water to a non maintenance-free battery and when carrying a battery. The electrolyte, even when diluted, is very corrosive and should not be allowed to contact clothing or skin.

Always wear eye protection when cleaning the battery to prevent the caustic deposits from entering your eyes.

HOUSEHOLD CURRENT

When using an electric power tool, inspection light, etc., which operates on household current, always make sure that the tool is correctly connected to its plug and that, where necessary, it is properly grounded. Do not use such items in damp conditions and, again, do not create a spark or apply excessive heat in the vicinity of fuel or fuel vapor.

SECONDARY IGNITION SYSTEM VOLTAGE

A severe electric shock can result from touching certain parts of the ignition system (such as the spark plug wires) when the engine is running or being cranked, particularly if components are damp or the insulation is defective. In the case of an electronic ignition system, the secondary system voltage is much higher and could prove fatal.

HYDROFLUORIC ACID

This extremely corrosive acid is formed when certain types of synthetic rubber, found in some O-rings, oil seals, fuel hoses, etc. are exposed to temperatures above 750-degrees F (400-degrees C). The rubber changes into a charred or sticky substance containing the acid. *Once formed, the acid remains dangerous for years. If it gets onto the skin, it may be necessary to amputate the limb concerned.*

When dealing with a vehicle which has suffered a fire, or with components salvaged from such a vehicle, wear protective gloves and discard them after use.

Troubleshooting

CONTENTS

This section provides an easy reference guide to the more common problems that may occur during the operation of your vehicle. These problems and possible causes are grouped under various components or systems; i.e. Engine, Cooling System, etc., and also refer to the Chapter and/or Section that deals with the problem.

Remember that successful troubleshooting is not a mysterious art practiced only by professional mechanics. It's simply the result of a bit of knowledge combined with an intelligent, systematic approach to the problem. Always work by a process of elimination, starting with the simplest solution and working through to the most complex - and never

overlook the obvious. Anyone can forget to fill the gas tank or leave the lights on overnight, so don't assume that you are above such oversights.

Finally, always get clear in your mind why a problem has occurred and take steps to ensure that it doesn't happen again. If the electrical system fails because of a poor connection, check all other connections in the system to make sure that they don't fail as well. If a particular fuse continues to blow, find out why - don't just go on replacing fuses. Remember, failure of a small component can often be indicative of potential failure or incorrect functioning of a more important component or system.

ENGINE

1 Engine will not rotate when attempting to start

1 Battery terminal connections loose or corroded. Check the cable terminals at the battery. Tighten the cable or remove corrosion as necessary.

2 Battery discharged or faulty. If the cable connections are clean and tight on the battery posts, turn the key to the On position and switch on the headlights and/or windshield wipers. If they fail to function, the battery is discharged.

3 Automatic transmission not completely engaged in Park or Neutral.

4 Broken, loose or disconnected wiring in the starting circuit. Inspect all wiring and connectors at the battery, starter solenoid and ignition switch.

5 Starter motor pinion jammed in driveplate ring gear. Remove starter and inspect pinion and driveplate at earliest convenience (Chapter 5).

6 Starter solenoid faulty (Chapter 5).

7 Starter motor faulty (Chapter 5).

8 Ignition switch faulty (Chapter 12).

2 Engine rotates but will not start

1 Fuel tank empty, fuel filter plugged or fuel line restricted.

2 Fault in the fuel injection system (Chapter 4).

3 Battery discharged (engine rotates slowly). Check the operation of electrical components as described in the previous Section.

4 Battery terminal connections loose or corroded (see previous Section).

5 Fuel pump faulty (Chapter 4).

6 Broken, loose or disconnected wiring in the starting circuit (see previous Section).

7 Fault in the ignition system (Chapter 5).

3 Starter motor operates without rotating engine

1 Starter pinion sticking. Remove the starter (Chapter 5) and inspect.

2 Starter pinion or driveplate teeth worn or broken. Remove the driveplate access cover and inspect.

4 Engine hard to start when cold

1 Discharged or low battery. Check as described in Section 1.

2 Fault in the fuel or ignition systems (Chapters 4 and 5).

5 Engine hard to start when hot

1 Air filter clogged (Chapter 1).

2 Fault in the fuel or ignition system (Chapters 4 and 5).

3 Low cylinder compression (Chapter 2).

4 Malfunctioning EVAP system (Chapter 6).

6 Starter motor noisy or excessively rough in engagement

1 Pinion or driveplate gear teeth worn or broken. Remove the cover at the rear of the engine (if equipped) and inspect.

2 Starter motor mounting bolts loose or missing.

7 Engine starts but stops immediately

1 Loose or faulty electrical connections at the ignition coils or alternator (Chapter 5).

2 Fault in the fuel or ignition system (Chapters 4 and 5).

3 Vacuum leak at the gasket surfaces of the intake manifold or throttle body. Make sure all mounting bolts/nuts are tightened securely and all vacuum hoses connected to the manifold are positioned properly and in good condition.

4 Restricted intake or exhaust systems (Chapter 4).

5 Vehicle Theft Deterrent system not receiving the correct code then denying injector immediately after start up.

8 Engine lopes while idling or idles erratically

1 Vacuum leakage. Check the mounting bolts/nuts at the throttle body and intake manifold for tightness. Make sure all vacuum hoses are connected and in good condition. Use a stethoscope or a length of fuel hose held against your ear to listen for vacuum leaks while the engine is running. A hissing sound will be heard. A soapy water solution will also detect leaks.

2 Fault in the fuel or ignition system (Chapters 4 and 5).

3 Plugged PCV valve or hose (see Chapters 1 and 6).

4 Air filter clogged (Chapter 1).

5 Fuel pump not delivering sufficient fuel to the fuel injectors (see Chapter 4).

6 Leaking head gasket. Perform a compression check (Chapter 2B).

7 Camshaft lobes worn (Chapter 2).

9 Engine misses at idle speed

1 Spark plugs worn, fouled or not gapped properly (Chapter 1).

2 Fault in the fuel or ignition systems (Chapters 4 and 5).

3 Faulty spark plug wires (Chapter 1).

4 Vacuum leaks at intake manifold or hose connections. Check as described in Section 8.

5 Uneven or low cylinder compression. Check compression as described in Chapter 2B.

10 Engine misses throughout driving speed range

1 Fuel filter clogged and/or impurities in the fuel system (Chapter 1).

2 Faulty or incorrectly gapped spark plugs (Chapter 1).

3 Fault in the fuel or ignition systems (Chapters 4 and 5).

4 Defective spark plug wires (Chapter 1).

5 Faulty emissions system components (Chapter 6).

6 Low or uneven cylinder compression pressures. Remove the spark plugs and test the compression with a gauge (Chapter 2B).

7 Vacuum leaks at the throttle body, intake manifold or vacuum hoses (see Section 8).

11 Engine stalls

1 Fuel filter clogged and/or water and impurities in the fuel system (Chapter 1).

2 Fault in the fuel system or sensors (Chapters 4 and 6).

3 Faulty emissions system components (Chapter 6).

4 Faulty or incorrectly gapped spark plugs (Chapter 1). Also check the spark plug wires (Chapter 1).

5 Vacuum leak at the throttle body, intake manifold or vacuum hoses. Check as described in Section 8.

12 Engine lacks power

1 Fault in the fuel or ignition systems (Chapters 4 and 5).
2 Faulty or incorrectly gapped spark plugs (Chapter 1).
3 Faulty coils (Chapter 5).
4 Brakes binding (Chapter 1).
5 Automatic transmission fluid level incorrect (Chapter 1).
6 Fuel filter clogged and/or impurities in the fuel system (Chapter 1).
7 Emissions control system not functioning properly (Chapter 6).
8 Use of substandard fuel. Fill the tank with the proper fuel.
9 Low or uneven cylinder compression pressures. Test with a compression tester, which will detect leaking valves and/or a blown head gasket (Chapter 2).
10 Restriction in the intake or exhaust system (Chapter 4).

13 Engine backfires

1 Emissions system not functioning properly (Chapter 6).
2 Fault in the fuel or ignition systems (Chapters 4 and 5).
3 Faulty secondary ignition system (cracked spark plug insulator or faulty plug wires) (Chapters 1 and 5).
4 Fuel injection system not functioning properly (Chapter 4).
5 Vacuum leak at the throttle body, intake manifold or vacuum hoses. Check as described in Section 8.
6 Valves sticking (Chapter 2).

14 Pinging or knocking engine sounds during acceleration or uphill

1 Incorrect grade of fuel. Fill the tank with fuel of the proper octane rating.
2 Fault in the fuel or ignition systems (Chapters 4 and 5).
3 Improper spark plugs. Check the plug type against the VECI label located in the engine compartment. Also check the plugs and wires for damage (Chapter 1).
4 Faulty emissions system (Chapter 6).
5 Vacuum leak. Check as described in Section 9.

15 Engine diesels (continues to run) after switching off

1 Fault in the fuel or ignition systems (Chapters 4 and 5).
2 Excessive engine operating temperature. Probable causes of this are a low coolant level (see Chapter 1), malfunctioning thermostat, clogged radiator or faulty water pump (see Chapter 3).

ENGINE ELECTRICAL SYSTEM

16 Battery will not hold a charge

1 Electrolyte level low or battery discharged (Chapter 1).
2 Battery terminals loose or corroded (Chapter 1).
3 Alternator not charging properly (Chapter 5).
4 Loose, broken or faulty wiring in the charging circuit (Chapter 5).
5 Short in the vehicle wiring causing a continuous drain on the battery (refer to Chapter 12 and the Wiring Diagrams).
6 Battery defective internally.

17 Alternator light fails to go out

1 Fault in the alternator or charging circuit (Chapter 5).
2 Alternator drivebelt defective or not properly adjusted (Chapter 1).

18 Alternator light fails to come on when key is turned on

1 Instrument cluster warning light bulb defective (Chapter 12).
2 Alternator faulty (Chapter 5).
3 Fault in the instrument cluster printed circuit, dashboard wiring or bulb holder (Chapter 12).

FUEL SYSTEM

19 Excessive fuel consumption

1 Dirty or clogged air filter element (Chapter 1).
2 Emissions system not functioning properly (Chapter 6).
3 Fault in the fuel or ignition systems (Chapters 4 and 5).
4 Low tire pressure or incorrect tire size (Chapter 1).
5 Restricted exhaust system (Chapter 4).

20 Fuel leakage and/or fuel odor

1 Leak in a fuel feed or vent line (Chapter 4).
2 Tank overfilled. Fill only to automatic shut-off.
3 Evaporative emissions system canister clogged (Chapter 6).
4 Vapor leaks from system lines or injectors (Chapter 4).

COOLING SYSTEM

21 Overheating

1 Insufficient coolant in the system (Chapter 1).
2 Water pump drivebelt defective or not adjusted properly (Chapter 1).
3 Radiator core blocked or radiator grille dirty and restricted (see Chapter 3).
4 Thermostat faulty (Chapter 3).
5 Fan blades broken or cracked (Chapter 3).
6 Radiator cap not maintaining proper pressure. Have the cap pressure tested by a gas station or repair shop.
7 Fault in electrical circuit for cooling fan (Chapter 3).

22 Overcooling

1 Thermostat faulty (Chapter 3).
2 Inaccurate temperature gauge (Chapter 12).
3 Fault in electrical circuit for cooling fan (Chapter 3).

23 External coolant leakage

1 Deteriorated or damaged hoses or loose clamps. Replace hoses and/or tighten the clamps at the hose connections (Chapter 1).
2 Water pump seals defective. If this is the case, water will drip from the weep hole in the water pump body (Chapter 3).
3 Leakage from the radiator core or side tank(s). This will require the radiator to be professionally repaired (see Chapter 3 for removal procedures).
4 Engine drain plug(s) leaking (Chapter 1) or water jacket core plugs leaking (see Chapter 2B).
5 Leakage at the heater core. Signs of leakage should show up on interior carpeting (Chapter 3).

24 Internal coolant leakage

➡Note: Internal coolant leaks can usually be detected by examining the oil. Check the dipstick and inside of the valve cover for water deposits and an oil consistency like that of a milkshake.

1 Leaking cylinder head gasket. Have the cooling system pressure tested.

2 Cracked cylinder bore or cylinder head. Remove the head and inspect (Chapter 2).

25 Coolant loss

1 Too much coolant in the system (Chapter 1).
2 Coolant boiling away due to overheating (see Section 15).
3 External or internal leakage (see Sections 23 and 24).
4 Faulty radiator cap. Have the cap pressure tested.

26 Poor coolant circulation

1 Inoperative water pump. A quick test is to pinch the top radiator hose closed with your hand while the engine is idling, then let it loose. You should feel the surge of coolant if the pump is working properly (see Chapter 1).

2 Restriction in the cooling system. Drain, flush and refill the system (Chapter 1). If necessary, remove the radiator (Chapter 3) and have it reverse flushed.

3 Drivebelt or tensioner broken (Chapter 1).
4 Thermostat sticking (Chapter 3).

AUTOMATIC TRANSMISSION

➡Note: Due to the complexity of the automatic transmission, it's difficult for the home mechanic to properly diagnose and service this component. For problems other than the following, the vehicle should be taken to a dealer service department or a transmission shop.

27 General shift mechanism problems

1 Chapter 7A deals with checking and adjusting the shift cable on automatic transmissions. Common problems that may be attributed to poorly adjusted cable are:

a) Engine starting in gears other than Park or Neutral.
b) Indicator on shifter pointing to a gear other than the one actually being selected.
c) Vehicle moves when in Park.

2 Refer to Chapter 7A to adjust the cable.
3 Problem with the electronic shift solenoid. Check for Diagnostic Trouble Codes (Chapter 6).

28 Transmission will not downshift with accelerator pedal pressed to the floor

Transmission pressure control solenoid valve faulty. Check for Diagnostic Trouble Codes (Chapter 6).

29 Transmission slips, shifts rough, is noisy or has no drive in forward or reverse gears

1 Of the many probable causes for the above problems, the home mechanic should be concerned with only one possibility - fluid level.

2 Before taking the vehicle to a repair shop, check the level and condition of the fluid as described in Chapter 1. Correct fluid level as necessary or change the fluid and filter if needed. If the problem persists, have a professional diagnose the probable cause.

3 If the transmission shifts late and the shifts are harsh, suspect a faulty transmission pressure control solenoid valve. Check for Diagnostic Trouble Codes (Chapter 6).

30 Fluid leakage

1 Automatic transmission fluid is a deep red color. Fluid leaks should not be confused with engine oil, which can easily be blown by airflow to the transmission.

2 To pinpoint a leak, first remove all built-up dirt and grime from around the transmission. Degreasing agents and/or steam cleaning will achieve this. With the underside clean, drive the vehicle at low speeds so airflow will not blow the leak far from its source. Raise the vehicle and determine where the leak is coming from. Common areas of leakage are:

a) Pan: Tighten the mounting bolts and/or replace the pan gasket as necessary (see Chapter 1).
b) Filler pipe: Replace the rubber seal where the pipe enters the transmission case.
c) Transmission oil lines: Tighten the connectors where the lines enter the transmission case and/or replace the lines.
d) Vent pipe: Transmission overfilled and/or water in fluid (see checking procedures, Chapter 1).
e) Speed sensor connector: Replace the O-ring where the vehicle speed sensor enters the transmission case (see Chapter 6).

TRANSFER CASE (4WD MODELS)

31 Transfer case won't shift into the desired range

1 Selector switch faulty (see Chapter 7B).
2 Control module faulty (see Chapter 7B).
3 Insufficient or incorrect grade of lubricant. Drain and refill the transfer case with the specified lubricant (Chapter 1).
4 Worn or damaged internal components. Disassembly and overhaul of the transfer case, by a qualified shop, may be necessary.
5 Fault in the electrical system of the front axle or automatic transfer case. Check for Diagnostic Trouble Codes (Chapter 6).

32 Transfer case noisy in all gears

Insufficient or incorrect grade of lubricant. Drain and refill (Chapter 1).

33 Noisy or jumps out of four-wheel drive Low range

1 Shift fork cracked, inserts worn or fork binding on the rail.
2 Fault in the electrical system of the front axle or automatic transfer case. Check for Diagnostic Trouble Codes (Chapter 6).

34 Lubricant leaks from the vent or output shaft seals

1 Transfer case is overfilled. Drain to the proper level (Chapter 1).
2 Vent is clogged or jammed closed. Clear or replace the vent.
3 Output shaft seal incorrectly installed or damaged. Replace the seal and check contact surfaces for nicks and scoring.

DRIVESHAFT

35   Oil leak at seal end of driveshaft

Defective transmission or transfer case oil seal. See Chapter 7 for replacement procedures. While this is done, check the splined yoke for burrs or a rough condition that may be damaging the seal. Burrs can be removed with crocus cloth or a fine whetstone.

36   Knock or clunk when the transmission is under initial load (just after transmission is put into gear)

1   Loose or disconnected rear suspension components. Check all mounting bolts, nuts and bushings (see Chapter 10).
2   Loose driveshaft bolts. Inspect all bolts and nuts and tighten them to the specified torque.
3   Worn or damaged universal joint bearings. Check for wear (see Chapter 8).

37   Metallic grinding sound consistent with vehicle speed

Pronounced wear in the universal joint bearings. Check as described in Chapter 8.

38   Vibration

➡**Note: Before assuming that the driveshaft is at fault, make sure the tires are perfectly balanced and perform the following test.**

1   Install a tachometer inside the vehicle to monitor engine speed as the vehicle is driven. Drive the vehicle and note the engine speed at which the vibration (roughness) is most pronounced. Now shift the transmission to a different gear and bring the engine speed to the same point.
2   If the vibration occurs at the same engine speed (rpm) regardless of which gear the transmission is in, the driveshaft is NOT at fault since the driveshaft speed varies.
3   If the vibration decreases or is eliminated when the transmission is in a different gear at the same engine speed, refer to the following probable causes.
4   Bent or dented driveshaft. Inspect and replace as necessary (see Chapter 8).
5   Undercoating or built-up dirt, etc. on the driveshaft. Clean the shaft thoroughly and recheck.
6   Worn universal joint bearings. Remove and inspect (see Chapter 8).
7   Driveshaft and/or companion flange out of balance. Check for missing weights on the shaft. Remove the driveshaft (see Chapter 8) and reinstall 180-degrees from original position, then retest. Have the driveshaft professionally balanced if the problem persists.

AXLES

39   Noise

1   Road noise. No corrective procedures available.
2   Tire noise. Inspect tires and check tire pressures (Chapter 1).
3   Rear wheel bearings worn or damaged (Chapter 8).

40   Vibration

See probable causes under Driveshaft. Proceed under the guidelines listed for the driveshaft. If the problem persists, check the rear wheel bearings by raising the rear of the vehicle and spinning the rear wheels by hand. Listen for evidence of rough (noisy) bearings. Remove and inspect (see Chapter 8).

41   Oil leakage

1   Pinion seal damaged (see Chapter 8).
2   Axleshaft oil seals damaged (see Chapter 8).
3   Differential cover leaking. Tighten the bolts or replace the gasket as required (see Chapter 8).

DRIVEAXLES (4WD MODELS)

42   Clicking noise on turns

Worn or damaged outboard CV joints (Chapter 8).

43   Shudder or vibration during acceleration

1   Excessive toe-in. Have alignment checked.
2   Worn or damaged inboard or outboard CV joints (Chapter 8).
3   Sticking inboard CV joint assembly (Chapter 8).

44   Vibration at highway speeds

1   Out-of-balance front wheels and/or tires (Chapters 1 and 10).
2   Out-of-round front tires (Chapters 1 and 10).
3   Worn CV joints (Chapter 8).

BRAKES

➡**Note: Before assuming that a brake problem exists, make sure that the tires are in good condition and inflated properly (see Chapter 1), that the front-end alignment is correct and that the vehicle is not loaded with weight in an unequal manner.**

45   Vehicle pulls to one side during braking

1   Defective, damaged or oil contaminated disc brake pads on one side. Inspect as described in Chapter 9.
2   Excessive wear of brake pad material or disc on one side. Inspect and correct as necessary.
3   Loose or disconnected front suspension components. Inspect and tighten all bolts to the specified torque (Chapter 10).
4   Defective brake caliper assembly. Remove the caliper and inspect for a stuck piston or other damage (Chapter 9).

46   Noise (high-pitched squeal with the brakes applied)

1   Disc brake pads worn out. The noise comes from the wear sensor rubbing against the disc (does not apply to all vehicles) or the actual pad backing plate itself if the material is completely worn away. Replace the pads with new ones immediately (Chapter 9). If the pad material has worn completely away, the brake discs should be inspected for damage as described in Chapter 9.
2   Linings contaminated with dirt or grease. Replace pads.
3   Incorrect linings. Replace with correct linings.

47   Excessive brake pedal travel

1   Partial brake system failure. Inspect the entire system (Chapter 9) and correct as required.
2   Insufficient fluid in the master cylinder. Check (Chapter 1), add fluid and bleed the system if necessary (Chapter 9).

48   Brake pedal feels spongy when depressed

1   Air in the hydraulic lines. Bleed the brake system (Chapter 9).
2   Faulty flexible hoses. Inspect all system hoses and lines. Replace parts as necessary.
3   Master cylinder mounting bolts/nuts loose.
4   Master cylinder defective (Chapter 9).

49   Excessive effort required to stop vehicle

1   Power brake booster not operating properly (see check in Chapter 1, repairs in Chapter 9).
2   Excessively worn pads. Inspect and replace if necessary (Chapter 9).
3   One or more caliper pistons seized or sticking. Inspect and rebuild as required (Chapter 9).
4   Brake pads contaminated with oil or grease. Inspect and replace as required (Chapter 9).
5   New pads installed and not yet seated. It will take a while for the new material to seat against the disc.

50   Pedal travels to the floor with little resistance

1   Little or no fluid in the master cylinder reservoir caused by leaking caliper piston(s), loose, damaged or disconnected brake lines. Inspect the entire system and correct as necessary.
2   Worn master cylinder seals (Chapter 9).

51   Brake pedal pulsates during brake application

Disc(s) defective. Remove (Chapter 9) and check for excessive lateral runout and parallelism. Have the discs resurfaced (always in pairs, front or rear) or replace with a new ones.

SUSPENSION AND STEERING SYSTEMS

52   Vehicle pulls to one side

1   Tire pressures uneven or tires mismatched (Chapter 1).
2   Defective tire (Chapter 1).
3   Excessive wear in suspension or steering components (Chapter 10).
4   Front end in need of alignment.
5   Front brakes dragging. Inspect the brakes as described in Chapter 9.

53   Shimmy, shake or vibration

1   Tire or wheel out-of-balance or out-of-round. Have professionally balanced.

2   Loose, worn or out-of-adjustment front wheel bearings (Chapter 1).
3   Shock absorbers and/or suspension components worn or damaged (Chapter 10).

54   Excessive pitching and/or rolling around corners or during braking

1   Defective shock absorbers. Replace as a set (Chapter 10).
2   Broken or weak springs and/or suspension components. Inspect as described in Chapters 1 and 10.

55   Excessively stiff steering

1   Lack of fluid in power steering fluid reservoir (Chapter 1).
2   Incorrect tire pressures (Chapter 1).
3   Front end out of alignment.
4   Lack of power assistance (see Section 57).
5   Steering gear defective (Chapter 10).

56   Excessive play in steering

1   Loose front wheel bearings (Chapters 1 and 10).
2   Excessive wear in suspension or steering components (Chapter 10).
3   Steering gear damaged or out of adjustment (Chapter 10).

57   Lack of power assistance

1   Drivebelt or tensioner faulty (Chapter 1).
2   Fluid level low (Chapter 1).
3   Hoses or lines restricted. Inspect and replace parts as necessary.
4   Air in power steering system. Bleed the system (Chapter 10).

58   Excessive tire wear (not specific to one area)

1   Incorrect tire pressures (Chapter 1).
2   Tires out-of-balance. Have professionally balanced.
3   Wheels damaged. Inspect and replace as necessary.
4   Suspension or steering components excessively worn (Chapter 10).

59   Excessive tire wear on outside edge

1   Inflation pressures incorrect (Chapter 1).
2   Excessive speed in turns.
3   Front-end alignment incorrect. Have the front end professionally aligned.
4   Suspension arm bent or twisted (Chapter 10).

60   Excessive tire wear on inside edge

1   Inflation pressures incorrect (Chapter 1).
2   Front-end alignment incorrect. Have the front end professionally aligned.
3   Loose or damaged steering components (Chapter 10).

61   Tire tread worn in one place

1   Tires out-of-balance.
2   Damaged or buckled wheel. Inspect and replace if necessary.
3   Defective tire (Chapter 1).

Notes

Section

1

TUNE-UP
AND ROUTINE
MAINTENANCE

Engine compartment components (six-cylinder model shown, V8 similar)

1	Brake fluid reservoir	6	Radiator cap	11	Windshield washer fluid reservoir
2	Underhood fuse/relay box	7	Upper radiator hose	12	Coolant reservoir
3	Battery	8	Air filter housing	13	Automatic transmission fluid dipstick
4	Engine oil filler cap	9	Power steering fluid reservoir	14	Spark plugs (underneath air intake
5	Drivebelt	10	Engine oil dipstick		resonator)

Typical engine compartment underside components (six-cylinder model shown, V8 similar)

1	Stabilizer bar	5	Lower control arm bushing	9	Automatic transmission fluid pan
2	Lower radiator hose	6	Brake caliper	10	Exhaust pipe
3	Engine oil drain plug	7	Tie-rod end	11	Shock absorber/coil spring assembly
4	Engine oil filter	8	Steering gear boot	12	Lower balljoint

Typical rear underside components

1	Resonator	4	Stabilizer bar	7	Rear universal joint
2	Shock absorber	5	Brake caliper	8	Muffler
3	Differential drain plug	6	Fuel tank		

Chevrolet TrailBlazer, Oldsmobile Bravada and GMC Envoy maintenance schedule

The following maintenance intervals are based on the assumption that the vehicle owner will be doing the maintenance or service work, as opposed to having a dealer service department do the work. These are the minimum maintenance intervals recommended by the factory for vehicles that are driven daily. If you wish to keep your vehicle in peak condition at all times, you may wish to perform some of these procedures even more often. Because frequent maintenance enhances the efficiency, performance and resale value of your car, we encourage you to do so. If you drive in dusty areas, tow a trailer, idle or drive at low speeds for extended periods or drive for short distances (less than four miles) in below freezing temperatures, shorter intervals are also recommended.

When the vehicle is new, follow the maintenance schedule to the letter, record the maintenance performed in your owners manual and keep all receipts to protect the new vehicle warranty. In many cases the initial maintenance check is done at no cost to the owner (check with your dealer service department for more information).

EVERY 250 MILES OR WEEKLY, WHICHEVER COMES FIRST

Check the engine oil level (Section 4)
Check the coolant level (Section 4)
Check the windshield washer fluid level (Section 4)
Check the brake fluid level (Section 4)
Check the tires and tire pressures (Section 5)

EVERY 3000 MILES OR 3 MONTHS, WHICHEVER COMES FIRST

All items listed above, plus . . .
Check the power steering fluid level (Section 6)
Check the automatic transmission fluid level (Section 7)
Change the engine oil and filter (Section 8)

EVERY 6000 MILES OR 6 MONTHS, WHICHEVER COMES FIRST

All items listed above, plus . . .
Check the seat belts (Section 9)
Inspect the windshield wiper blades (Section 10)
Check and service the battery (Section 11)
Check the engine drivebelt (Section 12)
Inspect underhood hoses (Section 13)
Check the cooling system (Section 14)
Rotate the tires (Section 15)
Check the lubricant level in the front (4WD) and rear axles
    (Section 16)

EVERY 15,000 MILES OR 12 MONTHS, WHICHEVER COMES FIRST

All items listed above, plus . . .
Lubricate the chassis (Section 17)
Check the fuel system (Section 18)
Check the brake system (Section 19)*
Check the exhaust system (Section 20)
Check the transfer case lubricant level (4WD) (Section 21)

EVERY 30,000 MILES OR 30 MONTHS, WHICHEVER COMES FIRST

All items listed above, plus . . .
Change the brake fluid (Section 22)
Replace the air filter (Section 23)
Replace the fuel filter (Section 24)
Replace the spark plugs (non-platinum type) (Section 25)
Check the steering, suspension and driveaxle boots (Section 26)
Change the automatic transmission fluid and filter (Section 27)**

EVERY 60,000 MILES OR 48 MONTHS, WHICHEVER COMES FIRST

Change the transfer case lubricant (Section 28)
Change the differential lubricant (Section 29)*

EVERY 100,000 MILES OR 60 MONTHS, WHICHEVER COMES FIRST

Replace the spark plugs (platinum type) (Section 25)
Service the cooling system (drain, flush and refill) (Section 30)

 *   This item is affected by "severe" operating conditions, as described below. If the vehicle is operated under severe conditions, perform all maintenance indicated with an asterisk (*) at half the indicated intervals. Severe conditions exist if you mainly operate the vehicle . . .

in dusty areas
towing a trailer
idling for extended periods
driving at low speeds when outside temperatures remain
    below freezing and most trips are less than four miles long

 ** Perform this procedure at half the recommended interval if operated under one or more of the following conditions:

in heavy city traffic where the outside temperature regularly reaches
    90-degrees F or higher in hilly or mountainous terrain
frequent trailer towing
if the vehicle has been driven through deep water

2 Introduction

This Chapter is designed to help the home mechanic maintain the Chevrolet TrailBlazer, GMC Envoy and Oldsmobile Bravada with the goals of maximum performance, economy, safety and reliability in mind.

Included is a master maintenance schedule, followed by procedures dealing specifically with each item on the schedule. Visual checks, adjustments, component replacement and other helpful items are included. Refer to the accompanying illustrations of the engine compartment and the underside of the vehicle for the locations of various components.

Servicing your vehicle in accordance with the mileage/time maintenance schedule and the step-by-step procedures will result in a planned maintenance program that should produce a long and reliable service life. Keep in mind that it's a comprehensive plan, so maintaining some items but not others at the specified intervals will not produce the same results.

As you service your vehicle, you will discover that many of the procedures can - and should - be grouped together because of the nature of the particular procedure you're performing or because of the close proximity of two otherwise unrelated components to one another.

For example, if the vehicle is raised for chassis lubrication, you should inspect the exhaust, suspension, steering and fuel systems while you're under the vehicle. When you're rotating the tires, it makes good sense to check the brakes since the wheels are already removed. Finally, let's suppose you have to borrow or rent a torque wrench. Even if you only need it to tighten the spark plugs, you might as well check the torque of as many critical fasteners as time allows.

The first step in this maintenance program is to prepare yourself before the actual work begins. Read through all the procedures you're planning to do, then gather up all the parts and tools needed. If it looks like you might run into problems during a particular job, seek advice from a mechanic or an experienced do-it-yourselfer.

OWNER'S MANUAL AND VECI LABEL INFORMATION

Your vehicle Owner's Manual was written for your year and model and contains very specific information on component locations, specifications, fuse ratings, part numbers, etc. The Owner's Manual is an important resource for the do-it-yourselfer to have; if one was not supplied with your vehicle, it can generally be ordered from a dealer parts department.

Among other important information, the Vehicle Emissions Control Information (VECI) label contains specifications and procedures for tune-up adjustments (if applicable) and, in some instances, spark plugs (see Chapter 6 for more information on the VECI label). The information on this label is the exact maintenance data recommended by the manufacturer. This data often varies by intended operating altitude, local emissions regulations, month of manufacture, etc.

This Chapter contains procedural details, safety information and more ambitious maintenance intervals than you might find in the manufacturer's literature. However, you may also find procedures and specifications in your Owner's Manual or VECI label that differ with what's printed here. In these cases, the Owner's Manual or VECI label can be considered correct, since it is specific to your particular vehicle.

3 Tune-up general information

The term tune-up is used in this manual to represent a combination of individual operations rather than one specific procedure that will maintain a gasoline engine in proper tune.

If, from the time the vehicle is new, the routine maintenance schedule is followed closely and frequent checks are made of fluid levels and high wear items, as suggested throughout this manual, the engine will be kept in relatively good running condition and the need for additional work will be minimized.

More likely than not, however, there may be times when the engine is running poorly due to lack of regular maintenance. This is even more likely if a used vehicle, which has not received regular and frequent maintenance checks, is purchased. In such cases, an engine tune-up will be needed outside of the regular routine maintenance intervals.

The first step in any tune-up or diagnostic procedure to help correct a poor running engine is a cylinder compression check. A compression check (see Chapter 2B) will help determine the condition of internal engine components and should be used as a guide for tune-up and repair procedures. If, for instance, the compression check indicates serious internal engine wear, a conventional tune-up won't improve the performance of the engine and would be a waste of time and money. Because of its importance, the compression check should be done by someone with the right equipment and the knowledge to use it properly.

The following procedures are those most often needed to bring a generally poor running engine back into a proper state of tune.

MINOR TUNE-UP

Check all engine related fluids (Section 4)
Clean, inspect and test the battery (Section 11)
Check and adjust the drivebelt (Section 12)
Check all underhood hoses (Section 13)
Check the cooling system (Section 14)
Check the air filter (Section 23)

MAJOR TUNE-UP

All items listed under Minor tune-up, plus . . .
Replace the air filter (Section 23)
Replace the spark plugs (Section 25)
Check the ignition system (Chapter 5)
Check the charging system (Chapter 5)

4 Fluid level checks (every 250 miles or weekly)

→Note: The following are fluid level checks to be done on a 250 mile or weekly basis. Additional fluid level checks can be found in specific maintenance procedures that follow. Regardless of intervals, be alert to fluid leaks under the vehicle, which would indicate a fault to be corrected immediately.

1 Fluids are an essential part of the lubrication, cooling, brake and windshield washer systems. Because the fluids gradually become depleted and/or contaminated during normal operation of the vehicle, they must be periodically replenished. See Recommended lubricants and fluids at the beginning of this Chapter before adding fluid to any of the following components.

→Note: The vehicle must be on level ground when fluid levels are checked.

ENGINE OIL

▶ Refer to illustrations 4.2, 4.4 and 4.6

2 The engine oil level is checked with a dipstick that extends through a tube and into the oil pan at the bottom of the engine (see illustration).

3 The oil level should be checked before the vehicle has been driven, or about 5 minutes after the engine has been shut off. If the oil is checked immediately after driving the vehicle, some of the oil will remain in the upper engine components, resulting in an inaccurate reading on the dipstick.

4 Pull the dipstick out of the tube and wipe all the oil from the end with a clean rag or paper towel. Insert the clean dipstick all the way back into the tube, then pull it out again. Note the oil at the end of the dipstick. Add oil as necessary to keep the level between the L and F marks or within the SAFE zone on the dipstick (see illustration).

5 Do not overfill the engine by adding too much oil since this may result in oil-fouled spark plugs, oil leaks or oil seal failures.

6 Oil is added to the engine after unscrewing a cap from the valve cover (see illustration). A funnel will help to reduce spills.

7 Checking the oil level is an important preventive maintenance step. A consistently low oil level indicates oil leakage through damaged seals, defective gaskets or past worn rings or valve guides. If the oil looks milky or has water droplets in it, the cylinder head gasket(s) may be blown or the head(s) or block may be cracked. The engine should be checked immediately. The condition of the oil should also be checked. Whenever you check the oil level, slide your thumb and index finger up the dipstick before wiping off the oil. If you see small dirt or metal particles clinging to the dipstick, the oil should be changed (see Section 8).

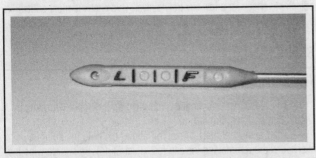

4.4 The oil level must be maintained between the marks at all times - it takes one quart of oil to raise the level from the L mark to the F mark

4.2 The engine oil dipstick is located at the right front of the engine (six-cylinder shown)

ENGINE COOLANT

▶ Refer to illustration 4.9

✳✳ WARNING 1:

Do not allow antifreeze to come in contact with your skin or painted surfaces of the vehicle. Rinse off spills immediately with plenty of water. Antifreeze is highly toxic if ingested. Never leave antifreeze lying around in an open container or in puddles on the floor; children and pets are attracted by its sweet smell and may drink it. Check with local authorities on disposing of used anti-freeze. Many communities have collection centers that will see that antifreeze is disposed of safely.

✳✳ WARNING 2:

Never remove the radiator cap when the engine is warm.

→Note: Non-toxic antifreeze is now manufactured and available at auto parts stores, but even this type should be disposed of properly.

4.6 Oil is added to the engine after unscrewing the oil filler cap - always make sure the area around the opening is clean before removing the cap to prevent dirt from contaminating the engine

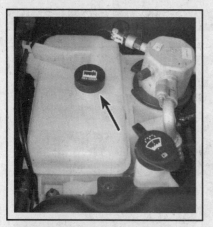

4.9 The coolant reservoir is located on the right side of the engine compartment

4.14 Flip open the cap to check the fluid level in the windshield washer tank

4.19 Never let the brake fluid level drop below the MIN mark

✳✳ CAUTION:

Never mix green-colored ethylene glycol anti-freeze and orange-colored "DEX-COOL" silicate-free coolant because doing so will destroy the efficiency of the "DEX-COOL" coolant which is designed to last for 100,000 miles or five years.

8 All vehicles covered by this manual are equipped with a coolant recovery tank, located at the right side of the engine compartment, and connected by hoses to the radiator and cooling system.

9 The coolant level in the reservoir should be checked regularly. When the engine is cold, the coolant level should be at or slightly above the COLD mark on the reservoir (see illustration). Once the engine has warmed up, the level should be at or near the HOT mark. If it isn't, add coolant to the reservoir. To add coolant simply twist open the cap and add a 50/50 mixture of "DEX-COOL" coolant and water (see the **Caution** at the beginning of this Section).

10 Drive the vehicle and recheck the coolant level. If only a small amount of coolant is required to bring the system up to the proper level, water can be used. However, repeated additions of water will dilute the antifreeze and water solution. In order to maintain the proper ratio of antifreeze and water, always top up the coolant level with the correct mixture. An empty plastic milk jug or bleach bottle makes an excellent container for mixing coolant. Do not use rust inhibitors or additives.

11 If the coolant level drops consistently, there may be a leak in the system. Inspect the radiator, hoses, filler cap, drain plugs and water pump (see Section 14). If no leaks are noted, have the pressure cap tested by a service station.

12 If you have to remove the radiator cap, wait until the engine has cooled completely, then wrap a thick cloth around the cap and slowly unscrew it. If coolant or steam escapes, let the engine cool down longer, then remove the cap.

13 Check the condition of the coolant as well. It should be relatively clear. If it is brown or rust colored, the system should be drained, flushed and refilled. Even if the coolant appears to be normal, the corrosion inhibitors wear out, so it must be replaced at the specified intervals. If the system is filled with standard green coolant/water, it must be flushed and replaced more frequently than if the original "DEX-COOL" coolant is retained.

WINDSHIELD WASHER FLUID

▶ **Refer to illustration 4.14**

14 Fluid for the windshield washer system is located in a plastic reservoir in the left side of the engine compartment (see illustration).

15 In milder climates, plain water can be used in the reservoir, but it should be kept no more than 2/3 full to allow for expansion if the water freezes. In colder climates, use windshield washer system antifreeze, available at any auto parts store, to lower the freezing point of the fluid. Mix the antifreeze with water in accordance with the manufacturer's directions on the container.

✳✳ CAUTION:

Don't use cooling system antifreeze - it will damage the vehicle's paint.

16 To help prevent icing in cold weather, warm the windshield with the defroster before using the washer.

BATTERY ELECTROLYTE

17 These vehicles are equipped with a battery which is permanently sealed (except for vent holes) and has no filler caps. Water doesn't have to be added to these batteries at any time. If a maintenance-type battery is installed, the caps on the top of the battery should be removed periodically to check for a low electrolyte level. This check is most critical during the warm summer months. Add only distilled water to any battery.

BRAKE FLUID

▶ **Refer to illustration 4.19**

18 The brake master cylinder is mounted on the upper left of the engine compartment firewall.

19 The translucent plastic reservoir allows the fluid inside to be checked without removing the cap (see illustration). Be sure to wipe the top of the reservoir cap with a clean rag to prevent contamination of the brake system before removing the cover.

20 When adding fluid, pour it carefully into the reservoir to avoid spilling it on surrounding painted surfaces. Be sure the specified fluid is used, since mixing different types of brake fluid can cause damage to the system. See *Recommended lubricants and fluids* at the back of this Chapter or your owner's manual.

✳✳ WARNING:

Brake fluid can harm your eyes and damage painted surfaces, so use extreme caution when handling or pouring it. Do not use brake fluid that has been standing open or is more than one year old. Brake fluid absorbs moisture from the air. Moisture in the system can cause a dangerous loss of brake performance.

21 At this time, the fluid and master cylinder can be inspected for contamination. The system should be drained and refilled if deposits, dirt particles or water droplets are seen in the fluid.

22 After filling the reservoir to the proper level, make sure the cover or cap is on tight to prevent fluid leakage.

23 The brake fluid level in the master cylinder will drop slightly as the pads at the front wheels wear down during normal operation. If the master cylinder requires repeated additions to keep it at the proper level, it's an indication of leakage in the brake system, which should be corrected immediately. Check all brake lines and connections (see Section 19 for more information).

24 If, upon checking the master cylinder fluid level, you discover one or both reservoirs empty or nearly empty, the brake system should be bled and thoroughly inspected (see Chapter 9).

5 Tire and tire pressure checks (every 250 miles or weekly)

▶ **Refer to illustrations 5.2, 5.3, 5.4a, 5.4b and 5.8**

1 Periodic inspection of the tires may spare you the inconvenience of being stranded with a flat tire. It can also provide you with vital information regarding possible problems in the steering and suspension systems before major damage occurs.

2 The original tires on this vehicle are equipped with 1/2-inch wide wear bands that will appear when tread depth reaches 1/16-inch, at which point the tires can be considered worn out. Tread wear can be monitored with a simple, inexpensive device known as a tread depth indicator (see illustration).

3 Note any abnormal tread wear (see illustration). Tread pattern irregularities such as cupping, flat spots and more wear on one side than the other are indications of front end alignment and/or balance problems. If any of these conditions are noted, take the vehicle to a tire shop or service station to correct the problem.

4 Look closely for cuts, punctures and embedded nails or tacks. Sometimes a tire will hold air pressure for a short time or leak down

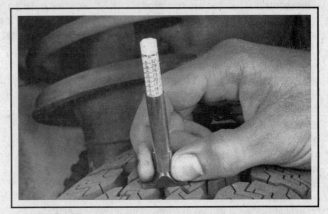

5.2 Use a tire tread depth indicator to monitor tire wear - they are available at auto parts stores and service stations and cost very little

UNDERINFLATION

CUPPING

Cupping may be caused by:
- Underinflation and/or mechanical irregularities such as out-of-balance condition of wheel and/or tire, and bent or damaged wheel.
- Loose or worn steering tie-rod or steering idler arm.
- Loose, damaged or worn front suspension parts.

INCORRECT TOE-IN OR EXTREME CAMBER

OVERINFLATION

FEATHERING DUE TO MISALIGNMENT

5.3 This chart will help you determine the condition of the tires and the probable cause(s) of abnormal wear

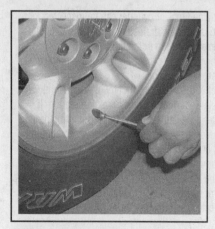

5.4a If a tire loses air on a steady basis, check the valve stem core first to make sure it's snug (special inexpensive wrenches are commonly available at auto parts stores)

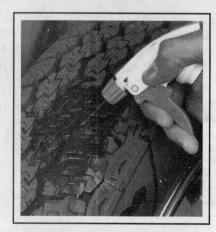

5.4b If the valve stem core is tight, raise the corner of the vehicle with the low tire and spray a soapy water solution onto the tread as the tire is turned slowly - leaks will cause small bubbles to appear

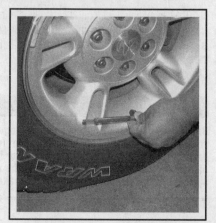

5.8 To extend the life of the tires, check the air pressure at least once a week with an accurate gauge (don't forget the spare!)

very slowly after a nail has embedded itself in the tread. If a slow leak persists, check the valve stem core to make sure it's tight (see illustration). Examine the tread for an object that may have embedded itself in the tire or for a "plug" that may have begun to leak (radial tire punctures are repaired with a plug that's installed in a puncture). If a puncture is suspected, it can be easily verified by spraying a solution of soapy water onto the puncture area (see illustration). The soapy solution will bubble if there's a leak. Unless the puncture is unusually large, a tire shop or service station can usually repair the tire.

5   Carefully inspect the inner sidewall of each tire for evidence of brake fluid leakage. If you see any, inspect the brakes immediately.

6   Correct air pressure adds miles to the lifespan of the tires, improves mileage and enhances overall ride quality. Tire pressure cannot be accurately estimated by looking at a tire, especially if it's a radial. A tire pressure gauge is essential. Keep an accurate gauge in the

vehicle. The pressure gauges attached to the nozzles of air hoses at gas stations are often inaccurate.

7   Always check tire pressure when the tires are cold. Cold, in this case, means the vehicle has not been driven over a mile in the three hours preceding a tire pressure check. A pressure rise of four to eight pounds is not uncommon once the tires are warm.

8   Unscrew the valve cap protruding from the wheel or hubcap and push the gauge firmly onto the valve stem (see illustration). Note the reading on the gauge and compare the figure to the recommended tire pressure shown on the placard on the driver's side door pillar. Be sure to reinstall the valve cap to keep dirt and moisture out of the valve stem mechanism. Check all four tires and, if necessary, add enough air to bring them up to the recommended pressure.

9   Don't forget to keep the spare tire inflated to the specified pressure (refer to your owner's manual or the tire sidewall).

6   Power steering fluid level check (every 3000 miles or 3 months)

6.2 The power steering fluid dipstick is located in the power steering pump reservoir - turn the cap counterclockwise to remove it

▶ **Refer to illustrations 6.2 and 6.6**

1   Unlike manual steering, the power steering system relies on fluid which may, over a period of time, require replenishing.

2   On all models, the fluid reservoir for the power steering pump is located on the pump body at the front of the engine (see illustration).

3   For the check, the front wheels should be pointed straight ahead and the engine should be off.

4   Use a clean rag to wipe off the reservoir cap and the area around the cap. This will help prevent any foreign matter from entering the reservoir during the check.

5   Twist off the cap and check the temperature of the fluid at the end of the dipstick with your finger.

6 Wipe off the fluid with a clean rag, reinstall the dipstick, then withdraw it and read the fluid level (see illustration). On six-cylinder engines, the level should be at the C (cold) mark. On V8 engines, the level should be at the FULL mark. Never allow the fluid level to drop below the lower mark on the dipstick.

7 If additional fluid is required, pour the specified type directly into the reservoir, using a funnel to prevent spills.

8 If the reservoir requires frequent fluid additions, all power steering hoses, hose connections, steering gear and the power steering pump should be carefully checked for leaks.

6.6 The power steering fluid dipstick has marks on it so the fluid can be checked hot or cold

7   Automatic transmission fluid level check (every 3000 miles or 3 months)

▶ **Refer to illustrations 7.3 and 7.6**

1 The automatic transmission fluid level should be carefully maintained. Low fluid level can lead to slipping or loss of drive, while overfilling can cause foaming and loss of fluid.

2 With the parking brake set, start the engine, then move the shift lever through all the gear ranges, ending in Park. The fluid level must be checked with the vehicle level and the engine running at idle.

➡**Note: Incorrect fluid level readings will result if the vehicle has just been driven at high speeds for an extended period, in hot weather in city traffic, or if it has been pulling a trailer. If any of these conditions apply, wait until the fluid has cooled (about 30 minutes).**

3 With the transmission at normal operating temperature, remove the dipstick from the filler tube. The dipstick is located at the rear of the engine compartment on the passenger's side (see illustration).

4 Wipe the fluid from the dipstick with a clean rag and push it back into the filler tube until the cap seats.

5 Pull the dipstick out again and note the fluid level.

6 If the fluid is warm, the level should be in the area between the COLD and HOT ranges (see illustration). If it's hot, the level should be in the crosshatched area in the HOT range. If additional fluid is required, add it directly into the tube using a funnel. It takes about one pint to raise the level from the COLD range to the HOT range with a hot transmission, so add the fluid a little at a time and keep checking the level until it's correct.

7 The condition of the fluid should also be checked along with the level. If the fluid at the end of the dipstick is a dark reddish-brown color, or if it smells burned, it should be changed. If you are in doubt about the condition of the fluid, purchase some new fluid and compare the two for color and smell.

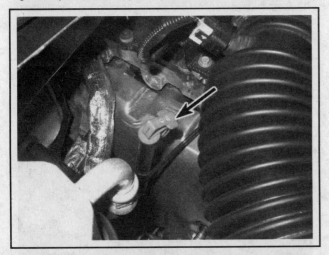

7.3 The automatic transmission dipstick is located at the right rear of the engine compartment - flip up the handle before pulling out the dipstick

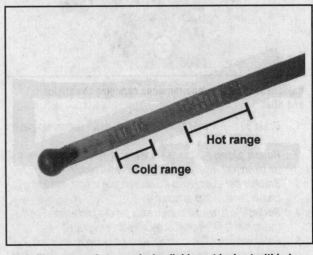

Hot range

Cold range

7.6 The automatic transmission fluid must be kept within in the appropriate marks, depending on the fluid temperature

8   Engine oil and filter change (every 3000 miles or 3 months)

◆ Refer to illustrations 8.3, 8.9, 8.14 and 8.18

➡Note: These vehicles are equipped with an oil life indicator system that illuminates a light on the instrument panel when the system deems it necessary to change the oil. A number of factors are taken into consideration to determine when the oil should be considered "worn out." Generally, this system will allow the vehicle to accumulate more miles between oil changes than the traditional 3000 mile interval, but we believe that frequent oil changes are "cheap insurance" and will prolong engine life. If you do decide not to change your oil every 3000 miles and rely on the oil life indicator instead, make sure you don't exceed 10,000 miles before the oil is changed, regardless of what the oil life indicator shows.

1   Frequent oil changes are the most important preventive maintenance procedures that can be done by the home mechanic. As engine oil ages, it becomes diluted and contaminated, which leads to premature engine wear.

2   Although some sources recommend oil filter changes every other oil change, we feel that the minimal cost of an oil filter and the relative ease with which it is installed dictate that a new filter be installed every time the oil is changed.

3   Gather together all necessary tools and materials before beginning this procedure (see illustration).

4   You should have plenty of clean rags and newspapers handy to mop up any spills. Access to the underside of the vehicle may be improved if the vehicle can be lifted on a hoist, driven onto ramps or supported by jackstands.

✳✳ WARNING:

Do not work under a vehicle which is supported only by a jack.

5   If this is your first oil change, familiarize yourself with the locations of the oil drain plug and the oil filter.

6   Warm the engine to normal operating temperature. If the new oil or any tools are needed, use this warm-up time to gather everything necessary for the job. The correct type of oil for your application can be found in *Recommended lubricants and fluids* at the end of this Chapter.

7   With the engine oil warm (warm engine oil will drain better and more built-up sludge will be removed with it), raise and support the vehicle. Make sure it's safely supported!

8   Remove the under-vehicle splash shield. Move all necessary tools, rags and newspapers under the vehicle. Set the drain pan under the drain plug. Keep in mind that the oil will initially flow from the pan with some force; position the pan accordingly.

9   Being careful not to touch any of the hot exhaust components, use a wrench to remove the drain plug near the bottom of the oil pan (see illustration). Depending on how hot the oil is, you may want to wear gloves while unscrewing the plug the final few turns.

10 Allow the oil to drain into the pan. It may be necessary to move the pan as the oil flow slows to a trickle.

11 After all the oil has drained, wipe off the drain plug with a clean rag. Small metal particles may cling to the plug and would immediately contaminate the new oil.

12 Clean the area around the drain plug opening and reinstall the plug. Tighten the plug securely with the wrench. If a torque wrench is

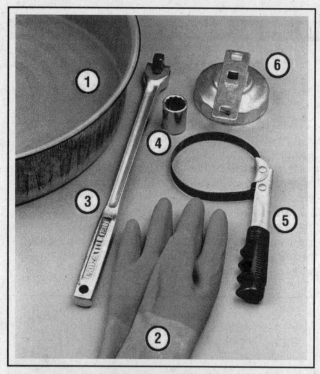

8.3 These tools are required when changing the engine oil and filter

1   Drain pan - It should be fairly shallow in depth, but wide to prevent spills
2   Rubber gloves - When removing the drain plug and filter, you will get oil on your hands (the gloves will prevent burns)
3   Breaker bar - Sometimes the oil drain plug is tight, and a long breaker bar is needed to loosen it
4   Socket - To be used with the breaker bar or a ratchet (must be the correct size to fit the drain plug - six-point preferred)
5   Filter wrench - This is a metal band-type wrench, which requires clearance around the filter to be effective
6   Filter wrench - This type fits on the bottom of the filter and can be turned with a ratchet or breaker bar (different-size wrenches are available for different types of filters)

8.9 Use a proper size box-end wrench or socket to remove the oil drain plug and avoid rounding it off

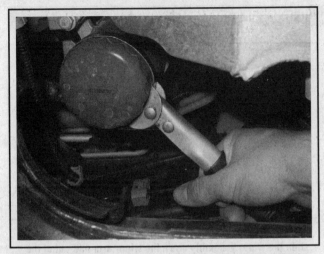

8.14 Since the oil filter is on very tight, you'll need a special wrench for removal - DO NOT use the wrench to tighten the new filter

8.18 Lubricate the oil filter gasket with clean engine oil before installing the filter on the engine

available, use it to tighten the plug to the torque listed in this Chapter's Specifications.

13 Move the drain pan into position under the oil filter.

14 Use the oil filter wrench to loosen the oil filter (see illustration).

15 Completely unscrew the old filter. Be careful; it's full of oil. Empty the oil inside the filter into the drain pan, then lower the filter.

16 Compare the old filter with the new one to make sure they're the same type.

17 Use a clean rag to remove all oil, dirt and sludge from the area where the oil filter mounts to the engine. Check the old filter to make sure the rubber gasket isn't stuck to the engine. If the gasket is stuck to the engine (use a flashlight if necessary), remove it.

18 Apply a light coat of clean oil to the rubber gasket on the new oil filter (see illustration).

19 Attach the new filter to the engine, following the tightening directions printed on the filter canister or packing box. Most filter manufacturers recommend against using a filter wrench due to the possibility of overtightening and damage to the seal.

20 Remove all tools, rags, etc. from under the vehicle, being careful not to spill the oil in the drain pan, then lower the vehicle.

21 Move to the engine compartment and locate the oil filler cap.

22 Pour the fresh oil through the filler opening. Use a funnel to prevent spills.

23 Refer to the engine oil capacity in this Chapter's Specifications and add the proper amount of fresh oil into the engine. Wait a few minutes to allow the oil to drain into the pan, then check the level on the oil dipstick (see Section 4 if necessary). If the oil level is above the upper mark, start the engine and allow the new oil to circulate.

24 Run the engine for only about a minute and then shut it off. Immediately look under the vehicle and check for leaks at the oil pan drain plug and around the oil filter.

25 With the new oil circulated and the filter now completely full, recheck the level on the dipstick and add more oil as necessary.

26 During the first few trips after an oil change, make it a point to check frequently for leaks and proper oil level.

27 The old oil drained from the engine cannot be reused in its present state and should be disposed of. Check with your local auto parts store, disposal facility or environmental agency to see if they will accept the oil for recycling. After the oil has cooled it can be drained into a container (capped plastic jugs, topped bottles, milk cartons, etc.) for transport to one of these disposal sites. Don't dispose of the oil by pouring it on the ground or down a drain!

OIL LIFE MONITOR

28 The Oil Life Monitor is a function of the PCM that tracks engine operating temperature and rpm. If the PCM determines that your engine's oil has been used long enough, an indicator that shows "Change Engine Oil" will light on the instrument panel.

29 When you change your engine oil and filter, whether you change it at the interval recommended in this Chapter or only when the light comes on, you will have to reset the system to make the indicator go out.

30 To reset, switch the ignition key to Run (engine not running) and depress/let up the throttle pedal quickly three times (within five seconds). The light should flash for five seconds, to let you know the system is reset properly. If the light does not flash for five seconds the procedure needs to be repeated.

31 If the vehicle is equipped with a Driver Information Center (DIC) on the instrument panel, reset the engine oil life system by pressing the fuel information button until ENGINE OIL LIFE is shown, then hold the select button down until the system is reset.

9 Seat belt check (every 6000 miles or 6 months)

1 Check seat belts, buckles, latch plates and guide loops for obvious damage and signs of wear.

2 Where the seat belt receptacle bolts to the floor of the vehicle, check that the bolts are secure.

3 See if the seat belt reminder light comes on when the key is turned to the Run or Start position. A chime should also sound.

10 Wiper blade inspection and replacement (every 6000 miles or 6 months)

♦ **Refer to illustration 10.3**

1 The windshield wiper blade elements should be checked periodically for cracks and deterioration.

2 Lift the wiper blade assembly away from the glass.

3 Press the release lever and slide the blade assembly out of the hook in the end of the wiper arm (see illustration).

4 Squeeze the two rubber prongs at the end of the blade element, then slide the element out of the frame.

➡**Note: These elements can be replaced by hand, without pliers.**

5 Compare the new element with the old for length, design, etc. Some replacement elements come in a three-piece design (two metal strips, one on either side of the rubber) that is held together by several small plastic sleeves. Keep the sleeves in place on this design until you start sliding the element into the frame. Remove each of the plastic sleeves as needed when they reach the frame.

6 Slide the new element into the frame, notched end last and secure the clips into the notches of the frame.

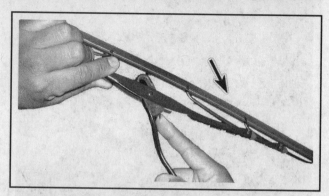

10.3 Depress the release lever (finger is on it here) and slide the wiper assembly down the wiper arm and out of the hook in the end of the arm

7 Reinstall the blade assembly on the arm, wet the windshield and test for proper operation.

11 Battery check, maintenance and charging (every 6000 miles or 6 months)

♦ **Refer to illustrations 11.1, 11.5, 11.7a, 11.7b and 11.7c**

❊❊ WARNING:

Refer to the Warning and Caution in Chapter 5, Section 1 under "Battery disconnection" before proceeding with the following Steps.

❊❊ WARNING:

Certain precautions must be followed when checking and servicing the battery. Hydrogen gas, which is highly flammable, is always present in the battery cells, so keep lighted tobacco and all other open flames and sparks away from the battery. The electrolyte inside the battery is actually dilute sulfuric acid, which will cause injury if splashed on your skin or in your eyes. It will also ruin clothes and painted surfaces. When removing the battery cables, always detach the negative cable first and hook it up last!

11.1 Tools and materials required for battery maintenance

1 ***Face shield/safety goggles*** - *When removing corrosion with a brush, the acidic particles can easily fly up into your eyes*

2 ***Rubber gloves*** - *Another safety item to consider when servicing the battery - remember that's acid inside the battery!*

3 ***Battery terminal/cable cleaner*** - *This wire brush cleaning tool will remove all traces of corrosion from the battery posts and cable clamps*

4 ***Treated felt washers*** - *Placing one of these on each post, directly under the cable clamps, will help prevent corrosion*

5 ***Baking soda*** - *A solution of baking soda and water can be used to neutralize corrosion*

6 ***Petroleum jelly*** - *A layer of this on the battery posts will help prevent corrosion*

1 A routine preventive maintenance program for the battery in your vehicle is the only way to ensure quick and reliable starts. But before performing any battery maintenance, make sure that you have the proper equipment necessary to work safely around the battery (see illustration).

➡**Note: Some of the covered models have an auxiliary battery in addition to the standard battery. All of the following care and maintenance should be applied to both batteries.**

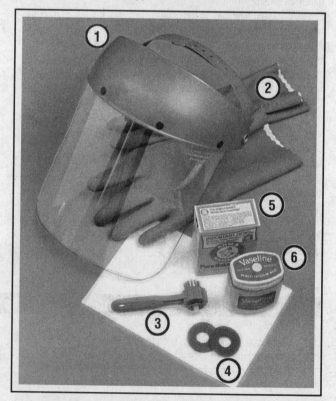

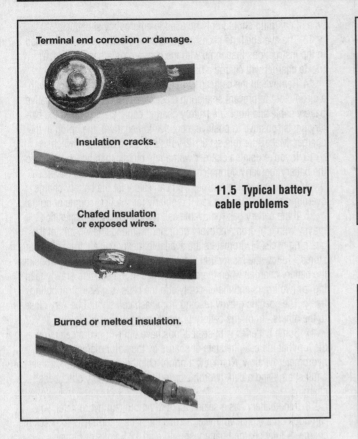

Terminal end corrosion or damage.

Insulation cracks.

11.5 Typical battery cable problems

Chafed insulation or exposed wires.

Burned or melted insulation.

11.7a A tool like this one (available at auto parts stores) is used to clean the side-terminal type battery-cable contact area

11.7b Use the brush side of the tool to finish the job

11.7c Regardless of the type of tool used on the battery and cables, a clean, shiny surface should be the result

2 There are also several precautions that should be taken whenever battery maintenance is performed. Before servicing the battery, always turn the engine and all accessories off and disconnect the cable from the negative terminal of the battery.

3 The battery produces hydrogen gas, which is both flammable and explosive. Never create a spark, smoke or light a match around the battery. Always charge the battery in a ventilated area.

4 Electrolyte contains poisonous and corrosive sulfuric acid. Do not allow it to get in your eyes, on your skin or on your clothes. Never ingest it. Wear protective safety glasses when working near the battery. Keep children away from the battery.

5 Note the external condition of the battery. If the positive terminal and cable clamp on your vehicle's battery is equipped with a rubber protector, make sure that it's not torn or damaged. It should completely cover the terminal. Look for any corroded or loose connections, cracks in the case or cover or loose hold-down clamps. Also check the entire length of each cable for cracks and frayed conductors (see illustration).

6 If corrosion, which looks like white, fluffy deposits is evident, particularly around the terminals, the battery should be removed for cleaning. Loosen the cable bolts with a wrench, being careful to remove the ground cable first, and slide them off the terminals. Then remove the hold-down clamp and lift the battery from the engine compartment.

7 Clean the cable ends thoroughly with a battery brush or a terminal cleaner and a solution of warm water and baking soda. Wash the terminals and the side of the battery case with the same solution but make sure that the solution doesn't get into the battery. When cleaning the cables, terminals and battery case, wear safety goggles and rubber gloves to prevent any solution from coming in contact with your eyes or hands. Wear old clothes too - even diluted, sulfuric acid splashed onto clothes will burn holes in them. If the terminals have been corroded, clean them up with a terminal cleaner (see illustrations). Thoroughly wash all cleaned areas with plain water.

8 Make sure that the battery tray is in good condition and the hold-down clamp is tight. If the battery is removed from the tray, make sure no parts remain in the bottom of the tray when the battery is reinstalled. When reinstalling the hold-down clamp bolts, do not overtighten them.

9 Any metal parts of the vehicle damaged by corrosion should be covered with a zinc-based primer, then painted.

10 Information on removing and installing the battery can be found in Chapter 5. Information on jump starting can be found at the front of this manual.

CHARGING

➡Note: The manufacturer recommends the battery be removed from the vehicle for charging because the gas that escapes during this procedure can damage the paint. Fast charging with the battery cables connected can result in damage to the electrical system.

11 Slow-rate charging is the best way to restore a battery that's discharged to the point where it will not start the engine. It's also a good way to maintain the battery charge in a vehicle that's only driven a few miles between starts. Maintaining the battery charge is particularly important in the winter when the battery must work harder to start the engine and electrical accessories that drain the battery are in greater use.

12 It's best to use a one or two-amp battery charger (sometimes called a "trickle" charger). They are the safest and put the least strain on the battery. They are also the least expensive. For a faster charge, you can use a higher amperage charger, but don't use one rated more than 1/10th the amp/hour rating of the battery. Rapid boost charges that claim to restore the power of the battery in one to two hours are hardest on the battery and can damage batteries not in good condition. This type of charging should only be used in emergency situations.

13 The average time necessary to charge a battery should be listed in the instructions that come with the charger. As a general rule, a trickle charger will charge a battery in 12 to 16 hours.

14 Remove all the cell caps (if equipped) and cover the holes with a clean cloth to prevent spattering electrolyte. Disconnect the negative battery cable and hook the battery charger cable clamps up to the battery posts (positive to positive, negative to negative), then plug in the charger. Make sure it is set at 12-volts if it has a selector switch.

15 If you're using a charger with a rate higher than two amps, check the battery regularly during charging to make sure it doesn't overheat. If you're using a trickle charger, you can safely let the battery charge overnight after you've checked it regularly for the first couple of hours.

16 If the battery has removable cell caps, measure the specific gravity with a hydrometer every hour during the last few hours of the charging cycle. Hydrometers are available inexpensively from auto parts stores - follow the instructions that come with the hydrometer. Consider the battery charged when there's no change in the specific gravity reading for two hours and the electrolyte in the cells is gassing (bubbling) freely. The specific gravity reading from each cell should be very close to the others. If not, the battery probably has a bad cell(s).

17 Some batteries with sealed tops have built-in hydrometers on the top that indicate the state of charge by the color displayed in the hydrometer window. Normally, a bright-colored hydrometer indicates a full charge and a dark hydrometer indicates the battery still needs charging.

18 If the battery has a sealed top and no built-in hydrometer, you can hook up a digital voltmeter across the battery terminals to check the charge. A fully charged battery should read 12.5 volts or higher.

19 Further information on the battery and jump-starting can be found in Chapter 5 and at the front of this manual.

12 Drivebelt and tensioner check and replacement (every 6000 miles or 6 months)

◆ Refer to illustrations 12.2, 12.4, 12.5 and 12.7

1 A serpentine drivebelt is located at the front of the engine and plays an important role in the overall operation of the engine and its components. Due to its function and material make up, the belt is prone to wear and should be periodically inspected. The serpentine belt drives the alternator, power steering pump, water pump and air conditioning compressor.

2 With the engine off, open the hood and use your fingers (and a flashlight, if necessary), to move along the belt checking for cracks and separation of the belt plies. Also check for fraying and glazing, which gives the belt a shiny appearance (see illustration). Both sides of the belt must be inspected.

3 Check the ribs on the underside of the belt. They should all be the same depth, with none of the surface uneven.

4 The tension of the belt is maintained by a spring-loaded tensioner assembly and isn't adjustable. The belt should be replaced when the indexing arrow is lined up with the indexing mark on the tensioner assembly (see illustrations).

5 To replace the belt, rotate the tensioner clockwise to release belt tension (see illustration).

6 Remove the belt from the tensioner and auxiliary components and slowly release the tensioner.

7 After verifying the new belt is the same length as the original belt route the new belt over the various pulleys, again rotating the tensioner to allow the belt to be installed, then release the belt tensioner.

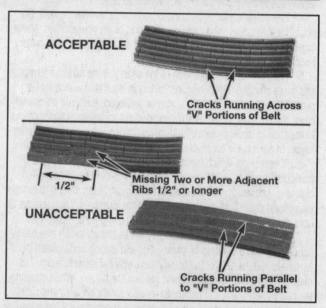

12.2 Check ribbed (serpentine) belts for signs of wear like these - if it looks worn, replace it

➡Note: A drivebelt routing decal is located on the radiator support to help during drivebelt installation (see illustration).

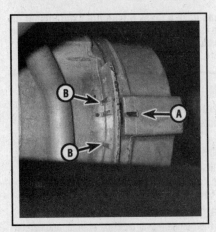

12.4 The indexing mark (A) on the drivebelt's tensioner must remain between the marks (B) on the tensioner assembly

12.5 Use a drivebelt tool to turn the tensioner clockwise for belt removal (there may not be room for a standard ratchet or breaker bar)

12.7 The drivebelt routing diagram is found on the radiator support

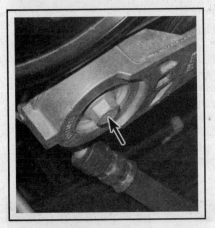

12.8a Drivebelt tensioner mounting bolt

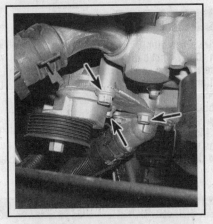

12.8b Main belt tensioner mounting bolts (arrows)

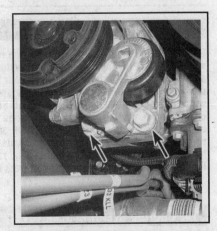

12.8c Mounting bolts (arrow) for air conditioning belt tensioner

TENSIONER REPLACEMENT

♦ **Refer to illustrations 12.8a, 12.8b and 12.8c**

8   To replace a tensioner that exhibits binding or a worn-out pulley/bearing, remove the belt. On a six-cylinder engine, remove the tensioner mounting bolt (see illustration). On V8 engines, remove the tensioner mounting bolts (see illustrations).

9   Installation is the reverse of the removal procedure.

➡**Note: On six-cylinder engines, be sure to get the indexing dowel on the tensioner inserted into the hole provided on the tensioner mounting surface.**

13   Underhood hose check and replacement (every 6000 miles or 6 months)

✳✳ CAUTION:

Replacement of air conditioning hoses must be left to a dealer service department or air conditioning shop that has the equipment to depressurize the system safely and recover the refrigerant. Never remove air conditioning components or hoses until the system has been depressurized.

1   High temperatures in the engine compartment can cause the deterioration of the rubber and plastic hoses used for engine, accessory and emission systems operation. Periodic inspection should be made for cracks, loose clamps, material hardening and leaks. Information specific to the cooling system hoses can be found in Section 14.

2   Some, but not all, hoses are secured to their fittings with clamps. Where clamps are used, check to be sure they haven't lost their tension, allowing the hose to leak. If clamps aren't used, make sure the hose has not expanded and/or hardened where it slips over the fitting, allowing it to leak.

VACUUM HOSES

3   It's quite common for vacuum hoses, especially those in the emissions system, to be color-coded or identified by colored stripes molded into them. Various systems require hoses with different wall thickness, collapse resistance and temperature resistance. When replacing hoses, be sure the new ones are made of the same material.

4   Often the only effective way to check a hose is to remove it completely from the vehicle. If more than one hose is removed, be sure to label the hoses and fittings to ensure correct installation.

5   When checking vacuum hoses, be sure to include any plastic T-fittings in the check. Inspect the fittings for cracks and the hose where it fits over the fitting for distortion, which could cause leakage.

6   A small piece of vacuum hose (1/4-inch inside diameter) can be used as a stethoscope to detect vacuum leaks. Hold one end of the hose to your ear and probe around vacuum hoses and fittings, listening for the "hissing" sound characteristic of a vacuum leak.

✳✳ WARNING:

When probing with the vacuum hose stethoscope, be very careful not to come into contact with moving engine components such as the drivebelt, cooling fan, etc.

FUEL HOSE

✳✳ WARNING:

Gasoline is extremely flammable, so take extra precautions when you work on any part of the fuel system. Don't smoke or allow open flames or bare light bulbs near the work area, and don't work in a garage where a gas-type appliance (such as a water heater or clothes dryer) is present. Since gasoline is carcinogenic, wear fuel-resistant gloves when there's a possibility of being exposed to fuel, and, if you spill any fuel on your skin, rinse it off immediately with soap and water. Mop up any spills immediately and do not store fuel-soaked rags where they could ignite. When you perform any kind of work on the fuel system, wear safety glasses and have a Class B type fire extinguisher on hand. The fuel system is under pressure, so if any lines must be disconnected, the pressure in the system must be relieved first (see Chapter 4 for more information).

7   Check all rubber fuel lines for deterioration and chafing. Check especially for cracks in areas where the hose bends and just before fittings, such as where a hose attaches to the fuel filter and fuel injection unit.

8   High quality fuel line, specifically designed for high-pressure fuel injection applications, must be used for fuel line replacement. Never, under any circumstances, use regular fuel line, unreinforced vacuum line, clear plastic tubing or water hose for fuel lines.

9   Spring-type (pinch) clamps are commonly used on fuel lines. These clamps often lose their tension over a period of time, and can be "sprung" during removal. Replace all spring-type clamps with screw clamps whenever a hose is replaced.

METAL LINES

10 Sections of metal line are routed along the frame, between the fuel tank and the engine. Check carefully to be sure the line has not been bent or crimped and no cracks have started in the line.

11 If a section of metal fuel line must be replaced, only seamless steel tubing should be used, since copper and aluminum tubing don't have the strength necessary to withstand normal engine vibration.

12 Check the metal brake lines where they enter the master cylinder and brake proportioning unit for cracks in the lines or loose fittings. Any sign of brake fluid leakage calls for an immediate and thorough inspection of the brake system.

---

14   Cooling system check (every 6000 miles or 6 months)

◆ **Refer to illustration 14.4**

✳✳ CAUTION:

Never mix green-colored ethylene glycol anti-freeze and orange-colored "DEX-COOL" silicate-free coolant because doing so will destroy the efficiency of the "DEX-COOL" coolant which is designed to last for 100,000 miles or five years.

1   Many major engine failures can be attributed to a faulty cooling system. If the vehicle is equipped with an automatic transmission, the cooling system also cools the transmission fluid and thus plays an important role in prolonging transmission life.

2   The cooling system should be checked with the engine cold. Do this before the vehicle is driven for the day or after it has been shut off for at least three hours.

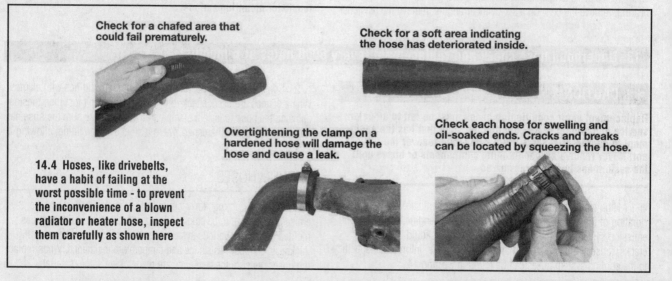

Check for a chafed area that could fail prematurely.

Check for a soft area indicating the hose has deteriorated inside.

Overtightening the clamp on a hardened hose will damage the hose and cause a leak.

Check each hose for swelling and oil-soaked ends. Cracks and breaks can be located by squeezing the hose.

14.4 Hoses, like drivebelts, have a habit of failing at the worst possible time - to prevent the inconvenience of a blown radiator or heater hose, inspect them carefully as shown here

3   Remove the radiator cap by slowly unscrewing it until it comes to a stop. If you hear any hissing sounds (indicating there is still pressure in the system), wait until it stops. If there is no hissing sound, depress the cap and continue unscrewing it. Thoroughly clean the cap, inside and out, with clean water. Also clean the filler neck on the radiator. All traces of corrosion should be removed. The coolant inside the coolant reservoir should be relatively transparent. If it is rust colored, the system should be drained and refilled (see Section 30). If the coolant level is not up to the top, add additional antifreeze/coolant mixture (see Section 4).

4   Carefully check the large upper and lower radiator hoses along with any smaller diameter heater hoses that run from the engine to the firewall. Inspect each hose along its entire length, replacing any hose that is cracked, swollen or shows signs of deterioration. Cracks may become more apparent if the hose is squeezed (see illustration).

5   Make sure all hose connections are tight. A leak in the cooling system will usually show up as white or rust-colored deposits on the areas adjoining the leak. If wire-type clamps are used at the ends of the hoses, it may be wise to replace them with more secure, screw-type clamps.

6   Use compressed air or a soft brush to remove bugs, leaves, etc. from the front of the radiator or air conditioning condenser. Be careful not to damage the delicate cooling fins or cut yourself on them.

7   Every other inspection, or at the first indication of cooling system problems, have the cap and system pressure tested. If you don't have a pressure tester, most gas stations and repair shops will do this for a minimal charge.

15 Tire rotation (every 6000 miles or 6 months)

▶ **Refer to illustrations 15.2a and 15.2b**

1   The tires should be rotated at the specified intervals and whenever uneven wear is noticed.

2   Tires must be rotated in the recommended pattern (see illustrations).

3   Refer to the information in *Jacking and towing* at the front of this manual for the proper procedures to follow when raising the vehicle and changing a tire. If the brakes are to be checked, don't apply the parking brake as stated. Make sure the tires are blocked to prevent the vehicle from rolling as it's raised.

4   Preferably, the entire vehicle should be raised at the same time. This can be done on a hoist or by jacking up each corner and then lowering the vehicle onto jackstands placed under the frame rails. Always use four jackstands and make sure the vehicle is safely supported.

5   After rotation, check and adjust the tire pressures as necessary. Tighten the lug nuts to the torque listed in this Chapter's Specifications.

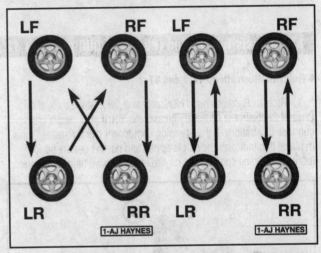

15.2a The recommended four-tire rotation pattern for non-directional radial tires

15.2b The recommended four-tire rotation pattern for directional radial tires

16 Differential lubricant level check (every 6,000 miles or 6 months)

▶ **Refer to illustrations 16.2a and 16.2b**

➡ **Note: 4WD vehicles have two differentials - one in the center of each axle. 2WD vehicles have one differential - in the center of the rear axle. On 4WD models, be sure to check the lubricant level in both differentials.**

1   The filler plug on all front and most rear differentials is a threaded metal type. If the vehicle is raised to gain access to the plug, be sure to support it safely on jackstands - DO NOT crawl under the vehicle when it's supported only by the jack. Be sure the vehicle is level or the check may not be accurate.

2   Remove the plug from the filler hole in the differential housing or cover (see illustrations).

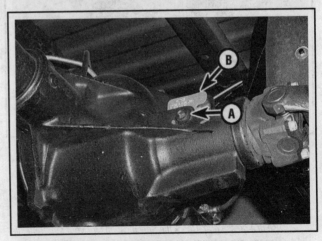

16.2a Remove the rear axle filler plug (A) to check the differential lubricant level - some models may have a tag with specific information about the required lubricant (B)

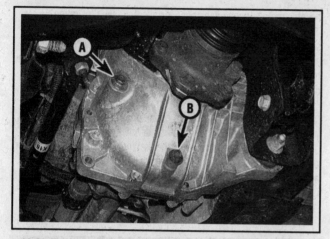

16.2b Remove the front (4WD) axle filler plug (A) to check the differential lubricant level - B is the drain plug (typical)

3   The lubricant level should be at the bottom of the filler hole. If you're checking the rear differential and it is filled with synthetic lubricant, the level should be below the fill-plug opening by 1/2 inch. If not, use a pump or squeeze bottle to add the recommended lubricant until it just starts to run out of the opening. On some models a tag is located in the area of the plug which gives information regarding lubricant type.

4   Install the plug securely into the filler hole.

17 Chassis lubrication (every 15,000 miles or 12 months)

♦ **Refer to illustrations 17.1 and 17.2**

1   Refer to *Recommended lubricants and fluids* at the back of this Chapter to obtain the necessary grease, etc. You'll also need a grease gun (see illustration). If a suspension component has no grease fitting in place, this indicates the part is sealed and doesn't require periodic lubrication. Some components on 4WD models have fittings that aren't on 2WD versions, and vice versa.

2   Look under the vehicle and look for the presence of grease fittings (see illustration).

3   For easier access under the vehicle, raise it with a jack and place jackstands under the frame. Make sure it's safely supported by the stands. If the wheels are to be removed at this interval for tire rotation or brake inspection, loosen the lug nuts slightly while the vehicle is still on the ground.

4   Before beginning, force a little grease out of the nozzle to remove any dirt from the end of the gun. Wipe the nozzle clean with a rag.

5   With the grease gun and plenty of clean rags, crawl under the vehicle and begin lubricating the components.

6   Wipe one of the grease fittings clean and push the nozzle firmly over it. Pump the gun until the component is completely lubricated. On balljoints, stop pumping when the rubber seal is firm to the touch. Do not pump too much grease into the fitting as it could rupture the seal. For all other suspension and steering components, continue pumping

17.1 Materials required for chassis and body lubrication

1   *Engine oil* - Light engine oil in a can like this can be used for door and hood hinges
2   *Graphite spray* - Used to lubricate lock cylinders
3   *Grease* - Grease, in a variety of types and weights, is available for use in a grease gun. Check the Specifications for your requirements
4   *Grease gun* - A common grease gun, shown here with a detachable hose and nozzle, is needed for chassis lubrication. After use, clean it thoroughly!

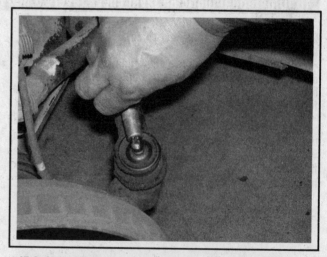

17.2 After cleaning the grease fitting, push the gun nozzle firmly into place and pump the grease into the component (usually about two pumps will be sufficient)

grease into the fitting until it oozes out of the joint between the two components. If it escapes around the grease gun nozzle, the fitting is clogged or the nozzle is not completely seated on the fitting. Resecure the gun nozzle to the fitting and try again. If necessary, replace the fitting with a new one.

7   Wipe the excess grease from the components and the grease fitting. Repeat the procedure for the remaining fittings.

8   Clean the fitting and pump grease into the driveline universal joints until the grease can be seen coming out of the contact points. The other U-joints are sealed and do not require lubrication.

➡Note: Most replacement driveshaft U-joints aren't permanently sealed, and are sold with grease fittings. If your U-joints have been replaced, make sure you include them in your routine chassis lubrication.

9   Also clean and lubricate the parking brake cable guides and levers.

✳✳ CAUTION:

Do not use chassis lubrication on the brake cables themselves. The grease will cause the cable housings to deteriorate.

18 Fuel system check (every 15,000 miles or 12 months)

▶ **Refer to illustration 18.7**

✳✳ WARNING:

Gasoline is extremely flammable, so take extra precautions when you work on any part of the fuel system. Don't smoke or allow open flames or bare light bulbs near the work area, and don't work in a garage where a gas-type appliance (such as a water heater or clothes dryer) is present. Since gasoline is carcinogenic, wear fuel-resistant gloves when there's a possibility of being exposed to fuel, and, if you spill any fuel on your skin, rinse it off immediately with soap and water. Mop up any spills immediately and do not store fuel-soaked rags where they could ignite. When you perform any kind of work on the fuel system, wear safety glasses and have a Class B type fire extinguisher on hand. The fuel system is under constant pressure, so, before any lines are disconnected, the fuel system pressure must be relieved (see Chapter 4).

1   If you smell gasoline while driving or after the vehicle has been sitting in the sun, inspect the fuel system immediately.

2   Remove the gas filler cap and inspect if for damage and corrosion. The gasket should have an unbroken sealing imprint. If the gasket is damaged or corroded, install a new cap.

3   Inspect the fuel feed and return lines for cracks. Make sure that the connections between the fuel lines and the fuel injection system are tight.

✳✳ WARNING:

Your vehicle is fuel injected, so you must relieve the fuel system pressure before servicing fuel system components. The fuel system pressure relief procedure is outlined in Chapter 4.

4   The fuel injectors are not visible on the 4.2L engine; signs of fuel leakage may be fuel contaminated oil, or an excessively long crank time before engine start, followed by black smoke from the tailpipe immediately after starting.

5   Since some components of the fuel system - the fuel tank and part of the fuel feed and return lines, for example - are underneath the vehicle, they can be inspected more easily with the vehicle raised on a hoist. If that's not possible, raise the vehicle and support it on jack stands.

6   With the vehicle raised and safely supported, inspect the gas tank and filler neck for punctures, cracks and other damage. The connection between the filler neck and the tank is particularly critical. Sometimes a rubber filler neck will leak because of loose clamps or deteriorated rubber. Inspect all fuel tank mounting brackets and straps to be sure that the tank is securely attached to the vehicle.

✳✳ WARNING:

Do not, under any circumstances, try to repair a fuel tank (except rubber components). A welding torch or any open flame can easily cause fuel vapors inside the tank to explode.

7   Carefully check all rubber hoses and metal lines leading away from the fuel tank (see illustration). Check for loose connections, deteriorated hoses, crimped lines and other damage. Repair or replace damaged sections as necessary (see Chapter 4).

8   The evaporative emissions control system can also be a source of fuel odors. The function of the system is to store fuel vapors from the fuel tank in a charcoal canister until they can be routed to the intake manifold where they mix with incoming air before being burned in the combustion chambers.

9   The most common symptom of a faulty evaporative emissions system is a strong odor of fuel coming from the area of the charcoal canister. If a fuel odor has been detected, and you have already checked the areas described above, check the charcoal canister, located near the fuel tank, and the hoses connected to it (see Chapter 6).

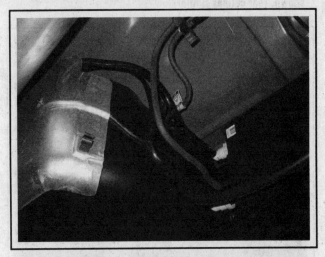

18.7 Inspect the fuel tank mounting straps and the various fuel and vapor lines

19 Brake system check (every 15,000 miles or 12 months)

➠Note: For detailed photographs of the brake system, refer to Chapter 9.

1   In addition to the specified intervals, the brakes should be inspected every time the wheels are removed or whenever a defect is suspected.

2   Any of the following symptoms could indicate a potential brake system defect: The vehicle pulls to one side when the brake pedal is depressed; the brakes make squealing or dragging noises when applied; brake pedal travel is excessive; the pedal pulsates; or brake fluid leaks, usually onto the inside of the tire or wheel.

3   Loosen the wheel lug nuts.

4   Raise the vehicle and place it securely on jackstands.

5   Remove the wheels (see *Jacking and towing* at the front of this book, or your owner's manual, if necessary).

DISC BRAKES

▶ **Refer to illustrations 19.7a, 19.7b, 19.9 and 19.11**

6   There are two pads (an outer and an inner) in each caliper. The pads are visible with the wheels removed. The vehicles covered by this manual have disc brakes front and rear, with a mechanical, drum-type parking brake mechanism inside the rear discs.

7   Check the pad thickness by looking at each end of the caliper and through the inspection window in the caliper body (see illustrations). If the lining material is less than the thickness listed in this Chapter's Specifications, replace the pads.

➠Note: Keep in mind that the lining material is riveted or bonded to a metal backing plate and the metal portion is not included in this measurement.

8   If it is difficult to determine the exact thickness of the remaining pad material by the above method, or if you are at all concerned about the condition of the pads, remove the caliper(s), then remove the pads from the calipers for further inspection (refer to Chapter 9).

9   Once the pads are removed from the calipers, clean them with brake cleaner and re-measure them with a ruler or a vernier caliper (see illustration).

10 Measure the disc thickness with a micrometer to make sure that it still has service life remaining. If any disc is thinner than the specified minimum thickness, replace it (refer to Chapter 9). Even if the disc has service life remaining, check its condition. Look for scoring, gouging and burned spots. If these conditions exist, remove the disc and have it resurfaced (see Chapter 9).

11 Before installing the wheels, check all brake lines and hoses for damage, wear, deformation, cracks, corrosion, leakage, bends and twists, particularly in the vicinity of the rubber hoses at the calipers (see illustration). Check the clamps for tightness and the connections for

19.7a With the wheel off, check the thickness of the inner pad through the inspection hole in the caliper (front caliper shown, rear caliper similar)

19.7b The outer pad is more easily checked at the edge of the caliper

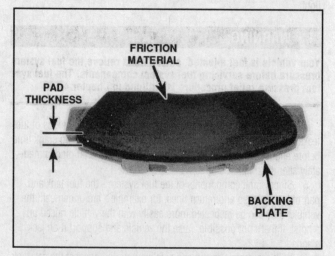

19.9 If a more precise measurement of pad thickness is necessary, remove the pads and measure the remaining friction material

19.11 Check along the brake hoses and at each fitting for deterioration, cracks and leakage

leakage. Make sure that all hoses and lines are clear of sharp edges, moving parts and the exhaust system. If any of the above conditions are noted, repair, reroute or replace the lines and/or fittings as necessary (see Chapter 9).

BRAKE BOOSTER CHECK

12 Sit in the driver's seat and perform the following sequence of tests.

13 With the brake fully depressed, start the engine - the pedal should move down a little when the engine starts.

14 With the engine running, depress the brake pedal several times - the travel distance should not change.

15 Depress the brake, stop the engine and hold the pedal in for about 30 seconds - the pedal should neither sink nor rise.

16 Restart the engine, run it for about a minute and turn it off. Then firmly depress the brake several times - the pedal travel should decrease with each application.

17 If your brakes do not operate as described, the brake booster has failed. Refer to Chapter 9 for the replacement procedure.

PARKING BRAKE

18 One method of checking the parking brake is to park the vehicle on a steep hill with the parking brake set and the transmission in Neutral (be sure to stay in the vehicle for this check). If the parking brake cannot prevent the vehicle from rolling, it's in need of attention (see Chapter 9).

20 Exhaust system check (every 15,000 miles or 12 months)

▶ Refer to illustrations 20.2a and 20.2b

1   With the engine cold (at least three hours after the vehicle has been driven), check the complete exhaust system from the manifold to the end of the tailpipe. Be careful around the catalytic converter, which may be hot even after three hours. The inspection should be done with the vehicle on a hoist to permit unrestricted access. If a hoist isn't available, raise the vehicle and support it securely on jackstands.

2   Check the exhaust pipes and connections for signs of leakage and/or corrosion indicating a potential failure. Make sure that all brackets and hangers are in good condition and tight (see illustrations).

3   Inspect the underside of the body for holes, corrosion, open seams, etc. which may allow exhaust gasses to enter the passenger compartment. Seal all body openings with silicone sealant or body putty.

4   Rattles and other noises can often be traced to the exhaust system, especially the hangers, mounts and heat shields. Try to move the pipes, mufflers and catalytic converter. If the components can come in contact with the body or suspension parts, secure the exhaust system with new brackets and hangers.

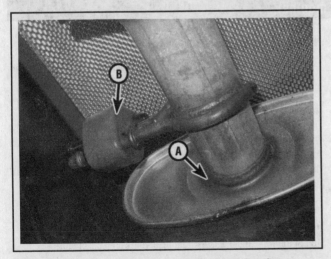

20.2a Inspect the muffler (A) for signs of deterioration, and all hangers (B)

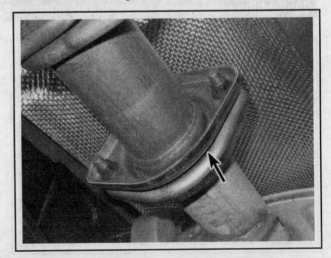

20.2b Inspect all flanged joints for signs of exhaust gas leakage

21 Transfer case lubricant level check (4WD models) (every 15,000 miles or 12 months)

▶ Refer to illustration 21.1

1 The transfer case lubricant level is checked by removing the upper plug located at the rear of the case (see illustration).

2 After removing the plug, reach inside the hole. The lubricant level should be just at the bottom of the hole. If not, add the appropriate lubricant through the opening.

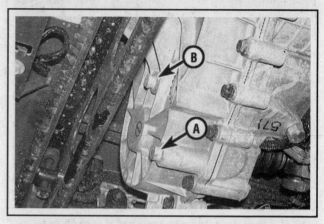

21.1 The drain plug (A) and fill plug (B) are on the rear cover of the transfer case (typical)

22 Brake fluid change (every 30,000 miles or 24 months)

✳✳ WARNING:

Brake fluid can harm your eyes and damage painted surfaces, so use extreme caution when handling or pouring it. Do not use brake fluid that has been standing open or is more than one year old. Brake fluid absorbs moisture from the air. Excess moisture can cause a dangerous loss of braking effectiveness.

1 At the specified intervals, the brake fluid should be drained and replaced. Since the brake fluid may drip or splash when pouring it, place plenty of rags around the master cylinder to protect any surrounding painted surfaces.

2 Before beginning work, purchase the specified brake fluid (see *Recommended lubricants and fluids* at the end of this Chapter).

3 Remove the cap from the master cylinder reservoir.

4 Using a hand suction pump or similar device, withdraw the fluid from the master cylinder reservoir.

5 Add new fluid to the master cylinder until it rises to the line indicated on the reservoir.

6 Bleed the brake system as described in Chapter 9 at all four brakes until new and uncontaminated fluid is expelled from the bleeder screw. Be sure to maintain the fluid level in the master cylinder as you perform the bleeding process. If you allow the master cylinder to run dry, air will enter the system.

7 Refill the master cylinder with fluid and check the operation of the brakes. The pedal should feel solid when depressed, with no sponginess.

✳✳ WARNING:

Do not operate the vehicle if you are in doubt about the effectiveness of the brake system.

23 Air filter replacement (every 30,000 miles or 24 months)

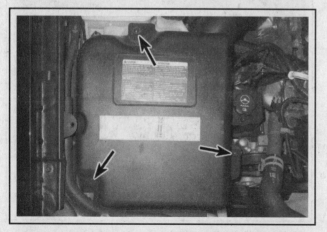

23.3a Loosen the screws and lift the air filter housing cover off

▶ Refer to illustrations 23.3a and 23.3b

1 At the specified intervals, the air filter element should be replaced with a new one.

2 On all models, the air filter is housed in a black plastic box mounted on the right side of the engine compartment. Attached to the intake tube on some models is a plastic gauge that measures the airflow through the filter and indicates when the filter should be changed. If you drive in conditions that are particularly dusty, the gauge may indicate the need for a filter change before the normally-recommended mileage interval.

3 On six-cylinder models, loosen the captive screws (3) and pull the housing cover up, then lift the air filter element out of the housing (see illustrations). Wipe out the inside of the air filter housing and the top of the windshield washer fluid reservoir with a clean rag.

4   On V8 models, remove the radiator support diagonal brace and the radiator air intake baffle. Loosen the captive screws (4) and pull the housing cover up, then lift the air filter element out of the housing. Separate the MAF/IAT unit from the air filter element. Wipe out the inside of the air filter housing and the top of the windshield washer fluid reservoir with a clean rag.

5   While the cover is off, be careful not to drop anything down into the air filter housing.

6   On six-cylinder models, push the new filter element onto the intake tube. Make sure it seats properly in the depression on top of the windshield washer fluid reservoir.

7   On V8 models, install the MAF/IAT unit onto the air filter element and make sure it seats properly.

8   Installation is the reverse of removal. After installing the air filter, push in on the top of the filter indicator to reset it.

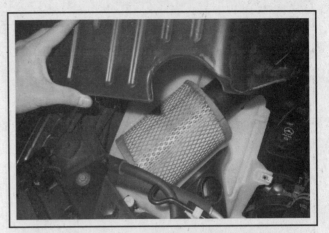

23.3b Holding the cover up, pull the filter element off the intake tube

24 Fuel filter replacement (2004 and earlier models) (every 30,000 miles or 30 months)

♦ Refer to illustration 24.5

✳✳ WARNING:

Gasoline is extremely flammable, so take extra precautions when you work on any part of the fuel system. Don't smoke or allow open flames or bare light bulbs near the work area, and don't work in a garage where a gas-type appliance (such as a water heater or clothes dryer) is present. Since gasoline is carcinogenic, wear fuel-resistant gloves when there's a possibility of being exposed to fuel, and, if you spill any fuel on your skin, rinse it off immediately with soap and water. Mop up any spills immediately and do not store fuel-soaked rags where they could ignite. The fuel system is under constant pressure, so, if any fuel lines are to be disconnected, the fuel pressure in the system must be relieved first (see Chapter 4 for more information). When you perform any kind of work on the fuel system, wear safety glasses and have a Class B type fire extinguisher on hand.

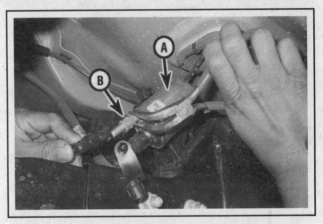

24.5 When changing the fuel filter (A), carefully squeeze the clips (B) to disconnect the fittings

➡Note: On 2005 and later models, the fuel filter is an integral part of the fuel pump module and is not serviceable.

1   Relieve the fuel system pressure (see Chapter 4). Disconnect the cable from the negative battery terminal.

2   Raise the vehicle and support it securely on jackstands.

3   The fuel filter is mounted in a bracket at the fuel tank.

4   Use compressed air or carburetor cleaner to clean any dirt surrounding the fuel inlet and outlet line fittings.

5   There are quick-connect fittings at each end of the filter, requiring finger pressure or a needle-nose pliers to remove. (see illustration).

➡Note: Have some rags or a small container to catch or wipe up extra gasoline that will spill from the filter assembly.

6   Remove the screw that holds the bracket to the tank.

➡Note: 4WD vehicles that are equipped with a tank shield have a small hole in the shield to access the bracket screw.

7   Squeeze the plastic clip together then separate the line from the filter. Most new filters will come with new clips.

8   Installation is the reverse of removal.

25 Spark plug replacement (see maintenance schedule for service intervals)

♦ Refer to illustrations 25.2, 25.5a, 25.5b, 25.8, 25.9a, 25.9b and 25.10

1   The spark plugs are threaded into the top of the cylinder head. For access, you'll have to remove the air intake resonator and the ignition coils.

2   In most cases, the tools necessary for spark plug replacement include a spark plug socket which fits onto a ratchet (spark plug sockets are padded inside to prevent damage to the porcelain insulators on the new plugs), various extensions and a gap gauge to check and adjust the gaps on the new plugs (see illustration). A torque wrench should be used to tighten the new plugs.

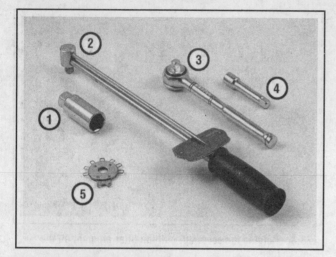

25.2 Tools required for changing spark plugs

1 *Spark plug socket* - This will have special padding inside to protect the spark plug's porcelain insulator

2 *Torque wrench* - Although not mandatory, using this tool is the best way to ensure the plugs are tightened properly

3 *Ratchet* - Standard hand tool to fit the spark plug socket

4 *Extension* - Depending on model and accessories, you may need special extensions and universal joints to reach one or more of the plugs

5 *Spark plug gap gauge* - This gauge for checking the gap comes in a variety of styles. Make sure the gap for your engine is included

➡**Note: The spark plugs on these models are 1/8-inch longer than standard plugs used on most earlier vehicles. Make sure your spark plug socket doesn't bottom-out on the longer plugs, which could crack the insulators.**

3 The best approach when replacing the spark plugs is to purchase the new ones in advance, adjust them to the proper gap and replace them one at a time. When buying the new spark plugs, be sure to obtain the correct plug type for your particular engine. This information can be found in your owner's manual and the *Specifications* at the back of this Chapter.

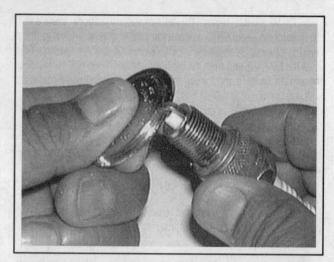

25.5a Spark plug manufacturers recommend using a tapered thickness gauge when checking the gap - slide the thin side into the gap and turn until the gauge just fills the gap, then read the thickness on the gauge - do not force the tool into the gap or use the tapered portion to widen a gap

4 Allow the engine to cool completely before attempting to remove any of the plugs. While you're waiting for the engine to cool, check the new plugs for defects and adjust the gaps.

5 The gap is checked by inserting the proper-thickness gauge between the electrodes at the tip of the plug (see illustration). The gap between the electrodes should be the same as the one specified on the Emissions Control Information label or in this Chapter's Specifications. The wire should just slide between the electrodes with a slight amount of drag. If the gap is incorrect, use the adjuster on the gauge body to bend the curved side electrode slightly until the proper gap is obtained (see illustration). If the side electrode is not exactly over the center electrode, bend it with the adjuster until it is. Check for cracks in the porcelain insulator (if any are found, the plug should not be used).

➡**Note: Manufacturers recommend using a tapered thickness gauge when checking platinum-type spark plugs. Other types of gauges may scrape the thin platinum coating from the electrodes, thus dramatically shortening the life of the plugs.**

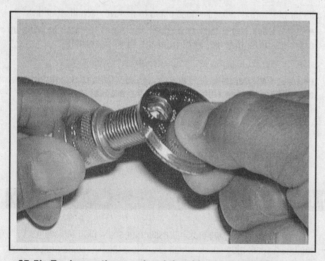

25.5b To change the gap, bend the side electrode only, using the adjuster hole in the tool, and be very careful not to crack or chip the porcelain insulator surrounding the center electrode

25.8 Use a socket and extension to unscrew the spark plugs - various length extensions and perhaps a flex-joint may be required to reach some plugs

A normally worn spark plug should have light tan or gray deposits on the firing tip.

A carbon fouled plug, identified by soft, sooty, black deposits, may indicate an improperly tuned vehicle. Check the air cleaner, ignition components and engine control system.

An oil fouled spark plug indicates an engine with worn piston rings and/or bad valve seals allowing excessive oil to enter the chamber.

This spark plug has been left in the engine too long, as evidenced by the extreme gap- Plugs with such an extreme gap can cause misfiring and stumbling accompanied by a noticeable lack of power.

A physically damaged spark plug may be evidence of severe detonation in that cylinder. Watch that cylinder carefully between services, as a continued detonation will not only damage the plug, but could also damage the engine.

A bridged or almost bridged spark plug, identified by a build-up between the electrodes caused by excessive carbon or oil build-up on the plug.

25.9a Inspect the spark plug to determine engine running conditions

6   With the engine cool, remove the ignition coils (see Chapter 5). Remove the spark plug boots by gently twisting and pulling straight up.

7   If compressed air is available, use it to blow any dirt or foreign material away from the spark plug hole. The idea here is to eliminate the possibility of debris falling into the cylinder as the spark plug is removed.

8   Place the spark plug socket over the plug and remove it from the engine by turning it in a counterclockwise direction (see illustration).

9   Compare the spark plug with this chart (see illustration) to get an indication of the general running condition of the engine. Before installing the new plugs, it is a good idea to apply a thin coat of anti-seize compound to the threads (see illustration).

10 Thread one of the new plugs into the hole until you can no longer turn it with your fingers, then tighten it with a torque wrench (if available) or the ratchet. It's a good idea to slip a short length of rubber hose over the end of the plug to use as a tool to thread it into place (see illustration). The hose will grip the plug well enough to turn it, but will start to slip if the plug begins to cross-thread in the hole - this will prevent damaged threads and the accompanying repair costs.

11 Attach the plug boot to the coil then the coil onto the spark plug.

12 Repeat the procedure for the remaining spark plugs.

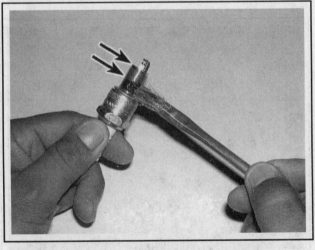

25.9b Apply a thin coat of anti-seize compound to the spark plug threads, being careful not to get any near the lower threads

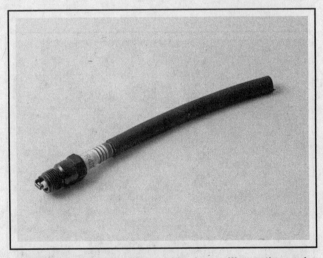

25.10 A length of snug-fitting rubber hose will save time and prevent damaged threads when installing the spark plugs

26 Suspension, steering and driveaxle boot check (every 30,000 miles or 30 months)

26.6 Check for signs of fluid leakage at this point on shock absorbers (front shock module shown)

26.9a Examine the mounting points for the upper . . .

26.9b . . . and lower control arms on the front suspension

➡Note: The steering linkage and suspension components should be checked periodically. Worn or damaged suspension and steering linkage components can result in excessive and abnormal tire wear, poor ride quality and vehicle handling and reduced fuel economy. For detailed illustrations of the steering and suspension components, refer to Chapter 10.

SHOCK ABSORBER CHECK

▶ **Refer to illustration 26.6**

1   Park the vehicle on level ground, turn the engine off and set the parking brake. Check the tire pressures.

2   Push down at one corner of the vehicle, then release it while noting the movement of the body. It should stop moving and come to rest in a level position within one or two bounces.

3   If the vehicle continues to move up-and-down or if it fails to return to its original position, a worn or weak shock absorber is probably the reason.

4   Repeat the above check at each of the three remaining corners of the vehicle.

5   Raise the vehicle and support it securely on jack stands.

6   Check the shock absorbers for evidence of fluid leakage (see illustration). A light film of fluid is no cause for concern. Make sure that any fluid noted is from the shocks and not from some other source. If leakage is noted, replace the shocks as a set.

7   Check the shocks to be sure that they are securely mounted and undamaged. Check the upper mounts for damage and wear. If damage or wear is noted, replace the shocks as a set (front or rear).

8   If the shocks must be replaced, refer to Chapter 10 for the procedure.

STEERING AND SUSPENSION CHECK

▶ **Refer to illustrations 26.9a, 26.9b, 26.9c, and 26.11**

9   Visually inspect the steering and suspension components (front and rear) for damage and distortion. Look for damaged seals, boots and bushings and leaks of any kind. Examine the bushings where the con-

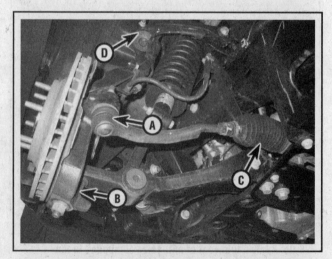

26.9c Inspect the tie-rod ends (A), the lower balljoints (B), the steering gear boots (C) and the upper balljoints (D)

26.11 With the steering wheel in the locked position and the vehicle raised, grasp the front tire as shown and try to move it back-and-forth - if any play is noted, check the steering gear mounts and tie-rod ends for looseness

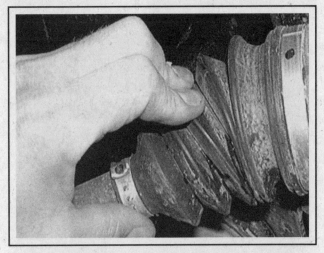

26.15 Inspect the inner and outer driveaxle boots on 4WD models for loose clamps, cracks or signs of leaking lubricant (inner boot shown)

trol arms meet the chassis (see illustrations).

10 Clean the lower end of the steering knuckle. Have an assistant grasp the lower edge of the tire and move the wheel in-and-out while you look for movement at the steering knuckle-to-control arm balljoint. If there is any movement the suspension balljoint(s) must be replaced.

11 Grasp each front tire at the front and rear edges, push in at the front, pull out at the rear and feel for play in the steering system components. If any freeplay is noted, check the idler arm and the tie-rod ends for looseness (see illustration).

12 On vehicles equipped with air suspension, inspect the air springs for physical damage as well as checking the air lines for cracks and leaks.

13 Additional steering and suspension system information and illustrations can be found in Chapter 10.

DRIVEAXLE BOOT CHECK (4WD MODELS)

▶ **Refer to illustration 26.15**

14 The driveaxle boots are very important because they prevent dirt, water and foreign material from entering and damaging the constant velocity (CV) joints. Oil and grease can cause the boot material to deteriorate prematurely, so it's a good idea to wash the boots with soap and water. Because it constantly pivots back and forth following the steering action of the front hub, the outer CV boot wears out sooner and should be inspected regularly.

15 Inspect the boots for tears and cracks as well as loose clamps (see illustration). If there is any evidence of cracks or leaking lubricant, they must be replaced as described in Chapter 8.

27 Automatic transmission fluid and filter change (every 30,000 miles or 30 months)

▶ **Refer to illustrations 27.5, 27.7, 27.11, 27.12 and 27.13**

1 At the specified intervals, the transmission fluid should be drained and replaced. Since the fluid will remain hot long after driving, perform this procedure only after the engine has cooled down completely.

2 Before beginning work, purchase the specified transmission fluid (see *Recommended lubricants and fluids* at the back of this Chapter) and a new filter and pan gasket.

3 Other tools necessary for this job include a floor jack, jackstands to support the vehicle in a raised position, a drain pan capable of holding at least eight quarts, newspapers and clean rags.

4 Raise the vehicle and support it securely on jackstands.

5 Place the drain pan underneath the transmission pan. If the fluid pan is equipped with a drain plug, remove the drain plug and allow the fluid to drain until it barely comes out, then reinsert the drain plug (see illustration).

6 If your vehicle does not have a drain plug it will be necessary to remove all the bolts except the ones in each corner, then slowly remove the front pan bolts allowing fluid to drain as the bolts are removed.

27.5 On models with a drain plug, drain the transmission fluid pan by removing the drain plug

27.7 Disconnect the shift cable end from the ballstud (A), then remove the two bolts securing the shift cable bracket to the transmission (B) (this allows room to access the fluid pan bolts)

27.12 Use a seal removal tool to remove the transmission filter seal from the valve body, then replace it with a new seal - be careful not to scratch the aluminum cavity

27.13 Clean the transmission pan, position the magnet back in place, and install the new pan gasket

27.11 Remove the filter from the transmission by pulling it straight down

7   On the driver's side of the transmission, the shift linkage must be removed to access the pan bolts (see illustration).

8   Remove the transmission pan mounting bolts, then carefully pry the transmission pan loose with a screwdriver.

❋❋ WARNING:

There is still some transmission fluid in the pan.

9   Carefully clean the gasket surface of the transmission to remove all traces of the old gasket and sealant.

10 Clean the pan with solvent and dry it with compressed air, if available.

➡**Note: Some models are equipped with magnets in the transmission pan to catch metal debris. Clean the magnet thoroughly. A small amount of metal material is normal at the magnet. If there is considerable debris, consult a dealer or transmission specialist.**

11 Remove the filter from the valve body inside the transmission (see illustration).

➡**Note: Be very careful not to gouge the delicate aluminum gasket surface on the valve body.**

12 Install a new seal and filter. On many replacement filters, the seal is attached to the filter to simplify installation (see illustration).

13 Make sure the gasket surface on the transmission pan is clean, then install a new gasket on the pan (see illustration). Put the pan in place against the transmission and install all of the bolts. Working around the pan, tighten each bolt a little at a time to the torque listed in this Chapter's Specifications.

14 Reinstall the components removed for access to the pan bolts.

15 Lower the vehicle and add approximately 4 quarts of the specified type of automatic transmission fluid through the filler tube (see Section 7).

16 With the transmission in Park and the parking brake set, run the engine at a fast idle, but don't race it.

17 Move the gear selector through each range and back to Park, then let the engine idle for a few minutes. Check the fluid level. It will probably be low. Add enough fluid to bring the level to the proper mark on the dipstick. Be careful not to overfill.

18 Check under the vehicle for leaks during the first few trips. Check the fluid level again when the transmission is hot (see Section 7).

28 Transfer case lubricant change (4WD models) (every 60,000 miles or 48 months)

1 This procedure should be performed after the vehicle has been driven so the lubricant will be warm and therefore will flow out of the transfer case more easily.

2 Raise the vehicle and support it securely on jackstands.

3 Remove the filler plug from the case (see illustration 21.1).

4 Remove the drain plug from the lower part of the case and allow the lubricant to drain completely.

5 After the case is completely drained, carefully clean and install the drain plug. Tighten the plug to the torque listed in this Chapter's Specifications.

6 Fill the case with the specified lubricant until it is level with the lower edge of the filler hole.

7 Install the filler plug and tighten it to the torque listed in this Chapter's Specifications.

8 Drive the vehicle for a short distance and recheck the lubricant level. In some instances a small amount of additional lubricant will have to be added.

29 Differential lubricant change (every 60,000 miles or 48 months)

◆ Refer to illustration 29.3

1 This procedure should be performed after the vehicle has been driven, so the lubricant will be warm and therefore will flow out of the differential more easily.

2 Raise the vehicle and support it securely on jackstands. You'll be draining the lubricant by removing the drain plug, so move a drain pan, rags, newspapers and wrenches under the vehicle.

3 Remove the fill plug (see illustration 16.2a [rear differential] or 16.2b [front differential]). Now remove the drain plug and allow the lubricant to drain into the pan (see illustration), then clean and reinstall the drain plug. Tighten the plug to the torque listed in this Chapter's Specifications.

4 Use a hand pump, syringe or squeeze bottle to fill the differential housing with the specified lubricant until it's level with the bottom of the fill-plug hole. If using synthetic axle lubricant, the level should be below the fill-plug opening by 1/2-inch.

➡Note: On some models with limited-slip differentials, a different lubricant or additive may be required.

5 Install the fill plug and tighten it to the torque listed in this Chapter's Specifications.

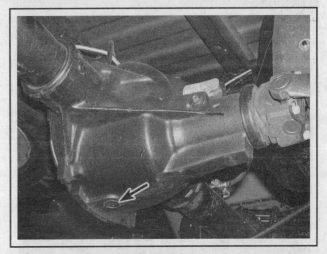

29.3 Remove the differential drain plug to drain the lubricant

30 Cooling system servicing (draining, flushing and refilling) (every 100,000 miles or 60 months)

❋❋ WARNING 1:

Wait until the engine is completely cool before beginning this procedure.

❋❋ WARNING 2:

Do not allow antifreeze to come in contact with your skin or painted surfaces of the vehicle. Rinse off spills immediately with plenty of water. Antifreeze is highly toxic if ingested. Never leave antifreeze lying around in an open container or in puddles on the floor; children and pets are attracted by its sweet smell and may drink it. Check with local authorities on disposing of used anti-freeze. Many communities have collection centers that will see that antifreeze is disposed of safely. Antifreeze is flammable under certain conditions - be sure to read the precautions on the container.

➡Note: Non-toxic coolant is available at local auto parts stores. Although the coolant is non-toxic when fresh, proper disposal is still required.

❋❋ CAUTION:

Never mix green-colored ethylene glycol anti-freeze and orange-colored "DEX-COOL" silicate-free coolant because doing so will destroy the efficiency of the "DEX-COOL" coolant, which is designed to last for 100,000 miles or five years.

DRAINING

◆ Refer to illustration 30.3

1 Periodically, the cooling system should be drained, flushed and refilled to replenish the antifreeze mixture and prevent formation of rust and corrosion, which can impair the performance of the cooling system and cause engine damage. When the cooling system is serviced, all hoses and the surge tank cap should be checked and replaced if necessary.

2 Apply the parking brake and block the wheels.

If the vehicle has just been driven, wait several hours to allow the engine to cool down before beginning this procedure.

Detach the coolant air bleed hose from the throttle body.

3   Move a large container under the radiator drain to catch the coolant. Loosen the hose clamp on the lower radiator hose, slide the hose back and allow the coolant to begin to drain (see illustration). Remove the radiator cap.

4   While the coolant is draining, check the condition of the radiator hoses, heater hoses and clamps (refer to Section 14 if necessary).

5   Replace any damaged clamps or hoses. Reconnect the lower radiator hose and reattach the coolant air bleed hose to the throttle body.

FLUSHING

6   Fill the cooling system with clean water, following the Refilling

30.3 The cooling system on these vehicle is drained by detaching the lower radiator hose from the radiator

procedure (see Step 12).

7   Start the engine and allow it to reach normal operating temperature, then rev up the engine a few times.

8   Turn the engine off and allow it to cool completely, then drain the system as described earlier.

9   Repeat Steps 6 through 8 until the water being drained is free of contaminants.

10 In severe cases of contamination or clogging of the radiator, remove the radiator (see Chapter 3) and have a radiator repair facility clean and repair it if necessary.

11 Many deposits can be removed by the chemical action of a cleaner available at auto parts stores. Follow the procedure outlined in the manufacturer's instructions.

➡**Note: When the coolant is regularly drained and the system refilled with the correct antifreeze/water mixture, there should be no need to use chemical cleaners or descalers.**

REFILLING

12 Reconnect the lower radiator hose to the radiator and install the clamp. Detach the air bleed hose from the throttle body.

13 Place the heater temperature control in the maximum heat position.

14 Be sure to use the proper coolant listed in this Chapter's Specifications. Slowly fill the radiator until it's full, then install the radiator cap.

15 Fill the coolant reservoir with the same mixture up to the FULL COLD mark, then install the cap on the reservoir.

16 Connect the air bleed hose to the throttle body.

17 Start the engine and run it at 2,000 rpm until normal operating temperature is reached, then let the engine speed down to idle for about three minutes.

18 Turn the engine off and allow it to cool completely.

19 With the engine completely cool, remove the radiator cap and add coolant if necessary. Reinstall the cap and add coolant, as necessary, to the coolant reservoir.

20 Check the cooling system for leaks.

Specifications

Recommended lubricants and fluids

Note: Listed here are manufacturer recommendations at the time this manual was written. Manufacturers occasionally upgrade their fluid and lubricant specifications, so check with your local auto parts store for current recommendations.

Engine oil	API "certified for gasoline engines"
Viscosity	
2002 through 2005	SAE 5W-30
2006 and later	
6.0L (VIN code H) engines	SAE 5W-30 GM Standard 4718M synthetic oil*
All others	SAE 5W-30
*GM recommends using GM Goodwrench synthetic oil or equivalent	
Fuel	Unleaded gasoline, 87 octane minimum
Automatic transmission fluid	
2002 through 2005	Dexron III
2006 and later	Dexron VI
Transfer Case	GM AUTO TRAK II fluid
Differential fluid	
2002 through 2005 (front and rear)	SAE 75W-90 synthetic axle lubricant
2006 and later	
Front differential	SAE 75W-90 synthetic axle lubricant
Rear differential	
SS models	SAE 75W-90 synthetic axle lubricant, add 4 ounces Limited Slip Axle Lubricant GM US #1052358**
All other models	SAE 75W-90 synthetic axle lubricant
** Canada models, use GM #992694	
Power steering fluid	GM power steering fluid, or equivalent
Brake fluid	DOT 3 brake fluid
Engine coolant	50/50 mixture of DEX-COOL coolant and demineralized water
Parking brake mechanism grease	White lithium-based grease NLGI no. 2
Chassis lubrication grease	NLGI Grade 2 GC or GC-LB chassis grease
Hood, door and trunk hinge lubricant	Lubriplate lubricant aerosol spray
Door hinge and check spring grease	NLGI no. 2 multi-purpose grease
Key lock cylinder lubricant	Graphite spray
Hood latch assembly lubricant	NLGI no. 2 multi-purpose grease
Door latch lubricant	NLGI no. 2 multi-purpose grease or equivalent

Capacities*

Engine oil (including filter)	
Six-cylinder engine	7.0 quarts
V8 engines	6.0 quarts
Automatic transmission (4L60E)	
Fluid and filter change	5.0 quarts
From dry, including torque converter	11.2 quarts
Differential	
Front (4WD models)	
2002 and 2003	2.6 pints
2004 and later	
Six-cylinder models (RPO LL8)	
with 18 inch wheels	4.3 pints
All other models	1.7 pints

Capacities*

Differential (continued)	
Rear	
2002 and 2003	4.0 pints
2004 and later	
Six-cylinder models	3.6 pints
5.3L models	4.3 pints
6.0L models**	5.5 pints
Transfer case	2.0 quarts
Cooling system	
Six-cylinder engines	
2002 and 2003	13.9 quarts
2004	
Standard wheelbase	13.9 quarts
Extended wheelbase	15.2 quarts
2005 and 2006	
Standard wheelbase	10.8 quarts
Extended wheelbase	13.8 quarts
2007 and later	13.9 quarts
V8 engines	
2002 and 2003	13.9 quarts
2004	
Standard wheelbase	15.3 quarts
Extended wheelbase	17.9 quarts
2005 and 2006	
Standard wheelbase	12.2 quarts
Extended wheelbase	15.3 quarts
2007 and later	15.3 quarts

*All capacities approximate. Add as necessary to bring to appropriate level
**Add 5w.5 ounces of Limited Slip Axle Lubricant

Brakes

Disc brake pad wear limit	3/32 inch
Parking brake shoe wear limit	1/16 inch

Ignition system

Six cylinder engine	
Spark plug type	
2002 and 2003	AC Delco 41-965
2004 and later	AC Delco 41-~~981~~ *103*
Spark plug gap	*GM 12598004*
2002 and 2003	0.050 inch
2004 through 2006	0.042 inch
2007 and later	0.040 inch
Firing order	1-5-3-6-4-2
V8 engines	
Spark plug type	AC Delco 41-985
Spark plug gap	0.040 inch
Firing order	1-8-7-2-6-5-4-3

INLINE 6-CYLINDER
Firing order
1-5-3-6-2-4

24072-1-0B HAYNES

Cylinder locations

24046-1SPECS.HAYNES

**V8 engine cylinder
numbering diagram**

Torque specifications   Ft-lbs (unless otherwise indicated)

➡Note: One foot-pound (ft-lb) of torque is equivalent to 12 inch-pounds (in-lbs) of torque. Torque values below approximately 15 ft-lbs are expressed in inch-pounds, since most foot-pound torque wrenches are not accurate at these smaller values.

Engine oil drain plug	19
Automatic transmission	
Fluid pan bolts	
2002 and 2003	120 in-lbs
2004 and later	97 in-lbs
Drain plug (if equipped)	156 in-lbs
Drivebelt tensioner bolt	37
Drivebelt idler pulley bolt	37
Differential drain/fill plugs	
2002 through 2005	
Front	24
Rear	36
2006 and later	
Front	24
Rear	
Drain plug	36
Fill plug	24
Transfer case drain/fill plugs	20
Spark plugs	
Six-cylinder engine	156 in-lbs
V8 engines	132 in-lbs
Wheel lug nuts	103

Notes

2A

INLINE SIX-CYLINDER ENGINE

Section

Reference to other Chapters

1   General information

This Chapter is devoted to in-vehicle repair procedures for the 4.2L inline six-cylinder engine. This engine utilizes a cast aluminum block with six cylinders arranged in a straight line. The dual overhead camshaft, aluminum cylinder head is equipped with four valves per cylinder. Roller-type rocker arms actuate the valves through direct contact with the camshaft, while hydraulic lash adjusters take up the play between the cam lobes, rocker arms and valves. The oil pump is located in the front cover and is driven directly from the crankshaft. The oil pan is made of cast aluminum. The crankshaft is made of nodular iron, and

the pistons are of a full floating design. Connecting rods are made from forged powdered metal.

To positively identify this engine, locate the Vehicle Identification Number (VIN) on the left front corner of the instrument panel. The VIN is visible from the outside of the vehicle through the windshield. The eighth character in the sequence is the engine designation:

S = 4.2 liter L6 engine

2   Repair operations possible with the engine in the vehicle

Many major repair operations can be accomplished without removing the engine from the vehicle.

Clean the engine compartment and the exterior of the engine with some type of pressure washer before any work is done. It will make the job easier and help keep dirt out of the internal areas of the engine. Do not direct high-pressure spray towards any electrical connector. Many of these are low voltage computer circuits and water may be forced past the seal, then causing a false reading, damage to the sensor or corrosion to occur.

Remove the hood, if necessary, to improve access to the engine as

repairs are performed (see Chapter 11 if necessary).

If vacuum, exhaust, oil or coolant leaks develop, indicating a need for gasket or seal replacement, the repairs can generally be made with the engine in the vehicle. The intake and exhaust manifold gaskets, front cover gasket, oil pan gasket, crankshaft oil seals and cylinder head gasket are all accessible with the engine in place.

Exterior engine components, such as the intake and exhaust manifolds, the oil pan and oil pump, the water pump, the starter motor, the alternator, the distributor and the fuel system components can be removed for repair with the engine in place.

3   Intake manifold - removal and installation

♦ **Refer to illustrations 3.6 and 3.10**

REMOVAL

1   Disconnect the cable from the negative terminal of the battery.
2   Remove the throttle body (see Chapter 4).
3   Remove the PCM (see Chapter 6).
4   Disconnect the electrical harnesses from their brackets and the MAP sensor connector.
5   Disconnect the front differential vent hose (if equipped) from its bracket clip.
6   Disconnect the crankcase vent hose from its port on the manifold (see illustration).

7   Remove the engine harness bracket.
8   Remove the alternator (see Chapter 5).
9   Disconnect the vacuum hose from the power brake booster.
10 Remove the intake manifold bolts and remove the manifold (see illustration).
11 Remove the old gasket, then clean and inspect the intake manifold for damage, cracks and warping.

INSTALLATION

12 Install a new gasket (no sealant is required).
13 Installation is the reverse of removal. Tighten the intake manifold bolts, a little at a time, to the torque listed in this Chapter's Specifications.

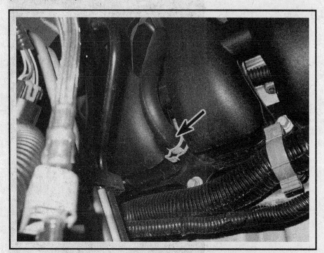

3.6 Disconnect the crankcase vent hose from the manifold

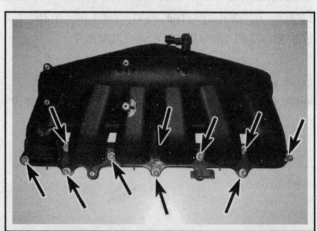

3.10 Intake manifold bolt locations

4 Valve cover - removal and installation

♦ Refer to illustrations 4.3, 4.5 and 4.7

REMOVAL

❋❋ **WARNING:**

Prior to removing the valve cover it will be necessary to discharge the air conditioning system. This must be performed by a licensed air conditioning technician with the proper knowledge and equipment to safely and correctly remove the refrigerant from the air conditioning system.

1 Have the air conditioning system discharged.
2 Remove the intake manifold (see Section 3).
3 Disconnect the air conditioning line at the accumulator (see Chapter 3). Also disconnect the air conditioning line bracket at the engine lift hook and the bracket at the oil level indicator tube (see illustration).
4 Remove the engine lift bracket.
5 Disconnect the injector connectors then carefully unclip the engine electrical harness from the valve cover (see illustration).
6 Remove the ignition coils (see Chapter 5).
7 Remove the valve cover bolts and valve cover (see illustration).
8 Clean and inspect the valve cover for cracks.

INSTALLATION

9 Install new ignition coil seals, if necessary (see Chapter 5), and a new valve cover seal.

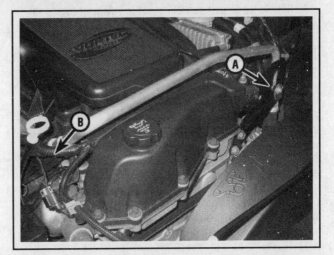

4.3 Air conditioning line bracket attachment at the engine lift hook (A) and the bracket at the oil level indicator tube (B)

10 Installation is the reverse of removal.
11 Tighten the valve cover bolts to the torque listed in this Chapter's Specifications. Tighten the ignition coil bolts to the torque listed in the Chapter 5 Specifications.
12 Have the air conditioning system recharged by the shop that discharged it.

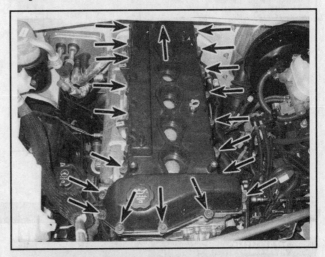

4.7 Valve cover bolt locations (not all bolts are visible in this photo)

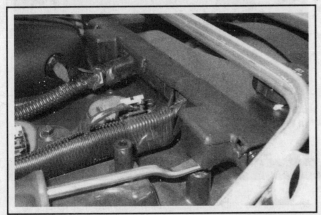

4.5 Carefully pry the engine harness off the valve cover

5 Exhaust manifold - removal and installation

REMOVAL

♦ Refer to illustrations 5.3, 5.5 and 5.6

❋❋ **WARNING:**

Use caution when working around the exhaust manifolds, the sheet metal heat shields can be sharp on the edges. Also, the engine should be cold when this procedure is performed.

1 Disconnect the cable from the negative terminal of the battery.
2 Raise the vehicle and support it securely on jackstands.
3 Working under the vehicle, apply penetrating oil to the exhaust pipe-to-manifold studs and nuts (they're usually rusty) (see illustration).
4 Wait a little while and let the penetrating oil soak in, then remove the nuts retaining the exhaust pipe to the manifold.
5 Unplug the oxygen sensor electrical connector. Remove the heat shield nuts, then remove the heat shield (see illustration).

6   Remove the exhaust manifold bolts and detach the manifold from the cylinder head (see illustration).

7   Remove the exhaust manifold gasket and clean the mating surfaces on the cylinder head and manifold.

INSTALLATION

8   Check the manifold for cracks and make sure the bolt threads are clean and undamaged. The manifold and cylinder head mating surfaces must be clean before the manifolds are reinstalled - use a gasket scraper to remove all carbon deposits. Check the manifold for warpage using a straightedge and feeler gauges. If it exceeds the limit listed in this Chapter's Specifications, have the manifold resurfaced or replace it with a new one.

9   Install a new gasket.

10 Install the manifold on the cylinder head, apply heat-resistant thread locking compound to the bolt threads then start the bolts by hand.

11 Tighten the bolts in three passes starting from the center bolt and working your way to the ends, to the torque listed in this Chapter's Specifications.

12 The remaining installation steps are the reverse of removal.

13 Start the engine and check for exhaust leaks.

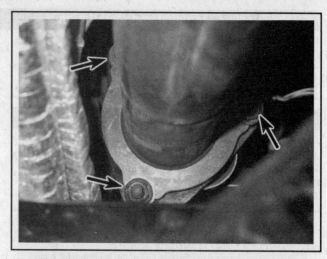

5.3 Access the exhaust pipe bolts/nuts from underneath the vehicle

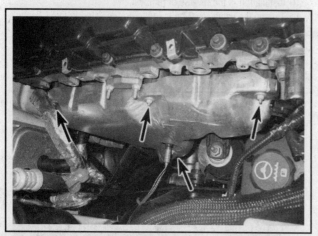

5.5 Exhaust manifold heat shield nuts

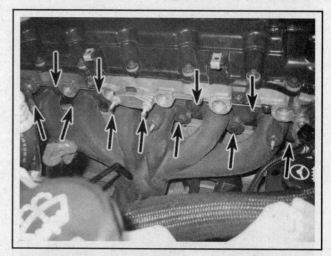

5.6 Exhaust manifold bolt locations (not all bolts are visible in this photo)

6   Front cover - removal and installation

❊❊ WARNING:

The engine must be completely cool before beginning this procedure.

REMOVAL

1   Drain the engine coolant (see Chapter 1).

2   Remove the drivebelt (see Chapter 1).

3   Remove the fan and fan shroud (see Chapter 3).

4   Remove the water pump (see Chapter 3) and the power steering pump (see Chapter 10).

5   Remove the crankshaft pulley (see Section 11).

6   Remove the oil pan (see Section 16).

7   Remove the front cover bolts, beginning with the 7 mm bolt in the center of the cover.

8   Install two bolts in the jackscrew holes on the front cover and evenly tighten the bolts until the cover comes off.

9   Remove the oil pump from the front cover, if necessary (see Section 12).

10 Clean the cover sealing area with solvent, remove all old gasket material, and inspect the cover for nicks and damage in the sealing area.

➡**Note: Do not use any powerdriven gasket removal tools such as wire wheels and cleaning disks, as this will damage the cover.**

INSTALLATION

11 Align the oil pump and the crankshaft splines (this will require you to temporarily install the cover without the sealant).

12 Remove the cover and apply a 3/16-inch bead of RTV sealant to

the cover sealing area and the three bolt hole areas on the inside of the cover.

13 Slide the front cover in place, making sure the oil pump and crankshaft splines remain in alignment. Temporarily install the crankshaft pulley and center the seal on it to align the front cover.

14 Tighten all the bolts finger tight, then tighten all the bolts to the torque listed in this Chapter's Specifications. Tighten the 7 mm center bolt (just above the crankshaft centerline) last.

15 The remainder of installation is the reverse of removal. Add engine oil and coolant (see Chapter 1), start the engine and check for leaks.

7 Timing chain, sprockets and tensioner - replacement

➡ **Note: A special camshaft holding tool (GM# J-44221 or equivalent) is required for this procedure.**

REMOVAL

> ※※ **CAUTION** ※※
>
> The timing system is complex. Severe engine damage will occur if you make any mistakes. Do not attempt this procedure unless you are highly experienced with this type of repair. If you are at all unsure of your abilities, consult an expert. Double-check all your work and be sure everything is correct before you attempt to start the engine.

▶ **Refer to illustrations 7.3, 7.4a, 7.4b, 7.5 and 7.6**

1 Position the engine at Top Dead Center for cylinder number one (see Chapter 2B). Remove the valve cover (see Section 4) and the engine front cover (see Section 6).

2 Collapse the timing chain tensioner and insert a drill bit or golf tee into the hole to hold it in place.

3 Remove the top chain guide (see illustration).

4 Remove the exhaust camshaft position actuator (see illustration). When loosening the bolt, hold the camshaft stationary by placing a wrench on the hex cast into the camshaft (see illustration).

5 Remove the intake camshaft sprocket (see illustration), then unhook the chain from the crankshaft sprocket and remove the chain. When loosening the sprocket bolt, hold the camshaft stationary by plac-

7.3 Unscrew these two bolts and remove the top chain guide

7.4a The exhaust camshaft actuator is retained by this Allen bolt

7.4b To prevent the camshafts from turning while loosening the sprocket bolts, place a wrench on these hexes cast into the shafts

7.5 Intake camshaft sprocket bolt

7.6 Use a hex bit to remove these two access plugs from the front of the cylinder head

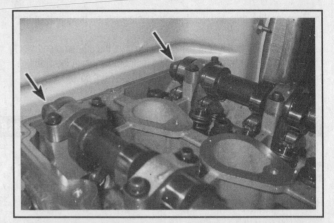

7.12 When the engine is at Top Dead Center for cylinder number one (on the compression stroke), the flats at the rear ends of the camshafts will be facing up, parallel with the top of the cylinder head (the camshaft holding tool engages these flats)

ing a wrench on the hex cast into the camshaft, just like in the previous step.

6 Remove the two access hole plugs from the front of the cylinder head (see illustration).

7 Remove the timing chain tensioner shoe bolt (right) and the timing chain guide bolt (left) then remove the guide and shoe. Remove the tensioner (if it is being replaced).

8 Remove the crankshaft sprocket.

INSTALLATION

> **✳✳ CAUTION ✳✳**
>
> Before starting the engine, carefully rotate the crankshaft by hand through at least two full revolutions (use a socket and breaker bar on the crankshaft pulley centerbolt). If you feel any resistance, STOP! There is something wrong - most likely, valves are contacting the pistons. You must find the problem before proceeding. Check your work and see if any updated repair information is available.

▶ Refer to illustrations 7.12, 7.21a and 7.21b

➡Note: Every seventh timing chain link is darkened to identify the alignment links.

9 If removed, install the tensioner and tighten it to the torque listed in this Chapter's Specifications.

10 Install the chain guide and shoe and tighten the bolts to the torque listed in this Chapter's Specifications.

11 Install the two access plugs and tighten them to the torque listed in this Chapter's Specifications.

12 Check to make sure cylinder number 1 is still at Top Dead Center, then install the camshaft holding tool. The lobes at the front of the camshafts will be pointing up and the flats on the back of each camshaft will be facing up (see illustration).

13 Install the crankshaft sprocket, then place the chain on the intake sprocket making sure to align the mark on the sprocket with a darkened link.

14 Feed the chain through the cylinder head and onto the crankshaft sprocket making sure the mark on the crankshaft sprocket is aligned with a darkened link.

15 Install the intake sprocket on to the intake camshaft.

➡Note: It may be necessary to remove the holding tool to allow slight movement of the camshaft to aid in sprocket to camshaft pin alignment.

Reinstall the holding tool.

7.21a When the timing chain is properly installed (with the engine at TDC for cylinder number one on the compression stroke) the mark on the intake camshaft sprocket will be aligned with a darkened link . . .

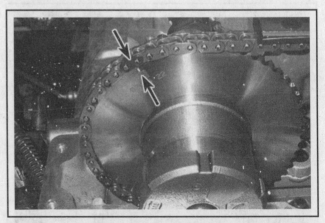

7.21b . . . and the mark on the exhaust camshaft actuator will be aligned with a darkened link (the mark on the crankshaft sprocket will also be aligned with a dark link)

16 Lift up the timing chain and guide the exhaust camshaft actuator into place, making sure the mark on the actuator sprocket is aligned with a darkened link.

17 Install the exhaust camshaft actuator onto the exhaust camshaft, but do not fully tighten the bolt.

➡Note: It may be necessary to remove the holding tool to allow slight movement of the camshaft to aid in sprocket to camshaft pin alignment.

Reinstall the holding tool.

18 Rotate the exhaust camshaft actuator clockwise (as you are facing it) until it stops.

❊❊ CAUTION:

The actuator must be installed in the full advance position (clockwise) or engine damage will occur.

Tighten the bolt to the torque listed in this Chapter's Specifications.

19 Tighten the intake camshaft sprocket bolt to the torque listed in this Chapter's Specifications.

20 Remove the drill bit or tee in the tensioner, then remove the camshaft holding tool.

21 Check the timing mark alignment (see illustrations).

22 The remainder of the installation is the reverse of removal.

8 Camshafts, rocker arms and lash adjusters - removal and installation

➡Note: A special camshaft holding tool (GM# J-44221 or equivalent) is required for this procedure.

REMOVAL

▶ Refer to illustration 8.2

➡Note: After removing the cam sprocket do not rotate the crankshaft or incorrect timing and engine damage can occur.

1 Remove the valve cover (see Section 4). Also remove the spark plugs (it'll make the engine easier to rotate - see Chapter 1).

2 Rotate the engine until the sprocket alignment marks are each aligned with a dark chain link (see illustration), and the flats at the rear of the camshafts are facing up (see illustration 7.12).

3 Following the procedure described in Section 7, Steps 4 and 5, remove the camshaft sprocket bolts, then carefully remove the sprockets from the camshafts.

❊❊ CAUTION:

Do not remove the sprockets from the chain, and be sure to suspend the sprockets and chain to prevent the bottom of the chain from coming off the crankshaft sprocket.

4 Check the camshaft caps for markings; if there are none, mark them with paint prior to removal to insure they are installed in the exact location they were prior to disassembly.

5 Remove the camshaft cap bolts, a little at a time, until they can be removed, then remove the camshafts. Keep the shafts separated so you don't get them mixed up. The rocker arms and lash adjusters can now be lifted out, if necessary. Keep these parts laid out in order, too, since they must all be returned to their original locations if they're going to be re-used.

INSPECTION

6 After the camshafts have been removed from the engine, cleaned with solvent and dried, inspect each camshaft for:

 a) Scored camshaft journals
 b) Check the camshaft lobes for heat discoloration, score marks, chipped areas, pitting and uneven wear
 c) Damaged camshaft sprocket locator pin slots
 d) Damaged threads

7 Measure the bearing journals with a micrometer to determine if they are excessively worn or out-of-round.

8.2 Correct timing mark alignment prior to camshaft sprocket removal

INSTALLATION

8 If removed, soak the lash adjusters and rocker arms in clean engine oil, then install the lash adjusters and rocker arms in their original locations.

9 Completely coat the camshaft with clean engine oil. Place the camshafts in their correct locations in the cylinder head.

10 Install the camshaft holding tool.

11 Install all the camshaft caps to their original locations and hand tighten them.

12 Working from center out, evenly tighten the caps to the torque listed in this Chapter's Specifications.

13 Remove the holding fixture.

14 Place the sprockets onto the camshafts and tighten the bolts to the torque listed in this Chapter's Specifications.

15 Using a large breaker bar and a socket placed on the crankshaft pulley bolt, rotate the crankshaft 720-degrees (two full revolutions) and re-check the sprocket and chain alignment; the darkened links must align with the sprocket marks (see illustration 8.2). If you feel any resistance while turning the crankshaft, stop immediately and find out what the problem is.

16 Install the spark plugs (see Chapter 1) and the valve cover (see Section 4).

9 Cylinder head - removal and installation

❊ WARNING:

Wait until the engine is completely cool before beginning this procedure.

REMOVAL

1 Drain the engine coolant (see Chapter 1).
2 Remove the valve cover (see Section 4).
3 Remove the exhaust manifold (see Section 5).
4 Remove the timing chain and sprockets (see Section 7).
5 Unscrew the seventeen cylinder head bolts working in the reverse order of the tightening sequence (see illustration 9.13).
6 Lift the cylinder head off the engine.

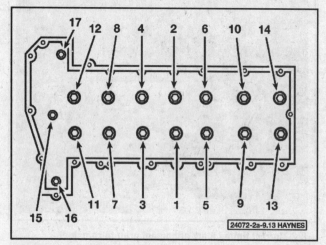

9.13 Cylinder head bolt tightening sequence

❊ CAUTION:

The cylinder head is heavy! Have an assistant help you do this. If the cylinder head is stuck, don't pry between the block and the head - instead, pry on a casting protrusion or use a wood block and a hammer to jar it loose.

7 Remove the cylinder head gasket.
8 Clean the surfaces of the engine block and cylinder head, taking care not to gouge the aluminum or lose the two alignment dowel pins.
9 Check the surface of the engine block and the cylinder head with a precision straightedge and feeler gauges and compare the readings with the Specifications in this Chapter.

INSTALLATION

▶ **Refer to illustration 9.13**

➡ **Note 1: It is important that number 1 cylinder is at top dead center.**

➡ **Note 2: Use new cylinder head bolts.**

10 Place a new head gasket on the engine block making sure the dowel pins are in the correct locations.
11 Place the cylinder head on the engine block.
12 Install new cylinder head bolts and hand tighten them.
13 Tighten the cylinder head bolts in sequence (see illustration) to the torque listed in this Chapter's Specifications.
14 The remaining assembly is the reverse of removal.
15 Change the engine oil and filter and replace the coolant (see Chapter 1).

10 Valves - servicing

1 Because of the complex nature of the job and the special tools and equipment needed, servicing of the valves, the valve seats and the valve guides, commonly known as a valve job, should be done by a professional.
2 The automotive machine shop, will remove the valves and springs, recondition or replace the valves and valve seats, recondition the valve guides, check and replace the valve springs, spring retainers or rotators and keepers (as necessary), replace the valve seals with new ones, reassemble the valve components and make sure the installed spring height is correct. The cylinder head gasket surface will also be resurfaced if it's warped. Note that some cylinder heads have a minimum resurfacing height (similar to a brake rotor or drum). If they're resurfaced past the minimum height they'll have to be replaced.
3 After the valve job has been performed by a professional, the head will be in like-new condition. When the head is returned, be sure to clean it again before installation on the engine to remove any metal particles and abrasive grit that may still be present from the valve service or head resurfacing operations. Use compressed air, if available, to blow out all the oil holes, bolt holes and coolant passages.

11 Crankshaft front oil seal - replacement

❊ CAUTION:

It is extremely important to avoid damaging the crankshaft threads. If the alternative setup described above does not readily remove the pulley, STOP. Obtain the special tools or have the work performed by a technician who does have the special tools. Be extremely careful not to damage the crankshaft end surface or the engine front cover.

➡ **Note 1: Special tools required: puller (GM # J-44226 or equivalent), crankshaft end protector (GM # J-41816-2 or equivalent), pulley installer (J-41478 or equivalent) and seal installer (GM # J- 44218 or equivalent). An alternative to these tools would be a three-jaw puller, a deep socket that just fits into the nose of the crankshaft and bottoms-out in the hole (for the puller screw to bear down against), and a press tool that threads into the end of the crankshaft and pushes the pulley into place.**

➡**Note 2: Due to its design the crank pulley has no keyway and can correctly be installed in any position on the crankshaft. A new shim should be used each time the pulley is removed**

REMOVAL

▶ **Refer to illustration 11.3**

1 Remove the radiator (see Chapter 3).

2 Remove the drivebelt (see Chapter 1).

3 Remove the torque converter access plate in the oil pan (see illustration); it will be necessary to have an assistant hold the flywheel from moving by using a large screwdriver braced against the ring gear as you loosen the pulley bolt.

4 Remove the crankshaft pulley bolt and install the crankshaft end protector.

5 Attach the puller and remove the pulley and pulley shim.

11.3 To prevent the crankshaft from turning when removing the crankshaft pulley bolt, remove this plug and wedge a screwdriver in the ring gear teeth to jam the driveplate

※※ **CAUTION:**

If you attempt to remove the pulley with a three-jaw puller, make sure the jaws of the puller grab the hub of the pulley only, not the outer circumference. Additionally, you'll have to insert an object such as a deep socket that is a close fit in the hole in the end of the crankshaft and bottoms-out in the hole; this is for the puller screw to push against. Never attempt to remove a crank pulley with a puller screw bearing down on the end of the crankshaft, since the threads in the end of the crankshaft will most likely be destroyed.

6 Using an appropriate tool, pry the oil seal out (notice the slots in the cover to access the outer edge of the seal).

INSTALLATION

7 Inspect the pulley for nicks and groves in the seal contact area. Also check the grooved drivebelt area on the circumference of the pulley for damage.

8 Lubricate the outside of the oil seal.

➡**Note: Unless specified by the seal manufacturer, do not lubricate the inside area that comes in contact with the crankshaft; it must be installed dry or the seal will leak.**

9 Using a seal installation tool, drive the seal into the front cover until it is seated.

10 Install a new pulley shim and slide it against the crankshaft sprocket.

11 Raise the vehicle and support it securely on jackstands.

12 Place the pulley on the crankshaft and push it into place until it is seated using the installer tool.

※※ **CAUTION:**

Don't try to drive it on with a hammer.

13 Remove the installer tool and install the pulley washer and bolt. While an assistant braces a screwdriver in the ring gear teeth, tighten the bolt to the torque listed in this Chapter's Specifications.

14 The remainder of the instillation is the reverse of removal.

12 Oil pump and relief valve - replacement

1 Remove the front cover (see Section 6).

2 Remove the oil pump cover and mark the gear orientation for assembly.

3 Remove the gears.

4 Remove the oil pump relief plug, relief valve and spring.

5 Install the new relief valve and spring, tightening the plug to the torque listed in this Chapter's Specifications.

6 Install the new oil pump in the same orientation as the original gears.

7 Install the oil pump cover and tighten the screws to the torque listed in this Chapter's Specifications.

8 Reinstall the front cover.

13 Driveplate - removal and installation

REMOVAL

1 Raise the vehicle and support it securely on jackstands, then refer to Chapter 7A and remove the transmission.

2 Mark the relationship between the driveplate and the crankshaft with a marking pen, then remove the bolts that secure the driveplate to the crankshaft. If the crankshaft turns, wedge a screwdriver in the ring gear teeth to jam the driveplate (see illustration 11.3).

➡**Note: If there is a retaining ring between the bolts and the driveplate, note which side faces the driveplate when removing it.**

3 Remove the driveplate from the crankshaft.

❄❄ CAUTION:

When removing a flywheel, wear gloves to protect your fingers - the edges of the ring gear teeth may be sharp.

4   Clean the driveplate to remove grease and oil. Inspect the surface for cracks, and check for cracked and broken ring gear teeth. Lay the driveplate on a flat surface to check for warpage.

5   Clean and inspect the mating surfaces of the driveplate and the crankshaft. If the rear main oil seal is leaking, replace it before reinstalling the driveplate.

INSTALLATION

6   Position the driveplate against the crankshaft. Be sure to align the marks made during removal. Note that some engines have an alignment dowel or staggered bolt holes to ensure correct installation. Before installing the bolts, apply thread-locking compound to the threads and place the retaining ring (if equipped) in position on the driveplate.

7   Wedge a screwdriver through the ring gear teeth to keep the driveplate from turning as you tighten the bolts in a criss-cross pattern to the torque listed in this Chapter's Specifications.

8   If the front pump seal/O-ring in the transmission is leaking, now would be a very good time to replace it.

9   The remainder of installation is the reverse of the removal procedure.

14   Rear main oil seal - replacement

REMOVAL

1   Remove the transmission (see Chapter 7A).
2   Remove the driveplate (see Section 13).
3   Inspect the oil seal, as well as the oil pan, engine block surface and oil seal housing for signs of leakage. Sometimes an oil pan gasket leak can appear to be a rear oil seal leak.
4   Remove the rear main seal housing bolts.
5   Install two bolts into the jackscrew holes provided in the housing. Carefully tighten each screw a little bit until the housing separates from the block, then remove the housing.
6   Remove the rear main oil seal from the housing. Inspect the crankshaft for nicks, grooves and damage.

INSTALLATION

7   Clean and inspect the oil seal housing.
8   Lubricate the outer seal surface with a very small amount of engine oil.

➡**Note: Unless specified by the seal manufacturer do not lubricate the inside area that comes in contact with the crankshaft, it must be installed dry or the seal will leak.**

Install the seal into the housing (make sure the lips of the seal point toward the engine) and carefully push it into place. A special aftermarket tool may be available at your local auto parts store. The tool just fits the diameter of the seal and, used with a hammer, drives the seal in.

➡**Note: Do not drive it in any further than the original seal was installed.**

9   Apply a 3/16-inch bead of RTV sealant to the housing-to-engine block mating surface.
10 Push the housing onto the block, making sure the lips of the seal slide over the rear of the crankshaft and don't fold under.
11 Install the bolts and tighten them to the torque listed in this Chapter's Specifications.
12 Install the driveplate (see Section 13).
13 Install the transmission (see Chapter 7).

15   Oil level tube - removal and installation

1   Disconnect the oxygen sensor connector and the air conditioning line bracket from the oil level tube bracket.
2   Remove the oil level tube stud from the cylinder head.

3   Remove the dipstick from the tube and twist and pull the tube out of the engine block.
4   Installation is the reverse of removal.

16   Oil pan - removal and installation

REMOVAL

1   Remove the oil level tube (see Section 15).
2   Loosen the top two air conditioning compressor bolts a few turns.
3   Loosen the front wheel lug nuts. Raise the front of the vehicle and support it securely on jackstands, then remove the front wheels.
4   Remove the under-vehicle splash shield.

5   Remove the steering gear crossmember (see Chapter 11).
6   If you're working on a 4WD model, remove the driveaxles and the intermediate shaft (see Chapter 8).
7   If you're working on a 4WD model, disconnect the front driveshaft from the differential companion flange (see Chapter 8).
8   Drain the engine oil (see Chapter 1).
9   Free the transmission cooler lines from the clip on the side of the engine.

10 If you're working on a 4WD model, unbolt the differential from the oil pan and secure it to the frame with heavy-gauge wire or rope.

11 Remove the bolts securing the oil pan to the transmission bellhousing, then remove the oil pan-to-engine block bolts.

12 Install two oil pan bolts in the jackscrew holes on the oil pan. Carefully and evenly tighten the bolts until the oil pan releases from the block.

13 Clean the pan with solvent.

➡**Note: Do not use any power-driven gasket removal tools such as wire wheels and cleaning disks, as this will damage the cover.**

14 Inspect the oil pan for nicks and cracks in the sealing areas. Also inspect the oil drain hole threads for damage.

INSTALLATION

15 Apply a 3/16-inch bead of RTV sealant to the engine block (not the pan) in the pan sealing area.

➡**Note: The pan must be installed within ten minutes of sealant application.**

16 Place the oil pan on the block and start the bolts. Tighten the pan-to-transmission bellhousing bolts first, then tighten the oil pan-to-engine block bolts. Tighten the bolts to the torque listed in this Chapter's Specifications.

17 The remainder of installation is the reverse of removal. Be sure to tighten all fasteners to the torque values listed in the relevant Chapters.

18 Change the engine oil filter and fill the crankcase with the correct type and capacity of oil (see Chapter 1).

17 Engine mounts - check and replacement

1 Engine mounts seldom require attention, but broken or deteriorated mounts should be replaced immediately or the added strain placed on the driveline components may cause damage.

CHECK

2 During the check, the engine must be raised slightly to remove the weight from the mounts.

3 Raise the vehicle and support it securely on jackstands, then position the jack under the engine oil pan. Place a large block of wood between the jack head and the oil pan, then carefully raise the engine just enough to take the weight off the mounts. Do not use the jack to support the entire weight of the engine.

4 Check the mounts to see if the rubber is cracked, hardened or separated from the metal plates. Sometimes the rubber will split right down the center. Rubber preservative or WD-40 can be applied to the mounts to slow deterioration.

5 Check for relative movement between the mount plates and the engine or frame (use a large screwdriver or pry bar to attempt to move the mounts). If movement is noted, check the tightness of the mount fasteners first before condemning the mounts. Usually when engine mounts are broken, they are very obvious as the engine will easily move away from the mount when pried or under load.

REPLACEMENT

▸ **Refer to illustration 17.9**

6 Disconnect the cable from the negative terminal of the battery.

7 Remove the cooling fan (see Chapter 3).

8 Disconnect the MAP sensor and remove the sensor.

9 Remove the left and right engine mount upper attaching nuts (even if only one mount is to be changed) (see illustration).

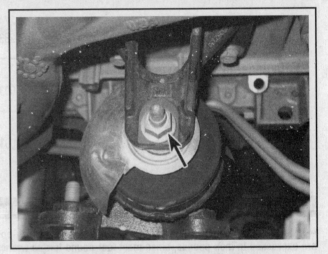

17.9 Removing both upper mount attaching nuts makes it easier to replace any one mount

10 Raise the vehicle and support it securely on jackstands.

11 Place a block of wood on top of a floor jack, position the floor jack under the oil pan.

12 Remove the mount lower attaching nut(s).

13 If your vehicle is equipped with an oil pan shield remove it at this time.

14 Lower the vehicle.

15 Raise the engine just high enough to allow the unbolted mounts to clear their brackets, then remove the mount(s).

16 Installation is the reverse of removal. Use non-hardening thread-locking compound on the mount fasteners and be sure to tighten them to the torque listed in this Chapter's Specifications.

Specifications

General

Displacement	256 cubic inches (4.2 liters)
Bore and stroke	3.66 x 4.02 inches
Compression Ratio	10:1
Cylinder numbers	1-2-3-4-5-6
Firing order	1-5-3-6-2-4

Camshaft

Journal diameter	
Exhaust, journal no. 1	1.1794 to 1.1804 inch
Exhaust journals 2 through 7 and all intake journals	1.0612 to 1.0622 inch
Endplay	
Intake	0.0020 to 0.0079 inch
Exhaust	0.0017 to 0.0084 inch
Lobe lift	
Intake	0.274 to 0.278 inch
Exhaust	0.283 to 0.287 inch

Cylinder head

Warpage limit	0.003 inch per 6 inches

Exhaust manifold

Warpage limit	0.003 inch

INLINE 6-CYLINDER

**Firing order
1-5-3-6-2-4**

24072-1-0B

Cylinder locations

Torque specifications   Ft-lbs (unless otherwise indicated)

➥**Note: One foot-pound (ft-lb) of torque is equivalent to 12 inch-pounds (in-lbs) of torque. Torque values below approximately 15 ft-lbs are expressed in inch-pounds, since most foot-pound torque wrenches are not accurate at these smaller values.**

Camshaft cap bolts	106 in-lbs
Camshaft sprocket bolt	
Intake	
Step 1	15
Step 2	Tighten an additional 100-degrees
Exhaust (camshaft actuator)	
Step 1	18
Step 2	Tighten an additional 135-degrees
Cylinder head bolts (in sequence - see illustration 9.13)	
Step 1 - Long cylinder head bolts (bolts 1 through 14)	22
Step 2 - Long cylinder head bolts (bolts 1 through 14)	Tighten an additional 155-degrees
Step 3 - Bolts 16 and 17	62 in-lbs plus an additional 60-degrees
Step 4 - Bolt 15	62 in-lbs plus an additional 120-degrees
Cylinder head access hole plugs	44 in-lbs
Crankshaft pulley bolt	
Step 1	110
Step 2	Tighten bolts an additional 180-degrees (1/2-turn)

Torque specifications   Ft-lbs (unless otherwise indicated)

Timing chain
- Tensioner shoe bolt — 18
- Tensioner guide bolt — 89 inch-lbs
- Tensioner bolts — 18
- Top chain guide bolts — 89 inch-lbs

Intake manifold bolts — 89 in-lbs

Exhaust manifold bolts
- 2002 through 2006 — 18
- 2007 and later — 15

Driveplate-to-crankshaft bolts
- Step 1 — 18
- Step 2 — Tighten an additional 50-degrees

Front cover bolts — 89 in-lbs

Rear main oil seal housing bolts — 89 in-lbs

Oil pan mounting bolts
- Sides — 18
- Ends — 89 in-lbs

Oil pump cover bolts — 89 in-lbs

Oil pump relief valve plug — 124 in-lbs

Engine mount nuts (upper and lower) — 52

Engine mount bracket-to-frame bolts — 81

Valve cover bolts — 89 in-lbs

Notes

2B

V8 ENGINES

1 General information

This Part of Chapter 2 is devoted to in-vehicle repair procedures for the 5.3L and 6.0L V8 engines. These engines utilize cast-iron blocks with eight cylinders arranged in a "V" shape at a 90-degree angle between the two banks. All V8 cylinder heads utilize an overhead valve arrangement. The 5.3L engine uses aluminum cylinder heads with pressed-in valve guides and hardened valve seats, while 6.0L V8 engines use cast iron cylinder heads with integral valve guides and pressed-in valve seats. Hydraulic roller lifters actuate the valves through tubular pushrods and rocker arms. The oil pump is mounted at the front of the engine behind the timing chain cover and is driven by the crankshaft. In addition, all 2005 and later V8 engines use a displacement on demand system that allows the engine to operate on four cylinders when driving conditions permit. This is accomplished with a valve lifter oil manifold and solenoids controlled buy the PCM. When commanded, the system deactivates lifters for cylinders 1, 7, 4 and 6.

To positively identify these engines, locate the Vehicle Identification Number (VIN) on the left front corner of the instrument panel. The VIN is visible from the outside of the vehicle through the windshield. The eighth character in the sequence is the engine designation:

P, M = 5.3 liter V8 engine
H = 6.0 liter V8 engine

Information concerning engine removal and installation and engine overhaul can be found in Part C of this Chapter. The following repair procedures are based on the assumption that the engine is installed in the vehicle. If the engine has been removed from the vehicle and mounted on a stand, many of the steps outlined in this Part of Chapter 2 will not apply.

2 Repair operations possible with the engine in the vehicle

Many major repair operations can be accomplished without removing the engine from the vehicle.

Clean the engine compartment and the exterior of the engine with some type of pressure washer before any work is done. A clean engine will make the job easier and will help keep dirt out of the internal areas of the engine.

Depending on the components involved, it may be a good idea to remove the hood to improve access to the engine as repairs are performed (refer to Chapter 11 if necessary).

If oil or coolant leaks develop, indicating a need for gasket or seal replacement, the repairs can generally be made with the engine in the vehicle. The oil pan gasket, the cylinder head gaskets, intake and exhaust manifold gaskets, timing chain cover gaskets and the crankshaft oil seals are all accessible with the engine in place.

Exterior engine components, such as the water pump, the starter motor, the alternator, the distributor and the fuel injection components, as well as the intake and exhaust manifolds, can be removed for repair with the engine in place.

Since the cylinder heads can be removed without removing the engine, valve component servicing can also be accomplished with the engine in the vehicle.

Replacement of, repairs to or inspection of the timing chain and sprockets and the oil pump are all possible with the engine in place.

In extreme cases caused by a lack of necessary equipment, repair or replacement of piston rings, pistons, connecting rods and rod bearings is possible with the engine in the vehicle. However, this practice is not recommended because of the cleaning and preparation work that must be done to the components involved.

3 Top Dead Center (TDC) for number one piston - locating

♦ **Refer to illustration 3.6**

1 Top Dead Center (TDC) is the highest point in the cylinder that each piston reaches as it travels up the cylinder bore. Each piston reaches TDC on the compression stroke and again on the exhaust stroke, but TDC generally refers to piston position on the compression stroke.

2 Positioning the piston(s) at TDC is an essential part of many procedures such as distributor and timing chain/sprocket removal.

3 Before beginning this procedure, be sure to place the transmission in Neutral and apply the parking brake or block the rear wheels. Also, disable the ignition system by disconnecting the primary electrical connectors at the ignition coil packs, then remove the spark plugs (see Chapter 1).

4 In order to bring any piston to TDC, the crankshaft must be turned using one of the methods outlined below. When looking at the front of the engine, normal crankshaft rotation is clockwise.

a) *The preferred method is to turn the crankshaft with a socket and ratchet attached to the bolt threaded into the front of the crankshaft. Apply pressure on the bolt in a clockwise direction only. Never turn the bolt counterclockwise.*

b) *A remote starter switch, which may save some time, can also be used. Follow the instructions included with the switch. Once the piston is close to TDC, use a socket and ratchet as described in the previous paragraph.*

c) *If an assistant is available to turn the ignition switch to the Start position in short bursts, you can get the piston close to TDC without a remote starter switch. Make sure your assistant is out of the vehicle, away from the ignition switch, then use a socket and ratchet as described in Paragraph (a) to complete the procedure.*

5 Place your finger partially over the number one spark plug hole and rotate the crankshaft using one of the methods described above until air pressure is felt at the spark plug hole. Air pressure at the spark plug hole indicates that the cylinder has started the compression stroke. Once the compression stroke has begun, TDC for the number one cylinder is obtained when the piston reaches the top of the cylinder on the compression stroke.

6 To bring the piston to the top of the cylinder, insert a long screwdriver into the number one spark plug hole until it touches the top of the piston.

➡**Note: Make sure to wrap the tip of the screwdriver with tape to avoid scratching the top of the piston and the cylinder walls.**

3.6 A long screwdriver inserted in the number one spark plug hole can be used to determine the highest point reached by that piston - make sure to wrap the tip of the screwdriver with tape to avoid scratching the top of the piston or the cylinder walls

Use the screwdriver (as a feeler gauge) to tell where the top of the piston is located in the cylinder while slowly rotating the crankshaft (see illustration). As the piston rises the screwdriver will be pushed out. The point at which the screwdriver stops moving outward is TDC.

➡️**Note: Always hold the screwdriver upright while the engine is being rotated so that the screwdriver will not get wedged as the piston travels upward.**

7   If you go past TDC, rotate the crank-shaft counterclockwise until the piston is approximately one inch below TDC, then slowly rotate the crankshaft clockwise again until TDC is reached.

8   After the number one piston has been positioned at TDC on the compression stroke, TDC for any of the remaining pistons can be located by turning the crankshaft 90-degrees (1/4 turn) at a time and following the firing order.

4   Valve covers - removal and installation

REMOVAL

▶ **Refer to illustrations 4.4 and 4.12**

1   Disconnect the cable from the negative terminal of the battery.

2   On models so equipped, remove the secondary air injection crossover pipe, then remove the air injection check valve and pipe assembly from the exhaust manifold on the side from which you wish to remove the valve cover (see Chapter 6). If both valve covers are being removed, both air injection check valves and pipe assemblies must be removed.

Right side

3   Remove the air filter housing (see Chapter 4).

4   Remove the heater hose bracket bolt and move the heater hoses aside without disconnecting them (see illustration).

5   Disconnect the electrical connectors from the ignition coils and the EGR valve. Unclip the wiring harness from the ignition coil bracket and lay it aside.

6   Remove the ignition coils from the valve cover (see Chapter 5). Be sure each plug wire is labeled before removal to ensure correct reinstallation.

7   Remove the valve cover bolts, then detach the cover from the cylinder head.

➡️**Note: If the cover is stuck to the cylinder head, bump one end with a block of wood and a hammer to jar it loose. If that doesn't work, try to slip a flexible putty knife between the cylinder head and cover to break the gasket seal. Don't pry at the cover-to-head joint or damage to the sealing surfaces may occur (leading to oil leaks in the future).**

Left side

8   Detach the clips securing the engine wiring harness to the valve cover and to positive battery cable junction block bracket and position the engine wiring harness aside.

4.4 Detach or lay aside the following components for valve cover removal - 2000 Silverado shown

A   Secondary Air Injection crossover pipe
B   Ignition coils (passenger side)
C   Heater hoses
D   EGR valve
E   Secondary Air Injection check valve and pipe assembly (driver side)
F   Wiring harness
G   Ignition coils (driver side)
H   Power brake booster hose

9   Remove the power brake booster vacuum hose from the power brake booster.

10 Remove the ignition coils from the valve cover (see Chapter 5). Be sure each plug wire is labeled before removal to ensure correct reinstallation.

11 Disconnect the PCV valve from the valve cover.

4.12 Valve cover mounting bolts (arrows) - arrow to the far right indicates location of the PCV valve (left valve cover shown)

12 Remove the valve cover bolts (see illustration), then detach the cover from the cylinder head.

➡**Note: If the cover is stuck to the cylinder head, bump one end with a block of wood and a hammer to jar it loose. If that doesn't work, try to slip a flexible putty knife between the cylinder head and cover to break the gasket seal. Don't pry at the cover-to-head joint or damage to the sealing surfaces may occur (leading to oil leaks in the future).**

INSTALLATION

▶ **Refer to illustration 4.15**

13 The mating surfaces of each cylinder head and valve cover must be perfectly clean when the covers are installed. Use a gasket scraper to remove all traces of sealant and old gasket material, then clean the mating surfaces with lacquer thinner or acetone. If there's sealant or oil on

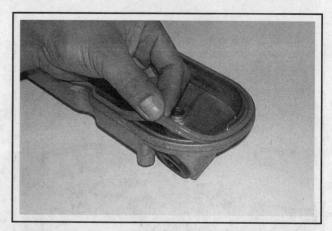

4.15 Position the new gasket in the valve cover lip

the mating surfaces when the cover is installed, oil leaks may develop.

14 Clean the mounting bolt threads with a die to remove any corrosion and restore damaged threads. Make sure the threaded holes in the cylinder head are clean - run a tap into them to remove corrosion and restore damaged threads.

15 The gaskets should be mated to the covers before the covers are installed. Position the gasket inside the cover lip (see illustration). If the gasket will not stay in place in the cover lip, apply a thin coat of RTV sealant to the cover flange, then and allow the sealant to set up so the gasket adheres to the cover.

16 Inspect the valve cover bolt grommets for damage. If the grommets aren't damaged they can be reused. Carefully position the valve cover(s) on the cylinder head and install the bolts and grommets. On 2001 and later models, remove the oil filler tube and replace it with a new one.

17 Tighten the bolts in three or four steps to the torque listed in this Chapter's Specifications.

18 The remaining installation steps are the reverse of removal.

19 Start the engine and check carefully for oil leaks as the engine warms up.

5 Rocker arms and pushrods - removal, inspection and installation

REMOVAL

▶ **Refer to illustrations 5.2 and 5.3**

1 Refer to Section 4 and detach the valve covers from the cylinder heads.

2 Loosen the rocker arm pivot bolts one at a time and detach the rocker arms and bolts, then detach the pivot support pedestal (see illustration). Keep track of the rocker arm positions, since they must be returned to the same locations. Store each set of rocker components separately in a marked plastic bag to ensure that they're reinstalled in their original locations.

3 Remove the pushrods and store them separately to make sure they don't get mixed up during installation (see illustration).

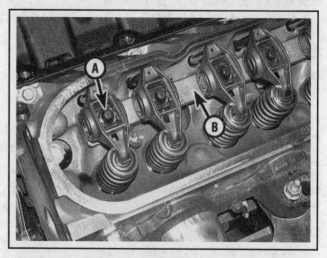

5.2 Remove the mounting bolts (A) and rocker arms, then remove the pivot support pedestal (B)

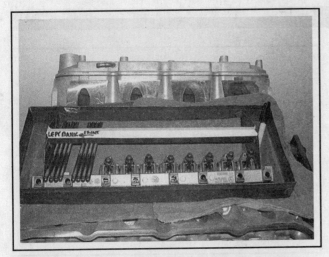

5.3 Store the pushrods and rocker arms in order to ensure they are reinstalled in their original locations - note the arrow indicating the front of the engine

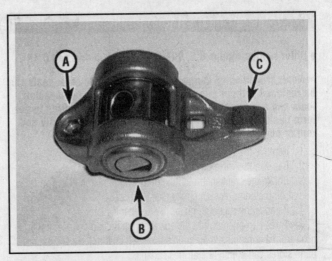

5.4 Rocker arm wear points

A	Pushrod socket	C	Valve stem contact point
B	Pivot bearings		

INSPECTION

♦ **Refer to illustration 5.4**

4   Check each rocker arm for wear, cracks and other damage, especially where the pushrods and valve stems contact the rocker arm (see illustration).

5   Check the pivot bearings for binding and roughness. If the bearings are worn or damaged, replacement of the entire rocker arm will be necessary.

➡**Note: Keep in mind that there is no valve adjustment on these engines, so excessive wear or damage in the valve train can easily result in excessive valve clearance, which in turn will cause valve noise when the engine is running. Also check the rocker arm pivot support pedestal for cracks and other obvious damage.**

6   Make sure the hole at the pushrod end of each rocker arm is open.

7   Inspect the pushrods for cracks and excessive wear at the ends, also check that the oil hole running through each pushrod is not clogged. Roll each pushrod across a piece of plate glass to see if it's bent (if it wobbles, it's bent).

INSTALLATION

♦ **Refer to illustration 5.9**

8   Lubricate the lower end of each pushrod with clean engine oil or engine assembly lube and install them in their original locations. Make sure each pushrod seats completely in the lifter socket.

9   Apply engine assembly lube to the ends of the valve stems and to the upper ends of the pushrods to prevent damage to the mating surfaces on initial start-up (see illustration). Also apply clean engine oil to the pivot shaft and bearing of each rocker arm and install the rocker arms loosely in their original locations. DO NOT tighten the bolts at this time!

5.9 Lubricate the pushrod ends and the valve stems with engine assembly lube before installing the rocker arms

10   Rotate the crankshaft until the number one piston is at TDC (see Section 3). With the number one piston is at TDC, tighten the intake valve rocker arms for the Number 1, 3, 4, and 5 cylinders and the exhaust rocker arms for the Number 1, 2, 7, and 8 cylinders. Tighten each of the specified rocker arm bolts to the torque listed in this Chapter's Specifications.

11   Rotate the crankshaft 360 degrees. Tighten the intake valve rocker arms for the Number 2, 6, 7, and 8 cylinders and the exhaust rocker arms for the Number 3, 4, 5, and 6 cylinders. Tighten each of the rocker arm bolts to the torque listed in this Chapter's Specifications.

12   Refer to Section 4 and install the valve covers. Start the engine, listen for unusual valve train noses and check for oil leaks at the valve cover gaskets.

6 Valve springs, retainers and seals - replacement

▶ Refer to illustrations 6.5, 6.8, 6.10, 6.15a, 6.15b and 6.19

➡Note: Broken valve springs and defective valve stem seals can be replaced without removing the cylinder head. Two special tools and a compressed air source are normally required to perform this operation, so read through this Section carefully and rent or buy the tools before beginning the job.

1 Remove the spark plugs (see Chapter 1).

2 Remove the valve covers (see Section 4).

3 Rotate the crankshaft until the number one piston is at Top Dead Center on the compression stroke (see Section 3).

4 Remove the rocker arms for the number 1 piston.

5 Thread an adapter into the spark plug hole and connect an air hose from a compressed air source to it (see illustration). Most auto parts stores can supply the air hose adapter.

➡Note: Many cylinder compression gauges utilize a screw-in fitting that may work with your air hose quick-disconnect fitting. If a cylinder compression gauge fitting is used it will be necessary to remove the schrader valve from the end of the fitting before using it in this procedure.

6 Apply compressed air to the cylinder. The valves should be held in place by the air pressure.

❋❋ WARNING:

If the cylinder isn't exactly at TDC, air pressure may force the piston down, causing the engine to quickly rotate. DO NOT leave a wrench on the crankshaft balancer bolt or you may be injured by the tool.

7 Stuff shop rags into the cylinder head holes around the valves to prevent parts and tools from falling into the engine.

8 Using a socket and a hammer, gently tap on the top of each valve spring retainer several times (this will break the seal between the valve keeper and the spring retainer and allow the keeper to separate from the valve spring retainer as the valve spring is compressed), then use a valve-spring compressor to compress the spring. Remove the keepers with small needle-nose pliers or a magnet (see illustration).

➡Note: Several different types of tools are available for compressing the valve springs with the head in place. One type grips

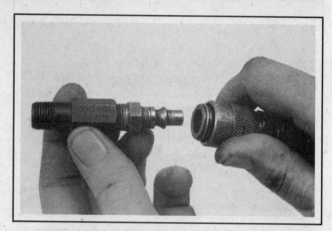

6.5 This is what the air hose adapter that fits into the spark plug hole looks like - they're commonly available from auto parts stores

the lower spring coils and presses on the retainer as the knob is turned, while the lever-type shown here utilizes the rocker arm bolt for leverage. Both types work very well, although the lever type is usually less expensive.

9 Remove the valve spring and retainer.

➡Note: If air pressure fails to retain the valve in the closed position during this operation, the valve face or seat may be damaged. If so, the cylinder head will have to be removed for repair.

10 Remove the old valve stem seals, noting differences between the intake and exhaust seals (see illustration).

11 Wrap a rubber band or tape around the top of the valve stem so the valve won't fall into the combustion chamber, then release the air pressure.

12 Inspect the valve stem for damage. Rotate the valve in the guide and check the end for eccentric movement, which would indicate that the valve is bent.

13 Move the valve up-and-down in the guide and make sure it does not bind. If the valve stem binds, either the valve is bent or the guide is damaged. In either case, the head will have to be removed for repair.

14 Reapply air pressure to the cylinder to retain the valve in the

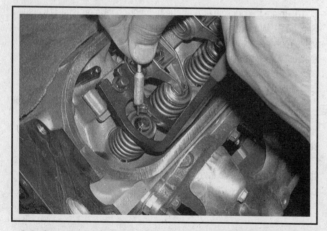

6.8 Once the spring is depressed, the keepers can be removed with a small magnet or needle-nose pliers (a magnet is preferred to prevent dropping the keepers)

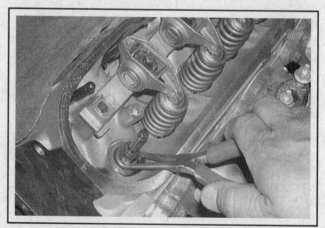

6.10 Use a pair of needle nose pliers to remove the valve seals

6.15a Be sure to install the seals on the correct valve stems

1 Intake valve seal
2 Exhaust valve seal

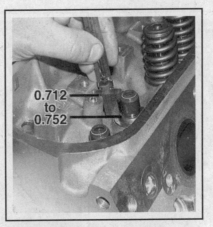

0.712
to
0.752

6.15b Install the intake and exhaust valve seals to the specified depth - measure from the spring seat to the top edge of the valve seal

6.19 Apply small dab of grease to each keeper as shown here before installation - it'll hold them in place on the valve stem as the spring is released

closed position, then remove the tape or rubber band from the valve stem.

15 If you're working on an exhaust valve, install the new exhaust valve seal on the valve stem and press it down over the valve guide to the specified depth. Don't force the seal against the top of the guide (see illustrations).

➡**Note: On aluminum heads be sure take this measurement from the steel spring seat to the top edge of the intake and exhaust valve seals, not from the aluminum seat on the head!**

16 If you're working on an intake valve, install a new intake valve stem seal over the valve stem and press it down over the valve guide to the specified depth. Don't force the intake valve seal against the top of the guide.

❋❋ **CAUTION:**

Do not install an exhaust valve seal on an intake valve, as high oil consumption will result.

17 Install the spring and retainer in position over the valve.
18 Compress the valve spring assembly only enough to install the keepers in the valve stem.
19 Position the keepers in the valve stem groove. Apply a small dab of grease to the inside of each keeper to hold it in place if necessary (see illustration). Remove the pressure from the spring tool and make sure the keepers are seated.
20 Disconnect the air hose and remove the adapter from the spark plug hole.
21 Repeat the above procedure on the remaining cylinders, following the firing order sequence (see this Chapter's Specifications). Bring each piston to Top Dead Center on the compression stroke before applying air pressure (see Section 3).
22 Reinstall the rocker arm assemblies and the valve covers (see Sections 4 and 5).
23 Start the engine, then check for oil leaks and unusual sounds coming from the valve cover area. Allow the engine to idle for at least five minutes before revving the engine.

7 Intake manifold - removal and installation

❋❋ **WARNING:**

Wait until the engine is completely cool before starting this procedure.

REMOVAL

▶ **Refer to illustrations 7.7a, 7.7b, 7.8a, 7.8b and 7.8c**

1 Disconnect the cable from the negative terminal of the battery.
2 Clamp off the coolant hoses leading to the throttle body.
3 Remove the air filter housing and on 6.0L models the intake manifold cover. Relieve the fuel system pressure (see Chapter 4).
4 Disconnect the accelerator linkage (see Chapter 4) and, if equipped, the cruise control linkage.
5 Disconnect the electrical connectors from the fuel injectors, EGR valve, EVAP solenoid, the MAP sensor and from the sensors on the

7.3 Intake manifold cover retaining screws (arrows)

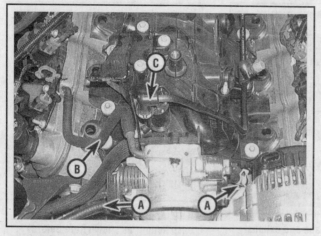

7.7a Disconnect the coolant hoses (A) and the crankcase breather hose (B) from the throttle body, then squeeze the retainer on the EVAP solenoid vent tube (C) and remove it from the top of the intake manifold

7.7b Detach the PCV hose (A) and the power brake booster vacuum hose (B) from the rear of the intake - PCV hose already removed in this photo

throttle body. Label each connector clearly to aid in the reassembly process. Detach the large wiring harness bracket from the stud on the top of the intake manifold and lay the harness aside.

6   Remove the fuel rails and injectors as an assembly (see Chapter 4). The two fuel rails can be pulled straight up with the injectors still attached, but it will take some force to dislodge the injectors from the intake manifold.

➡**Note: This Step is not absolutely necessary but it will help prevent subsequent damage to the fuel injectors as the intake manifold is removed.**

7   Disconnect any vacuum hoses attached to the intake manifold or throttle body such as the power brake booster, the PCV and the EVAP purge control solenoid. Also disconnect the coolant hoses from the throttle body (see illustrations).

8   Remove the EGR valve and pipe assembly from the engine (see illustrations).

9   Disconnect any remaining electrical connectors or vacuum hoses connected to the intake manifold or throttle body.

10 Loosen the intake manifold mounting bolts in 1/4-turn increments in the reverse order of the tightening sequence until they can be removed by hand (see illustration 7.16). The manifold will probably be stuck to the cylinder heads and force may be required to break the gas-

ket seal. A pry bar can be positioned between the front of the manifold and the valley tray to break the bond made by the gasket.

✳✳ CAUTION:

Do not pry between the manifold and the heads or damage to the gasket sealing surfaces may result and vacuum leaks could develop. Also, don't use too much force - the manifold is made of a plastic composite and could crack.

11 Remove the intake manifold. As the manifold is lifted from the engine, be sure to check for and disconnect anything still attached to the manifold.

INSTALLATION

◆ **Refer to illustrations 7.14 and 7.16**

➡**Note: The mating surfaces of the cylinder heads, block and manifold must be perfectly clean when the manifold is installed.**

12 Carefully remove all traces of old gasket material. Note that the intake manifold is made of a composite material and the cylinder heads on the 5.3L engine is made of aluminum, therefore aggressive scraping

7.8a EGR pipe-to-intake manifold mounting bolts (arrows)

7.8b EGR valve mounting bracket-to-cylinder head mounting bolts (arrows)

7.8c EGR pipe-to-exhaust manifold mounting bolts (arrows)

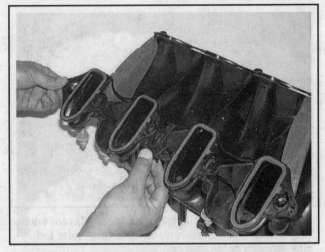

7.14 Align the tabs on the intake gaskets with the tabs on the manifold and snap the gasket into place

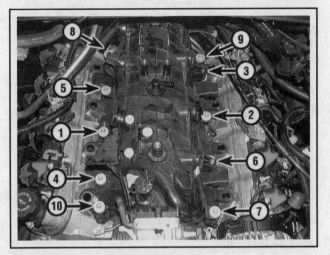

7.16 Intake manifold bolt tightening sequence - all V8 engines

is not suggested and will damage the sealing surfaces. After the gasket surfaces are cleaned and free of any gasket material wipe the mating surfaces with a cloth saturated with safety solvent. If there is old sealant or oil on the mating surfaces when the manifold is installed, oil or vacuum leaks may develop. Use a vacuum cleaner to remove any gasket material that falls into the intake ports in the heads.

13 Use a tap of the correct size to chase the threads in the bolt holes, then use compressed air (if available) to remove the debris from the holes.

✳✳ WARNING:

Wear safety glasses or a face shield to protect your eyes when using compressed air.

14 Position the new gaskets on the intake manifold (see illustration). Note that the gaskets are equipped with installation tabs that must snap into place on the intake manifold. The words "Manifold Side" may appear on the gasket, If so, this will ensure proper installation. Make sure the gaskets snap into place and all intake port openings align.

15 Carefully set the manifold in place.

16 Apply medium-strength threadlocking compound to the threads of the bolts. Install the bolts and tighten them following the recommended sequence (see illustration) to the torque listed in this Chapter's Specifications. Do not overtighten the bolts or gasket leaks may develop.

17 The remaining installation steps are the reverse of removal. Check the coolant level, adding as necessary (see Chapter 1). Start the engine and check carefully for vacuum leaks at the intake manifold joints.

8 Exhaust manifolds - removal and installation

REMOVAL

▶ **Refer to illustrations 8.4, 8.8 and 8.9**

✳✳ WARNING:

Use caution when working around the exhaust manifolds - the sheetmetal heat shields can be sharp on the edges. Also, the engine should be cold when this procedure is followed.

1 Disconnect the cable from the negative terminal of the battery.

2 Raise the vehicle and support it securely on jackstands.

3 Working under the vehicle, apply penetrating oil to the exhaust pipe-to-manifold studs and nuts (they're usually rusty). Disconnect the electrical connector for oxygen sensor.

4 Remove the nuts retaining the exhaust pipe(s) to the manifold(s) (see illustration). Note that both exhaust manifolds are more easily accessed with the front tires and the inner fenderwells removed, but it's not absolutely necessary (see Chapter 11).

8.4 Remove the exhaust pipe-to-manifold nuts

5   Detach the spark plug wires and remove the spark plugs from the side being worked on (see Chapter 1), If both manifolds are being removed, detach all the spark plug wires and remove all the spark plugs.

6   Remove the secondary air injection pipe (if equipped) from the exhaust manifold being removed (see Chapter 6).

Right side manifold

7   Remove the air cleaner assembly (see Chapter 4).

8   Remove the oil dipstick, unbolt the dipstick tube bracket and move the dipstick tube (see illustration).

9   Remove the EGR valve and pipe assembly (see illustrations 7.8a, 7.8b and 7.8c). Remove the mounting bolts and separate the exhaust manifold from the cylinder head (see illustration). Remove the heat shields from the manifold after the manifold has been removed.

Left side manifold

10 Disconnect the electrical connector from the Engine Coolant Temperature (ECT) sensor (see Chapter 6).

11 Remove the mounting bolts and separate the exhaust manifold from the cylinder head. Remove the heat shields from the manifold after the manifold has been removed.

INSTALLATION

12 Check the manifold for cracks and make sure the bolt threads are clean and undamaged. The manifold and cylinder head mating surfaces must be clean before the manifolds are reinstalled - use a gasket scraper to remove all carbon deposits and gasket material.

➡**Note: The cylinder heads on 4.8L and 5.3L engines are made of aluminum, therefore aggressive scraping is not suggested and will damage the sealing surfaces.**

13 Install the heat shields, then install the bolts and gaskets onto the manifold. Retaining tabs surrounding the gasket bolt holes should hold the assembly together as the manifold is installed.

14 Starting at the fourth thread, apply a 1/4-inch wide band of medium-strength threadlocking compound to the threads of the bolts.

➡**Note: The manufacturer recommends not applying threadlocking compound on the first three threads.**

15 Place the manifold on the cylinder head and install the mounting bolts finger tight.

16 When tightening the mounting bolts, work from the center to the

8.8 Remove the oil dipstick tube mounting bolt (A) and tube - (B) indicates the secondary air injection check valve and pipe assembly on the right manifold

8.9 Exhaust manifold fastener locations (right side shown, left side similar)

ends and be sure to use a torque wrench. Tighten the bolts in two steps to the torque listed in this Chapter's Specifications. If required, bend the exposed end of the exhaust manifold gasket back against the cylinder head.

17 The remaining installation steps are the reverse of removal. Always use new O-rings and gaskets on the EGR valve and pipe assembly.

18 Start the engine and check for exhaust leaks.

---

9   Cylinder heads - removal and installation

➡**Note: It will be necessary to purchase a new set of 11 mm head bolts before or during this procedure.**

REMOVAL

▶ **Refer to illustrations 9.2, 9.4a, 9.4b, 9.8 and 9.10**

1   Disconnect the cable from the negative terminal of the battery and drain the cooling system (see Chapter 1).

2   Remove the intake manifold (see Section 7) and the coolant pipe (see illustration).

3   On 1999 through 2004 models, remove the knock sensors from the valley cover (see Chapter 6).

4   On 1999 through 2004 models, remove the mounting screws and remove the valley cover and gasket (see illustration). On 2005 and later models, disconnect the electrical connector from the oil pressure regulator, then, remove the mounting screws and remove the valve lifter oil manifold and gasket (see illustration).

5   Detach both exhaust manifolds from the cylinder heads (see Section 8).

6   Remove the valve covers (see Section 4).

7   Remove the rocker arms and pushrods (see Section 5).

※※ **CAUTION:**

Again, as mentioned in Section 5, keep all the parts in order so they are reinstalled in the same location.

9.2 The coolant pipe is retained by two bolts at the front and two bolts at the rear of the cylinder heads

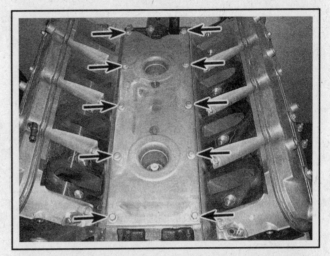

9.4a Valley cover mounting bolts (1999 through 2004 models)

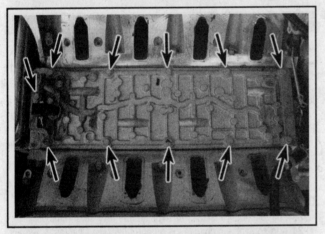

9.4b Locations of the screws for the valve lifter oil manifold (2005 and later models)

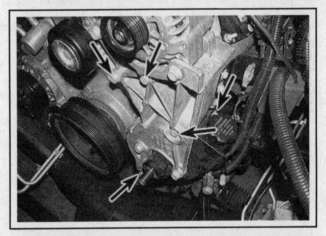

9.8 Alternator/power steering pump mounting bracket bolts (arrows) - remove the bolts and lay the bracket aside with the components attached

9.10 Using a prybar inserted into an intake port to break the head loose - do not use excessive force or damage to the head may result

8   Disconnect the wiring from the back of the alternator, then remove the power steering pump/alternator mounting bracket from the engine. Lay the bracket aside (with the components attached), without disconnecting the lines from the steering pump (see illustration).

9   Loosen the head bolts in 1/4-turn increments in the reverse order of the tightening sequence (see illustration 9.17) until they can be removed by hand.

➡Note: There will be different length and size head bolts for different locations. Make a note of the different sizes and lengths and where they go when removing the bolts to ensure correct installation of the new bolts.

10   Lift the heads off the engine. If resistance is felt, do not pry between the head and block as damage to the mating surfaces will result. To dislodge the head, place a pry bar or long screwdriver into the intake port and carefully pry the head off the engine (see illustration). Store the heads on blocks of wood to prevent damage to the gasket sealing surfaces.

11   Cylinder head disassembly and inspection procedures are covered in detail in Chapter 2, Part C.

INSTALLATION

▸ **Refer to illustrations 9.16, 9.19 and 9.22**

12   The mating surfaces of the cylinder heads and block must be perfectly clean when the heads are installed. Gasket removal solvents are available at auto parts stores and may prove helpful.

9.16 Position the head gasket over the dowels at each end of the cylinder head with the mark (arrow) facing the front of the vehicle

13 Use a gasket scraper to remove all traces of carbon and old gasket material, then wipe the mating surfaces with a cloth saturated with lacquer thinner or acetone.

➡Note: The cylinder heads on 4.8L and 5.3L engines are made of aluminum, therefore aggressive scraping is not suggested and will damage the sealing surfaces. If there is oil on the mating surfaces when the heads are installed, the gaskets may not seal correctly and leaks may develop. When working on the block, use a vacuum cleaner to remove any debris that falls into the cylinders.

14 Check the block and head mating surfaces for nicks, deep scratches and other damage. If damage is slight, it can be removed with emery cloth. If it is excessive, machining may be the only alternative.

15 Use a tap of the correct size to chase the threads in the head bolt holes in the block. If a tap is not available, spray a liberal amount of brake cleaner into each hole. Use compressed air (if available) to remove the debris from the holes.

※※ **WARNING:**

Wear safety glasses or a face shield to protect your eyes when using compressed air. All cylinder head bolts should be replaced with New bolts.

16 Position the new gaskets over the dowels in the block (see illustration).

17 Carefully position the heads on the block without disturbing the gaskets.

18 Before installing the 8mm head bolts, coat the threads with a medium-strength threadlocking compound. Then install the New 8mm head bolts (bolts 11 through 15).

19 Install New 11 mm head bolts (bolts 1 through 10) and tighten them finger tight. Following the recommended sequence (see illustration), tighten

9.19 Cylinder head bolt tightening sequence - all V8 engines

the bolts in four steps to the torque listed in this Chapter's Specifications.

※※ **WARNING:**

DO NOT reuse head bolts - always replace them with new ones.

20 On 1999 through 2004 models, install a new gasket and the valley cover and gasket (see illustration 9.2). On 2005-on models, install a new gasket and the valve lifter oil manifold and gasket. Tighten the bolts to the torque listed in this Chapter's Specifications

21 On 1999 through 2004 models, install the knock sensors onto the valley cover (see Chapter Six).

22 Install the coolant pipe, using new gaskets, onto the cylinder heads (see illustration). Tighten the bolts to the torque listed in this Chapter's Specifications.

23 The remaining installation steps are the reverse of removal.

24 Add coolant and change the oil and filter (see Chapter 1). Start the engine and check for proper operation and coolant or oil leaks.

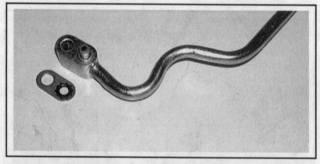

9.22 Be sure to use new gaskets at each cylinder head-to-coolant pipe joint - position the O-ring seal over the coolant pipe nipple

10 Crankshaft balancer - removal and installation

◆ **Refer to illustrations 10.5, 10.6 and 10.9**

➡Note: This procedure requires a special balancer installation tool that is available through specialized tool manufacturers only and a new crankshaft balancer bolt. Read through the entire procedure and obtain the tool and materials before proceeding.

1 Disconnect the cable from the negative terminal of the battery.

2 Raise the front of the vehicle and support it securely on jackstands. Then apply the parking brake.

3 Remove the drivebelt (see Chapter 1) and the cooling fan (see Chapter 3).

10.5 Use strap wrench to hold the crankshaft balancer while removing the center bolt (a chain-type wrench may be used if you wrap a section of old drivebelt or rag around the balancer first)

10.6 The use of a three jaw puller will be necessary to remove the crankshaft balancer - always place the puller jaws around the hub, not the outer ring

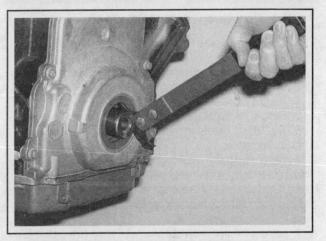

10.9 Before the new crankshaft bolt is installed and tightened, the balancer must be measured for proper installation - when properly installed, the balancer hub should extend 3/32 to 11/64-inch past the crankshaft snout

4   Working under the vehicle, remove the stone shield from below the engine (if equipped).

5   Use a strap wrench around the crankshaft pulley to hold it while using a breaker bar and socket to remove the crankshaft pulley center bolt (see illustration).

6   Pull the balancer off the crankshaft with a puller (see illustration).

⁕⁕ CAUTION:

The jaws of the puller must only contact the hub of the balancer - not the outer ring.

➡Note: A long Allen-head bolt should be inserted into the crankshaft nose for the puller's tapered tip to push against to prevent damage to the crankshaft threads.

7   Position the crankshaft pulley/balancer on the crankshaft and slide it on as far as it will go. Note that the slot (keyway) in the hub must be aligned with the Woodruff key in the end of the crankshaft.

8   Using the specialized crankshaft balancer installation tool, press the crankshaft pulley/balancer onto the crankshaft.

9   Install the old crankshaft balancer bolt and tighten the crankshaft bolt to 240 ft-lbs. Remove the old bolt and measure the distance from the snout of the crankshaft to the balancer hub (see illustration). When properly installed, the balancer hub should extend 3/32 to 11/64-inch past the crankshaft snout. If the measurement is incorrect, reinstall the balancer installation tool and press the balancer on the crankshaft until the measurement is correct.

10 Install a New crankshaft balancer bolt and tighten it in two steps to the torque and angle of rotation listed in this Chapter's Specifications.

11 The remaining installation steps are the reverse of removal.

11 Crankshaft front oil seal - removal and installation

◗ Refer to illustrations 11.2, 11.4 and 11.5

1   Remove the crankshaft balancer (see Section 10).

2   Note how the seal is installed - the new one must be installed to the same depth and facing the same way. Carefully pry the oil seal out of the cover with a seal puller or a large screwdriver (see illustration). Be very careful not to distort the cover or scratch the crankshaft! Wrap electrician's tape around the tip of the screwdriver to avoid damage to the crankshaft.

3   If the seal is being replaced with the timing chain cover removed, support the cover on top of two blocks of wood and drive the seal out from the backside with a hammer and punch.

⁕⁕ CAUTION:

Be careful not to scratch, gouge or distort the area that the seal fits into or a leak will develop.

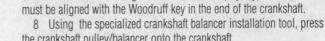

11.2 Carefully pry the old seal out of the timing chain cover - don't damage the crankshaft in the process

11.4 Drive the new seal into place with a large socket and hammer

11.5 If the sealing surface of the pulley hub has a wear groove from contact with the seal, repair sleeves are available at most auto parts stores

4   Apply clean engine oil or multi-purpose grease to the outer edge of the new seal, then install it in the cover with the lip (spring side) facing IN. Drive the seal into place (see illustration) with a large socket and a hammer (if a large socket isn't available, a piece of pipe will also work). Make sure the seal enters the bore squarely and stop when the front face is at the proper depth.

5   Check the surface on the balancer hub that the oil seal rides on. If the surface has been grooved from long-time contact with the seal,

a press-on sleeve may be available to renew the sealing surface (see illustration). This sleeve is pressed into place with a hammer and a block of wood and is commonly available at auto parts stores for various applications.

6   Lubricate the balancer hub with clean engine oil and reinstall the crankshaft balancer as described in Section 10.

7   The remainder of installation is the reverse of the removal.

12 Timing chain - removal, inspection and installation

REMOVAL AND INSPECTION

> ✳✳ **CAUTION** ✳✳
>
> The timing system is complex. Severe engine damage will occur if you make any mistakes. Do not attempt this procedure unless you are highly experienced with this type of repair. If you are at all unsure of your abilities, consult an expert. Double-check all your work and be sure everything is correct before you attempt to start the engine.

▶ **Refer to illustrations 12.6, 12.10 and 12.14**

1   Disconnect the cable from the negative terminal of the battery.

2   Refer to Chapter 1 and drain the cooling system and engine oil.

3   Refer to Chapter 3 and remove the upper and lower fan shrouds, drivebelt, cooling fan and water pump.

4   Remove the crankshaft balancer (see Section 10).

5   Remove the oil pan (see Section 14).

6   On 2005-on models, remove the mounting bolts and the camshaft position sensor.

7   Remove the timing chain cover mounting bolts and separate the timing chain cover from the block (see illustration). The cover may be stuck; if so, use a putty knife to break the gasket seal. Since the cover is made of aluminum it can easily be damaged, so DO NOT attempt to pry it off.

8   Remove the oil pick-up tube and the oil pump (see Section 15).

9   Measure the timing chain freeplay. If it is more than 5/8 inch, the chain and both sprockets should be replaced.

10   Loosen the camshaft sprocket bolts one turn, then screw the crankshaft balancer bolt into the end of the crankshaft and rotate the crankshaft in the normal direction of rotation (clockwise) until the timing marks align (see illustration). Verify that the number one piston is at TDC.

11   Remove the three bolts from the end of the camshaft, then detach the camshaft sprocket and chain as an assembly.

➡ **Note: 2007 models are equipped with a single camshaft sprocket bolt.**

12.6 Timing chain cover mounting bolts (arrows)

12.10 Timing chain alignment marks (arrows) - when properly aligned, the crankshaft gear should be in the 12 o'clock position, the camshaft gear should be in the 6 o'clock position and the number one piston should be at TDC

12.18 Slip the chain and camshaft sprocket in place over the crankshaft sprocket with the camshaft sprocket timing mark (arrow) at the bottom

12.22 Install the front cover with a new gasket onto the engine block LOOSELY - the cover must be aligned properly before final installation

12.14 The sprocket on the crankshaft can be removed with a two or three-jaw puller

12 On 2005-on models, remove the two mounting bolts and the timing chain damper.

13 Inspect the camshaft and crankshaft sprockets for damage or wear.

14 If replacement of the timing chain is necessary, remove the sprocket on the crankshaft with a two-or three-jaw puller, but be careful not to damage the threads in the end of the crankshaft (see illustration).

INSTALLATION

> ※ **CAUTION** ※
>
> Before starting the engine, carefully rotate the crankshaft by hand through at least two full revolutions (use a socket and breaker bar on the crankshaft pulley centerbolt). If you feel any resistance, STOP! There is something wrong - most likely, valves are contacting the pistons. You must find the problem before proceeding. Check your work and see if any updated repair information is available.

▶ **Refer to illustrations 12.18, 12.22 and 12.23**

➡**Note: Timing chains must be replaced as a set with the camshaft and crankshaft sprockets. Never put a new chain on old sprockets.**

15 Use a gasket scraper to remove all traces of old gasket material and sealant from the cover and engine block.

16 On 2005-on models, install the timing chain damper and tighten the bolts to the torque listed in this Chapter's Specifications.

17 Align the crankshaft sprocket with the Woodruff key and press the sprocket onto the crankshaft (if removed) with the vibration damper bolt, a large socket and some washers or tap it gently into place until it is completely seated.

> ※ **CAUTION:**
>
> **If resistance is encountered, do not hammer the sprocket onto the crankshaft. It may eventually move onto the shaft, but it may be cracked in the process and fail later, causing extensive engine damage.**

18 Loop the new chain over the camshaft sprocket, then turn the sprocket until the timing mark is at the bottom (see illustration). Mesh the chain with the crankshaft sprocket and position the camshaft sprocket on the end of the camshaft. If necessary, turn the camshaft so the dowel in the camshaft fits into the hole in the sprocket with the timing mark in the 6 o'clock position (see illustration 12.12). When the chain is installed, the timing marks MUST align as shown.

19 Apply a thread locking compound to the camshaft sprocket bolt threads and tighten the bolts to the torque listed in this Chapter's Specifications.

20 Lubricate the chain with clean engine oil.

21 Install the oil pump and the oil pick up tube onto the engine (see Section 15). Now would be a good time to replace the crankshaft front oil seal (see Section 11).

22 Install the timing chain cover on the engine loosely using a new gasket (see illustration).

23 Align the timing chain cover as follows:

a) *Install the crankshaft balancer on the engine as described in Section 10. This Step will align the front oil seal with the balancer hub.*

b) *Place a straightedge on the engine block oil pan rail. Measure the distance on each side of the block from the oil pan rail to the timing chain cover with a feeler gauge (see illustration). This Step measures the difference between the sealing surface of the oil pan and the sealing surface of the timing chain cover in relationship to each other.*

c) *Tilt the front timing cover as necessary to achieve an even measurement on each side. This Step properly aligns the front timing cover to oil pan sealing surfaces. Typically 0.000 to 0.020 inch is an acceptable tolerance.*

➡Note: Ideally the timing chain cover should be flush with the oil pan rail, but because of the differences in seal thickness, this may not always be obtainable. That is why there is a tolerance of 0.000 to 0.020 inch. Always let the front seal center itself around the crankshaft balancer hub and tilt the cover from

12.23 With the crankshaft balancer in place and the front cover bolts installed LOOSELY, measure the distance between the oil pan rail and the front cover sealing surface on each side (arrows) - then adjust the cover so the measurements are even on both sides before tightening the cover bolts

side to side to even up the measurement at both oil pan rails. Never push downward on the front timing cover in an attempt to make the oil pan sealing surface flush, as this will distort the front oil seal and eventually lead to an oil leak!

d) *With the timing chain cover properly aligned, tighten the cover bolts to the torque listed in this Chapter's Specifications.*

24 Apply a thin layer of RTV sealant to the areas where the timing chain cover and cylinder block meet, then install the oil pan as described in Section 14.

25 The remaining installation steps are the reverse of removal.

26 Add coolant and oil to the engine (see Chapter 1). Run the engine and check for oil and coolant leaks.

13 Camshaft and lifters - removal and installation

➡Note 1: The camshaft should always be thoroughly inspected before installation and camshaft endplay should always be checked prior to camshaft removal. Refer to Chapter 2C for the camshaft and lifter inspection procedures.

➡Note 2: If the camshaft is being replaced, always install new lifters as well. Do not use old lifters on a new camshaft.

REMOVAL

▶ Refer to illustrations 13.2a, 13.2b and 13.5

1 Refer to the appropriate Sections and remove the intake manifold, valve covers, rocker arms, pushrods, valley cover (2002 through 2004) or valve lifter oil manifold (2005 and later) timing chain and the cylinder heads. Also remove the radiator and air conditioning condenser (see Chapter 3) and the camshaft position sensor (see Chapter 6).

2 Before removing the lifters, arrange to store them in a clearly labeled box to ensure that they're reinstalled in their original locations. Remove the lifter retainers and lifters and store them where they won't get dirty (see illustrations). On 2005 and later 5.3L Displacement on

13.2a The roller lifters are held in place by retainers - remove the retainer bolts and remove the retainers and the lifters as an assembly - note that each retainer houses four individual lifters and they must be installed back in their original locations if they're going to be reused

13.2b Once the lifters and retainers are removed from the block they can be marked (for location and installation purposes) and inspected

13.5 Remove the bolts (arrows) and take off the camshaft retainer plate, noting which side faces the block

Demand models, these specific lifters are installed in the notched areas of the retainer. DO NOT attempt to withdraw the camshaft with the lifters in place.

3   If the lifters are built up with gum and varnish they may not come out with the retainer. If so, there are several ways to extract the lifters from the bores. A special tool designed to grip and remove lifters is manufactured by many tool companies and is widely available, but it may not be required in every case. On newer engines without a lot of varnish buildup, the lifters can often be removed with a small magnet or even with your fingers. A machinist's scribe with a bent end can be used to pull the lifters out by positioning the point under the retainer ring in the top of each lifter.

✳✳ CAUTION:

Don't use pliers to remove the lifters unless you intend to replace them with new ones. The pliers will damage the precision machined and hardened lifters, rendering them useless.

4   On 5.3L models, remove the mounting bolt and camshaft sensor from the rear top surface of the cylinder block.

5   Remove the bolts and the camshaft retainer plate, noting which direction faces the block (see illustration).

6   Thread three 6-inch long bolts into the camshaft sprocket bolt holes to use as a "handle" when removing the camshaft from the block.

7   Carefully pull the camshaft out. Support the cam near the block so the lobes don't nick or gouge the bearings as it's withdrawn.

INSTALLATION

▶ **Refer to illustration 13.8**

8   Lubricate the camshaft bearing journals and cam lobes with camshaft and lifter assembly lube (see illustration).

9   Slide the camshaft into the engine. Support the cam near the block and be careful not to scrape or nick the bearings.

10   Turn the camshaft until the dowel pin is in the 3 o'clock position, and install the camshaft thrust plate, tighten the bolts to the torque

13.8 Be sure to apply camshaft assembly lube to the cam lobes and bearing journals before installing the camshaft

listed in this Chapter's Specifications. Make sure the gasket surface on the camshaft thrust plate and the engine block are free from oil and dirt.

11   Install the timing chain and sprockets (see Section 12). Also install the camshaft position sensor using a new O-ring (see Chapter 6).

12   Lubricate the lifters with clean engine oil and install them in the lifter retainers. Be sure to align the flats on the lifters with the flats in the lifter retainers. On 2005-on 5.3L Displacement on Demand models, align the raised surface of the lifter with the notched area of the retainer. Install the retainer and lifters into the engine block as an assembly. If the original lifters are being reinstalled, be sure to return them to their original locations. If a new camshaft is being installed, install new lifters as well. Tighten the lifter retainer bolts to the torque listed in this Chapter's Specifications.

13   The remaining installation steps are the reverse of removal.

14   Before starting and running the engine, change the oil and install a new oil filter (see Chapter 1).

14 Oil pan - removal and installation

REMOVAL

▶ **Refer to illustrations 14.4 and 14.9**

1 Disconnect the cable from the negative terminal of the battery.

2 Raise the vehicle and support it securely on jackstands, then refer to Chapter 1 and drain the engine oil and remove the oil filter.

3 Remove the oil pan skid plate, if equipped.

4 Remove the lower control arm crossmember from below the oil pan, if equipped (see illustration).

5 On 4WD vehicles, unbolt and lower the front differential carrier with a floorjack (see Chapter 8).

6 Disconnect the front exhaust Y pipe from the engine and the exhaust system and remove it from the vehicle. This step is not absolutely necessary, but it will help facilitate removal of the oil pan.

7 Remove the starter motor (see Chapter 5).

8 On 2005-on models, remove the air conditioning compressor (see Chapter 3).

9 Remove the wiring harness bracket from the front of the oil pan and the bracket on the passenger side of the oil pan securing the transmission oil cooler lines (if equipped) and the starter motor wiring. Also disconnect the electrical connector from the oil level sensor (see illustration).

10 Remove the transmission to oil pan bolts (see Chapter 7).

11 If the vehicle is equipped with an engine oil cooler, remove the engine oil cooler lines and adapter from the driver's side of the oil pan.

12 Remove the access plugs covering the nuts at the rear of the oil pan (if equipped).

13 Remove all the oil pan bolts, then lower the pan from the engine. The pan will probably stick to the engine, so strike the pan with a rubber mallet until it breaks the gasket seal.

❋❋ CAUTION:

Before using force on the oil pan, be sure all the bolts have been removed.

Carefully slide the oil pan down and out, to the rear.

INSTALLATION

▶ **Refer to illustrations 14.14 and 14.17**

14 Drill out the rivets securing the oil pan gasket to the oil pan and remove the old gasket (see illustration). Wash out the oil pan with solvent.

15 Thoroughly clean the mounting surfaces of the oil pan and engine block of old gasket material and sealer. Wipe the gasket surfaces clean with a rag soaked in lacquer thinner, acetone or brake system cleaner.

16 Apply a 3/16-inch wide, one inch long bead of RTV sealant to the corners of the block where the front cover and the rear cover meet the engine block. Then attach the new gasket to the pan, install the pan and tighten the bolts finger-tight. Be sure the oil gallery passages in the pan and the gasket are aligned properly.

➡**Note: Oil pan gasket rivets do not need to be installed on assembly.**

17 The alignment of the rear face of the aluminum pan to the rear of the block is important. Measure the distance between the rear face of

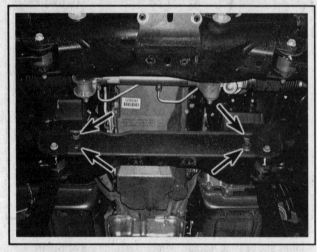

14.4 Remove the bolts (arrows) and the lower control arm support crossmember

14.8 The oil level sensor is located on the passenger side of the oil pan

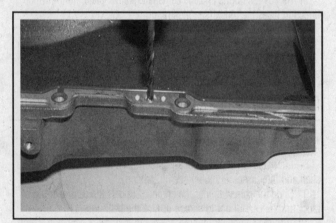

14.14 The manufacturer uses rivets to hold the gasket to the oil pan during assembly - carefully drill them out (it isn't necessary to rivet the new gasket to the oil pan)

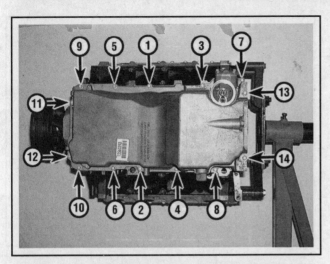

14.17 Oil pan TIGHTENING sequence - all V8 engines

the pan and the front face of the transmission bellhousing with feeler gauges. Clearance should ideally be flush, but a gap of up to 0.010-inch is allowable. If the clearance is OK, tighten the pan bolts/studs in sequence to the torque listed in this Chapter's Specifications (see illustration). If the clearance is not acceptable, install the two lower oil pan-to-bellhousing bolts and tighten them finger tight. This should draw the oil pan flush with the bellhousing.

> ✳ **CAUTION:**
>
> **The rear of the oil pan should never protrude rearward of the bellhousing plane of the block.**

18 The remainder of installation is the reverse of removal. Tighten the bolts to the torque listed in this Chapter's Specifications.
19 Add the proper type and quantity of oil (see Chapter 1), start the engine and check for leaks before placing the vehicle back in service.

15 Oil pump - removal, inspection and installation

REMOVAL

▶ **Refer to illustrations 15.2a, 15.2b and 15.3**

1 Refer to the Section 12, Steps 1 through 6 and remove the timing chain cover.
2 Remove the oil pump pick-up tube mounting nuts and bolts and lower the pick-up tube and screen assembly from the vehicle (see illustrations).
3 Remove the oil pump retaining bolts and slide the pump off the end of the crankshaft (see illustration).

INSPECTION

▶ **Refer to illustration 15.4**

4 Remove the oil pump cover and withdraw the rotors from the pump body (see illustration). Clean the components with solvent, dry

15.2a Oil pick-up tube-to-main stud retaining nuts (arrows)

15.2b Remove the bolt (arrow) securing the oil pick-up tube to the oil pump and remove it from the engine

15.3 Oil pump mounting bolts (arrows)

15.4 Oil pump cover-to-oil pump housing mounting bolts (arrows)

15.8 Always install a new O-ring on the oil pump pick up tube

them thoroughly and inspect for any obvious damage. Also check the bolt holes for damaged threads and the splined surfaces on the crankshaft sprocket for any apparent damage. If any of the components are scored, scratched or worn, replace the entire oil pump assembly. There are no serviceable parts currently available.

INSTALLATION

▶ **Refer to illustration 15.8**

5   Prime the pump by pouring clean motor oil into the pick-up tube hole, while turning the pump by hand.

6   Position the oil pump over the end of the crankshaft and align the teeth on the crankshaft sprocket with the teeth on the oil pump drive gear. Making sure the pump is fully seated against the block.

7   Install the oil pump mounting bolts and tighten them to the torque listed in this Chapter's Specifications.

8   Install a new O-ring on the oil pump pick-up tube, then fasten it to the oil pump and the engine block main studs (see illustration).

❊❊ **CAUTION:**

Be absolutely certain that the pick-up tube-to-oil pump bolts are properly tightened so that no air can be sucked into the oiling system at this connection.

9   Install and align the timing chain cover, then install the oil pan. Refer to Sections 12 and 14 for the installation procedures.

10   The remainder of installation is the reverse of removal.

11   Add oil and coolant as necessary. Run the engine and check for oil and coolant leaks. Also check the oil pressure as described in Chapter 2C.

16 Driveplate - removal and installation

The flywheel/driveplate replacement for V8 engines is identical to the flywheel/driveplate replacement procedure for the V6 engines. Refer to Chapter 2 Part A for the procedure and use the torque figures in this Chapter's Specifications.

➡**Note: If the spacer between the driveplate and the crankshaft must be removed and it's stuck, insert bolts (M11 bolts, 1.5 mm long) into the two threaded holes in the spacer. Tightening the bolts will force the spacer off the crankshaft.**

17 Rear main oil seal - replacement

▶ **Refer to illustrations 17.3 and 17.4**

➡**Note: If you're installing a new rear seal during a complete engine overhaul, refer to the procedure in Chapter 2C.**

1   Remove the transmission (see Chapter 7).

2   Remove the flywheel/driveplate (see Section 16).

3   Pry the oil seal from the rear cover with a screwdriver (see illustration). Be careful not to nick or scratch the crankshaft or the seal bore. Be sure to note how far it's recessed into the housing bore before removal so the new seal can be installed to the same depth. Thoroughly clean the seal bore in the block with a shop towel. Remove all traces of oil and dirt.

4   Lubricate the outside diameter of the seal and install the seal over the end of the crankshaft. Make sure the lip of the seal points toward the engine. Preferably, a seal installation tool (available at most auto parts store) should be used to press the new seal back into place. If the proper seal installation tool is unavailable, use a large socket, section of pipe or a blunt tool and carefully drive the new seal squarely into the seal bore and flush with the rear cover (see illustration).

5   Install the flywheel/driveplate (see Section 16).

6   Install the transmission (see Chapter 7).

17.3 Carefully pry the old seal out with a screwdriver at the notches provided in the rear cover

17.4 The rear oil seal can be pressed into place with a seal installation tool, a section of pipe or a blunt object shown here - in any case be sure the seal is installed squarely into the seal bore and flush with the rear cover

18 Engine mounts - check and replacement

1 Engine mounts seldom require attention, but broken or deteriorated mounts should be replaced immediately or the added strain placed on the driveline components may cause damage.

CHECK

2 During the check, the engine must be raised slightly to remove the weight from the mounts.

3 Raise the vehicle and support it securely on jackstands, then position the jack under the engine oil pan. Place a large block of wood between the jack head and the oil pan, then carefully raise the engine just enough to take the weight off the mounts. Do not use the jack to support the entire weight of the engine.

4 Check the mounts to see if the rubber is cracked, hardened or separated from the metal plates. Sometimes the rubber will split right down the center. Rubber preservative or WD-40 can be applied to the mounts to slow deterioration.

5 Check for relative movement between the mount plates and the engine or frame (use a large screwdriver or prybar to attempt to move the mounts). If movement is noted, check the tightness of the mount

fasteners first before condemning the mounts. Usually when engine mounts are broken, they are very obvious as the engine will easily move away from the mount when pried or under load.

REPLACEMENT

▶ **Refer to illustrations 18.7a, 18.7b and 18.9**

6 Disconnect the cable from the negative terminal of the battery, then raise the vehicle and support it securely on jackstands.

✳✳ CAUTION:

On models equipped with the Theftlock audio system, be sure the lockout feature is turned off before performing any procedure which requires disconnecting the battery (see the front of this manual).

7 Working in the engine compartment remove the engine mount-to-frame bracket bolts. There are three bolts on each side securing the mounts to the frame bracket (see illustrations).

18.7a Driver's side engine mount-to-frame bracket bolts (arrows)

18.7b Passenger side engine mount-to-frame bracket bolts (arrows)

8   Attach an engine hoist to the top of the engine for lifting; do not use a jack under the oil pan to support the entire weight of the engine or the oil pump pick-up could be damaged.

➡**Note: If a hoist is not available, casting lugs on each side of the engine block can be used to support the entire weight of the engine while the engine mounts are being replaced.**

9   Raise the engine slightly until the engine mount can be unbolted from the block. Unbolt the mount from the engine block and remove it from the vehicle (see illustration).

10 Installation is the reverse of removal. Use non-hardening thread-locking compound on the mount bolts and be sure to tighten them to the torque listed in this Chapter's Specifications.

18.9 Engine mount-to-engine block mounting bolts (arrows)

Specifications

General

Displacement	
5.3L	325 cubic inches
6.0L	364 cubic inches
Bore and stroke	
5.3L	3.779 x 3.622 inches
6.0L	4.001 x 3.622 inches
Cylinder numbers (front-to-rear)	
Left (driver's) side	1-3-5-7
Right side	2-4-6-8
Firing order	1-8-7-2-6-5-4-3
Cylinder compression pressure	
Minimum	100 psi
Maximum variation between cylinders	25 percent from the highest reading

Camshaft

Journal diameters	2.164 to 2.166 inches
Camshaft endplay	0.001 to 0.012 inch
5.3L engines	
Intake	0.268 inch
Exhaust	0.274 inch
6.0L engines	
Intake	0.274 inch
Exhaust	0.281 inch

Torque specifications   Ft-lbs (unless otherwise indicated)

➡ **Note: One foot-pound (ft-lb) of torque is equivalent to 12 inch-pounds (in-lbs) of torque. Torque values below approximately 15 ft-lbs are expressed in inch-pounds, since most foot-pound torque wrenches are not accurate at these smaller values.**

Camshaft sensor bolt (5.3L engines)	18
Camshaft sprocket bolt(s)	
2002 through 2004	26
2005 and 2006	18
2007 and later	
Step 1	55
Step 2	Tighten an additional 50-degrees
Camshaft retainer bolts	18
Crankshaft balancer bolt**	
Step one (use old bolt)	240
Step two (use new bolt)	37
Step three (use new bolt)	Tighten an additional 140 degrees
Cylinder head bolts (in sequence)** (see illustration 9.19)	
2002 and 2003 models	
Step 1	
All 11 mm bolts	22
Step 2	
All 11 mm bolts	Tighten an additional 90-degrees
Step 3	
11 mm bolts (1 through 8)	Tighten an additional 90-degrees
11 mm bolts (9 and 10)	Tighten an additional 50-degrees
Step 4	
All 8 mm bolts (11 through 15)	22
2004 models	
Design I (equipped with two different length 11 mm bolts; 3.94 inches and 6.1 inches)	
Step 1	
All 11 mm bolts	22
Step 2	
All 11 mm bolts	Tighten an additional 90-degrees
Step 3	
11 mm bolts (1 through 8)	Tighten an additional 90-degrees
11 mm bolts (9 and 10)	Tighten an additional 50-degrees
Step 4	
All 8 mm bolts	
(11 through 15)	22
Design II (equipped with one length 11 mm bolt; 3.94 inches)	
Step 1	
All 11 mm bolts	
(1 through 10)	22
Step 2	
All 11 mm bolts	
(1 through 10)	Tighten an additional 90-degrees
Step 3	
All 11 mm bolts	
(1 through 10)	Tighten an additional 70-degrees
Step 4	
All 8 mm bolts	
(11 through 15)	22

24017-1-B HAYNES

Cylinder numbering - V8 engines

Torque specifications (continued) Ft-lbs (unless otherwise indicated)

➡ **Note: One foot-pound (ft-lb) of torque is equivalent to 12 inch-pounds (in-lbs) of torque. Torque values below approximately 15 ft-lbs are expressed in inch-pounds, since most foot-pound torque wrenches are not accurate at these smaller values.**

2005 and later models	
Step 1	
All 11 mm bolts (1 through 10)	22
Step 2	
All 11 mm bolts (1 through 10)	Tighten an additional 90-degrees
Step 3	
All 11 mm bolts (1 through 10)	Tighten an additional 70-degrees
Step 4	
All 8 mm bolts (11 through 15)	22
Engine mount retaining bolts	37
Exhaust manifold bolts	
Step one	132 in-lbs
Step two	18
Exhaust manifold heat shield bolt	80 in-lbs
Exhaust pipe flange nuts	20 to 25
Driveplate bolts	
Step one	15
Step two	37
Step three	74
Intake manifold bolts	
Step one	44 in-lbs
Step two	89 in-lbs
Oil pan baffle bolts	106 in-lbs
Oil pan drain plug	18
Oil pan rear access plugs	80 in-lbs
Oil pan bolts	
Step 1 (to engine and front cover)	18
Step 2 (to rear cover)	106 in-lbs
Step 3 (bellhousing, converter cover and	
transmission bolts)	37
Oil pump cover bolts	106 in-lbs
Oil pump mounting bolts	18
Rocker arm bolts	22
Front timing chain cover bolts	18
Timing chain tensioner (2005 and later)	18
Valley cover bolts (2002 through 2004)	18
Valve lifter oil manifold (2005 and later)	18
Valve cover bolts	106 in-lbs
Vapor vent pipe bolts	106 in-lbs

*Note: Refer to Part C for additional specifications.

** Use new bolt(s)

2C

GENERAL ENGINE OVERHAUL PROCEDURES

Reference to other Chapters

SERVICE ENGINE SOON light on - See Chapter 6

1 General information - engine overhaul

▶ **Refer to illustrations 1.2, 1.3, 1.4, 1.5, 1.6 and 1.7**

Included in this portion of Chapter 2 are general information and diagnostic testing procedures for determining the overall mechanical condition of your engine.

The information ranges from advice concerning preparation for an overhaul and the purchase of replacement parts and/or components to detailed, step-by-step procedures covering removal and installation.

The following Sections have been written to help you determine whether your engine needs to be overhauled and how to remove and install it once you've determined it needs to be rebuilt. For information concerning in-vehicle engine repair, see Chapter 2A or 2B.

The Specifications included in this Part are general in nature and include only those necessary for testing the oil pressure and checking the engine compression. Refer to Chapter 2A or 2B for additional engine Specifications.

It's not always easy to determine when, or if, an engine should be completely overhauled, because a number of factors must be considered.

High mileage is not necessarily an indication that an overhaul is needed, while low mileage doesn't preclude the need for an overhaul. Frequency of servicing is probably the most important consideration. An engine that's had regular and frequent oil and filter changes, as well

as other required maintenance, will most likely give many thousands of miles of reliable service. Conversely, a neglected engine may require an overhaul very early in its service life.

Excessive oil consumption is an indication that piston rings, valve seals and/or valve guides are in need of attention. Make sure that oil leaks aren't responsible before deciding that the rings and/or guides are bad. Perform a cylinder compression check to determine the extent of the work required (see Section 3). Also check the vacuum readings under various conditions (see Section 3).

Check the oil pressure with a gauge installed in place of the oil pressure sending unit and compare it to this Chapter's Specifications (see Section 2). If it's extremely low, the bearings and/or oil pump are probably worn out.

Loss of power, rough running, knocking or metallic engine noises, excessive valve train noise and high fuel consumption rates may also point to the need for an overhaul, especially if they're all present at the same time. If a complete tune-up doesn't remedy the situation, major mechanical work is the only solution.

An engine overhaul involves restoring the internal parts to the specifications of a new engine. During an overhaul, the piston rings are replaced and the cylinder walls are reconditioned (rebored and/or honed) (see illustrations 1.2 and 1.3). If a rebore is done by an

1.2 An engine block being bored. A engine rebuilder will use special machinery to recondition the cylinder bores

1.3 If the cylinders are bored, the machine shop will normally hone the engine on a machine like this

automotive machine shop, new oversize pistons will also be installed. The main bearings, connecting rod bearings and camshaft bearings are generally replaced with new ones and, if necessary, the crankshaft may be reground to restore the journals (see illustration 1.4). Generally, the valves are serviced as well, since they're usually in less-than-perfect condition at this point. While the engine is being overhauled, other components, such as the starter and alternator, can be rebuilt as well. The end result should be a like new engine that will give many trouble free miles.

➡ **Note: Critical cooling system components such as the hoses, drivebelt, thermostat and water pump should be replaced with new parts when an engine is overhauled. The radiator should be checked carefully to ensure that it isn't clogged or leaking (see Chapter 3). If you purchase a rebuilt engine or short block, some rebuilders will not warranty their engines unless the radiator has been professionally flushed. Also, we don't recommend overhauling the oil pump - always install a new one when an engine is rebuilt.**

Overhauling the internal components on today's engines is a difficult and time-consuming task which requires a significant amount of specialty tools and is best left to a professional engine rebuilder (see illustrations 1.5, 1.6 and 1.7). A competent engine rebuilder will handle the inspection of your old parts and offer advice concerning the reconditioning or replacement of the original engine, never purchase parts or have machine work done on other components until the block has been thoroughly inspected by a professional machine shop. As a general rule, time is the primary cost of an overhaul, especially since

1.4 A crankshaft having a main bearing journal ground

the vehicle may be tied up for a minimum of two weeks or more. Be aware that some engine builders only have the capability to rebuild the engine you bring them while other rebuilders have a large inventory of rebuilt exchange engines in stock. Also be aware that many machine shops could take as much as two weeks time to completely rebuild your engine depending on shop workload. Sometimes it makes more sense to simply exchange your engine for another engine that's already rebuilt to save time.

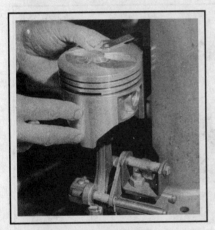

1.5 A machinist checks for a bent connecting rod, using specialized equipment

1.6 A bore gauge being used to check the main bearing bore

1.7 Uneven piston wear like this indicates a bent connecting rod

2   Oil pressure check

▶ **Refer to illustrations 2.2a and 2.2b**

1   Low engine oil pressure can be a sign of an engine in need of rebuilding. A "low oil pressure" indicator (often called an "idiot light") is not a test of the oiling system. Such indicators only come on when the oil pressure is dangerously low. Even an original pressure gauge in the instrument panel is only a relative indication, although it's much better for driver information than a warning light. An accurate test can only be performed with a mechanical (not electrical) oil pressure gauge. When used in conjunction with an accurate tachometer, the engine's oil pressure performance can be compared to the manufacturer's Specifications for that year and model.

2   Locate the oil pressure indicator sending unit (see illustration).

3   Remove the oil pressure sending unit and install a fitting which will allow you to directly connect your hand-held, mechanical oil pres-

2.2a The oil pressure sending unit is located above the oil filter - six-cylinder engine . . .

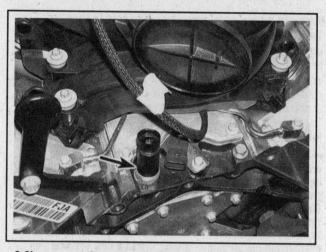

2.2b . . . or at the rear of the cylinder block - V8 engine

sure gauge. Use Teflon tape or sealant on the threads of the adapter and the fitting on the end of your gauge's hose.

4   Connect an accurate tachometer to the engine, according to the tachometer manufacturer's instructions.

5   Check the oil pressure with the engine running (full operating temperature) at the specified engine speed, and compare it to this Chapter's Specifications. If it's extremely low, the bearings and/or oil pump are probably worn out.

3   Compression check and vacuum gauge diagnostic checks

COMPRESSION CHECK

▶ **Refer to illustration 3.5**

1   A compression check will tell you what mechanical condition the upper end (pistons, rings, valves, head gaskets) of your engine is in. Specifically, it can tell you if the compression is down due to leakage caused by worn piston rings, defective valves and seats or a blown head gasket.

➡**Note: The engine must be at normal operating temperature and the battery must be fully charged for this check.**

2   Begin by cleaning the area around the spark plugs before you remove them (compressed air should be used, if available). The idea is to prevent dirt from getting into the cylinders as the compression check is being done.

3   Remove all of the ignition coils and spark plugs from the engine (see Chapters 5 and 1, respectively).

4   The fuel pump circuit should be disabled by removing the fuel pump relay (it's located in the underhood fuse/relay box - see Chapter 4, illustration 3.3).

5   Install the compression gauge in the number one spark plug hole (see illustration).

6   Crank the engine over at least four compression strokes and watch the gauge. The compression should build up quickly in a healthy engine. Low compression on the first stroke, followed by gradually increasing pressure on successive strokes, indicates worn piston rings. A low compression reading on the first stroke, which doesn't build up during successive strokes, indicates leaking valves or a blown head gasket (a cracked head could also be the cause). Deposits on the undersides of the valve heads can also cause low compression. Record the highest gauge reading obtained.

7   Repeat the procedure for the remaining cylinders and compare the results to this Chapter's Specifications.

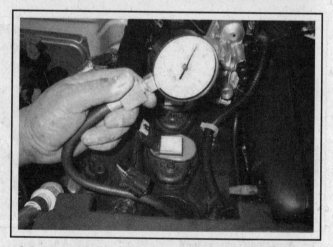

3.5 A compression gauge with a threaded fitting for the spark plug hole is preferred over the type that requires hand pressure to maintain the seal

8   Add some engine oil (about three squirts from a plunger-type oil can) to each cylinder, through the spark plug hole, and repeat the test.

9   If the compression increases after the oil is added, the piston rings are definitely worn. If the compression doesn't increase significantly, the leakage is occurring at the valves or head gasket. Leakage past the valves may be caused by burned valve seats and/or faces or warped, cracked or bent valves.

10   If two adjacent cylinders have equally-low compression, there's a strong possibility that the head gasket between them is blown. The appearance of coolant in the combustion chambers or the crankcase would verify this condition.

11   If one cylinder is slightly lower than the others, and the engine has a rough idle, a worn lobe on the camshaft could be the cause.

12 If the compression is unusually high, the combustion chambers are probably coated with carbon deposits. If that's the case, the cylinder head(s) should be removed and decarbonized.

13 If compression is way down or varies greatly between cylinders, it would be a good idea to have a leak-down test performed by an automotive repair shop. This test will pinpoint exactly where the leakage is occurring and how severe it is.

VACUUM GAUGE DIAGNOSTIC CHECKS

▶ **Refer to illustrations 3.17 and 3.19**

14 A vacuum gauge provides valuable information about the condition of internal engine components. You can check for worn rings or cylinder walls, leaking head or intake manifold gaskets, restricted exhaust, stuck or burned valves, weak valve springs, improper ignition or valve timing and ignition problems.

15 Unfortunately, vacuum gauge readings are easy to misinterpret, so they should be used in conjunction with other tests to confirm the diagnosis.

16 Both the absolute readings and the rate of needle movement are important for accurate interpretation. Most gauges measure vacuum in inches of mercury (in-Hg). The following references to vacuum assume the diagnosis is being performed at sea level. As elevation increases (or atmospheric pressure decreases), the reading will decrease. For every 1,000 foot increase in elevation above approximately 2000 feet, the gauge readings will decrease about one inch of mercury.

17 Connect the vacuum gauge directly to intake manifold vacuum,

3.17 An inexpensive vacuum gauge can tell you a lot about an engine's condition

not to ported (throttle body) vacuum (see illustration). Be sure no hoses are left disconnected during the test or false readings will result.

18 Before you begin the test, allow the engine to warm up completely. Block the wheels and set the parking brake. With the transmission in Park or Neutral, start the engine and allow it to run at normal idle speed.

❋❋ WARNING:

Always keep your hands, loose clothing and tools clear of the fan and do not stand in front of the vehicle or in line with the fan when the engine is running.

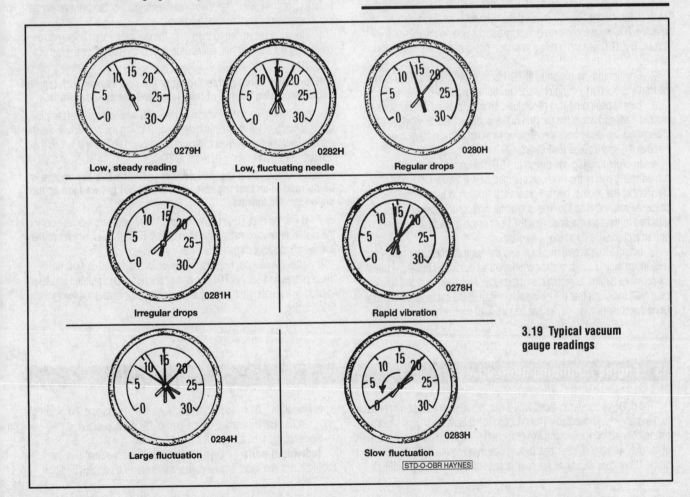

Low, steady reading   Low, fluctuating needle   Regular drops

Irregular drops   Rapid vibration

Large fluctuation   Slow fluctuation

3.19 Typical vacuum gauge readings

STD-O-OBR HAYNES

19 Read the vacuum gauge; an average, healthy engine should normally produce about 17 to 22 inches of vacuum with a fairly steady needle (see illustration). Refer to the following vacuum gauge readings and what they indicate about the engine's condition:

a) A low steady reading usually indicates a leaking gasket between the intake manifold and throttle body, a leaky vacuum hose, late ignition timing or incorrect camshaft timing. Check ignition timing with a timing light and eliminate all other possible causes, utilizing the tests provided in this Chapter before you remove the timing chain cover to check the timing marks.

b) If the reading is three to eight inches below normal and it fluctuates at that low reading, suspect an intake manifold gasket leak at an intake port or a faulty fuel injector.

c) If the needle has regular drops of about two-to-four inches at a steady rate, the valves are probably leaking. Perform a compression check or leak-down test to confirm this.

d) An irregular drop or down-flick of the needle can be caused by a sticking valve or an ignition misfire. Perform a compression check or leak-down test and read the spark plugs.

e) A rapid vibration of about four inches Hg vibration at idle combined with exhaust smoke indicates worn valve guides. Perform a leak-down test to confirm this. If the rapid vibration occurs with an increase in engine speed, check for a leaking intake manifold gasket or head gasket, weak valve springs, burned valves or ignition misfire.

f) A slight fluctuation, say one inch up and down, may mean ignition problems. Check all the usual tune-up items and, if necessary, run the engine on an ignition analyzer.

g) If there is a large fluctuation, perform a compression or leak-down test to look for a weak or dead cylinder or a blown head gasket.

h) If the needle moves slowly through a wide range, check for a clogged PCV system, incorrect idle fuel mixture, carburetor/throttle body or intake manifold gasket leaks.

i) Check for a slow return after revving the engine by quickly snapping the throttle open until the engine reaches about 2,500 rpm and let it shut. Normally the reading should drop to near zero, rise above normal idle reading (about 5 in.-Hg over) and then return to the previous idle reading. If the vacuum returns slowly and doesn't peak when the throttle is snapped shut, the rings may be worn. If there is a long delay, look for a restricted exhaust system (often the muffler or catalytic converter). An easy way to check this is to temporarily disconnect the exhaust ahead of the suspected part and re-test.

4 Top Dead Center (TDC) for number one piston - locating

1 Top Dead Center (TDC) is the highest point in the cylinder that each piston reaches as it travels up the cylinder bore. Each piston reaches TDC on the compression stroke and again on the exhaust stroke, but TDC generally refers to piston position on the compression stroke.

2 Positioning the piston(s) at TDC is an essential part of certain procedures such as timing chain/sprocket removal.

3 Before beginning this procedure, be sure to place the transmission in Park and apply the parking brake or block the rear wheels. Also, disconnect the cable from the negative terminal of the battery, then remove the spark plugs (see Chapter 1).

4 In order to bring any piston to TDC, the crankshaft must be turned using one of the methods outlined below. When looking at the front of the engine, normal crankshaft rotation is clockwise. The preferred method is to turn the crankshaft with a socket and ratchet attached to the bolt threaded into the front of the crankshaft. Turn the bolt in a clockwise direction.

5 Install a compression gauge into the number one spark plug hole (see illustration 3.5). Rotate the crankshaft as described in Step 4 until air pressure begins to register on the gauge. Air pressure at the spark plug hole indicates that the cylinder has started the compression stroke. Once the compression stroke has begun, TDC for the number one cyl-inder is obtained when the piston reaches the top of the cylinder on the compression stroke. Remove the gauge.

6 To bring the piston to the top of the cylinder, insert a long screwdriver into the number one spark plug hole until it touches the top of the piston.

→ **Note: Make sure to wrap the tip of the screwdriver with tape to avoid scratching the top of the piston and the cylinder walls.**

Use the screwdriver (as a feeler gauge) to tell where the top of the piston is located in the cylinder while slowly rotating the crankshaft. As the piston rises the screwdriver will be pushed out. The point at which the screwdriver stops moving outward is TDC.

→ **Note: Always hold the screwdriver upright while the engine is being rotated so that the screwdriver will not get wedged as the piston travels upward.**

7 If you go past TDC, rotate the crankshaft counterclockwise until the piston is approximately one inch below TDC, then slowly rotate the crankshaft clockwise again until TDC is reached.

8 After the number one piston has been positioned at TDC on the compression stroke, TDC for any of the remaining pistons can be located by repeating the procedure described above and following the firing order.

5 Engine rebuilding alternatives

The do-it-yourselfer is faced with a number of options when performing an engine overhaul. The decision to replace the engine block, piston/connecting rod assemblies and crankshaft depends on a number of factors, with the number one consideration being the condition of the block. Other considerations are cost, access to machine shop facilities, parts availability, time required to complete the project and the extent of prior mechanical experience on the part of the do-it-yourselfer.

Some of the rebuilding alternatives include:

Individual parts - If the inspection procedures reveal that the engine block and most engine components are in reusable condition, purchasing individual parts may be the most economical alternative. The block, crankshaft and piston/connecting rod assemblies should all be inspected carefully. Even if the block shows little wear, the cylinder bores should be surface-honed.

Crankshaft kit - This rebuild package consists of a reground crankshaft and a matched set of pistons and connecting rods. The pistons will already be installed on the connecting rods. Piston rings and the necessary bearings will be included in the kit. These kits are commonly available for standard cylinder bores, as well as for engine blocks which have been bored to a regular oversize.

Short block - A short block consists of an engine block with renewed crankshaft and piston/connecting rod assemblies already installed. All new bearings are incorporated and all clearances will be correct. The existing cylinder head(s), camshaft, valve train components and external parts can be bolted to the short block with little or no machine shop work necessary.

Long block - A long block consists of a short block plus an oil pump, oil pan, cylinder heads, valve covers, camshaft and valve train components, timing sprockets, timing chain and timing cover. All components are installed with new bearings, seals and gaskets incorporated throughout. The installation of manifolds and external parts is all that is necessary.

Used engine assembly - While overhaul provides the best assurance of a like-new engine, used engines available from wrecking yards and importers are often a very simple and economical solution. Many used engines come with warranties, but always give any engine a thorough diagnostic check-out before purchase. Check compression, vacuum and also for signs of oil leakage. If possible, have the seller run the engine, ether in the vehicle or on a test stand so you can be sure it runs smoothly with no knocking or other noises.

Give careful thought to which alternative is best for you and discuss the situation with local automotive machine shops, auto parts dealers or parts store countermen before ordering or purchasing replacement parts.

6   Engine removal - methods and precautions

♦ **Refer to illustrations 6.1, 6.2, 6.3 and 6.4**

If you've decided that an engine must be removed for overhaul or major repair work, several preliminary steps should be taken.

Locating a suitable place to work is extremely important. Adequate work space, along with storage space for the vehicle, will be needed. If a shop or garage isn't available, at the very least a flat, level, clean work surface made of concrete or asphalt is required.

Cleaning the engine compartment and engine before beginning the removal procedure will help keep your tools and your hands clean (see illustrations 6.1 and 6.2).

An engine hoist or A-frame will also be necessary. Make sure the equipment is rated in excess of the combined weight of the engine and accessories. Safety is of primary importance, considering the potential hazards involved in lifting the engine out of the vehicle.

If the engine is being removed by a novice, a helper should be available. Advice and aid from someone more experienced would also be helpful. There are many instances when one person cannot simultaneously perform all of the operations required when lifting the engine out of the vehicle.

6.1 After tightly wrapping water-vulnerable components, use a spray cleaner on everything, with particular concentration on the greasiest areas, usually around the valve cover and lower edges of the block. If one section dries out, apply more cleaner

6.2 Depending on how dirty the engine is, let the cleaner soak in according to the directions and then hose off the grime and cleaner. Get the rinse water down into every area you can get at; then dry important components with a hair dryer or paper towels

6.3 Get an engine hoist that's strong enough to easily lift your engine in and out of the engine compartment; an adapter, like the one shown here, can be used to change the angle of the engine as it's being removed or installed

Plan the operation ahead of time. Arrange for or obtain all of the tools and equipment you'll need prior to beginning the job (see illustrations 6.3 and 6.4). Some of the equipment necessary to perform engine removal and installation safely and with relative ease are (in addition to an engine hoist) a heavy duty floor jack, complete sets of wrenches and

6.4 Get an engine stand sturdy enough to firmly support the engine while you're working on it. Stay away from three-wheeled models: they have a tendency to tip over more easily, so get a four-wheeled unit

sockets as described in the front of this manual, wooden blocks and plenty of rags and cleaning solvent for mopping up spilled oil, coolant and gasoline. If the hoist must be rented, make sure that you arrange for it in advance and perform all of the operations possible without it beforehand. This will save you money and time.

Plan for the vehicle to be out of use for quite a while. A machine shop will be required to perform some of the work which the do-it-yourselfer can't accomplish without special equipment. These shops often have a busy schedule, so it would be a good idea to consult them before removing the engine in order to accurately estimate the amount of time required to rebuild or repair components that may need work.

Always be extremely careful when removing and installing the engine. Serious injury can result from careless actions. Plan ahead, take your time and a job of this nature, although major, can be accomplished successfully.

7 Engine - removal and installation

✳✳ WARNING 1:

The air conditioning system is under high pressure. Do not loosen any hose fittings or remove any components until after the system has been discharged. Air conditioning refrigerant must be properly discharged into an EPA-approved recov-ery/recycling unit at a dealer service department or an automotive air conditioning repair facility. Always wear eye protection when disconnecting air conditioning system fittings.

✳✳ WARNING 2:

Gasoline is extremely flammable, so take extra precautions when you work on any part of the fuel system. Don't smoke or allow open flames or bare light bulbs near the work area, and don't work in a garage where a gas-type appliance (such as a water heater or a clothes dryer) is present. Since gasoline is carcinogenic, wear fuel-resistant gloves when there's a possibil-

ity of being exposed to fuel, and, if you spill any fuel on your skin, rinse it off immediately with soap and water. Mop up any spills immediately and do not store fuel-soaked rags where they could ignite. The fuel system is under constant pressure, so, if any fuel lines are to be disconnected, the fuel pressure in the system must be relieved first (see Chapter 4 for more information). When you perform any kind of work on the fuel system, wear safety glasses and have a Class B type fire extinguisher on hand.

✳✳ WARNING 3:

The models covered by this manual are equipped with airbags. Always disable the airbag system before working in the vicinity of any airbag system components to avoid the possibility of accidental deployment of the airbag(s), which could cause personal injury (see Chapter 12).

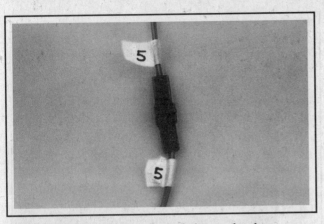

7.5a Label both ends of each wire before unplugging the connector

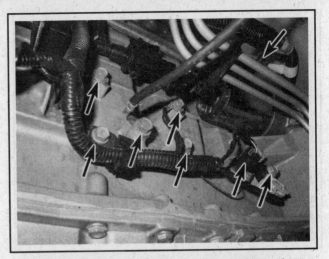

7.5b There are a number of ground straps, brackets and electrical connectors attached to the engine block (left rear of the engine shown)

REMOVAL

▶ **Refer to illustrations 7.5a, 7.5b, 7.6, 7.19, 7.26a, 7.26b, 7.27 and 7.29**

1 Have the air conditioning system discharged by an air conditioning specialist.

2 Refer to Chapter 4 and relieve the fuel system pressure, then disconnect the cable from the negative terminal of the battery.

3 Cover the fenders and cowl and remove the hood (see Chapter 11). Special pads are available to protect the fenders, but an old bedspread or blanket will also work.

4 Remove the air cleaner assembly (see Chapter 4). Drain the cooling system (see Chapter 1).

5 Label the vacuum lines, emissions system hoses, wiring connectors, ground straps and fuel lines, to ensure correct reinstallation, then detach them (see illustrations). If there's any possibility of confusion, make a sketch of the engine compartment and clearly label the lines, hoses and wires. Detach the wiring harness brackets from the engine and set the engine wiring harness aside.

➡**Note: Some components will be easier to disconnect once the vehicle is raised and supported by jackstands.**

6 Label and detach all coolant hoses from the engine. The heater hoses, however, should be detached at the heater core tubes on the firewall (see illustration).

7 Remove the MAP sensor (see Chapter 4).

8 Remove the throttle body (see Chapter 4).

9 Disconnect the air conditioning lines at the condenser and accumulator (see the **Warning** at the beginning of this Section).

10 Remove the radiator (see Chapter 3).

11 Remove the drivebelt (see Chapter 1) and the power steering pump mounting bolts (see Chapter 10), then wire the pump aside.

12 Disconnect the transmission fill tube bracket nut from the engine.

13 On 4WD models, disconnect the front axle electrical connector.

14 Remove the bolt holding the transmission line bracket to the right side of the engine, then move the lines away from the engine.

15 Remove the PCM (see Chapter 6).

16 Raise the vehicle and support it securely on jackstands. Working under the vehicle, drain the engine oil (see Chapter 1).

17 If the vehicle is a 4WD model, remove the engine skid plate, front driveaxles and front driveshaft (see Chapter 8). Also remove the fuel tank skid plate, if equipped.

18 Disconnect the exhaust pipe from the manifold (see Chapter 2A or 2B), then slide the pipe to the rear.

19 Remove the torque converter access cover, mark the torque converter to the driveplate, then remove the torque converter bolts (see illustration).

7.6 Be sure to disconnect the heater hoses at the heater core

7.19 Mark the torque converter to the driveplate, then remove the bolts

7.26a Connect the engine lifting chain to the lifting hook at the front of the engine (six-cylinder engine) . . .

7.27 On V8 engines, attach a sling or chain to the cylinder heads

7.29 Pull the engine forward as far as possible to clear the transmission and the cowl, then lift the engine high enough to clear the body (six-cylinder engine shown, V8 engine similar)

7.26b . . . and to the cylinder head at the right rear of the engine (use a bolt that is longer than the original exhaust manifold bolt and a washer, if necessary). As an alternative, you can wrap the chain around one of the manifold runners and bolt it together

20 Support the transmission with a floor jack.

➡**Note: Place a block of wood between the jack and transmission oil pan.**

21 Remove the transmission crossmember (see Chapter 7A).

22 There are four bolts at the top of the bellhousing. To access these bolts for removal, lower the transmission just enough to reach the bolts. Unclip the engine harness from two of the bolts and remove all four bolts, then raise the transmission and reinstall the crossmember using only two bolts.

23 Remove the remaining bellhousing bolts.

24 Remove the lower engine mount nuts.

25 Lower the vehicle and remove the upper engine mount nuts. Reposition the jack under the vehicle to support the transmission.

26 On six cylinder engines, attach an engine sling or a length of chain to the lifting bracket at the front of the engine (see illustration). Attach the other end of the chain to the right rear of the engine; remove an exhaust manifold bolt and, using a longer bolt of the same size and thread pitch as the original, attach the chain to the cylinder head (see illustration).

✳✳ **CAUTION:**

DO NOT lift the engine by the intake manifold. Lift the engine by the block or the cylinder head only.

27 On V8 engines, attach an engine sling to the exhaust manifold bolts or directly to the cylinder heads (see illustration).

28 Roll the hoist into position and connect the sling to it. Take up the slack in the sling or chain, but don't lift the engine.

✳✳ **WARNING:**

DO NOT place any part of your body under the engine when it's supported only by a hoist or other lifting device.

29 Raise the engine slightly. Carefully work it forward to separate it from the transmission. Be sure the torque converter stays in the trans-

mission (clamp a pair of vise-grips to the housing to keep the converter from sliding out). Slowly raise the engine out of the engine compartment (see illustration). Check carefully to make sure nothing is hanging up.

30 Remove the driveplate and mount the engine on an engine stand.

INSTALLATION

31 Install the driveplate on the engine (see Chapter 2A or 2B). Check the engine and transmission mounts. If they're worn or damaged, replace them.

32 Carefully lower the engine into the engine compartment - make sure the engine mounts line up.

33 Guide the torque converter into the crankshaft following the procedure outlined in Chapter 7A.

34 Install the transmission-to-engine bolts and tighten them securely.

❋❋ CAUTION:

DO NOT use the bolts to force the transmission and engine together!

35 Reinstall the remaining components in the reverse order of removal.

36 Add coolant, oil, power steering and transmission fluid as needed (see Chapter 1).

37 Run the engine and check for leaks and proper operation of all accessories, then install the hood and test drive the vehicle.

38 Have the air conditioning system recharged and leak tested by the shop that discharged it.

8 Engine overhaul - disassembly sequence

1 It's much easier to disassemble and work on the engine if it's mounted on a portable engine stand. A stand can often be rented quite cheaply from an equipment rental yard. Before the engine is mounted on a stand, the flywheel/driveplate should be removed from the engine.

2 If a stand isn't available, it's possible to disassemble the engine with it blocked up on the floor. Be extra careful not to tip or drop the engine when working without a stand.

3 If you're going to obtain a rebuilt engine, all external components must come off first to be transferred to the replacement engine, just as they will if you're doing a complete engine overhaul yourself. These include:

Alternator and brackets
Emissions control components
Thermostat and housing cover
Water pump
Fuel injection components
Intake/exhaust manifold
Oil filter
Engine mounts
Driveplate

➡Note: **When removing the external components from the engine, pay close attention to details that may be helpful or important during installation. Note the installed position of gaskets, seals, spacers, pins, brackets, washers, bolts and other small items.**

4 If you're obtaining a short block, which consists of the engine block, crankshaft, pistons and connecting rods all assembled, then the cylinder head, oil pan and oil pump will have to be removed as well. See *Engine rebuilding alternatives* for additional information regarding the different possibilities to be considered.

5 If you're planning a complete overhaul, the engine must be disassembled and the internal components removed in the following order:

Valve cover
Intake and exhaust manifolds
Timing chain cover
Oil pan
Oil pump
Timing chain and sprockets
Camshaft
Cylinder head
Piston/connecting rod assemblies
Rear main oil seal retainer
Crankshaft and main bearings

6 Before beginning the disassembly and overhaul procedures, make sure the following items are available. Also, refer to Section 11 for a list of tools and materials needed for engine reassembly.

Common hand tools
Small cardboard boxes or plastic bags for storing parts
Gasket scraper
Ridge reamer
Crankshaft balancer puller
Micrometers
Telescoping gauges
Dial-indicator set
Valve spring compressor
Cylinder surfacing hone
Piston ring groove-cleaning tool
Electric drill motor
Tap and die set
Wire brushes
Oil gallery brushes
Cleaning solvent

ENGINE BEARING ANALYSIS

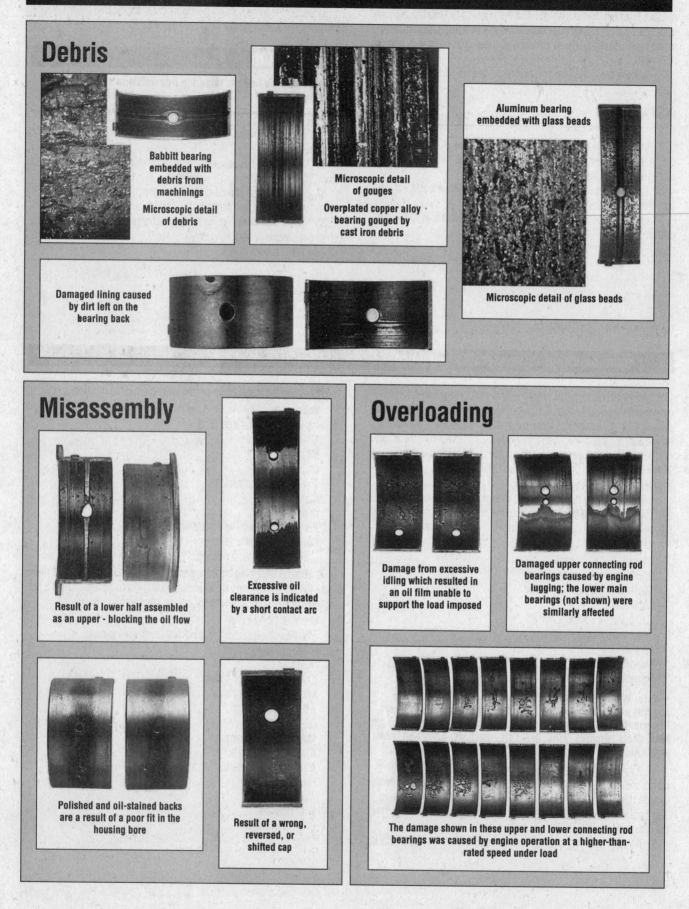

Debris

Babbitt bearing embedded with debris from machinings

Microscopic detail of debris

Microscopic detail of gouges

Overplated copper alloy bearing gouged by cast iron debris

Aluminum bearing embedded with glass beads

Microscopic detail of glass beads

Damaged lining caused by dirt left on the bearing back

Misassembly

Result of a lower half assembled as an upper - blocking the oil flow

Excessive oil clearance is indicated by a short contact arc

Polished and oil-stained backs are a result of a poor fit in the housing bore

Result of a wrong, reversed, or shifted cap

Overloading

Damage from excessive idling which resulted in an oil film unable to support the load imposed

Damaged upper connecting rod bearings caused by engine lugging; the lower main bearings (not shown) were similarly affected

The damage shown in these upper and lower connecting rod bearings was caused by engine operation at a higher-than-rated speed under load

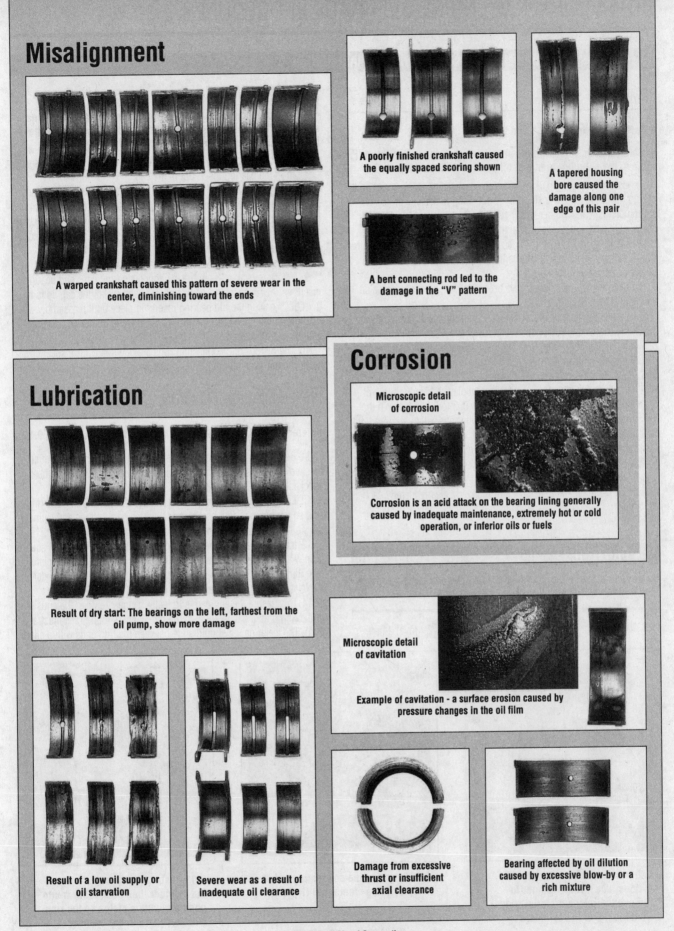

Misalignment

A warped crankshaft caused this pattern of severe wear in the center, diminishing toward the ends

A poorly finished crankshaft caused the equally spaced scoring shown

A tapered housing bore caused the damage along one edge of this pair

A bent connecting rod led to the damage in the "V" pattern

Lubrication

Result of dry start: The bearings on the left, farthest from the oil pump, show more damage

Result of a low oil supply or oil starvation

Severe wear as a result of inadequate oil clearance

Corrosion

Microscopic detail of corrosion

Corrosion is an acid attack on the bearing lining generally caused by inadequate maintenance, extremely hot or cold operation, or inferior oils or fuels

Microscopic detail of cavitation

Example of cavitation - a surface erosion caused by pressure changes in the oil film

Damage from excessive thrust or insufficient axial clearance

Bearing affected by oil dilution caused by excessive blow-by or a rich mixture

9 Pistons and connecting rods - removal and installation

REMOVAL

▶ **Refer to illustrations 9.1 and 9.3**

➡**Note: Prior to removing the piston/connecting rod assemblies, remove the cylinder head and oil pan (see Chapter 2A or 2B).**

1   Use your fingernail to feel if a ridge has formed at the upper limit of ring travel (about 1/4-inch down from the top of each cylinder). If carbon deposits or cylinder wear have produced ridges, they must be completely removed with a special tool (see illustration). Follow the manufacturer's instructions provided with the tool. Failure to remove the ridges before attempting to remove the piston/connecting rod assemblies may result in piston breakage.

2   After the cylinder ridges have been removed, turn the engine so the crankshaft is facing up.

3   Before the main bearing caps and connecting rods are removed, check the connecting rod endplay with feeler gauges. Slide them between the first connecting rod and the crankshaft throw until the play is removed (see illustration). Repeat this procedure for each connecting rod. The endplay is equal to the thickness of the feeler gauge(s). Check with an automotive machine shop for the endplay service limit (a typical endplay limit should measure between 0.005 to 0.015 inch). If the play exceeds the service limit, new connecting rods will be required. If new rods (or a new crankshaft) are installed, the endplay may fall under the minimum allowable. If it does, the rods will have to be machined to restore it. If necessary, consult an automotive machine shop for advice.

4   Check the connecting rods and caps for identification marks. If they aren't plainly marked, use paint or marker to clearly identify each rod and cap (1, 2, 3, etc., depending on the cylinder they're associated with).

✳✳ CAUTION:

Do not use a punch and hammer to mark the connecting rods or they may be damaged.

5   Loosen each of the connecting rod cap bolts 1/2-turn at a time until they can be removed by hand.

➡**Note: New connecting rod cap bolts must be used when reassembling the engine, but save the old bolts for use when checking the connecting rod bearing oil clearance.**

6   Remove the number one connecting rod cap and bearing insert. Don't drop the bearing insert out of the cap.

7   Remove the bearing insert and push the connecting rod/piston assembly out through the top of the engine. Use a wooden or plastic hammer handle to push on the upper bearing surface in the connecting rod. If resistance is felt, double-check to make sure that all of the ridge was removed from the cylinder.

8   Repeat the procedure for the remaining cylinders.

9   After removal, reassemble the connecting rod caps and bearing inserts in their respective connecting rods and install the cap bolts finger tight. Leaving the old bearing inserts in place until reassembly will help prevent the connecting rod bearing surfaces from being accidentally nicked or gouged.

10 The pistons and connecting rods are now ready for inspection and overhaul at an automotive machine shop.

PISTON RING INSTALLATION

▶ **Refer to illustrations 9.13, 9.14, 9.15, 9.19a, 9.19b and 9.22**

11 Before installing the new piston rings, the ring end gaps must be checked. It's assumed that the piston ring side clearance has been checked and verified correct.

12 Lay out the piston/connecting rod assemblies and the new ring sets so the ring sets will be matched with the same piston and cylinder during the end gap measurement and engine assembly.

13 Insert the top (number one) ring into the first cylinder and square it up with the cylinder walls by pushing it in with the top of the piston (see illustration). The ring should be near the bottom of the cylinder, at the lower limit of ring travel.

14 To measure the end gap, slip feeler gauges between the ends of the ring until a gauge equal to the gap width is found (see illustration). The feeler gauge should slide between the ring ends with a slight

9.1 Before you try to remove the pistons, use a ridge reamer to remove the raised material (ridge) from the top of the cylinders

9.3 Checking the connecting rod endplay (side clearance) (typical)

9.13 Install the piston ring into the cylinder then push it down into position using a piston so the ring will be square in the cylinder

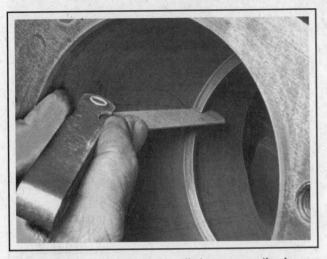

9.14 With the ring square in the cylinder, measure the ring end gap with a feeler gauge

9.15 If the ring end gap is too small, clamp a file in a vise as shown and file the piston ring ends - be sure to remove all raised material

amount of drag. A typical ring gap should fall between 0.010 and 0.020 inch for compression rings and up to 0.030 inch for the oil ring steel rails. If the gap is larger or smaller than specified, double-check to make sure you have the correct rings before proceeding.

15 If the gap is too small, it must be enlarged or the ring ends may come in contact with each other during engine operation, which can cause serious damage to the engine. If necessary, increase the end gaps by filing the ring ends very carefully with a fine file. Mount the file in a vise equipped with soft jaws, slip the ring over the file with the ends contacting the file face and slowly move the ring to remove material from the ends. When performing this operation, file only by pushing the ring from the outside end of the file towards the vise (see illustration).

16 Excess end gap isn't critical unless it's greater than 0.040 inch. Again, double-check to make sure you have the correct ring type.

17 Repeat the procedure for each ring that will be installed in the first cylinder and for each ring in the remaining cylinders. Remember to keep rings, pistons and cylinders matched up.

18 Once the ring end gaps have been checked/corrected, the rings can be installed on the pistons.

19 The oil control ring (lowest one on the piston) is usually installed first. It's composed of three separate components. Slip the spacer/

expander into the groove (see illustration). If an anti-rotation tang is used, make sure it's inserted into the drilled hole in the ring groove. Next, install the upper side rail in the same manner (see illustration). Don't use a piston ring installation tool on the oil ring side rails, as they may be damaged. Instead, place one end of the side rail into the groove between the spacer/expander and the ring land, hold it firmly in place and slide a finger around the piston while pushing the rail into the groove. Finally, install the lower side rail.

20 After the three oil ring components have been installed, check to make sure that both the upper and lower side rails can be rotated smoothly inside the ring grooves.

21 The number two (middle) ring is installed next. It's usually stamped with a mark which must face up, toward the top of the piston. Do not mix up the top and middle rings, as they have different cross-sections.

➡**Note: Always follow the instructions printed on the ring package or box - different manufacturers may require different approaches.**

22 Use a piston ring installation tool and make sure the identification mark is facing the top of the piston, then slip the ring into the middle

9.19a Installing the spacer/expander in the oil ring groove

9.19b DO NOT use a piston ring installation tool when installing the oil control ring side rails

9.22 Use a piston ring installation tool to install the number 2 and the number 1 (top) rings - be sure the directional mark on the piston ring(s) is facing toward the top of the piston

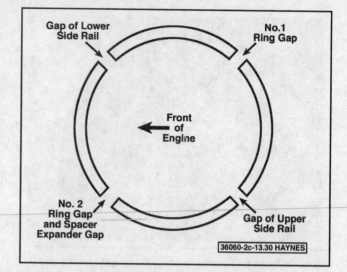

9.30 Position the piston ring end gaps as shown

groove on the piston (see illustration). Don't expand the ring any more than necessary to slide it over the piston.

23 Install the number one (top) ring in the same manner. Make sure the mark is facing up. Be careful not to confuse the number one and number two rings.

24 Repeat the procedure for the remaining pistons and rings.

INSTALLATION

25 Before installing the piston/connecting rod assemblies, the cylinder walls must be perfectly clean, the top edge of each cylinder bore must be chamfered, and the crankshaft must be in place.

26 Remove the cap from the end of the number one connecting rod (refer to the marks made during removal). Remove the original bearing inserts and wipe the bearing surfaces of the connecting rod and cap with a clean, lint-free cloth. They must be kept spotlessly clean.

Connecting rod bearing oil clearance check
▶ **Refer to illustrations 9.30, 9.35, 9.37 and 9.41**

27 Clean the back side of the new upper bearing insert, then lay it in place in the connecting rod.

28 Make sure the tab on the bearing fits into the recess in the rod. Don't hammer the bearing insert into place and be very careful not to nick or gouge the bearing face. Don't lubricate the bearing at this time.

29 Clean the back side of the other bearing insert and install it in the rod cap. Again, make sure the tab on the bearing fits into the recess in the cap, and don't apply any lubricant. It's critically important that the mating surfaces of the bearing and connecting rod are perfectly clean and oil free when they're assembled.

30 Position the piston ring gaps at 90-degree intervals around the piston as shown (see illustration).

31 Lubricate the piston and rings with clean engine oil and attach a piston ring compressor to the piston. Leave the skirt protruding about 1/4-inch to guide the piston into the cylinder. The rings must be compressed until they're flush with the piston.

32 Rotate the crankshaft until the number one connecting rod journal is at BDC (bottom dead center) and apply a liberal coat of engine oil to the cylinder walls.

33 With the mark, or notch, on top of the piston and the flat side of

the connecting rod on V8 engines facing the front (timing chain end) of the engine, gently insert the piston/connecting rod assembly into the number one cylinder bore and rest the bottom edge of the ring compressor on the engine block.

34 Tap the top edge of the ring compressor to make sure it's contacting the block around its entire circumference.

35 Gently tap on the top of the piston with the end of a wooden or plastic hammer handle (see illustration) while guiding the end of the connecting rod into place on the crankshaft journal. The piston rings may try to pop out of the ring compressor just before entering the cylinder bore, so keep some downward pressure on the ring compressor. Work slowly, and if any resistance is felt as the piston enters the cylinder, stop immediately. Find out what's hanging up and fix it before proceeding. Do not, for any reason, force the piston into the cylinder - you might break a ring and/or the piston.

36 Once the piston/connecting rod assembly is installed, the connecting rod bearing oil clearance must be checked before the rod cap is permanently installed.

37 Cut a piece of the appropriate size Plastigage slightly shorter than the width of the connecting rod bearing and lay it in place on the

9.35 Use a plastic or wooden hammer handle to push the piston into the cylinder

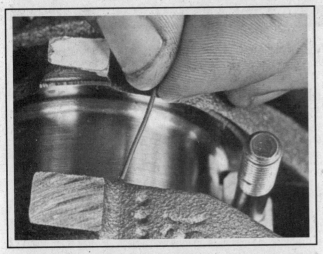

9.37 Place Plastigage on each connecting rod bearing journal parallel to the crankshaft centerline

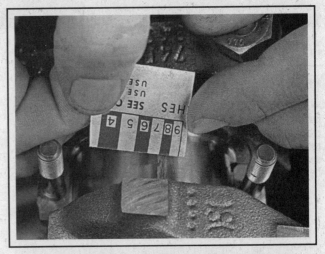

9.41 Use the scale on the Plastigage package to determine the bearing oil clearance - be sure to measure the widest part of the Plastigage and use the correct scale; it comes with both standard and metric scales

number one connecting rod journal, parallel with the journal axis (see illustration).

38 Clean the connecting rod cap bearing face and install the rod cap. Make sure the mating mark on the cap is on the same side as the mark on the connecting rod (see illustration 9.4).

39 Install the old rod bolts, at this time, and tighten them to the torque listed in this Chapter's Specifications.

➡**Note: Use a thin-wall socket to avoid erroneous torque readings that can result if the socket is wedged between the rod cap and the bolt. If the socket tends to wedge itself between the fastener and the cap, lift up on it slightly until it no longer contacts the cap. DO NOT rotate the crankshaft at any time during this operation.**

40 Remove the fasteners and detach the rod cap, being very careful not to disturb the Plastigage. Discard the cap bolts at this time as they cannot be reused.

➡**Note: You MUST use new connecting rod bolts.**

41 Compare the width of the crushed Plastigage to the scale printed on the Plastigage envelope to obtain the oil clearance (see illustration). The connecting rod oil clearance is usually about 0.001 to 0.002 inch. Consult an automotive machine shop for the clearance specified for the rod bearings on your engine.

42 If the clearance is not as specified, the bearing inserts may be the wrong size (which means different ones will be required). Before deciding that different inserts are needed, make sure that no dirt or oil was between the bearing inserts and the connecting rod or cap when the clearance was measured. Also, recheck the journal diameter. If the Plastigage was wider at one end than the other, the journal may be tapered. If the clearance still exceeds the limit specified, the bearing will have to be replaced with an undersize bearing.

✲✲ CAUTION:

When installing a new crankshaft always use a standard size bearing.

Final installation

43 Carefully scrape all traces of the Plastigage material off the rod

journal and/or bearing face. Be very careful not to scratch the bearing – use your fingernail or the edge of a plastic card.

44 Make sure the bearing faces are perfectly clean, then apply a uniform layer of clean moly-base grease or engine assembly lube to both of them. You'll have to push the piston into the cylinder to expose the face of the bearing insert in the connecting rod.

✲✲ CAUTION:

Install new connecting rod cap bolts. Do NOT reuse old bolts - they have stretched and cannot be reused.

45 Slide the connecting rod back into place on the journal, install the rod cap, install the nuts or new bolts and tighten them to the torque listed in this Chapter's Specifications. Again, work up to the torque in three steps.

46 Repeat the entire procedure for the remaining pistons/connecting rods.

47 The important points to remember are:

a) *Keep the back sides of the bearing inserts and the insides of the connecting rods and caps perfectly clean when assembling them.*
b) *Make sure you have the correct piston/rod assembly for each cylinder.*
c) *The mark on the piston must face the front of the engine.*
d) *Lubricate the cylinder walls liberally with clean oil.*
e) *Lubricate the bearing faces when installing the rod caps after the oil clearance has been checked.*

48 After all the piston/connecting rod assemblies have been correctly installed, rotate the crankshaft a number of times by hand to check for any obvious binding.

49 As a final step, check the connecting rod endplay again.

50 Compare the measured endplay to the tolerance listed in this Chapter's Specifications to make sure it's acceptable. If it was correct before disassembly and the original crankshaft and rods were reinstalled, it should still be correct. If new rods or a new crankshaft were installed, the endplay may be inadequate. If so, the rods will have to be removed and taken to an automotive machine shop for resizing.

10 Crankshaft - removal and installation

REMOVAL

▶ **Refer to illustrations 10.1 and 10.3**

➡**Note: The crankshaft can be removed only after the engine has been removed from the vehicle. It's assumed that the driveplate, crankshaft pulley, oil pan, timing chain and piston/connecting rod assemblies have already been removed. The rear main oil seal retainer must be unbolted and separated from the block before proceeding with crankshaft removal.**

1   Before the crankshaft is removed, measure the endplay. Mount a dial indicator with the indicator in line with the crankshaft and just touching the end of the crankshaft as shown (see illustration).

2   Pry the crankshaft all the way to the rear and zero the dial indicator. Next, pry the crankshaft to the front as far as possible and check the reading on the dial indicator. The distance traveled is the endplay. A typical crankshaft endplay will fall between 0.003 to 0.010 inch. If it is greater than that, check the crankshaft thrust surfaces for wear after it's removed. If no wear is evident, new main bearings should correct the endplay.

3   If a dial indicator isn't available, feeler gauges can be used. Gently pry the crankshaft all the way to the front of the engine. Slip feeler gauges between the crankshaft and the front face of the thrust bearing or washer to determine the clearance (see illustration).

4   Loosen the main bearing cap bolts 1/4-turn at a time each, until they can be removed by hand.

5   Remove the main bearing cap stiffener, then check for marks on the main bearing caps indicating their positions. If there aren't any, number them from front to rear and also add an arrow to each one pointing to the front of the engine. Now remove the main bearing caps. Try not to drop the bearing inserts if they come out with the caps.

6   Carefully lift the crankshaft out of the engine. It's a good idea to have an assistant available, since the crankshaft is quite heavy and awkward to handle. With the bearing inserts in place inside the engine block and main bearing caps, reinstall the main bearing caps and stiffener onto the engine block and tighten the bolts finger tight. Make sure

you install the main bearing caps in their proper positions and facing the proper direction.

INSTALLATION

7   Crankshaft installation is the first step in engine reassembly. It's assumed at this point that the engine block and crankshaft have been cleaned, inspected and repaired or reconditioned.

8   Position the engine block with the bottom facing up.

9   Remove the mounting bolts and lift off the stiffener and main bearing caps.

10 If they're still in place, remove the original bearing inserts from the block and from the main bearing caps. Wipe the bearing surfaces of the block and main bearing caps with a clean, lint-free cloth. They must be kept spotlessly clean. This is critical for determining the correct bearing oil clearance.

MAIN BEARING OIL CLEARANCE CHECK

▶ **Refer to illustrations 10.17, 10.19 and 10.21**

11 Without mixing them up, clean the back sides of the new upper main bearing inserts (with grooves and oil holes) and lay one in each main bearing saddle in the block. Each upper bearing has an oil groove and oil hole in it.

✳✳ CAUTION:

The oil holes in the block must line up with the oil holes in the upper bearing inserts.

The thrust washer or thrust bearing insert must be installed in the number 5 crankshaft journal (counting from the front). Clean the back sides of the lower main bearing inserts and lay them in their corresponding locations in the main bearing caps. Make sure the tab on the bearing insert fits into the recess in the block or main bearing cap assembly. The upper bearings with the oil holes are installed into the engine block while the lower bearings without the oil holes are installed in the main bearing caps.

10.1 Checking crankshaft endplay with a dial indicator (typical)

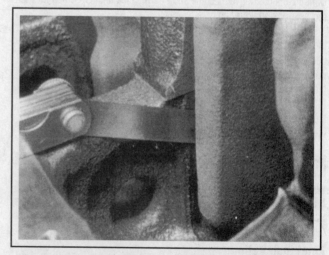

10.3 Checking crankshaft endplay with feeler gauges at the thrust bearing journal

10.17 Place the Plastigage onto the crankshaft bearing journal as shown

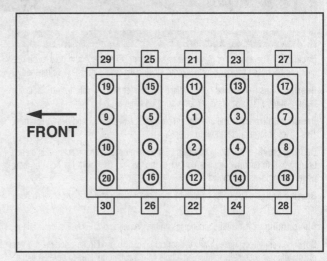

10.19 Main bearing cap bolt tightening sequence - V8 engines

❊❊ **CAUTION:**

Do not hammer the bearing insert into place and don't nick or gouge the bearing faces. DO NOT apply any lubrication at this time.

---

12 Clean the faces of the bearing inserts in the block and the crank-shaft main bearing journals with a clean, lint-free cloth.

13 Check or clean the oil holes in the crankshaft, as any dirt here can go only one way - straight through the new bearings.

14 Once you're certain the crankshaft is clean, carefully lay it in position in the cylinder block.

15 Before the crankshaft can be permanently installed, the main bearing oil clearance must be checked.

16 Cut several strips of the appropriate size of Plastigage. They must be slightly shorter than the width of the main bearing journal.

17 Place one piece on each crankshaft main bearing journal, parallel with the journal axis as shown (see illustration).

18 Clean the faces of the bearing inserts in the main bearing cap assembly. Hold the bearing inserts in place and install the assembly onto the crankshaft and cylinder block. DO NOT disturb the Plastigage. Make sure you install the main bearing caps with the arrows facing the front of the engine, then install the stiffener.

19 Apply a light coat of oil to the bolt threads and the under sides of the bolt heads, then install all bolts finger tight (see the old bolts for this step). On six-cylinder engines, tighten the main bearing cap bolts, starting in the center and working towards the ends, in two steps, to the torque listed in this Chapter's Specifications. Don't rotate the crankshaft at any time during this operation! On V8 engines, the main bearing tightening procedure is done in five steps. First, tighten the inner bolts (bolts 1 through 10) in two steps to the torque and angle of rotation listed in this Chapter's Specifications, then tighten the outer bolts (bolts 11 through 20) in two steps to the torque and angle of rotation listed in this Chapter's Specifications (see illustration). The fifth step is tightening the side bolts, but DO NOT use the new side bolts during the oil clearance check as this will damage the O-ring on the new side bolts.

20 Remove the bolts in the reverse order of the tightening sequence, remove the stiffener and carefully lift the main bearing caps straight up and off the block. Do not disturb the Plastigage or rotate the crankshaft.

21 Compare the width of the crushed Plastigage on each journal to the scale printed on the Plastigage envelope to determine the main

bearing oil clearance (see illustration). Check with an automotive machine shop for the oil clearance for your engine.

22 If the clearance is not as specified, the bearing inserts may be the wrong size (which means different ones will be required). Before deciding if different inserts are needed, make sure that no dirt or oil was between the bearing inserts and the cap assembly or block when the clearance was measured. If the Plastigage was wider at one end than the other, the crankshaft journal may be tapered. If the clearance still exceeds the limit specified, the bearing insert(s) will have to be replaced with an undersize bearing insert(s).

❊❊ **CAUTION:**

When installing a new crankshaft always install a standard bearing insert set.

---

23 Carefully scrape all traces of the Plastigage material off the main bearing journals and/or the bearing insert faces. Be sure to remove all residue from the oil holes. Use your fingernail or the edge of a plastic card - don't nick or scratch the bearing faces.

10.21 Use the scale on the Plastigage package to determine the bearing oil clearance - be sure to measure the widest part of the Plastigage and use the correct scale; it comes with both standard and metric scales

GLOSSARY

B

Backlash - The amount of play between two parts. Usually refers to how much one gear can be moved back and forth without moving the gear with which it's meshed.

Bearing Caps - The caps held in place by nuts or bolts which, in turn, hold the bearing surface. This space is for lubricating oil to enter.

Bearing clearance - The amount of space left between shaft and bearing surface. This space is for lubricating oil to enter.

Bearing crush - The additional height which is purposely manufactured into each bearing half to ensure complete contact of the bearing back with the housing bore when the engine is assembled.

Bearing knock - The noise created by movement of a part in a loose or worn bearing.

Blueprinting - Dismantling an engine and reassembling it to EXACT specifications.

Bore - An engine cylinder, or any cylindrical hole; also used to describe the process of enlarging or accurately refinishing a hole with a cutting tool, as to bore an engine cylinder. The bore size is the diameter of the hole.

Boring - Renewing the cylinders by cutting them out to a specified size. A boring bar is used to make the cut.

Bottom end - A term which refers collectively to the engine block, crankshaft, main bearings and the big ends of the connecting rods.

Break-in - The period of operation between installation of new or rebuilt parts and time in which parts are worn to the correct fit. Driving at reduced and varying speed for a specified mileage to permit parts to wear to the correct fit.

Bushing - A one-piece sleeve placed in a bore to serve as a bearing surface for shaft, piston pin, etc. Usually replaceable.

C

Camshaft - The shaft in the engine, on which a series of lobes are located for operating the valve mechanisms. The camshaft is driven by gears or sprockets and a timing chain. Usually referred to simply as the cam.

Carbon - Hard, or soft, black deposits found in combustion chamber, on plugs, under rings, on and under valve heads.

Cast iron - An alloy of iron and more than two percent carbon, used for engine blocks and heads because it's relatively inexpensive and easy to mold into complex shapes.

Chamfer - To bevel across (or a bevel on) the sharp edge of an object.

Chase - To repair damaged threads with a tap or die.

Combustion chamber - The space between the piston and the cylinder head, with the piston at top dead center, in which air-fuel mixture is burned.

Compression ratio - The relationship between cylinder volume (clearance volume) when the piston is at top dead center and cylinder volume when the piston is at bottom dead center.

Connecting rod - The rod that connects the crank on the crankshaft with the piston. Sometimes called a con rod.

Connecting rod cap - The part of the connecting rod assembly that attaches the rod to the crankpin.

Core plug - Soft metal plug used to plug the casting holes for the coolant passages in the block.

Crankcase - The lower part of the engine in which the crankshaft rotates; includes the lower section of the cylinder block and the oil pan.

Crank kit - A reground or reconditioned crankshaft and new main and connecting rod bearings.

Crankpin - The part of a crankshaft to which a connecting rod is attached.

Crankshaft - The main rotating member, or shaft, running the length of the crankcase, with offset throws to which the connecting rods are attached; changes the reciprocating motion of the pistons into rotating motion.

Cylinder sleeve - A replaceable sleeve, or liner, pressed into the cylinder block to form the cylinder bore.

D

Deburring - Removing the burrs (rough edges or areas) from a bearing.

Deglazer - A tool, rotated by an electric motor, used to remove glaze from cylinder walls so a new set of rings will seat.

E

Endplay - The amount of lengthwise movement between two parts. As applied to a crankshaft, the distance that the crankshaft can move forward and back in the cylinder block.

F

Face - A machinist's term that refers to removing metal from the end of a shaft or the face of a larger part, such as a flywheel.

Fatigue - A breakdown of material through a large number of loading and unloading cycles. The first signs are cracks followed shortly by breaks.

Feeler gauge - A thin strip of hardened steel, ground to an exact thickness, used to check clearances between parts.

Free height - The unloaded length or height of a spring.

Freeplay - The looseness in a linkage, or an assembly of parts, between the initial application of force and actual movement. Usually perceived as slop or slight delay.

Freeze plug - See Core plug.

G

Gallery - A large passage in the block that forms a reservoir for engine oil pressure.

Glaze - The very smooth, glassy finish that develops on cylinder walls while an engine is in service.

H

Heli-Coil - A rethreading device used when threads are worn or damaged. The device is installed in a retapped hole to reduce the thread size to the original size.

I

Installed height - The spring's measured length or height, as installed on the cylinder head. Installed height is measured from the spring seat to the underside of the spring retainer.

J

Journal - The surface of a rotating shaft which turns in a bearing.

K

Keeper - The split lock that holds the valve spring retainer in position on the valve stem.

Key - A small piece of metal inserted into matching grooves machined into two parts fitted together - such as a gear pressed onto a shaft - which prevents slippage between the two parts.

Knock - The heavy metallic engine sound, produced in the combustion chamber as a result of abnormal combustion - usually detonation. Knock is usually caused by a loose or worn bearing. Also referred to as detonation, pinging and spark knock. Connecting rod or main bearing knocks are created by too much oil clearance or insufficient lubrication.

L

Lands - The portions of metal between the piston ring grooves.

Lapping the valves - Grinding a valve face and its seat together with lapping compound.

Lash - The amount of free motion in a gear train, between gears, or in a mechanical assembly, that occurs before movement can begin. Usually refers to the lash in a valve train.

Lifter - The part that rides against the cam to transfer motion to the rest of the valve train.

M

Machining - The process of using a machine to remove metal from a metal part.

Main bearings - The plain, or babbitt, bearings that support the crankshaft.

Main bearing caps - The cast iron caps, bolted to the bottom of the block, that support the main bearings.

O

O.D. - Outside diameter.

Oil gallery - A pipe or drilled passageway in the engine used to carry engine oil from one area to another.

Oil ring - The lower ring, or rings, of a piston; designed to prevent excessive amounts of oil from working up the cylinder walls and into the combustion chamber. Also called an oil-control ring.

Oil seal - A seal which keeps oil from leaking out of a compartment. Usually refers to a dynamic seal around a rotating shaft or other moving part.

O-ring - A type of sealing ring made of a special rubberlike material; in use, the O-ring is compressed into a groove to provide the sealing action.

Overhaul - To completely disassemble a unit, clean and inspect all parts, reassemble it with the original or new parts and make all adjustments necessary for proper operation.

P

Pilot bearing - A small bearing installed in the center of the flywheel (or the rear end of the crankshaft) to support the front end of the input shaft of the transmission.

Pip mark - A little dot or indentation which indicates the top side of a compression ring.

Piston - The cylindrical part, attached to the connecting rod, that moves up and down in the cylinder as the crankshaft rotates. When the fuel charge is fired, the piston transfers the force of the explosion to the connecting rod, then to the crankshaft.

Piston pin (or wrist pin) - The cylindrical and usually hollow steel pin that passes through the piston. The piston pin fastens the piston to the upper end of the connecting rod.

Piston ring - The split ring fitted to the groove in a piston. The ring contacts the sides of the ring groove and also rubs against the cylinder wall, thus sealing space between piston and wall. There are two types of rings: Compression rings seal the compression pressure in the combustion chamber; oil rings scrape excessive oil off the cylinder wall.

Piston ring groove - The slots or grooves cut in piston heads to hold piston rings in position.

Piston skirt - The portion of the piston below the rings and the piston pin hole.

Plastigage - A thin strip of plastic thread, available in different sizes, used for measuring clearances. For example, a strip of plastigage is laid across a bearing journal and mashed as parts are assembled. Then parts are disassembled and the width of the strip is measured to determine clearance between journal and bearing. Commonly used to measure crankshaft main-bearing and connecting rod bearing clearances.

Press-fit - A tight fit between two parts that requires pressure to force the parts together. Also referred to as drive, or force, fit.

Prussian blue - A blue pigment; in solution, useful in determining the area of contact between two surfaces. Prussian blue is commonly used to determine the width and location of the contact area between the valve face and the valve seat.

R

Race (bearing) - The inner or outer ring that provides a contact surface for balls or rollers in bearing.

Ream - To size, enlarge or smooth a hole by using a round cutting tool with fluted edges.

Ring job - The process of reconditioning the cylinders and installing new rings.

Runout - Wobble. The amount a shaft rotates out-of-true.

S

Saddle - The upper main bearing seat.

Scored - Scratched or grooved, as a cylinder wall may be scored by abrasive particles moved up and down by the piston rings.

Scuffing - A type of wear in which there's a transfer of material between parts moving against each other; shows up as pits or grooves in the mating surfaces.

Seat - The surface upon which another part rests or seats. For example, the valve seat is the matched surface upon which the valve face rests. Also used to refer to wearing into a good fit; for example, piston rings seat after a few miles of driving.

Short block - An engine block complete with crankshaft and piston and, usually, camshaft assemblies.

Static balance - The balance of an object while it's stationary.

Step - The wear on the lower portion of a ring land caused by excessive side and back-clearance. The height of the step indicates the ring's extra side clearance and the length of the step projecting from the back wall of the groove represents the ring's back clearance.

Stroke - The distance the piston moves when traveling from top dead center to bottom dead center, or from bottom dead center to top dead center.

Stud - A metal rod with threads on both ends.

T

Tang - A lip on the end of a plain bearing used to align the bearing during assembly.

Tap - To cut threads in a hole. Also refers to the fluted tool used to cut threads.

Taper - A gradual reduction in the width of a shaft or hole; in an engine cylinder, taper usually takes the form of uneven wear, more pronounced at the top than at the bottom.

Throws - The offset portions of the crankshaft to which the connecting rods are affixed.

Thrust bearing - The main bearing that has thrust faces to prevent excessive endplay, or forward and backward movement of the crankshaft.

Thrust washer - A bronze or hardened steel washer placed between two moving parts. The washer prevents longitudinal movement and provides a bearing surface for thrust surfaces of parts.

Tolerance - The amount of variation permitted from an exact size of measurement. Actual amount from smallest acceptable dimension to largest acceptable dimension.

U

Umbrella - An oil deflector placed near the valve tip to throw oil from the valve stem area.

Undercut - A machined groove below the normal surface.

Undersize bearings - Smaller diameter bearings used with re-ground crankshaft journals.

V

Valve grinding - Refacing a valve in a valve-refacing machine.

Valve train - The valve-operating mechanism of an engine; includes all components from the camshaft to the valve.

Vibration damper - A cylindrical weight attached to the front of the crankshaft to minimize torsional vibration (the twist-untwist actions of the crankshaft caused by the cylinder firing impulses). Also called a harmonic balancer.

W

Water jacket - The spaces around the cylinders, between the inner and outer shells of the cylinder block or head, through which coolant circulates.

Web - A supporting structure across a cavity.

Woodruff key - A key with a radiused backside (viewed from the side).

FINAL INSTALLATION

24 Carefully lift the crankshaft out of the cylinder block.

25 Clean the bearing insert faces in the cylinder block, then apply a thin, uniform layer of moly-base grease or engine assembly lube to each of the bearing surfaces. Be sure to coat the thrust faces as well as the journal face of the thrust bearing.

26 Make sure the crankshaft journals are clean, then lay the crankshaft back in place in the cylinder block.

27 Clean the bearing insert faces and then apply the same lubricant to them. Clean the engine block and the main bearing caps thoroughly. The surfaces must be free of oil residue.

28 Install the main bearing caps and stiffener.

29 Prior to installation, apply clean engine oil to the threads of the new main bearing cap bolts, wiping off any excess, then install all bolts finger-tight.

30 Tighten the main bearing cap bolts, working from the center out, to the torque listed in this Chapter's Specifications.

31 Recheck crankshaft endplay with a feeler gauge or a dial indicator. The endplay should be correct if the crankshaft thrust faces aren't worn or damaged and if new bearings have been installed.

32 Rotate the crankshaft a number of times by hand to check for any obvious binding. It should rotate with a running torque of 50 in-lbs or less (without the pistons and connecting rods installed). If the running torque is too high, correct the problem at this time.

33 Install the new rear main oil seal (see Chapter 2A or 2B).

11 Engine overhaul - reassembly sequence

1 Before beginning engine reassembly, make sure you have all the necessary new parts, gaskets and seals as well as the following items on hand:

Common hand tools
A 1/2-inch drive torque wrench
New engine oil
Gasket sealant
Thread locking compound

2 If you obtained a short block it will be necessary to install the cylinder head, the oil pump and pick-up tube, the water pump, the timing chain and front cover, the oil pan, and the valve cover (see Chapter 2A or 2B). In order to save time and avoid problems, the external components must be installed in the following general order:

Thermostat and housing cover
Water pump
Intake and exhaust manifolds
Fuel injection components
Emission control components
Spark plug wires and spark plugs
Ignition coils
Oil filter
Engine mounts and mount brackets
Driveplate

12 Initial start-up and break-in after overhaul

✳✳ WARNING:

Have a fire extinguisher handy when starting the engine for the first time.

1 Once the engine has been installed in the vehicle, double-check the engine oil and coolant levels.

2 With the spark plugs out of the engine and the ignition and fuel systems disabled (see Section 3), crank the engine until oil pressure registers on the gauge or the light goes out.

3 Install the spark plugs, coils and restore the ignition and fuel system functions.

4 Start the engine. It may take a few moments for the fuel system to build up pressure, but the engine should start without a great deal of effort.

5 After the engine starts, it should be allowed to warm up to normal operating temperature. Do not allow the engine to exceed a fast idle until the hydraulic lifters pump up and become quiet again (usually about five minutes).

6 While the engine is warming up, make a thorough check for fuel, oil and coolant leaks. If a new camshaft and lifters have been installed during the overhaul, the engine should run at a fast idle for 15 minutes after the lifters pump up and become quiet (keep an eye on the temperature gauge and don't allow the engine to overheat) to "break in" the cam and lifters.

7 Shut the engine off and recheck the engine oil and coolant levels.

8 Drive the vehicle to an area with minimum traffic, accelerate from 30 to 50 mph, then allow the vehicle to slow to 30 mph with the throttle closed. Repeat the procedure 10 or 12 times. This will load the piston rings and cause them to seat properly against the cylinder walls. Check again for oil and coolant leaks.

9 Drive the vehicle gently for the first 500 miles (no sustained high speeds) and keep a constant check on the oil level. It is not unusual for an engine to use oil during the break-in period.

10 At approximately 500 to 600 miles, change the oil and filter.

11 For the next few hundred miles, drive the vehicle normally. Do not pamper it or abuse it.

12 After 2000 miles, change the oil and filter again and consider the engine broken in.

Specifications

4.2L inline six-cylinder engine

General

Displacement	256 cubic centimeters
Compression ratio	10:1
Cylinder compression pressure	
Minimum	150 psi
Typical	215 psi
Lowest allowable between cylinders	10 percent of the highest reading
Oil pressure (minimum warm engine)	12 psi @ 1200 rpm

V8 engines

General

Displacement	
5.3L	325 cubic centimeters
6.0L	364 cubic centimeters
Compression ratio	
5.3L	9.49:1
6.0L	10.86:1
Cylinder compression pressure	
Minimum	100 psi
Lowest allowable between cylinders	30 percent of the highest reading
Oil pressure (minimum warm engine)	6 psi @ 1000 rpm

Torque specifications   Ft-lbs (unless otherwise indicated)

➡**Note: One foot-pound (ft-lb) of torque is equivalent to 12 inch-pounds (in-lbs) of torque. Torque values below approximately 15 ft-lbs are expressed in inch-pounds, since most foot-pound torque wrenches are not accurate at these smaller values.**

4.2L inline six-cylinder engine

Connecting rod cap bolts	
Step one	18
Step two	Turn an additional 110-degrees
Main bearing cap bolts	
Step one	18
Step two	Turn an additional 180-degrees

V8 engines

Connecting rod cap bolts	
Step one	15
Step two	Turn an additional 75-degrees
Main bearing cap bolts (see illustration 10.19)	
Inner bolts (1 through 10)	
Step 1	15
Step 2	Tighten an additional 80-degrees
Outer stud nuts (11 through 20)	
Step 1	15
Step 2	Tighten an additional 51-degrees
Side bolts (21 through 30)	18

* **Note: Refer to Part A or B for additional torque specifications.**

Notes

3

COOLING, HEATING AND AIR CONDITIONING SYSTEMS

Section

Reference to other Chapters

1 General information

All vehicles covered by this manual employ a pressurized engine cooling system with thermostatically controlled coolant circulation. Coolant is drawn from the radiator by an impeller-type water pump mounted at the front of the block. The coolant is then circulated through the engine block where it passes around the individual cylinders. After exiting the cylinder block, the coolant then enters the cylinder head where it quenches the combustion chamber area. The coolant flows out of the cylinder head and into the thermostat where, depending on the coolant temperature, it is either blocked until the desired temperature is obtained or allowed to pass through the thermostat into the radiator.

During the coolant flow cycle some coolant is directed into the heater core for passenger compartment heating, and some coolant is directed to the throttle body to allow the throttle body to operate at a consistent temperature.

A wax pellet type thermostat is located in the thermostat housing on the engine. During warm up, the closed thermostat prevents coolant from circulating through the radiator. When the engine reaches normal operating temperature, the thermostat opens and allows hot coolant to travel through the radiator, where it is cooled before returning to the engine.

The cooling system is pressurized by the radiator cap, which contains a blow-off pressure valve and a vacuum atmospheric valve. By maintaining higher atmospheric pressure, it increases the boiling point of the coolant. If the coolant temperature goes above this increased boiling point, the extra pressure in the system forces the cap valve off its seat and allows excess pressure to escape the system.

The coolant reservoir serves as a holding tank that contains coolant which, as the engine cools, is drawn into the radiator, and when hot allows for normal coolant expansion out of the radiator into the coolant reservoir.

These vehicles incorporate an electro-viscous fan clutch. This fan/clutch system is controlled by the PCM and is dependent on various vehicle sensor inputs for its correct operation.

The heating system works by directing air through the heater core mounted in the dash and then to the interior of the vehicle by a system of ducts. Rear heating systems are equipped with separate heater core located at the rear of the vehicle. Temperature is controlled by mixing heated air with fresh air, using a system of doors in the ducts, and a blower motor.

Air conditioning is standard on all models and consists of an evaporator core located under the dash, a condenser in front of the radiator, an accumulator in the engine compartment and a belt-driven compressor mounted at the front of the engine. Rear air conditioning systems are equipped with a separate evaporator core located at the rear of the vehicle.

2 Antifreeze - general information

♦ **Refer to illustration 2.4**

The cooling system should be filled with a water/DEX-COOL based antifreeze solution which will prevent freezing down to at least -20-degrees F. It also provides protection against corrosion and increases the coolant boiling point.

The cooling system should be drained, flushed and refilled according to the vehicle maintenance schedule (see Chapter 1). The use of antifreeze solutions for periods of longer than recommended is likely to cause damage and encourage the formation of rust and scale in the system.

Before adding antifreeze, check all hose connections, because antifreeze tends to leak through very minute openings. Engines don't normally consume coolant, so if the level goes down, find the cause and correct it.

The exact mixture of antifreeze to water which you should use depends on the relative weather conditions. The mixture should contain at least 50-percent antifreeze, but should never contain more than 70-percent antifreeze. Consult the mixture ratio chart on the antifreeze container before adding coolant. Hydrometers are available at most auto parts stores to test the coolant (see illustration). Always use antifreeze which meets the vehicle manufacturer's specifications.

2.4 An inexpensive hydrometer can be used to test the condition of your coolant

3 Thermostat - check and replacement

➡Note: The thermostat is part of the thermostat housing and must be replaced as a unit.

CHECK

1 Before assuming the thermostat is to blame for a cooling system problem, check the coolant level, drivebelt tension (see Chapter 1) and temperature gauge (or light) operation.

2 If the engine seems to be taking a long time to warm up (based on heater output or temperature gauge operation), the thermostat is probably stuck open. Replace the thermostat with a new one.

3 If the engine runs hot, use your hand to check the temperature of the lower radiator hose. If the hose isn't hot, but the engine is, the thermostat is probably stuck closed, preventing the coolant inside the engine from escaping to the radiator. Replace the thermostat

✳✳ CAUTION:

Don't drive the vehicle without a thermostat. The computer may stay in open loop and emissions and fuel economy will suffer.

4 If the lower radiator hose is hot, it means the coolant is flowing and the thermostat is open. Consult the *Troubleshooting* Section at the front of this manual for cooling system diagnosis.

REPLACEMENT

▶ Refer to illustrations 3.7, 3.8 and 3.12

✳✳ WARNING:

The engine must be completely cool when this procedure is performed.

5 Disconnect the cable from the negative terminal of the battery. Partially drain the cooling system. If the coolant is relatively new or in good condition, save it and reuse it. If it is to be replaced, see Section 2 for cautions about proper handling of used antifreeze.

3.7 The thermostat housing is located on the left side of the engine (alternator removed for clarity); note that the thermostat is part of the housing and will have to be replaced as a unit

6 Remove the alternator (see Chapter 5).

7 On six-cylinder models, follow the upper radiator hose to the engine to locate the thermostat housing. The thermostat housing is located at the left side of the engine block (see illustration).

8 On V8 models, follow the lower radiator hose to the engine to locate the thermostat housing. The thermostat housing is located at the right side of the water pump (see illustration).

9 Loosen the hose clamp, then detach the radiator hose from the thermostat housing. If the hose sticks, grasp it near the end with a pair of adjustable pliers and twist it to break the seal, then pull it off. If the hose is old or deteriorated, cut it off and install a new one.

10 If the outer surface of the fitting that mates with the hose is deteriorated (corroded, pitted, etc.) it may be damaged further by hose removal. If it is, the thermostat housing will have to be replaced.

11 Remove the bolts and detach the thermostat housing. If the housing is stuck, tap it with a soft-face hammer to jar it loose. Be prepared for some coolant to spill as the gasket seal is broken.

12 Clean the mating surfaces on the engine and the thermostat housing. Install a new O-ring in the groove in the housing (see illustration).

3.8 The thermostat housing is located adjacent to the water pump inlet

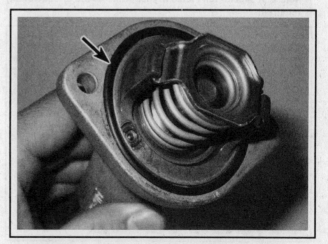

3.12 After the housing is cleaned, or a new thermostat/ housing is used, a new O-ring should always be used

13 Reattach the thermostat housing to the intake manifold (six-cylinder models) or water pump housing (V8 models) and tighten the bolts to the torque listed in this Chapter's Specifications.

14 The remaining steps are the reverse of the removal procedure. Now would be a good time to check and replace the hoses and clamps (see Chapter 1).

15 Refer to Chapter 1 and refill the cooling system, then run the engine and check carefully for leaks.

16 Repeat steps 1 through 4 to be sure the repairs corrected the previous problem(s).

4 Engine cooling fan and clutch - check

✳✳ WARNING 1:

Keep your hands, tools and clothing away from the fan. To avoid injury or damage DO NOT operate the engine with a damaged fan. Do not attempt to repair fan blades - replace a damaged fan with a new one.

✳✳ WARNING 2:

If the fan is damaged in any way, don't attempt to repair it. Replace the fan with a new one.

1 The vehicles covered by this manual are equipped with electro-viscous PCM controlled fan clutches.

2 Remove the key from the ignition switch for safety purposes.

3 Begin the check with a visual inspection. With the engine cold, inspect the fan blades for cracks or damage; replace any fan that shows signs of either.

4 Wiggle the fan blade from side-to-side - there should be 1/4-inch or less play in the fan. Replace the clutch if play is excessive.

5 Inspect the electro-viscous clutch for signs of leakage and proper tightness to the water pump. Replace the clutch if leakage is present.

6 Turn the fan blades and note the resistance. There should be less resistance with a cold engine.

7 Drive the vehicle until the engine is warmed up. Shut it off and remove the key.

8 Turn the fan blades and again note the resistance. There should be a noticeable increase in resistance.

9 If the fan clutch fails this check or is locked up solid, replacement is indicated.

5 Engine cooling fan, clutch and shroud - removal and installation

▶ **Refer to illustrations 5.5 and 5.7**

✳✳ WARNING:

The engine must be completely cool when this procedure is performed.

➡**Note 1: These models are equipped with an electronically controlled viscous fan that uses the PCM to control the operation of the fan. If the engine is overheating because the fan is not coming on, have the electronically controlled viscous fan checked by a dealer service department or other qualified automotive repair facility.**

➡**Note 2: A special fan clutch wrench (GM# 46406 or equivalent) is required.**

1 Remove the bolts and push pins that attach the intake air baffle to the radiator support, then remove the baffle.

2 Disconnect the transmission cooler lines at the engine bracket and fan shroud.

3 Disconnect the electro-viscous clutch electrical connector from the shroud.

4 Remove the upper radiator hose from the radiator; be prepared for coolant spillage.

5 Use a large wrench to remove the fan clutch retaining nut and detach the fan clutch assembly from the engine. The drivebelt should keep the nut from rotating while the fan nut is loosened (counterclockwise). If the water pump pulley slips on the belt, it will be necessary to remove the drivebelts (see Chapter 1) and use a strap wrench to hold the pulley (see illustration).

5.5 Loosening the fan clutch retaining nut while holding the pulley with a strap wrench

5.7 Carefully lift the fan, clutch and shroud out as an assembly

6   Unclip the shroud from the radiator side panels then tilt the condenser and radiator forward. This will be easier if someone assists you.

7   Remove the fan and shroud as one unit by lifting straight up as the condenser and radiator are being held in the forward position (see illustration).

8   The fan can now be unbolted from the clutch, if necessary. Be sure to tighten the fan-to-clutch bolts to the torque listed in this Chapter's Specifications.

9   Installation is the reverse of removal. Tighten the fan hub nut to the torque listed in this Chapter's Specifications.

10 Check the coolant, adding as necessary to bring it to the appropriate level (see Chapter 1).

6   Radiator - removal and installation

▶ Refer to illustrations 6.7 and 6.9

✳✳ WARNING 1:

The air conditioning system is under high pressure. Do not loosen any hose fittings or remove any components until after the system has been discharged. Air conditioning refrigerant must be properly discharged into an EPA-approved recovery/ recycling unit at a dealer service department or an automotive air conditioning repair facility. Always wear eye protection when disconnecting air conditioning system fittings.

✳✳ WARNING 2:

The engine must be completely cool before beginning this procedure.

➡**Note: The vehicles covered by this manual use spring-type radiator hose clamps. If you decide to reuse them, make sure that the hose is installed on a connection that is clean and dry. Don't try to reuse these clamps on aftermarket hoses. Replace them with conventional worm-drive type clamps.**

1   If you're working on a model without an auxiliary (rear) air conditioning system, have the air conditioning system discharged (see the **Warning** above).

2   Disconnect the cable from the negative terminal of the battery.

3   Drain the cooling system as described in Chapter 1, then remove the fan shroud and electro-viscous clutch (see section 5)

4   Raise the vehicle and support on jackstands.

5   Remove the lower radiator hose from the radiator.

6   Remove the radiator support shield (if equipped).

7   Detach the transmission cooler lines from the radiator (see illustration). To disconnect the lines from the radiator, simply unsnap the plastic collar from the quick-connect fitting, then remove the retaining clip and pull out the lines. Plug the ends of the lines to prevent fluid from leaking out after you disconnect them. Have a drip pan ready to catch any spills. Always be sure to inspect the O-rings on the cooler lines before reinstallation.

➡**Note: Do not remove the clips by pulling straight out. Hold one side in with your fingers while using a pick (with a bent tip) to pull the other side out, then rotate the clip off. Install clips the same way, not straight on.**

8   Lower the vehicle.

9   Remove the radiator support brace (see illustration) and the coolant reservoir line.

10 Disconnect the radiator side panels and remove the radiator

➡**Note: On models without a rear air conditioning system, the condenser is removed with the radiator and then separated from the radiator by removing the condenser bracket bolts.**

11 Prior to installation of the radiator, replace any damaged radiator hoses and hose clamps.

6.7 Unsnap the plastic collar, then remove the retaining clip from the quick-connect fitting to disconnect the transmission cooler lines (typical)

12 Radiator installation is the reverse of removal. When installing the radiator, make sure that the radiator seats properly in the lower saddles and that the upper brackets are secure. Install the transmission cooler line retaining clips onto the quick-connect fitting before installing the lines, then snap the cooler lines into place on the quick connect fittings. Be sure to reinstall the plastic collars on the quick connect fittings as they lock the retaining clip in place.

➡**Note: If the plastic collars don't easily fit over the retaining clips the quick disconnect fitting is not assembled correctly.**

13 After installation, refill the cooling system (see Chapter 1), then check the engine oil and automatic transmission fluid levels.

14 On models without a rear air conditioning system, have the air conditioning system charged by the shop that discharged it.

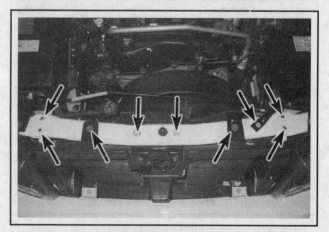

6.9 Radiator support brace fasteners

7   Water pump (main) and auxiliary water pump - check and replacement

☀ WARNING:

Wait until the engine is completely cool before starting this procedure.

➡Note: Some models are equipped with an auxiliary water pump that is mounted in the engine compartment near the frame rail. This pump delivers coolant from the engine cooling system to the rear heater core for heating the rear passenger compartment.

WATER PUMP (MAIN)

Check

◆ **Refer to illustration 7.2**

1   Water pump (main) failure can cause overheating and serious damage to the engine. There are three ways to check the operation of the water pump while it is installed on the engine. If any one of the following quick checks indicate water pump problems, it should be replaced immediately.

2   A seal protects the water pump impeller shaft bearing from contamination by engine coolant. If this seal fails, a weep hole in the water pump snout will leak coolant (see illustration) (an inspection mirror can be used to look at the underside of the water pump if the hole is not on top). If the weep hole is leaking, shaft bearing failure will follow. Replace the water pump immediately.

3   The water pump impeller shaft bearing can also wear out prematurely. When the bearing wears out, it emits a high pitched squealing sound. If such a noise is coming from the water pump during engine operation, the shaft bearing has failed. Replace the water pump immediately.

➡Note: Do not confuse belt noise with bearing noise.

4   To identify excessive bearing wear, remove the drivebelt (see Chapter 1), grasp the water pump pulley and try to force it up and down or from side-to-side. If the pulley can be moved either vertically or horizontally, the bearing is nearing the end of its service life. Replace the water pump.

5   It is possible for the water pump to be bad even if it does not howl or leak water. Sometimes the fins on the back of the impeller can corrode away until the pump is no longer effective. The only way to check for this is to remove the pump for examination.

7.2 The weep hole is located on the bottom of the water pump (typical)

7.10 To remove the water pump pulley, prevent it from turning with a pin spanner (or a strap wrench wrapped around the pulley) and unscrew the bolts

Replacement

◆ **Refer to illustrations 7.10, 7.11a and 7.11b**

6   Disconnect the cable from the negative terminal of the battery.

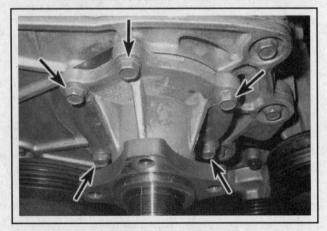

7.11a Water pump mounting bolts (arrows) - six-cylinder engine

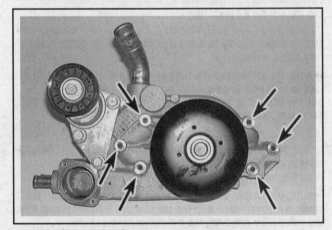

7.11b Water pump mounting bolt locations (arrows) - V8 engines

7 Drain the coolant (see Chapter 1) and remove the air intake duct and resonator (see Chapter 1).

8 Remove the radiator shroud and the fan clutch assembly (see Section 5).

9 Remove the drivebelt (see Chapter 1).

10 Remove the water pump pulley (see illustration).

11 Remove the water pump bolts (see illustrations). It may be necessary to tap the pump with a soft-faced hammer to break the gasket seal. Inspect the pump's impeller blades on the backside for corrosion. If any fins are missing or badly corroded, replace the pump with a new one.

12 Clean the sealing surfaces of all gasket material on both the water pump and block. Wipe the mating surfaces with a rag soaked with lacquer thinner or acetone.

13 Apply a thin layer of RTV sealant to both sides of the new gasket and install the gasket on the water pump.

14 Place the water pump in position and install the bolts finger tight. Use caution to ensure the gasket does not slip out of position. Now tighten the bolts to the torque listed in this Chapter's Specifications.

15 Install the pulley and tighten the bolts to the torque listed in this Chapter's Specifications.

16 The remainder of the installation procedure is the reverse of removal. Refill and bleed the cooling system (see Chapter 1), start the engine and check for the proper coolant level. Also check for coolant leaks around the water pump and hoses.

AUXILIARY WATER PUMP

17 Disconnect the cable from the negative terminal of the battery.

18 Drain the coolant (see Chapter 1) and remove the air intake duct and resonator (see Chapter 1).

19 On six cylinder models, remove the air filter housing (see Chapter 4).

20 On V8 models, remove the air conditioning accumulator (see Section 14).

21 Remove the heater hose clamps and separate the heater hoses from the pump.

➡Note: It will be necessary to use a special tool to open the spring clamp. Be sure to install new clamps.

22 Disconnect the auxiliary water pump connector.

23 Remove the water pump bracket nuts and remove the water pump.

24 Remove the auxiliary water pump clips and remove the pump from the bracket.

25 Installation is the reverse of removal.

26 Refill and bleed the cooling system (see Chapter 1), start the engine and check for the proper coolant level. Also check for coolant leaks around the auxiliary water pump and hoses.

8   Coolant temperature gauge sending unit - check and replacement

1 The coolant temperature indicator system is composed of a temperature gauge or warning light mounted in the dash and a coolant temperature sensor mounted on the engine. This coolant temperature sensor doubles as an information sensor for the fuel and emissions systems (see Chapter 6) and as a sending unit for the temperature gauge.

2 If an overheating indication occurs, check the coolant level in the system and then make sure the wiring between the gauge and the sending unit is secure and all fuses are intact.

3 Check the operation of the coolant temperature sensor (see Chapter 6). If the sensor is defective, replace it by following the procedure in that Chapter.

4 If the coolant temperature sensor is good, have the temperature gauge checked by a dealer service department or other properly equipped repair shop. This test will require a scan tool to access the information as it is processed by the Powertrain Control Module (PCM).

9   Blower motor and circuit - check

▸ Refer to illustration 9.4

✳✳ WARNING:

These models have airbags. Always disable the airbag system before working in the vicinity of any airbag system component to avoid the possibility of accidental deployment of the airbag, which could cause personal injury (see Chapter 12).

➡Note: This procedure applies to the front blower motor and circuit on all models covered by this manual. Some models are equipped with rear auxiliary heating and air conditioning systems which can't be tested using conventional equipment. Due to the use of an integrated electronic control module that can only be tested with specialized equipment it will be necessary to take these vehicles to dealer service department or other qualified repair shop for diagnosis.

1 Check the fuse (marked HVAC) and all connections in the circuit for looseness and corrosion. Make sure the battery is fully charged.

➡Note: The heater/blower relay is located on the blower motor housing in the passenger compartment and the HVAC fuse is located in the fuse panel on the left side of the dash.

9.4 Backprobe the blower motor connector terminals with a voltmeter. Check the running voltage in each of the fan speed switch positions

2 With the transmission in Park, set the parking brake securely and turn the ignition switch to the Run position. It isn't necessary to start the vehicle.

3 Remove the heater/air conditioning assembly cover (below the glove box) for access to the blower motor, then remove the glove box.

4 Backprobe the blower motor electrical connector with a voltmeter (see illustration).

5 Move the blower switch through each of its positions and note the voltage readings. Changes in voltage indicate that the motor speeds will also vary as the switch is moved to the different positions.

6 If there is voltage present, but the blower motor does not operate, the blower motor is probably faulty. Disconnect the blower motor connector, then hook one side of the blower motor terminals to a chassis ground and the other to a fused source of battery voltage. If the blower doesn't operate, it is faulty.

7 If there was no voltage present at the blower motor, and the motor itself tested OK, follow the blower motor ground wire to the splice pack near the right front of the lower console. Check the ground terminal for continuity to ground against the chassis metal. If no continuity exists, repair the ground circuit as necessary.

8 If the blower still doesn't operate properly, the resistor, control panel or related wiring is probably faulty.

➡**Note: These models are equipped with a blower motor resistor module mounted on the blower motor housing. The front blower motor mounts the resistor module near the blower motor cover. On the rear blower motor (if equipped), the resistor module is mounted on the top of the assembly.**

10 Blower motor - removal and installation

✳✳ WARNING:

These models have airbags. Always disable the airbag system before working in the vicinity of any airbag system component to avoid the possibility of accidental deployment of the airbag, which could cause personal injury (see Chapter 12).

FRONT BLOWER MOTOR

▸ **Refer to illustration 10.4**

1 Remove the right instrument panel insulator.
2 Remove the glove box door.
3 Disconnect the electrical connector from the blower motor.
4 Remove the blower motor screws and cooling tube (see illustration).
5 Remove the blower motor and separate it from the cover.
6 If you're replacing the blower motor with a new one, remove the fan from the blower motor. The fan is pressed onto the blower motor shaft and can be pried off with two screwdrivers.
7 Install the fan onto the new motor and install the blower motor into the heater housing.

AUXILIARY BLOWER MOTOR (IF EQUIPPED)

✳✳ WARNING 1:

Wait until the engine is completely cool before beginning this procedure.

✳✳ WARNING 2:

The air conditioning system is under high pressure. Do not loosen any hose fittings or remove any components until after

10.4 Blower motor screws and vent tube

the system has been discharged. Air conditioning refrigerant must be properly discharged into an EPA-approved recovery/recycling unit at a dealer service department or an automotive air conditioning repair facility. Always wear eye protection when disconnecting air conditioning system fittings.

8 Have the air conditioning system discharged (see the **Warning** above). Drain the cooling system (see Chapter 1).
9 Remove the HVAC module. Disconnect the electrical connector from the HVAC auxiliary module.
10 Remove the air outlet duct.
11 Remove the blower motor screws and remove the blower motor.
12 Installation is the reverse of removal.
13 Refill the cooling system (see Chapter 1). Have the air conditioning system charged by the shop that discharged it.

11 Heater and air conditioning control assembly - removal and installation

✳✳ WARNING:

These models have airbags. Always disable the airbag system before working in the vicinity of any airbag system component to avoid the possibility of accidental deployment of the airbag, which could cause personal injury (see Chapter 12).

➡**Note: After control assembly replacement the control module will need to be recalibrated. To achieve this, first replace the module, then turn the ignition Off, start the vehicle and let it idle for one minute. Do not interrupt this process or incorrect HVAC operation will occur.**

11.4a Remove the screws (A), pinch the retaining tabs (B) and pull the control assembly outward . . .

11.4b . . . then disconnect the electrical connectors

FRONT HEATER CONTROLS (ALL MODELS)

▶ **Refer to illustrations 11.4a and 11.4b**

1   Disconnect the cable from the negative terminal of the battery.
2   Remove the console (see Chapter 11).
3   Remove the accessory trim plate (see Chapter 11).
4   Remove the control assembly retaining screws, then depress the tabs and pull the unit from the dash (see illustrations). It can be pulled out just far enough to allow disconnecting the electrical connections and control cables (if equipped) from the control head. Use a small screwdriver to release the clips.

5   To install the control assembly, reverse the removal procedure.
6   Perform a module recalibration (see the **Note** above).

REAR AUXILIARY HEATER CONTROLS

7   Using a small screwdriver pry out the rear control panel(s).
8   Pull the control head downward from the center console, disconnect the electrical connections and remove it from the vehicle. Use a small screwdriver to release the clips.
9   To install the control assembly, reverse the removal procedure. Be sure the control head snaps securely into place on the center console.
10 Perform a module recalibration (see the **Note** above).

12 Heater core - removal and installation

▶ **Refer to illustrations 12.3, 12.5, 12.7a and 12.7b**

❋❋ WARNING 1:

These models have airbags. Always disable the airbag system before working in the vicinity of any airbag system component to avoid the possibility of accidental deployment of the airbag, which could cause personal injury (see Chapter 12).

❋❋ WARNING 2:

The air conditioning system is under high pressure. DO NOT loosen any fittings or remove any components until after the system has been discharged. Air conditioning refrigerant must be properly discharged into an EPA-approved container at a dealership service department or an automotive air conditioning facility. Always wear eye protection when disconnecting air conditioning system fittings.

❋❋ WARNING 3:

Wait until the engine is completely cool before beginning the procedure.

1   Have the air conditioning system discharged by a dealership service department or an automotive air conditioning facility (see **Warning** above).

12.3 After having the air conditioning system discharged, disconnect the evaporator lines at the firewall. Cap the fittings to prevent moisture from entering the system. Heater hoses may be cut off if you are unable to remove them easily

2   Disconnect the cable at the negative terminal of the battery.
3   Drain the cooling system (see Chapter 1). then remove the heater hoses and air conditioning lines from the fittings at the firewall (see illustration). Be sure to plug the lines line to avoid coolant spillage and contamination of the air conditioning system.

12.5 The HVAC module must be removed along with the instrument panel carrier

12.7a Separate the cover from the HVAC housing and remove the screw and clamp that retains the heater core ...

4   Remove the instrument panel assembly (see Chapter 11).

5   Remove the instrument panel carrier and heater/air conditioning assembly (HVAC module) assembly (see illustration).

6   Separate the HVAC module from the instrument panel carrier.

7   Remove the screws and separate the HVAC module halves. Remove the screw and clamp and carefully remove the heater core (see illustrations).

8   Installation is the reverse of removal.

➡**Note: When reinstalling the heater core, make sure any original insulating/sealing materials are in place around the heater core pipes and around the core.**

9   Refill the cooling system (see Chapter 1). Have the air conditioning system charged by the shop that discharged it.

10 Start the engine and check for proper operation.

12.7b ... and remove the heater core

13 Air conditioning and heating system - check and maintenance

▶ **Refer to illustration 13.1**

✳✳ **WARNING:**

The air conditioning system is under high pressure. Do not loosen any hose fittings or remove any components until after the system has been discharged. Air conditioning refrigerant must be properly discharged into an EPA-approved recovery/recycling unit at a dealer service department or an automotive air conditioning repair facility. Always wear eye protection when disconnecting air conditioning system fittings.

✳✳ **CAUTION 1:**

All models covered by this manual use environmentally friendly R-134a. This refrigerant (and its appropriate refrigerant oils) are not compatible R-12 refrigerant system components and must never be mixed or the components will be damaged.

✳✳ **CAUTION 2:**

When replacing entire components, additional refrigerant oil should be added equal to the amount that is removed with the component being replaced. Be sure to read the can before adding any oil to the system, to make sure it is compatible with the R-134a system.

1   The following maintenance checks should be performed on a regular basis to ensure that the air conditioning continues to operate at peak efficiency.

   a) Inspect the condition of the drivebelt. If it is worn or deteriorated, replace it (see Chapter 1).
   b) Check the drivebelt tension (see Chapter 1).
   c) Inspect the system hoses. Look for cracks, bubbles, hardening and deterioration. Inspect the hoses and all fittings for oil bubbles or seepage. If there is any evidence of wear, damage or leakage, replace the hose(s).

d) *Inspect the condenser fins for leaves, bugs and any other foreign material that may have embedded itself in the fins. Use a "fin comb" or compressed air to remove debris from the condenser.*

e) *Make sure the system has the correct refrigerant charge.*

f) *If you hear water sloshing around in the dash area or have water dripping on the carpet, check the evaporator housing drain tube (see illustration) and insert a piece of wire into the opening to check for blockage.*

2   It's a good idea to operate the system for about ten minutes at least once a month. This is particularly important during the winter months because long term non-use can cause hardening, and subsequent failure, of the seals. Note that using the Defrost function operates the compressor.

3   If the air conditioning system is not working properly, proceed to Step 6 and perform the general checks outlined below.

4   Because of the complexity of the air conditioning system and the special equipment necessary to service it, in-depth troubleshooting and repairs beyond checking the refrigerant charge and the compressor clutch operation are not included in this manual. However, simple checks and component replacement procedures are provided in this Chapter.

5   The most common cause of poor cooling is simply a low system refrigerant charge. If a noticeable drop in system cooling ability occurs, one of the following quick checks will help you determine whether the refrigerant level is low. Should the system lose its cooling ability, the following procedure will help you pinpoint the cause.

CHECK

6   Warm the engine up to normal operating temperature.

7   Place the air conditioning temperature selector at the coldest setting and put the blower at the highest setting. Open the doors (to make sure the air conditioning system doesn't cycle off as soon as it cools the passenger compartment).

8   After the system reaches operating temperature, feel the two pipes connected to the evaporator at the firewall.

9   The pipe leading from the accumulator to the evaporator should be cold, and the evaporator outlet line (the tubing that leads back to the compressor) should be slightly warmer (about 3 to 10 degrees F warmer). If the evaporator outlet is considerably warmer than the inlet, or if the evaporator inlet isn't cold, the system needs a charge. Insert a thermometer in the center air distribution duct while operating the air conditioning system at its maximum setting - the temperature of the output air should be 35 to 40 degrees F below the ambient air temperature (down to approximately 40 degrees F). If the ambient (outside) air temperature is very high, say 110 degrees F, the duct air temperature may be as high as 60 degrees F, but generally the air conditioning is 35 to 40 degrees F cooler than the ambient air.

10   If the air isn't as cold as it used to be, the system probably needs a charge.

11   If the air is warm and the system doesn't seem to be operating properly check the operation of the compressor clutch.

12   Have an assistant switch the air conditioning On while you observe the front of the compressor. The clutch will make an audible click and the center of the clutch should rotate. If it doesn't, shut the engine off and disconnect the air conditioning system low pressure switch (see illustration 13.22). Bridge the terminals of the connector with a jumper wire and turn the air conditioning On again. If it works now, the system pressure is too high or too low. Have your system tested by a dealer service department or air conditioning shop.

13.1 Check that the evaporator housing drain tube at the firewall is clear of any blockage - the view here is from above the engine looking down

13   If the clutch still didn't operate, check the appropriate fuses. Inspect the fuses in the interior fuse panel.

14   Remove the compressor clutch (A/C) relay from the engine compartment relay panel and test it (see Chapter 12). With the relay out and the ignition On, check for battery power at two of the relay terminals (refer to the wiring diagrams for wire color designations to determine which terminals to check). There should be battery power with the key On, at the terminals for the relay control and power circuits.

15   Using a jumper wire, connect the terminals in the relay box from the relay power circuit to the terminal that leads to the compressor clutch (refer to the wiring diagrams for wire color designations to determine which terminals to connect). Listen for the clutch to click as you make the connection. If the clutch doesn't respond, disconnect the clutch connector at the compressor and check for battery voltage at the compressor clutch connector. Check for continuity to ground on the black wire terminal of the compressor clutch connector. If power and ground are available and the clutch doesn't operate when connected, the compressor clutch is defective.

16   If the compressor clutch, relay and related circuits are good and the system is fully charged with refrigerant and the compressor does not operate under normal conditions, have the PCM and related circuits checked by a dealer service department or other properly equipped repair facility.

17   Further inspection or testing of the system is beyond the scope of the home mechanic and should be left to a professional.

ADDING REFRIGERANT

▶ **Refer to illustrations 13.18, 13.21 and 13.22**

❄ CAUTION:

Make sure any refrigerant, refrigerant oil or replacement component your purchase is designated as compatible with environmentally friendly R-134a systems.

18   Purchase an R-134a automotive charging kit at an auto parts store (see illustration). A charging kit includes a 12-ounce can of refrigerant, a tap valve and a short section of hose that can be attached

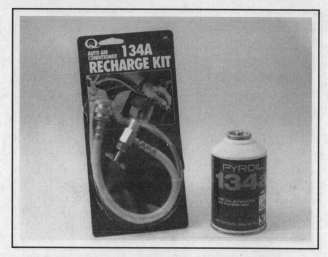

13.18 A basic charging kit for 134a systems is available at most auto parts stores - it must say 134a (not R-12) and so must the can of refrigerant

13.21 Attach the refrigerant kit to the low-side charging port - it's on the accumulator - the cap may be marked with an "L"

between the tap valve and the system low side service valve. Because one can of refrigerant may not be sufficient to bring the system charge up to the proper level, it's a good idea to buy an additional can.

> ❋❋ WARNING:
>
> **Never add more than two cans of refrigerant to the system.**

19 Hook up the charging kit by following the manufacturer's instructions.

> ❋❋ WARNING:
>
> **DO NOT hook the charging kit hose to the system high side! The fittings on the charging kit are designed to fit only on the low side of the system.**

20 Back off the valve handle on the charging kit and screw the kit onto the refrigerant can, making sure first that the O-ring or rubber seal inside the threaded portion of the kit is in place.

> ❋❋ WARNING:
>
> **Wear protective eyewear when dealing with pressurized refrigerant cans.**

21 Remove the dust cap from the low-side charging port and attach the quick-connect fitting on the kit hose (see illustration).

22 Warm up the engine and turn on the air conditioning. Keep the charging kit hose away from the fan and other moving parts.

➡**Note 1: The charging process requires the compressor to be running. If the clutch cycles off, you can put the air conditioning switch on High and leave the car doors open to keep the clutch on and compressor working.**

➡**Note 2: The compressor can be kept on during the charging by removing the connector from the low pressure switch and bridging it with a paper clip or jumper wire during the procedure (see illustration).**

23 Turn the valve handle on the kit until the stem pierces the can,

then back the handle out to release the refrigerant. You should be able to hear the rush of gas. Add refrigerant to the low side of the system, keeping the can upright at all times, but shaking it occasionally. Allow stabilization time between each addition.

➡**Note: The charging process will go faster if you wrap the can with a hot-water-soaked shop rag to keep the can from freezing up.**

24 If you have an accurate thermometer, you can place it in the center air conditioning duct inside the vehicle and keep track of the output air temperature. A charged system that is working properly should cool down to approximately 40-degrees F. If the ambient (outside) air temperature is very high, say 110 degrees F, the duct air temperature may be as high as 60 degrees F, but generally the air conditioning is 30-40 degrees F cooler than the ambient air.

25 When the can is empty, turn the valve handle to the closed position and release the connection from the low-side port. Replace the dust cap.

26 Remove the charging kit from the can and store the kit for future use with the piercing valve in the UP position, to prevent inadvertently piercing the can on the next use.

13.22 The air conditioning low pressure switch is located on the accumulator - if the compressor will not stay engaged, disconnect the connector and bridge the terminals (on the harness side) with a jumper wire during the charging procedure

HEATING SYSTEMS

27 If the carpet under the heater core is damp, or if antifreeze vapor or steam is coming through the vents, the heater core is leaking. Remove it (see Section 12) and install a new unit (most radiator shops will not repair a leaking heater core).

28 If the air coming out of the heater vents isn't hot, the problem could stem from any of the following causes:

a) *The thermostat is stuck open, preventing the engine coolant from warming up enough to carry heat to the heater core. Replace the thermostat (see Section 3).*

b) *There is a blockage in the system, preventing the flow of coolant through the heater core. Feel both heater hoses at the firewall. They should be hot. If one of them is cold, there is an obstruction in one of the hoses or in the heater core, or the heater control valve is shut. Detach the hoses and back flush the heater core with a water hose. If the heater core is clear but circulation is impeded, remove the two hoses and flush them out with a water hose.*

c) *If flushing fails to remove the blockage from the heater core, the core must be replaced (see Section 12).*

ELIMINATING AIR CONDITIONING ODORS

▶ **Refer to illustration 13.32**

29 Unpleasant odors that often develop in air conditioning systems are caused by the growth of a fungus, usually on the surface of the evaporator core. The warm, humid environment there is a perfect breeding ground for mildew to develop.

30 The evaporator core on most vehicles is difficult to access, and dealerships have a lengthy, expensive process for eliminating the fungus by opening up the evaporator case and using a powerful disinfectant and rinse on the core until the fungus is gone. You can service your own system at home, but it takes something much stronger than basic household germ-killers or deodorizers.

31 Aerosol disinfectants for automotive air conditioning systems are available in most auto parts stores, but remember when shopping for them that the most effective treatments are also the most expensive. The basic procedure for using these sprays is to start by running the system in the RECIRC mode for ten minutes with the blower on its highest speed. Use the highest heat mode to dry out the system and keep the compressor from engaging by disconnecting the wiring connector at the compressor (see Section 15).

32 The disinfectant can usually comes with a long spray hose. Remove the passenger's side lower dash trim panel, then remove the

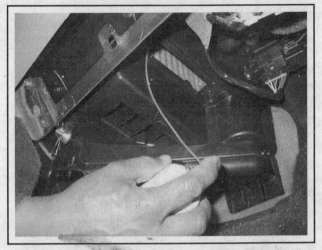

13.32 Spray the disinfectant at the evaporator core - the carpet directly under the area you are spraying should be protected by covering it with plastic or a towel

small access cover from the HVAC housing. Point the nozzle inside the hole and to the left towards the evaporator core, and spray according to the manufacturer's recommendations (see illustration). Try to cover the whole surface of the evaporator core, by aiming the spray up, down and sideways. Follow the manufacturer's recommendations for the length of spray and waiting time between applications.

33 Once the evaporator has been cleaned, the best way to prevent the mildew from coming back again is to make sure your evaporator housing drain tube is clear (see illustration 13.1).

AUTOMATIC HEATING AND AIR CONDITIONING SYSTEMS

34 Some models are equipped with an optional automatic climate control system. This system has its own computer that receives inputs from various sensors in the heating and air conditioning system. This computer, like the PCM, has self-diagnostic capabilities to help pinpoint problems or faults within the system. Vehicles equipped with automatic heating and air conditioning systems are very complex and considered beyond the scope of the home mechanic. Vehicles equipped with automatic heating and air conditioning systems should be taken to dealer service department or other qualified facility for repair.

---

14 Air conditioning accumulator/drier - removal and installation

REMOVAL

▶ **Refer to illustration 14.2**

✷✷ WARNING:

The air conditioning system is under high pressure. DO NOT loosen any fittings or remove any components until after the system has been discharged. Air conditioning refrigerant must be properly discharged into an EPA-approved container at a dealership service department or an automotive air conditioning

repair facility. Always wear eye protection when disconnecting air conditioning system fittings.

1 Have the air conditioning system discharged (see **Warning** above). Disconnect the cable from the negative terminal of the battery.

2 Disconnect the refrigerant inlet and outlet lines (see illustration). Loosen each nut and remove the fittings from the retaining stud(s). Cap or plug the open lines immediately to prevent the entry of dirt or moisture.

3 Disconnect the electrical connector from the low pressure switch,

then remove the switch.

4   Remove the clamp bolt on the mounting bracket and remove the accumulator/drier assembly up and out of the engine compartment.

INSTALLATION

5   If you are replacing the accumulator/drier with a new one, add one ounce of fresh refrigerant oil to the new unit (oil must be R-134a compatible).

6   Place the new accumulator/drier into position in the bracket, then position the accumulator and bracket on the mounting stud.

7   Install the inlet and outlet lines, using clean refrigerant oil on the new O-rings. Tighten the mounting bolt securely.

8   Install the pressure cycling switch and reattach the connector.

9   Connect the cable to the negative terminal of the battery.

10 Have the system evacuated, recharged and leak tested by the shop that discharged it.

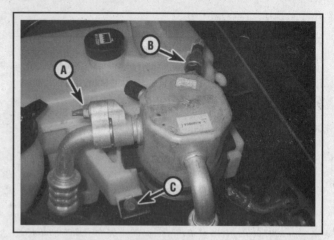

14.2 Accumulator mounting details

| A | Refrigerant line fitting nut | C | Mounting bracket bolt |
| B | Low pressure switch | | |

15 Air conditioning compressor - removal and installation

REMOVAL

▶ **Refer to illustrations 15.6a and 15.6b**

✳✳ WARNING:

The air conditioning system is under high pressure. DO NOT loosen any fittings or remove any components until after the system has been discharged. Air conditioning refrigerant must be properly discharged into an EPA-approved container at a dealership service department or an automotive air conditioning repair facility. Always wear eye protection when disconnecting air conditioning system fittings.

➡**Note: The accumulator/drier (see Section 14) and the expansion (orifice) tube (see Section 18) should be replaced whenever the compressor is replaced.**

1   Have the air conditioning system discharged (see **Warning** above).

2   Disconnect the cable from the negative terminal of the battery.

3   Clean the compressor thoroughly around the refrigerant line fittings.

Six-cylinder engines

4   Remove the drivebelt (see Chapter 1).

5   Remove the alternator (see Chapter 5) and the drivebelt idler pulley bracket.

6   Disconnect the electrical connector(s) from the air conditioning compressor (see illustrations).

7   Disconnect the suction and discharge block from the compressor. Both lines are mounted to the compressor with a manifold secured by one bolt. Plug the open fittings to prevent the entry of dirt and moisture, and discard the seals between the plate and compressor.

8   Remove the compressor mounting bolts, then remove the compressor.

V8 engines

9   Remove the air cleaner housing assembly, including the windshield washer fluid reservoir and duct to the throttle body (see Chapter 1).

10 Remove the cooling fan shroud (see Section 5) and the drivebelt (see Chapter 1).

11 Disconnect the lower radiator hose from the engine, then remove the refrigerant suction and discharge hoses from the compressor. Discard the seals and use new ones on installation.

12 Remove the upper compressor mounting bolts.

13 Raise the vehicle and support it securely on jackstands.

14 Working from underneath the vehicle, disconnect the compressor electrical connector(s), then remove the remaining compressor mounting bolts.

15 Lower the vehicle. Remove any remaining bracket bolts and remove the compressor.

INSTALLATION (ALL MODELS)

16 If a new compressor is being installed, pour the oil from the old compressor into a graduated container and add that exact amount of new refrigerant oil to the new compressor. Also follow any directions included with the new compressor.

➡**Note: Some replacement compressors come with refrigerant oil in them. Follow the directions with the compressor regarding the draining of excess oil prior to installation. Caution: The oil used must be labeled as compatible with R-134a refrigerant systems.**

17 Installation is the reverse of the disassembly. When installing the lines or line fitting block to the compressor, use new seals lubricated with clean refrigerant oil, and tighten the nut securely.

18 Reconnect the cable to the negative terminal of the battery.

19 Have the system evacuated, recharged and leak tested by the shop that discharged it.

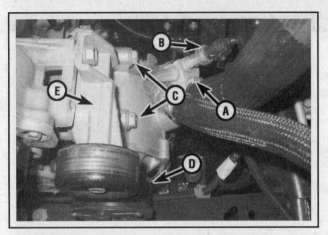

15.6a Air conditioning compressor mounting details - six-cylinder engine

A   *Refrigerant line fitting bolt*
B   *Refrigerant pressure sensor*
C   *Compressor mounting bolts (lower two bolts not visible)*
D   *Compressor clutch electrical connector*
E   *Drive belt pulley bracket*

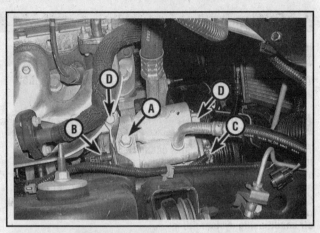

15.6b Air conditioning compressor mounting details - V8 engines

A   *Refrigerant line mounting bolt*
B   *High pressure cycling switch electrical connector*
C   *Compressor clutch electrical connector*
D   *Compressor mounting bolts (lower two bolts not visible)*

16 Air conditioning condenser - removal and installation

▶ Refer to illustrations 16.3a and 16.3b

❋❋ WARNING:

The air conditioning system is under high pressure. DO NOT loosen any fittings or remove any components until after the system has been discharged. Air conditioning refrigerant must be properly discharged into an EPA-approved container at a dealership service department or an automotive air conditioning repair facility. Always wear eye protection when disconnecting air conditioning system fittings.

➡**Note: The accumulator/drier should be replaced if the condenser was damaged, causing the system to be open for some time (see Section 14).**

1   Have the air conditioning system discharged (if equipped) at a dealer service department or service station. Drain the engine coolant (see Chapter 1).

2   Disconnect the cable from the negative terminal of the battery.

3   Disconnect the refrigerant lines from the condenser (see illustration). Plug the open ends of the condenser and the disconnected refrigerant lines to prevent entry of dirt or moisture.

4   Remove the radiator (see Section 6).

5   Remove the condenser mounting bolts.

6   Inspect the rubber insulator pads (on the lower cross member) on which the radiator sits. Replace them if they're dried or cracked.

7   If the original condenser will be reinstalled, store it with the line fittings on top to prevent oil from draining out. If a new condenser is being installed, pour one ounce of R-134a-compatible refrigerant oil into it prior to installation.

8   Reinstall the components in the reverse order of removal. Be sure the rubber pads are in place under the condenser.

9   Refill the cooling system (see Chapter 1).

10 Have the system evacuated, recharged and leak tested by the shop that discharged it.

16.3a Remove the nut and detach the refrigerant line from the left side of the condenser . . .

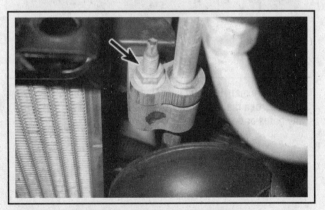

16.3b . . . and from the right side of the condenser

17 Evaporator core - replacement

⁕⁕ WARNING 1:

Wait until the engine is completely cool before beginning the procedure.

⁕⁕ WARNING 2:

The air conditioning system is under high pressure. DO NOT loosen any fittings or remove any components until after the system has been discharged. Air conditioning refrigerant must be properly discharged into an EPA-approved container at a dealership service department or an automotive air conditioning repair facility. Always wear eye protection when disconnecting air conditioning system fittings.

1 Drain the cooling system (see Chapter 1). Remove the front HVAC module assembly (see Section 12).

2 Remove the screws and separate the HVAC module halves. Use caution not to damage the seal.

3 Remove the evaporator core.

4 If a new evaporator core is used, add 2 oz. of refrigerant oil.

5 The remaining installation is the reverse of removal.

6 Refill the cooling system (see Chapter 1).

7 Have the system evacuated, recharged and leak tested by the shop that discharged it.

18 Air conditioning expansion (orifice) tube - removal and installation

▶ Refer to illustration 18.6

⁕⁕ WARNING 1:

The air conditioning system is under high pressure. DO NOT loosen any fittings or remove any components until after the system has been discharged. Air conditioning refrigerant must be properly discharged into an EPA-approved container at a dealership service department or an automotive air conditioning repair facility. Always wear eye protection when disconnecting air conditioning system fittings.

⁕⁕ WARNING 2:

The engine must be completely cool before beginning this procedure.

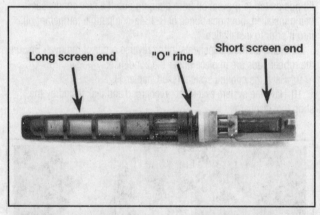

18.6 The expansion tube is equipped with a tapered mesh screen that must be clean and must not have any holes or damage

1 Have the air conditioning system discharged (see **Warning** above).

2 Remove the accumulator and cap the fittings to prevent moisture and dirt from entering the system.

3 Remove the air filter and the coolant reservoir (the reservoir is actually the lower half of the air filter housing - see Chapter 4).

4 Remove the evaporator tube nut and block fitting. Discard the seal - a new one must be used on reassembly

5 Follow the line to its other end and detach it, too. Remove the line from the engine compartment.

6 The expansion tube is a tube with a fixed-diameter orifice and a mesh filter at each end (see illustration). You will see one end of the orifice tube inside the pipe leading to the evaporator. Use needle-nose pliers to remove the orifice tube; notice the direction it was installed.

7 The orifice tube acts to meter the refrigerant, changing it from a high-pressure liquid to a low-pressure gas. It is possible to reuse the orifice tube if:

    a) *The screens aren't plugged with grit or foreign material*

    b) *Neither screen is torn*

    c) *The plastic housing over the screens is intact*

    d) *The brass orifice inside the plastic housing is unrestricted*

8 Installation is the reverse of removal. Be sure to insert the expansion tube with the shorter end in first.

⁕⁕ CAUTION:

Always use a new O-ring when installing the expansion (orifice) tube.

9 Reinstall the refrigerant line (using new seals) and tighten the fittings securely, then have the system evacuated, recharged and leak-tested by the shop that discharged it.

Specifications

General

Coolant capacity

    Six-cylinder engine

2002 and 2003	13.9 quarts
2004	
Standard wheelbase	13.9 quarts
Extended wheelbase	15.2 quarts
2005 and 2006	
Standard wheelbase	10.8 quarts
Extended wheelbase	13.8 quarts
2007 and later	13.9 quarts

    V8 engines

2002 and 2003	13.9 quarts
2004	
Standard wheelbase	15.3 quarts
Extended wheelbase	17.9 quarts
2005 and 2006	
Standard wheelbase	12.2 quarts
Extended wheelbase	15.3 quarts
2007 and later	15.3 quarts

Radiator pressure cap rating	15 psi
Refrigerant type	R-134a
Refrigerant oil type	PAG

Oil capacity

2002 through 2006 models	
Standard	7.4 ounces
With rear air conditioning	8.45 ounces
2007 and later models	8 ounces

Refrigerant capacity

Standard	1.9 pounds
With rear air conditioning	2.65 pounds

Torque specifications   Ft-lbs (unless otherwise indicated)

➡**Note: One foot-pound (ft-lb) of torque is equivalent to 12 inch-pounds (in-lbs) of torque. Torque values below approximately 15 ft-lbs are expressed in inch-pounds, since most foot-pound torque wrenches are not accurate at these smaller values.**

Air conditioning compressor mounting bolts	37
Cooling fan hub nut	41
Fan blade bolts	20
Thermostat housing bolts	
Six-cylinder engine	89 in-lbs
V8 engines	132 in-lbs
Water pump mounting bolts	
Six-cylinder engine	89 in-lbs
V8 engines	
Step 1	132 in-lbs
Step 2	22
Water pump pulley bolts	18

Notes

Section

Reference to other Chapters

4

FUEL AND EXHAUST SYTEMS

1 General information

▶ **Refer to illustration 1.1**

❈❈ WARNING:

Gasoline is extremely flammable, so take extra precautions when you work on any part of the fuel system. Don't smoke or allow open flames or bare light bulbs near the work area, and don't work in a garage where a gas-type appliance (such as a water heater or a clothes dryer) is present. Since gasoline is carcinogenic, wear fuel-resistant gloves when there's a possibility of being exposed to fuel, and, if you spill any fuel on your skin, rinse it off immediately with soap and water. Mop up any spills immediately and do not store fuel-soaked rags where they could ignite. The fuel system is under constant pressure, so, if any fuel lines are to be disconnected, the fuel pressure in the system must be relieved first. When you perform any kind of work on the fuel system, wear safety glasses and have a Class B type fire extinguisher on hand.

All models covered by this manual are equipped with a Sequential Multi Port Fuel Injection (SFI) system (see illustration). This system uses timed impulses to sequentially inject the fuel directly into the intake ports of each cylinder. The injectors are controlled by the Powertrain Control Module (PCM). The PCM monitors various engine parameters and delivers the exact amount of fuel, in the correct sequence, into the intake ports.

All models are equipped with an electric fuel pump, mounted in the fuel tank. It is necessary to remove the fuel tank for access to the fuel pump. The fuel level sending unit is an integral component of the fuel pump module and it must be removed from the fuel tank in the same manner.

Fuel pressure is controlled by the fuel pressure regulator and it is mounted in various locations depending on the year and model. On 2002 through 2004 models, the fuel pressure regulator is mounted in the corner of the engine compartment on six-cylinder models or on the fuel rail on V8 models. On 2005 and later models (and some 2004 5.3L V8 models), the fuel pressure regulator is an integral component of the fuel pump/fuel level sending unit that is located in the fuel tank.

The exhaust system consists of exhaust manifolds, a catalytic converter, exhaust pipes and a muffler. Each of these components is replaceable. For further information regarding the catalytic converter, refer to Chapter 6.

1.1 Typical fuel system components (six cylinder model shown)

1   Throttle body
2   Fuel pump relay (inside underhood electrical center)
3   Air filter housing
4   Air intake duct and resonator
5   Fuel rail and injectors (not visible)

2 Fuel pressure relief procedure

❈❈ WARNING:

See the Warning in Section 1.

➡ **Note: After the fuel pressure has been relieved, it's a good idea to lay a shop towel over any fuel connection to be disas-** sembled, to absorb the residual fuel that may leak out when servicing the fuel system.

1   Before servicing any fuel system component, you must relieve the fuel pressure to minimize the risk of fire or personal injury.

2   Remove the fuel filler cap - this will relieve any pressure built up in the tank.

3 Remove the fuel pump relay located in the underhood fuse box (see illustration 3.3).

4 Start the engine and allow it to stall, then continue to crank the engine an additional 5 to 10 seconds.

5 Disconnect the negative battery cable from the battery.

6 Place shop towels around the fuel fitting to be disconnected to absorb any residual fuel that may spill out.

3 Fuel pump/fuel pressure - check

✳✳ WARNING:

See the Warning in Section 1.

PRELIMINARY CHECK

▶ **Refer to illustration 3.3**

1 If you suspect insufficient fuel delivery, first inspect all fuel lines to ensure that the problem is not simply a leak in a line. Be certain there is adequate fuel in the fuel tank before proceeding.

2 Set the parking brake and have an assistant turn the ignition switch to the ON position while you listen to the fuel pump (inside the fuel tank). You should hear a whirring sound, lasting for approximately two seconds, indicating the fuel pump is operating. If the fuel pump is operating, proceed to the pressure check.

3 If there is no sound, turn the ignition key Off and remove the cover from the underhood electrical center. Check the fuel pump fuse (PCM B) and the fuel pump relay (see illustration). If the fuse and relay are good, check the fuel pump relay control circuit from the electrical center to the PCM. If the circuit is good, have the PCM diagnosed by a dealer service department or other qualified repair shop.

4 If the pump does not run, disconnect the electrical connector from the fuel pump module at the fuel tank (see Section 5). Using a test light or voltmeter, check for power at the harness connector. Using a continuity tester or ohmmeter, check for continuity to a good chassis ground at the black wire terminal. If power is not indicated on the gray wire terminal or the ground circuit is open, repair the wiring harness.

5 If power is present at the connector, the ground circuit is good and the fuel pump does not operate when connected, replace the fuel pump (see Section 7).

PRESSURE CHECK

➡**Note: In order to perform the fuel pressure test, you will need a fuel pressure gauge capable of measuring high fuel pressure. The fuel gauge must be equipped with the proper fitting required to attach it to the test port. To test the fuel pressure regulator on 2002 through 2004 models, a fuel shut off valve must be installed in the fuel return line with the necessary adapters.**

2002 through 2004 models

Refer to illustrations 3.6a, 3.6b and 3.6c

➡**Note: On 2005 and later models (and some late 2004 5.3L V8 models), the fuel pressure regulator is an integral component of the fuel pump/fuel level sending unit that is located in the fuel tank. This updated fuel supply system does not return fuel to the fuel tank. Instead, the returnless fuel system bleeds off excess fuel directly at the fuel pressure regulator.**

6 Relieve the fuel pressure (see Section 2). Remove the cap from the fuel pressure test port and attach a fuel pressure gauge (see illustrations). Six-cylinder models with a fuel tank shield have an access hole in the shield.

3.3 Refer to the schematic under the electrical center cover for the relay location on your model

3.6a Fuel pressure test port location on the fuel filter (six-cylinder model)

3.6b Fuel pressure test port on the fuel rail (V8 model)

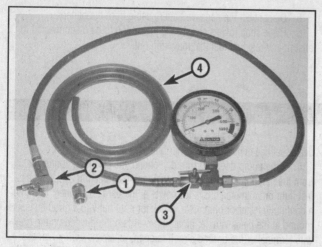

3.6c A typical fuel pressure gauge set up

1 Screw on adapter for the Schrader valve on the fuel rail
2 Hose with fitting to connect to the adapter
3 Bleeder valve (optional)
4 Bleeder hose (optional)

7   Turn the ignition key On (engine not running); the fuel pump should run for approximately two seconds then shut off. Note the pressure indicated on the gauge and compare your reading with the pressure listed in this Chapter's Specifications. Cycle the ignition key On and Off several times, if necessary, to obtain the highest reading.

8   If the fuel pressure is lower than specified, turn the ignition key Off and relieve the fuel system pressure (see Section 2). Install a fuel shut-off valve in the fuel return line and close the valve.

> ❊❊ **CAUTION:**
>
> **Do not pinch the flexible fuel line shut or damage to the fuel line may occur.**

Turn the ignition key On and note the fuel pressure.

> ❊❊ **CAUTION:**
>
> **Do not allow the fuel pressure to rise above 75 psi or damage to the fuel system may occur.**

If the fuel pressure is now above the specified pressure, replace the fuel pressure regulator (see Section 13). If the fuel pressure is lower than specified, check the fuel lines and the fuel filter for restrictions. If no restriction is found, remove the fuel pump module (see Section 7) and check the fuel strainer for restrictions, check the fuel flex pipe for leaks and check the fuel pump wiring for high resistance. If no problems are found, replace the fuel pump.

9   If the fuel pressure recorded in Step 7 is higher than specified, check the fuel return line for restrictions. If no restrictions are found, replace the fuel pressure regulator (see Section 13).

10 If the fuel pressure is within specifications, start the engine. With the engine running, the fuel pressure should be 3 to 10 psi below the

pressure recorded in Step 7. If it isn't, remove the vacuum hose from the fuel pressure regulator and verify there is 12 to 14 in-Hg of vacuum present at the hose. If vacuum is not present at the hose, check the hose for a restriction or a broken hose. If vacuum is present, reconnect the hose to the fuel pressure regulator. If the fuel pressure regulator does not decrease the fuel pressure with vacuum applied, replace the fuel pressure regulator.

11 Turn the engine off and monitor the fuel pressure for five minutes. The fuel pressure should not drop more than 5 psi within five minutes. If it does, there is a leak in the fuel line, a fuel injector is leaking, the pressure regulator diaphragm or the fuel pump module check valve is defective. The first check made for an internal leak is at the pressure regulator - simply disconnect the vacuum line and check for the presence of fuel; the line may be wet or fuel may run out of it. Cycle the ignition key several times with the line disconnected and check for a drop of fuel at the pressure regulator vacuum fitting. If any fuel is present at the vacuum line or regulator, replace the regulator. To determine if the fuel injectors are leaking, cycle the ignition key On and Off several times to obtain the highest fuel pressure reading, then immediately shut off both the fuel supply and return lines. If the pressure drops below 5 psi within five minutes, a fuel injector (or injectors) is leaking (or the fuel line or fuel rail may be leaking, but such a leak would be very apparent). If the fuel injectors hold pressure, the main fuel line is leaking or the fuel pump is defective.

12 Relieve the fuel pressure before removing the gauge (see Section 2).

2005 and later models

▶ Refer to illustration 3.15

13 To measure the fuel pressure, you'll need a fuel pressure gauge compatible with high-pressure fuel injection systems, and a hose and fitting suitable for connecting the gauge to the Schrader valve-type test port on the fuel feed line (see illustration 3.6b).

14 Relieve the fuel pressure (see Section 2).

15 Locate the fuel pressure test port (see illustrations 3.6a and 3.6b), unscrew the cap and connect a fuel pressure gauge.

16 Turn the ignition key On (engine not running). Note the gauge reading as soon as the pressure stabilizes, and compare it with the pressure listed in this Chapter's Specifications.

   a) If the pressure is lower than specified, check for a restriction in the fuel system. Two likely suspects are the fuel inlet strainer at the base of the fuel pump module, or a faulty fuel pressure regulator.

➡️**Note: Neither of these components can be inspected or replaced separately. It's also possible that there is a restriction in the fuel line (a blockage or a kink).**

   b) If the fuel pressure is higher than specified, replace the fuel pressure regulator, which is part of the fuel pump module (see Section 7).

17 Turn off the engine. Verify that the fuel pressure loses no more than 8 psi for five minutes after the engine is turned off.

18 Relieve the fuel pressure (see Section 2), then disconnect the fuel pressure gauge and screw on the test port cap. Clean up any spilled gasoline.

19 Start the engine and verify that there are no fuel leaks.

4 Fuel lines and fittings - repair and replacement

▶ **Refer to illustrations 4.2, 4.11a, 4.11b, 4.11c and 4.11d**

❋❋ WARNING:

See the Warning in Section 1.

1   Always relieve the fuel pressure before servicing fuel lines or fittings (see Section 2).

2   Metal fuel supply and vapor lines extend from the fuel tank to the engine compartment. The lines are secured to the underbody or frame with plastic retainers (see illustration). Flexible hose connects the metal lines to the fuel tank, fuel filter and fuel rail. Fuel lines must be occasionally inspected for leaks or damage.

3   In the event of any fuel line damage, metal lines may be repaired with steel tubing of the same diameter, provided the correct fittings are used. Flexible lines, on the other hand, must be replaced with factory replacement parts; others may fail from the high pressures of this system. Never repair a damaged section of steel line with rubber hose and hose clamps.

4   If evidence of contamination is found in the system or fuel filter during disassembly, the line should be disconnected and blown out. Check the fuel strainer on the fuel pump module for damage and deterioration.

5   Don't route fuel line or hose within four inches of any part of the exhaust system or within ten inches of the catalytic converter. Fuel line must never be allowed to chafe against the engine, body or frame. A minimum of 1/4-inch clearance must be maintained around a fuel line.

6   When replacing a fuel line, remove all fasteners attaching the fuel line to the vehicle body.

7   Because fuel lines used on fuel-injected vehicles are under high pressure, they require special consideration.

STEEL TUBING

8   If replacement of a steel fuel line or emission line is called for, use genuine replacement parts or equivalent only.

9   Never use copper or aluminum tubing to replace steel tubing. These materials cannot withstand normal vehicle vibration.

10   Some fuel lines have threaded fittings with O-rings. Any time the

4.2 The fuel lines are secured to the underbody with plastic retainers

fittings are loosened to service or replace components:

a) Use a flare-nut wrench on the fitting nut and a backup wrench on the stationary portion of the fitting while loosening and tightening the fittings.

b) Metal quick disconnect fittings require the use of a special tool GM#J37088-A or equivalent (available at most auto parts stores).

c) Check all O-rings for cuts, cracks and deterioration. Replace any that appear hardened, worn or damaged.

d) If the lines are replaced, always use original equipment parts, or parts that meet the original equipment standards.

FLEXIBLE HOSE

11   There are various methods of disconnecting the fittings, depending upon the type of quick-connect fitting installed on the fuel line (see illustrations). Clean any debris from around the fitting. Disconnect the fitting and carefully remove the fuel line from the vehicle.

❋❋ CAUTION:

The quick-connect fittings are not serviced separately. Do not attempt to repair these types of fuel lines in the event the fitting or line becomes damaged. Replace the entire fuel line as an assembly.

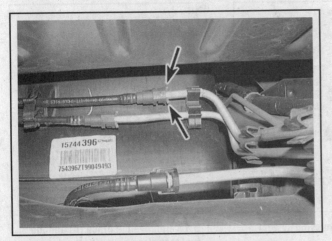

4.11a To disconnect a plastic collar two-tab type fitting, squeeze the two tabs together and pull the lines apart

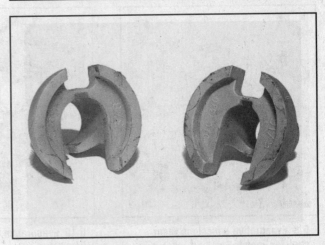

4.11b A special tool (available at most auto parts stores) is required to disconnect the metal collar type fitting

4.11c To disconnect a metal collar type fitting, remove the safety tether from the fitting . . .

4.11d . . . place the tool over the fuel line, insert it squarely into the fitting and pull the lines apart (the tool is not required to connect the lines)

12 Installation is the reverse of removal with the following additions:

a) *Clean the quick-connect fittings with a lint-free cloth and apply clean engine oil the fittings.*

b) *After connecting a quick-connect fitting, check the integrity of the*

connection by attempting to pull the lines apart.

c) *Use new O-rings at the threaded fittings (if equipped).*

d) *Cycle the ignition key On and Off several times and check for leaks at the fitting, before starting the engine.*

5   Fuel tank - removal and installation

▶ **Refer to illustrations 5.8, 5.10 and 5.12**

✳✳ WARNING:

See the Warning in Section 1.

➡**Note: If necessary, clean the fuel tank and areas surrounding the fuel lines and hoses to prevent contaminating the fuel system.**

1 Remove the fuel tank filler cap to relieve fuel tank pressure.
2 Relieve the fuel system pressure (see Section 2).

3 Disconnect the cable from the negative battery terminal.
4 Using a siphoning kit (available at most auto parts stores), siphon the fuel into an approved gasoline container.

✳✳ WARNING:

Do not start the siphoning action by mouth!

5 Raise the vehicle and support it securely on jackstands.
6 Remove the frame brace.
7 On models so equipped, remove the bolts and the shield over the fuel tank.

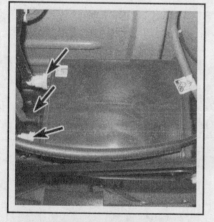

5.8 Evaporative emissions vapor canister lines

5.10 Evaporative emission system vent valve

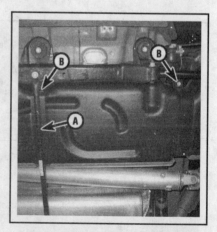

5.12 Remove the brace (A) and the fuel tank strap bolts (B), then remove the straps

8   Disconnect the fuel supply and return lines and evap vapor lines from the vapor canister (see Section 4) (see illustration).

9   Remove the fuel filler hose from the tank.

10 Disconnect the electrical connectors from the tank pressure sensor and the evap vent valve (see illustration).

11 Position a transmission jack under the fuel tank and support the tank.

12 Remove the brace that passes under the fuel tank. Also unscrew the fuel tank strap bolts and remove the straps (see illustration).

13 Lower the tank slightly and disconnect the electrical connectors from the fuel pump module.

14 Lower the jack and remove the tank from the vehicle.

15 Installation is the reverse of removal.

6   Fuel tank cleaning and repair - general information

1   The fuel tanks installed in the vehicles covered by this manual are not repairable. If the fuel tank becomes damaged, it must be replaced.

2   Cleaning the fuel tank (due to fuel contamination) should be performed by a professional with the proper training to carry out this critical and potentially dangerous work. Even after cleaning and flushing, explosive fumes may remain inside the fuel tank.

3   If the fuel tank is removed from the vehicle, it should not be placed in an area where sparks or open flames could ignite the fumes coming out of the tank. Be especially careful inside a garage where a gas-type appliance is located.

7   Fuel pump module - removal and installation

▶ Refer to illustrations 7.5 and 7.6

❈❈ WARNING:

See the Warning in Section 1.

❈❈ WARNING:

Some fuel may remain in the module reservoir and spill as the module is removed. Have several shop towels ready and a drain pan nearby to place the module in.

1   Relieve the fuel system pressure (see Section 2).

2   Disconnect the cable from the negative battery terminal.

3   Remove the fuel tank from the vehicle (see Section 5).

4   Disconnect the fuel lines and EVAP line from the fuel pump module.

5   While prying the locking tab out, rotate the fuel pump module retaining ring counterclockwise until it's loose (see illustration).

6   Remove the fuel pump module from the tank (see illustration). Angle the assembly slightly to avoid damaging the fuel level sending unit float.

7   The electric fuel pump is not serviced separately. In the event of failure, the complete assembly must be replaced. Transfer the fuel pressure sensor and fuel level sending unit to the new fuel pump module assembly, if necessary (see Section 8).

8   Clean the fuel tank sealing surface and install a new seal on the fuel pump module.

9   Install the fuel pump module, aligning the fuel line fittings with the fuel lines.

10 Press the fuel pump module down until seated and install the retaining ring. Make sure the retaining ring is fully seated and the locking tab is engaged with the slot.

11 The remainder of installation is the reverse of removal.

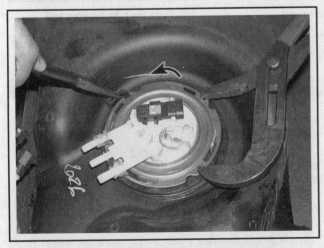

7.5 Release the locking tab and loosen the fuel pump module retaining ring by rotating it counterclockwise

7.6 Carefully remove the fuel pump module from the tank and drain the fuel from the reservoir

8 Fuel level sending unit - check and replacement

CHECK

▶ **Refer to illustration 8.2**

1 Remove the fuel tank and the fuel pump module (see Sections 5 and 7).

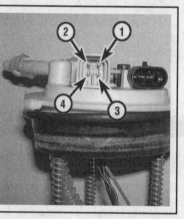

8.2 Fuel pump module connector terminal identification

1 Fuel level sending unit signal
2 Fuel pump 12-volt supply (from fuel pump relay)
3 Ground
4 Fuel level sending unit ground

2 Connect the probes of an ohmmeter to the two fuel level sensor terminals (1 and 4) of the fuel pump module electrical connector (see illustration).

3 Position the float in the down (empty) position and note the reading on the ohmmeter.

4 Move the float up to the full position while watching the meter.

5 If the fuel level sending unit resistance does not change smoothly as the float travels from empty to full, replace the fuel level sending unit assembly.

REPLACEMENT

▶ **Refer to illustrations 8.7, 8.8 and 8.9**

6 Remove the fuel tank and the fuel pump module (see Sections 5 and 7).

7 Disconnect the fuel level sending unit electrical connector from the module cover (see illustration).

8 Remove the sending unit retaining clip (see illustration).

9 Pinch the tabs together and slide the fuel level sending unit off the module (see illustration). Note the routing of the wiring for installation.

10 Installation is the reverse of removal.

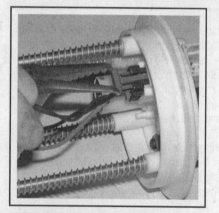

8.7 Disconnect the fuel pump/ fuel level sending unit electrical connector from the fuel pump module

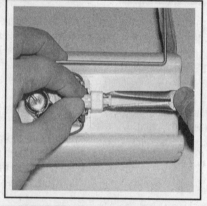

8.8 Remove the sending unit retaining clip

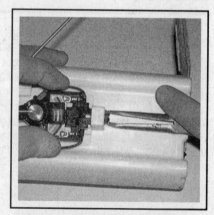

8.9 Pinch the tabs together and remove the fuel level sending unit from the module

9 Air filter housing and resonator - removal and installation

SIX-CYLINDER MODEL

▶ **Refer to illustrations 9.3, 9.6 and 9.9**

1 Remove the radiator diagonal brace (if equipped).

2 Loosen the three screws that retain the air cleaner cover, then remove the air filter and tube from the lower housing (the lower housing also serves as the windshield washer fluid tank) (see Chapter 1).

3 Remove the two air filter housing/washer fluid tank nuts (see illustration).

4 Disconnect all the electrical connectors.

5 Grasp the housing and pull it straight up lifting the lower hous-

ing/washer solvent tank off the studs. Remove the assembly from the engine compartment.

6 To remove the resonator, disconnect the Intake Air Temperature sensor connector, loosen the clamps securing the resonator to the air intake duct and throttle body, then detach the duct (see illustration).

7 Disconnect the fuel pressure regulator vacuum line at the resonator.

8 Remove the resonator mounting bolts.

9 Lift the resonator up and disconnect the crankcase ventilation hose from the valve cover (see illustration).

10 Installation is the reverse of removal.

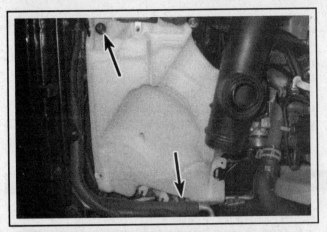

9.3 Locations of the lower air filter housing/washer fluid reservoir retaining nuts

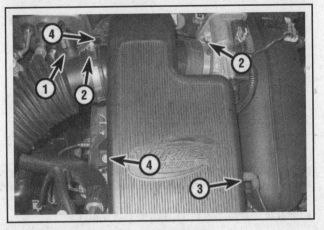

9.6 Air intake resonator mounting details

1 Intake Air Temperature sensor connector
2 Hose clamps
3 Fuel pressure regulator vacuum line
4 Mounting bolts

V8 MODELS

11 Remove the radiator diagonal brace.

12 Remove the radiator air intake baffle.

13 Loosen the captive screws (4) and pull the housing cover up, then lift the air filter element out of the housing. Separate the MAF/IAT unit from the air filter element.

14 Disconnect the headlamp washer hose (if equipped).

15 Disconnect the following electrical connectors:

   a) Windshield washer.
   b) Headlamp washer (if equipped).
   c) Low fluid level.
   d) Liftgate washer pump (if equipped).

16 Disconnect the forward lamp harness clips from the housing.

17 Disconnect the windshield washer solvent hose.

18 Loosen the clamp securing the MAF/IAT sensor to the housing

19 Remove the housing mounting nuts, and remove the housing.

20 Installation is the reverse of removal.

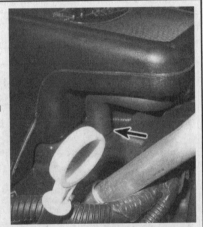

9.9 When lifting off the air intake resonator, detach the PCV hose from the valve cover

10 Fuel injection system - general information

The Sequential Multi Port Fuel Injection (SFI) system consists of three sub-systems: air intake, engine control and fuel delivery. The system uses a Powertrain Control Module (PCM) along with the sensors (Coolant Temperature Sensor, Throttle Position Sensor, Mass Airflow sensor, oxygen sensor, etc.) to determine the proper air/fuel ratio under all operating conditions.

The fuel injection system and the engine control system are closely linked in function and design. For additional information, refer to Chapter 6.

AIR INTAKE SYSTEM

The air intake system consists of the air filter, the air intake ducts, the throttle body, and the intake manifold.

When the engine is idling, the air/fuel ratio is controlled by the idle air control system, which consists of the Powertrain Control Module (PCM) and the Idle Air Control valve. This idle air control regulates the amount of airflow past the throttle plate and into the intake manifold, thus increasing or decreasing the engine idle speed. The PCM receives information from the sensors (vehicle speed, coolant temperature, air conditioning, power steering mode etc.) and adjusts the idle according to the demands of the engine and driver. Refer to Chapter 6 for information on the Idle Air Control valve.

EMISSIONS AND ENGINE CONTROL SYSTEM

The emissions and engine control system is described in detail in Chapter 6.

FUEL DELIVERY SYSTEM

The fuel delivery system consists of these components: the fuel pump, the fuel pressure regulator, the fuel rail and the fuel injectors. The fuel pump is an electric type. Fuel is drawn through an inlet screen into the pump, flows through the one-way valve, passes through the fuel filter and is delivered to the fuel rail and injectors. The pressure regulator maintains a constant fuel pressure to the injectors. Excess fuel is routed back to the fuel tank through the fuel pressure regulator and fuel return line.

The injectors are solenoid-actuated pintle types consisting of a solenoid, plunger, needle valve and housing. When current is applied to the solenoid coil, the needle valve raises and pressurized fuel sprays out the nozzle. The injection quantity is determined by the length of time the valve is open (the length of time during which current is supplied to the solenoid coils).

The fuel pump relay is located in the engine compartment electrical center. The PCM controls the relay by supplying battery voltage to the relay coil. When energized, the fuel pump relay connects battery voltage to the fuel pump. If the PCM senses there is NO signal from the camshaft or crankshaft sensors (as with the engine not running or cranking), the PCM will de-energize the relay.

11 Fuel injection system - check

▶ **Refer to illustrations 11.7a, 11.7b, 11.8 and 11.9**

➡**Note: The following procedure is based on the assumption that the fuel pressure is adequate (see Section 3).**

1   Check all electrical connectors that are related to the system. Check the ground wire connections for tightness. Loose connectors and poor grounds can cause many problems that resemble more serious malfunctions.

2   Check to see that the battery is fully charged, as the control unit and sensors depend on an accurate supply voltage in order to properly meter the fuel.

3   Check the air filter element - a dirty or partially blocked filter will severely impede performance and economy (see Chapter 1).

4   Check the related fuses. If a blown fuse is found, replace it and see if it blows again. If it does, search for a wire shorted to ground in the harness.

5   Check the air intake duct from the air filter housing to the throttle body for leaks, which will result in an excessively lean mixture. Also check the condition of all vacuum hoses connected to the intake manifold and/or throttle body.

6   Remove the resonator and air intake duct from the throttle body (see Section 9) and check for dirt, carbon or other residue build-up on the throttle bore and throttle plate. If it's dirty, clean it with carburetor cleaner spray, a toothbrush and a shop towel.

✳✳ CAUTION:

Do not use a solvent containing Methyl Ethyl Ketone or damage to the throttle body may occur.

7   On six-cylinder models, locate and disconnect the 8-way injector harness connector (see illustration). Measure the resistance of each injector by attaching an ohmmeter to the injector side of the disconnected harness, between terminal A and the corresponding terminals B, C, D, F, G and H (see illustration). Compare the measurements with the resistance values listed in this Chapter's Specifications. If the resistance of one of the injectors is way out of range (shorted or open), replace that injector.

8   On V8 models, start the engine and place an automotive stethoscope against each injector, one at a time, and listen for a clicking sound, indicating operation (see illustration). If you don't have a stethoscope, place the tip of a screwdriver against the injector and listen through the handle

11.7a Fuel injector harness connector

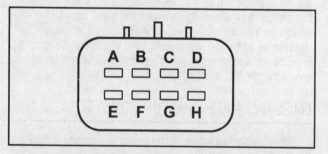

11.7b Terminal guide for the injector 8-way harness connector (injector side of connector, looking into unplugged connector)

A   Ignition voltage (pink)
B   Injector 4 (lt-blue/black)
C   Injector 5 (black/white)
D   Injector 6 (yellow/black)
E   Empty
F   Injector 1 (black)
G   Injector 2 (lt-green/black)
H   Injector 3 (pink/black)

11.8 On V8 models, use a stethoscope to determine if the injectors are working properly - they should make a steady clicking sound that rises and falls with engine speed changes

9 On V8 models, locate and disconnect the fuel injector electrical connectors and measure the resistance of each fuel injector by attaching an ohmmeter to the injector terminals (see illustration). Compare the measurements with the resistance values listed in this Chapter's Specifications. If the resistance of one of the injectors is way out of range (shorted or open), replace that injector.

10 Turn the ignition key On and check for battery voltage at the pink wire terminal A of the injector harness connector (on the engine harness side - the terminal that corresponds to terminal A in illustration 11.7b). If battery voltage is not present, check the fuel injector fuse and related wiring (see Chapter 12).

11 The remainder of the engine control system checks can be found in Chapter 6.

11.9 Measure the resistance of each injector across the two terminals of the injector

12 Throttle body - removal and installation

SIX-CYLINDER MODELS

▶ **Refer to illustration 12.3**

> ❊❊ **WARNING:**
>
> **Wait until the engine is completely cool before beginning this procedure.**

1 Remove the air intake duct and resonator (see Section 9).

2 Disconnect the electrical connector from the throttle body.

3 Disconnect the evap canister purge line from the throttle body (see illustration).

4 Remove the mounting bolts and remove the throttle body and gasket.

5 Remove all traces of old gasket material from the throttle body and intake manifold and install a new gasket.

> ❊❊ **CAUTION:**
>
> **Do not use solvent or a sharp tool to clean the throttle body gasket surface or damage to the throttle body may occur.**

6 Install the throttle body and tighten the bolts to the torque listed in this Chapter's Specifications.

7 The remainder of installation is the reverse of removal.

V8 MODELS

▶ **Refer to illustration 12.14**

> ❊❊ **WARNING:**
>
> **Wait until the engine is completely cool before beginning this procedure.**

8 Partially drain the cooling system (see Chapter 1).

9 Remove the air intake duct and resonator.

10 Disconnect the electrical connectors from the throttle body.

11 Label and detach the vacuum hoses from the throttle body.

12 Detach the accelerator cable and, if equipped, the cruise control cable.

13 Detach the coolant hoses from the throttle body.

14 Remove the mounting bolt/nuts and remove the throttle body and gasket (see illustration). Discard the O-ring gasket.

15 Install the throttle body and tighten the bolts to the torque listed in this Chapter's Specifications.

16 The remainder of the installation is the reverse of removal.

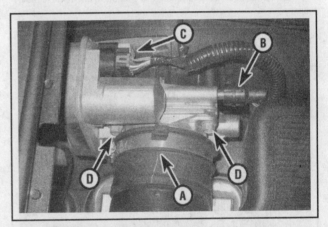

12.3 Throttle body mounting details

A   Air intake resonator duct
B   Canister purge line
C   Electrical connector
D   Mounting bolts (two of four shown)

12.14 Throttle body mounting bolt/nuts (arrows) - V8 models

13 Fuel pressure regulator - replacement

See the Warning in Section 1.

➡Note: 2005 and later models are equipped with a returnless fuel system that utilizes a fuel pressure regulator as an integral component of the fuel pump module (see Section 7).

1   Relieve the fuel system pressure (see Section 2).
2   Disconnect the cable from the negative battery terminal.

SIX-CYLINDER MODELS

◆ **Refer to illustrations 13.5 and 13.8**

➡Note: The fuel pressure regulator is mounted in the corner of the engine compartment near the air conditioning lines.

3   Remove the air intake resonator (see Section 9).
4   Clean any dirt and debris from around the fuel pressure regulator and fuel lines.
5   Disconnect the fuel pressure regulator vacuum line and unclip the engine wiring harness at the front of the engine (see illustration).
6   Disconnect the fuel return line (see Section 4) and remove the retainer.
7   Remove the fuel pressure regulator mounting screw and remove the fuel pressure regulator.

Have a towel placed around the pressure regulator area to catch the fuel that will spill as the regulator is removed.

8   Install a new O-ring and lubricate it with clean engine oil (see illustration).
9   The remainder of installation is the reverse of removal.
10 Tighten the fuel pressure regulator screw to the torque listed in this Chapter's Specifications.

V8 MODELS

➡Note: The fuel pressure regulator is mounted on the fuel rail on the right (passenger side) of the engine.

11 Remove the air intake resonator (see Section 9).
12 Clean any dirt and debris from around the fuel pressure regulator and fuel lines.
13 Disconnect the fuel pressure regulator retainer clip.
14 Remove the fuel pressure regulator.
15 Be sure to install a new back-up ring, regulator seal O-rings (two total) and a regulator filter.
16 Install a new fuel pressure regulator retainer clip.
17 The remainder of the installation is the reverse of removal.

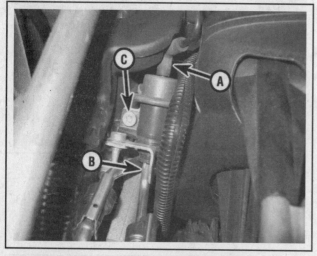

13.5 Fuel pressure regulator mounting details

A	Vacuum line	C	Mounting screw
B	Fuel return line		

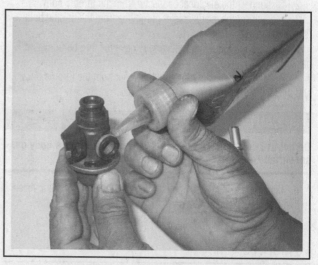

13.8 Lubricate the O-ring with a light coat of engine oil

14 Fuel rail and injectors - removal and installation

See the Warning in Section 1.

➡Note: When replacing components of the fuel rail/injector assembly, refer to the identification numbers on the fuel injectors. Fuel injectors are calibrated with different flow rates and must not be interchanged with injectors from a different application.

14.6 The fuel rail and injectors are removed as a unit, then the individual injectors can be serviced

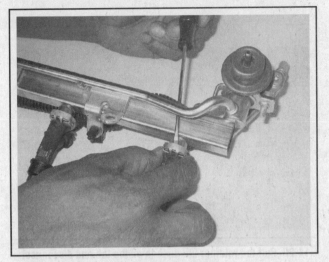

14.8 The retaining clip must be removed prior to removing the injector.

SIX-CYLINDER MODELS

Removal

♦ **Refer to illustrations 14.6 and 14.8**

1 Relieve the fuel system pressure (see Section 2).
2 Disconnect the cable from the negative battery terminal.
3 Remove the intake manifold (see Chapter 2A).
4 Before proceeding, clean the fuel rail/fuel injector area with degreaser or other appropriate solvent, then blow dry with compressed air.

❄❄ **CAUTION:**

Wear eye protection.

5 Disconnect the fuel pressure regulator vacuum line, the fuel injector harness connector (see illustration 11.7a) and the fuel line fittings (see Section 4).
6 Remove the fuel rail attaching bolts and apply gentle and even outward pressure on the fuel rail to free it from the cylinder head (see illustration).
7 Disconnect the electrical connector from the injector(s) to be removed.
8 Remove the retaining clip(s) and remove the injector(s) from the fuel rail assembly (see illustration). Remove and discard the O-rings and seals.

➡**Note: Whether you're replacing an injector or a leaking O-ring, it's a good idea to remove all the injectors from the fuel rail and replace all the O-rings (two per injector).**

INSTALLATION

9 Replace the injector O-rings. Apply a light coat of clean engine oil to the O-rings and press the injector into the fuel rail until seated.
10 Install the injector retaining clips.
11 Inspect the cylinder head injector holes and clean them out if necessary, then lubricate the injector O-rings with clean engine oil.
12 The remainder of installation is the reverse of removal. Tighten the fuel rail mounting bolts to the torque listed in this Chapter's Specifications.
13 After installation is complete, turn the ignition switch to On, but don't operate the starter (this activates the fuel pump for about two seconds, which builds up fuel pressure in the fuel lines and the fuel meter body). Cycle the ignition On and Off several times, then check the fuel lines, fuel rail and injector for fuel leakage.

V8 MODELS

❄❄ **WARNING:**

See the Warning in Section 1.

➡**Note: When replacing components of the fuel rail/injector assembly, refer to the identification numbers on the fuel rail and injectors. Fuel injectors are calibrated with different flow rates and must not be interchanged with injectors from a different application.**

Removal

♦ **Refer to illustrations 14.20, 14.22, 14.24a and 14.24b**

14 Relieve the fuel system pressure (see Section 2).
15 Disconnect the cable from the negative battery terminal.
16 Remove the air intake duct and resonator (see Section 9). On 6.0L models, remove the upper intake manifold cover and the cover mounting bracket.
17 Disconnect any electrical connectors that will interfere with fuel rail removal. Detach the upper engine wiring harness from the retainers and position the wiring harness aside.
18 Disconnect the accelerator cable and cruise control cable (if equipped) from the throttle body. Detach the cables from the bracket and position the cables aside.
19 Before proceeding, clean the fuel rail/injector area with degreaser or other appropriate solvent, then blow dry with compressed air.

❄❄ **CAUTION:**

Wear eye protection.

14.20 Pull the retainer up, push in on the tab and disconnect the electrical connector from the fuel injector

14.22 Using the proper fuel line disconnecting tool, disconnect the fuel supply and return lines (arrows) from the fuel rail pipes

20 Disconnect the fuel injector electrical connectors (see illustration).

➡**Note: Apply a numbering tag to each connector with the corresponding cylinder number.**

21 Disconnect and remove the PCV valve and hose.

22 Disconnect the fuel supply and return lines from the fuel rail (see illustration). Disconnect the fuel vacuum line from the fuel pressure regulator.

23 Clean all debris from around the injectors. Remove the fuel rail mounting bolts (see illustration). Loosen (but do not remove) the crossover tube retaining screw at the right (passenger) side fuel rail. Gently rock the fuel rail and injectors to loosen the injectors. Remove the fuel rail and fuel injectors as an assembly.

24 Remove the retaining clip and remove the injector(s) from the fuel rail assembly (see illustrations). Remove and discard the O-rings and seals.

➡**Note: Whether you're replacing an injector or a leaking O-ring, it's a good idea to remove all the injectors from the fuel rail and replace all the O-rings.**

Installation

25 Replace the injector O-rings. Apply a light coat of clean engine oil to the O-rings and press the injector into the fuel rail until seated. Install the injector retaining clips.

26 Install the injector and fuel rail assembly on the intake manifold and fully seat the injectors. Apply thread locking compound to the fuel rail mounting bolts and tighten them to the torque listed in this Chapter's Specifications. Tighten the crossover tube retainer screw at the right fuel rail.

27 Connect the fuel supply and return lines and make sure they're securely installed.

28 Connect the electrical connectors to each injector, referring to the number tags.

29 The remainder of the installation is the reverse of removal.

30 After installation is complete, turn the ignition switch to On, but don't operate the starter (this activates the fuel pump for about two seconds, which builds up fuel pressure in the fuel supply line). Cycle the ignition switch On and Off several times, then check the fuel lines, fuel rail and injectors for fuel leakage.

14.24a Remove the fuel injector retaining clip . . .

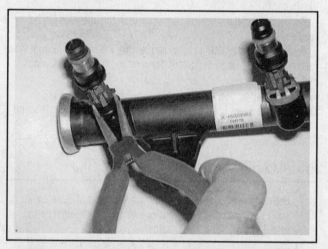

14.24b . . . and pry the fuel injector out of the fuel rail with a forked tool

15 Exhaust system servicing - general information

WARNING:

Inspection and repair of exhaust system components should be done only after enough time has elapsed after driving the vehicle to allow the system components to cool completely. Also, when working under the vehicle, make sure it is securely supported on jackstands.

1   The exhaust system consists of the exhaust manifolds, catalytic converters, muffler, resonators, the tailpipe and all connecting pipes, brackets, hangers and clamps. The exhaust system is attached to the body with mounting brackets and rubber hangers. If any of the parts are improperly installed, excessive noise and vibration will be transmitted to the body.

MUFFLER AND PIPES

▶ **Refer to illustrations 15.2a and 15.2b**

2   Conduct regular inspections of the exhaust system to keep it safe and quiet. Look for any damaged or bent parts, open seams, holes, loose connections, excessive corrosion or other defects which could allow exhaust fumes to enter the vehicle (see illustrations). Also check the catalytic converter when you inspect the exhaust system (see below). Deteriorated exhaust system components should not be repaired; they should be replaced with new parts.

3   If the exhaust system components are extremely corroded or rusted together, welding equipment will probably be required to remove them. The convenient way to accomplish this is to have a muffler repair shop remove the corroded sections with a cutting torch. If, however, you want to save money by doing it yourself (and you don't have a welding outfit with a cutting torch), simply cut off the old components with a hacksaw. If you have compressed air, special pneumatic cutting chisels can also be used. If you do decide to tackle the job at home, be sure to wear safety goggles to protect your eyes from metal chips and work gloves to protect your hands.

4   Here are some simple guidelines to follow when repairing the exhaust system:

a) *Work from the back to the front when removing exhaust system components.*

b) *Apply penetrating oil to the exhaust system component fasteners to make them easier to remove.*

c) *Use new gaskets, hangers and clamps when installing exhaust systems components.*

d) *Apply anti-seize compound to the threads of all exhaust system fasteners during reassembly.*

e) *Be sure to allow sufficient clearance between newly installed parts and all points on the underbody to avoid overheating the floor pan and possibly damaging the interior carpet and insulation. Pay particularly close attention to the catalytic converter and heat shield.*

CATALYTIC CONVERTER

WARNING:

The converter gets very hot during operation. Make sure it has cooled down before you touch it.

➡**Note: See Chapter 6 for additional information on the catalytic converter.**

5   Periodically inspect the heat shield for cracks, dents and loose or missing fasteners.

6   Inspect the converter for cracks or other damage.

7   If the catalytic converter requires replacement, refer to Chapter 6.

15.2a Inspect the exhaust system connections for leakage

15.2b Inspect the rubber hangers for damage

Specifications

General

Fuel pressure (key on, engine off)	
2002 and 2003 models	
Six-cylinder engine	48 to 54 psi
V8 engines	
VIN V, T and U	55 to 62 psi
VIN Z	48 to 54 psi
2004 through 2006 models	
Six-cylinder engine	50 to 57 psi
V8 engines	
VIN V, T and U	55 to 62 psi
VIN Z	48 to 54 psi
2007 and later models	50 to 60 psi
Fuel injector resistance	11 to 14 ohms

Torque specifications   Ft-lbs (unless otherwise indicated)

➡**Note: One foot-pound (ft-lb) of torque is equivalent to 12 inch-pounds (in-lbs) of torque. Torque values below approximately 15 ft-lbs are expressed in inch-pounds, since most foot-pound torque wrenches are not accurate at these smaller values.**

Fuel pressure regulator screw	71 in-lbs
Fuel rail mounting bolts	89 in-lbs
Fuel tank mounting strap bolts	24
Throttle body mounting bolt/nuts	
Six cylinder models	80 in-lbs
V8 models	53 in-lbs

Section

Reference to other Chapters

5

ENGINE ELECTRICAL SYSTEMS

1 General information and precautions

GENERAL INFORMATION

▶ **Refer to illustration 1.1**

The engine electrical systems include all ignition, charging and starting components (see illustration). Because of their engine-related functions, these components are discussed separately from body electrical devices such as the lights, the instruments, etc. (which are included in Chapter 12).

PRECAUTIONS

Always observe the following precautions when working on the electrical system:

a) Be extremely careful when servicing engine electrical components. They are easily damaged if checked, connected or handled improperly.
b) Never leave the ignition switched on for long periods of time when the engine is not running.
c) Never disconnect the battery cables while the engine is running.
d) Maintain correct polarity when connecting battery cables from another vehicle during jump starting - see the "Booster battery (jump) starting" section at the front of this manual.
e) Always disconnect the negative battery cable before working on the electrical system.

It's also a good idea to review the safety-related information regarding the engine electrical systems located in the "Safety first!" section at the front of this manual, before beginning any operation included in this Chapter.

BATTERY DISCONNECTION

✳✳ WARNING:

On 2006 and later models with OnStar, make absolutely sure the ignition key is in the Off position and Retained Accessory Power (RAP) has been depleted before disconnecting the cable from the negative battery terminal. Also, never remove the OnStar fuse with the ignition key in any position other than Off. If these precautions are not taken, the OnStar system's back-up battery will be activated, and remain activated, until it goes dead. If this happens, the OnStar system will not function as it should in the event that the main vehicle battery power is cut off (as might happen during a collision).

Several systems on the vehicle require battery power to be available at all times, either to ensure their continued operation (such as the clock) or to maintain control unit memories (such as that in the engine management system's Powertrain Control Module) which would be wiped out if the battery were to be disconnected. Therefore, whenever the battery is to be disconnected, first note the following to ensure that there are no unforeseen consequences of this action:

a) First, on any vehicle with power door locks, it is a wise precaution to remove the key from the ignition and to keep it with you, so that it does not get locked inside if the power door locks should engage accidentally when the battery is reconnected!
b) The engine management system's PCM will lose the information stored in its memory when the battery is disconnected. This includes idling and operating values, and any fault codes detected (see Chapter 6). Whenever the battery is disconnected, the information relating to idle speed control and other operating values will have to be re-programmed into the unit's memory. The PCM does this by itself, but until then, there may be surging, hesitation, erratic idle and a generally inferior level of performance. To allow the PCM to relearn these values, start the engine and run it as close to idle speed as possible until it reaches its normal operating temperature, then run it for approximately two minutes at 1200 rpm. Next, drive the vehicle as far as necessary - approximately 5 miles of varied driving conditions is usually sufficient - to complete the relearning process.

Devices known as "memory-savers" can be used to avoid some of the above problems. Precise details vary according to the device used. Typically, it is plugged into the cigarette lighter, and is connected by its own wires to a spare battery; the vehicle's own battery is then disconnected from the electrical system, leaving the "memory-saver" to pass sufficient current to maintain audio unit security codes and PCM memory values, and also to run permanently live circuits such as the clock, all the while isolating the battery in the event of a short-circuit occurring while work is carried out.

✳✳ WARNING 1:

Some of these devices allow a considerable amount of current to pass, which can mean that many of the vehicle's systems are still operational when the main battery is disconnected. If a "memory-saver" is used, ensure that the circuit concerned is actually "dead" before carrying out any work on it!

✳✳ WARNING 2:

If work is to be performed around any of the airbag system components, the battery must be disconnected and no "memory saver" can be used. If a memory saver is used, power will be supplied to the airbag system and personal injury may result if the airbag is accidentally deployed.

To disconnect the battery for service procedures requiring power to be cut from the vehicle, first open the driver's door to disable Retained Accessory Power (RAP), then loosen the cable end bolt and disconnect the cable from the negative battery terminal. Isolate the cable end to prevent it from coming into accidental contact with the battery terminal.

2 Battery - emergency jump starting

Refer to the *Booster battery (jump) starting* procedure at the front of this manual.

1.1 Typical engine electrical system components (six-cylinder model shown)

1   *Ignition coils (under air intake resonator)*
2   *Underhood Electrical Center*
3   *Battery*
4   *Alternator*

3   Battery - check and replacement

※※ WARNING:

Hydrogen gas is produced by the battery, so keep open flames and lighted cigarettes away from it at all times. Always wear eye protection when working around a battery. Rinse off spilled electrolyte immediately with large amounts of water.

CHECK

▶ **Refer to illustrations 3.2 and 3.3**

1   The battery's surface charge must be removed before accurate voltage measurements can be made. Turn On the high beams for ten seconds, then turn them Off, let the vehicle stand for two minutes. Remove the battery from the vehicle (see Steps 4 through 10).

2   Check the battery state of charge. Visually inspect the indicator eye on the top of the battery, if the indicator eye is clear, charge the battery as described in Chapter 1. Next perform an open voltage circuit test using a digital voltmeter (see illustration). With the engine and all accessories Off, connect the negative probe of the voltmeter to the negative terminal of the battery and the positive probe to the positive terminal of the battery. The battery voltage should be 12.4 volts or more. If the battery is less than the specified voltage, charge the battery before proceeding to the next test. Do not proceed with the battery load test unless the battery charge is correct.

3   Perform a battery load test. An accurate check of the battery condition can only be performed with a load tester (available at most auto parts stores). This test evaluates the ability of the battery to operate the starter and other accessories during periods of heavy amperage draw (load). Install a special battery load testing tool onto the terminals (see illustration). Load test the battery according to the tool manufacturer's

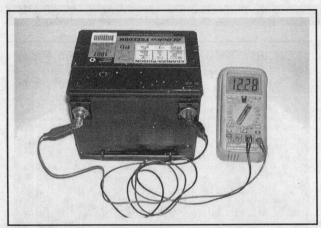

3.2 To test the open circuit voltage of the battery, connect a voltmeter to the battery - a fully charged battery should measure at least 12.4 volts (depending on outside air temperature)

3.3 Connect a battery load tester to the battery and check the battery condition under load following the tool manufacturers instructions

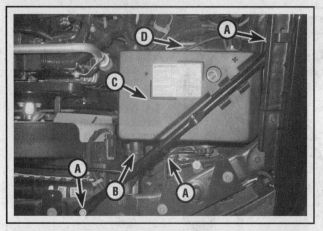

3.7 Before removing the battery, remove the brace bolts (A) and brace, the air duct (B), battery cover (C) and hold-down bolt and retainer (D)

3.11 Inspect the tray, retainer brackets and related fasteners for corrosion or damage - if necessary, remove the bolts (holding the tray to the inner fender panel) and the battery tray

instructions. This tool utilizes a carbon pile to increase the load demand (amperage draw) on the battery. Maintain the load on the battery for 15 seconds or less and observe that the battery voltage does not drop below 9.6 volts. If the battery condition is weak or defective, the tool will indicate this condition immediately.

➡**Note: Cold temperatures will cause the minimum voltage requirements to drop slightly. Follow the chart given in the tool manufacturer's instructions to compensate for cold climates. Minimum load voltage for freezing temperatures (32-degrees F) should be approximately 9.1 volts.**

REPLACEMENT

◆ **Refer to illustrations 3.7 and 3.11**

⁂ **WARNING:**

Refer to the Warning and Caution in Chapter 5, Section 1 under "Battery disconnection" before proceeding with the following Steps.

4 Disconnect the cable from the negative battery terminal.

5 Disconnect the positive battery cable.

6 On vehicles equipped with an engine block heater, remove the heater cord retainer from the battery cover.

7 Remove the battery brace bolts and the battery air duct from the cover (see illustration).

8 To remove the battery cover lift it straight up.

9 Remove the battery retainer nut and the retainer.

10 Lift the battery straight up to remove it.

11 If corrosion is evident, remove the battery tray and use a baking soda/water solution to clean the corroded area to prevent further oxidation (see illustration). Repaint the area as necessary using rust-resistant paint.

12 Clean and service the battery and cables (see Chapter 1).

13 If you are replacing the battery, make sure you purchase one that is identical to yours, with the same dimensions, amperage rating, cold cranking amps rating, etc. Make sure it is fully charged prior to installation in the vehicle.

14 Installation is the reverse of removal. Connect the positive cable first and the negative cable last.

15 After connecting the cables to the battery, apply a light coating of petroleum jelly or grease to the connections to help prevent corrosion.

4 Battery cables - replacement

◆ **Refer to illustrations 4.4a, 4.4b, 4.4c and 4.4d**

⁂ **WARNING:**

Refer to the Warning and Caution in Chapter 5, Section 1 under "Battery disconnection" before proceeding with the following Steps.

1 Periodically inspect the entire length of each battery cable for damage, cracked or burned insulation and corrosion. Poor battery cable connections can cause starting problems and decreased engine performance.

2 Check the cable-to-terminal connections at the ends of the cables for cracks, loose wire strands and corrosion. The presence of white, fluffy deposits under the insulation at the cable terminal connection is a sign that the cable is corroded and should be replaced. Check the

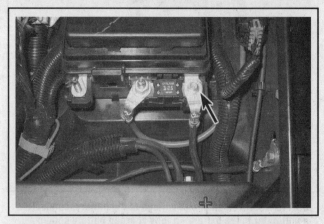

4.4a One branch of the positive cable is connected to the underhood electrical center

4.4b Disconnect the lead from the alternator

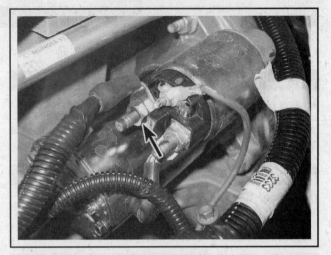

4.4c Disconnect the cable at the starter

terminals for distortion, missing mounting bolts and corrosion.

3   When removing the cables, always disconnect the negative cable first and hook it up last or the battery may be shorted by the tool used to loosen the cable clamps. Even if only the positive cable is being replaced, be sure to disconnect the negative cable first (see Chapter 1 for further information regarding battery cable maintenance).

4   Disconnect the old cables from the battery, then disconnect them at the opposite end. Detach the cables from the starter solenoid, underhood electrical center and ground terminals, as necessary (see illustrations). Note the routing of each cable to ensure correct installation.

5   If you are replacing either or both of the battery cables, take them with you when buying new cables. It is vitally important that you replace the cables with identical parts. Cables have characteristics that make them easy to identify: positive cables are usually red and larger in cross-section; ground cables are usually black and smaller in cross-section.

6   Clean the threads of the starter solenoid or ground connection with a wire brush to remove rust and corrosion. Apply a light coat of battery terminal corrosion inhibitor or petroleum jelly to the threads to prevent future corrosion.

7   Attach the cable to the terminal and tighten the mounting nut/

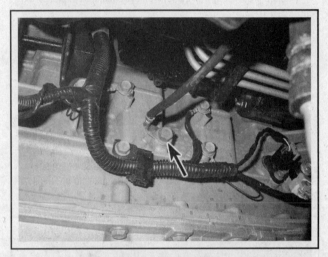

4.4d The negative cable is fastened to the engine block

bolt securely.

8   Before connecting a new cable to the battery, make sure that it reaches the battery without having to be stretched.

5   Ignition system - general information

All models are equipped with a distributorless ignition system. The ignition system consists of the battery, six or eight ignition coils (one per cylinder), spark plug boots, spark plugs, camshaft position sensor, crankshaft position sensor and the Powertrain Control Module (PCM).

On all models, the PCM controls the ignition timing and spark advance characteristics for the engine. The ignition timing is not adjustable.

The crankshaft position sensor produces a signal voltage to indicate crankshaft position and crankshaft speed. This signal is used by the Powertrain Control Module (PCM) to control the ignition system and ignition timing, and for misfire detection.

The camshaft position sensor operation is similar to a crankshaft

position sensor. The PCM uses the camshaft position sensor signal for fuel synchronization and, on the six-cylinder engine, camshaft actuator position phasing.

The ignition system is also equipped with a knock sensor to detect detonation, or spark knock (usually caused by the use of sub-standard fuel). The system uses a knock sensor in conjunction with the Powertrain Control Module (PCM) to control spark timing. If a knock signal is received, the PCM will retard the timing until the knock is eliminated. The knock sensor system allows the engine to use maximum spark advance without spark knock, which improves driveability and fuel economy.

6 Ignition system - check

▶ **Refer to illustration 6.4**

1   Before proceeding with the ignition system, check the following items:

   a) *Make sure the battery cable clamps, where they connect to the battery, are clean and tight.*
   b) *Test the condition of the battery (see Section 3). If it does not pass all the tests, replace it with a new battery.*
   c) *Check the ignition coil and ignition control module external wiring and connections.*
   d) *Check the related fuses inside the underhood electrical center (see Chapter 12). If they're burned, determine the cause and repair the circuit.*

2   If the engine turns over but won't start or has a severe misfire, make sure there is sufficient secondary ignition voltage to fire the spark plugs.

6.4 To use a calibrated ignition tester, remove an ignition coil, connect the tester to the spark plug boot and clip the tester to a convenient ground. Crank the engine over; if there's enough power to fire the plug, bright blue sparks will be visible between the electrode tip and the tester body (weak spark or intermittent spark are the same as no spark)

3   Disable the fuel system by removing the fuel pump relay from the underhood electrical center (see Chapter 12).

4   Remove an ignition coil (see Section 7) from one of the spark plugs and attach a calibrated ignition system tester (available at most auto parts stores) to the spark plug boot. Connect the clip on the tester to a bolt or metal bracket on the engine (see illustration). Crank the engine and watch the end of the tester to see if bright blue, well-defined sparks occur (weak spark or intermittent spark is the same as no spark).

5   If spark occurs, sufficient voltage is reaching the plug to fire it. Repeat the check at the remaining cylinders to verify that the ignition coil(s), spark plug boots and control systems are functioning properly. If the ignition system is operating properly the problem lies elsewhere; i.e., a mechanical or fuel system problem. However, the spark plugs may be fouled, so remove and check them as described in Chapter 1.

6   If none of the cylinders has spark check the PCM I fuse in the underhood fuse box.

7   If no spark occurs at one or more cylinders, check for battery voltage to the ignition coils from the ignition switch. Attach a 12 volt test light to the battery negative (-) terminal or other good ground. Disconnect the electrical connector from one of the ignition coils and check for power at the pink wire terminal. Battery voltage should be available with the ignition key On. If there is no battery voltage present, check the wiring and/or circuit between the underhood electrical center and ignition coil connector (don't forget to check the fuses). Also check the black wire terminal for continuity to battery ground. If there is battery voltage at the coil, but there is no spark from the coil, the coil, crankshaft position sensor, PCM or wiring are likely culprits.

8   Check for a trigger signal from the PCM. Attach the lead of a test light to the positive battery terminal and touch the probe of the test light to the ignition control circuit terminal of an ignition coil (it's the center terminal in the connector). Crank the engine. The test light should blink with the engine cranking if a trigger signal is present. Check each coil, if necessary. If a trigger signal is present at the coil, the power and ground circuits are good and there is no spark, replace the ignition coil. If a trigger signal is not present, check the crankshaft position sensor (see Chapter 6). If the crankshaft position sensor is good, check the circuits from the coil to the PCM. If the circuits are good, have the PCM checked by a dealer service department or other qualified repair shop.

7   Ignition coils - removal and installation

SIX-CYLINDER MODELS

▶ **Refer to illustrations 7.3, 7.4a, 7.4b and 7.5**

1   Disconnect the cable from the negative battery terminal.

2   Remove the air intake duct and resonator from the throttle body (see Chapter 4).

3   Disconnect the electrical connector from the ignition coil (see illustration).

4   Remove the ignition coil mounting bolt and remove the assembly from the valve cover (see illustrations).

5   Check the seals on the coils for cracks or other signs of damage, replacing them as necessary (see illustration). Installation is otherwise the reverse of removal. Tighten the mounting bolt to the torque listed in this Chapter's Specifications.

V8 MODELS

▶ **Refer to illustration 7.9**

6   Disconnect the cable from the negative battery terminal.

7   The ignition coils may be removed from each cylinder bank as a complete assembly or removed from the mounting bracket individually.

8   If removing the complete assembly, disconnect the ignition coil main electrical connector. Disconnect the spark plug wires from the spark plugs. Remove the ignition coil bracket mounting nuts/bolts and remove the assembly from the engine.

9   If removing the individual coil, disconnect the spark plug wire from the coil. Remove the ignition coil mounting screws and remove the ignition coil from the bracket (see illustration).

10   Installation is the reverse of removal

7.3 Disengage the connector lock then unplug the electrical connector . . .

7.4a . . . remove the ignition coil mounting bolt . . .

7.4b . . . then pull the coil from the valve cover

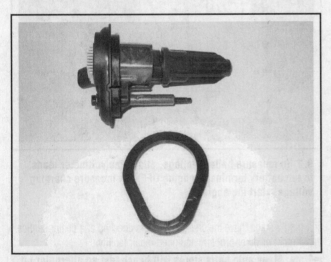

7.5 Install new seal(s) on the ignition coil(s) if they are damaged or hardened

7.9 Remove the ignition coil mounting screws (arrows)

8   Charging system - general information and precautions

The main components of the charging system are an alternator (with an integral voltage regulator), the battery and the wiring connecting the components. The components work together to supply electrical power for the electrical system and maintain the battery in a charged condition. The alternator is driven by the drivebelt at the front of the engine.

All models are equipped with either a model AD-230 or AD-244 alternator. AD type alternators should be considered non-serviceable and, if defective, exchanged as cores for new or rebuilt units. An identification number and amperage rating is stamped on the alternator housing. Refer to these numbers to obtain the correct replacement alternator, if necessary.

The purpose of the voltage regulator is to limit the alternator voltage output to a preset value. This prevents power surges and circuit overloads during peak voltage output. On all models with which this manual is concerned, the voltage regulator is integral with the alternator.

The charging system doesn't ordinarily require periodic maintenance. However, the drivebelt, battery and wires and connections should be inspected at the intervals outlined in Chapter 1.

The instrument panel warning light should come on when the ignition key is turned to START, then go off immediately after the engine has started. If the warning light stays on or comes on when the engine is running, a charging system problem has occurred (see Section 9).

2007 and later models are equipped with Electrical Power Management (EPM). This system monitors and controls the charging system, runs continuous diagnostics, and alerts the driver of any concerns within the charging system. Components of the system include the alternator, alternator-battery control module, Powertrain Control Module (PCM), and the instrument cluster. If a fault in the system is detected, the instrument cluster will display "CHARGING SYSTEM FAILURE" or "SERVICE CHARGING SYSTEM." Corresponding diagnostic trouble codes will be set and retained in the Body Control Module (BCM).

Be very careful when making electrical circuit connections to a vehicle equipped with an alternator and note the following:

a) *When reconnecting wires to the alternator from the battery, be sure to note the polarity.*

b) *Before using arc welding equipment to repair any part of the vehicle, disconnect the wires from the alternator and the battery terminals.*

c) *Always disconnect both battery leads before using a battery charger.*

d) *The alternator is turned by an engine drivebelt which could cause serious injury if your hands, hair or clothes become entangled in it with the engine running.*

e) *Because the alternator is connected directly to the battery, it could arc or cause a fire if overloaded or shorted out.*

f) *Wrap a plastic bag over the alternator and secure it with rubber bands before steam cleaning the engine.*

9   Charging system - check

▶ **Refer to illustration 9.2**

➡ **Note: These vehicles are equipped with an On-Board Diagnostic (OBD) system that is useful for detecting charging system problems. Refer to Chapter 6 for the list of diagnostic codes and procedures for obtaining the codes.**

1   If a malfunction occurs in the charging circuit, do not immediately assume that the alternator is causing the problem. First check the following items:

a) *The battery cables where they connect to the battery. Make sure the connections are clean and tight.*

b) *The battery electrolyte specific gravity (by observing the charge indicator on the battery). If it is low, charge the battery.*

c) *Check the external alternator wiring and connections.*

d) *Check the drivebelt condition and tension (see Chapter 1).*

e) *Check the alternator mounting bolts for tightness.*

f) *Run the engine and check the alternator for abnormal noise.*

2   Connect a voltmeter to the positive and negative battery terminals (see illustration). Check the battery voltage with the engine off. It should be approximately 12.4 to 12.6 volts, if the battery is fully charged.

3   Start the engine and check the battery voltage again. It should now be greater than the voltage recorded in Step 2, but not more than 14.7 volts.

4   If the indicated voltage reading is less or more than the specified

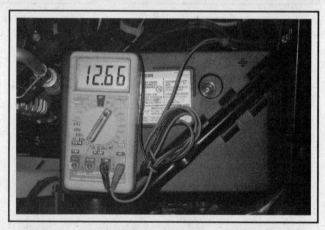

9.2 To measure battery voltage, attach the voltmeter leads to the battery terminals (engine OFF) - to measure charging voltage, start the engine

charging voltage, have the charging system checked at a dealer service department or other properly equipped repair facility.

➡ **Note: Many auto parts stores will bench test an alternator off the vehicle. Refer to your local auto parts store regarding their policy, many will perform this service free of charge.**

10 Alternator - removal and installation

▶ **Refer to illustrations 10.3a, 10.3b, 10.3c, 10.3d, 10.4a and 10.4b**

1 Disconnect the cable from the negative battery terminal.
2 Remove the drivebelt (see Chapter 1).
3 On six-cylinder models, unbolt the air conditioning line mounting bracket located at the engine lift hook (see illustration). Remove the right engine lift hook and the alternator mounting bolts, then remove the alternator from the engine (see illustrations). Disconnect the electrical connectors from the alternator (see illustration).

4 On V8 models, disconnect the output wire and the electrical connector from the alternator (see illustration). Remove the mounting bolts and remove the alternator from the engine (see illustration).

10.3a Remove the bolt securing the air conditioning line to the engine lifting hook

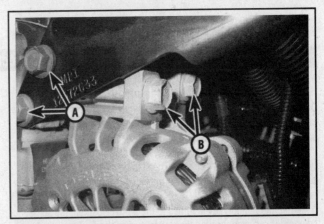

10.3b Remove the engine lift hook bolts (A), the alternator upper mounting bolts (B) . . .

10.3c . . . and the lower mounting bolt

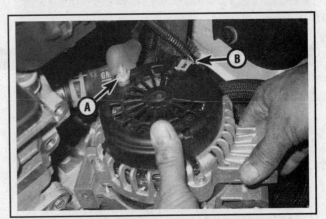

10.3d Lift the alternator away from its mount, remove the nut and wire terminal from the output terminal (A) and disconnect the alternator electrical connector (B)

10.4a Remove the nut and wire terminal from the output terminal (A) and disconnect the alternator electrical connector (B)

10.4b Remove the alternator mounting bolts (arrows)

5   If you are replacing the alternator, take the old one with you when purchasing a replacement unit. Make sure the new/rebuilt unit looks identical to the old alternator. Look at the terminals - they should be the same in number, size and location as the terminals on the old alternator. Finally, look at the identification numbers - they will be stamped into the housing. Make sure the numbers are the same on both alternators.

6   Many new/rebuilt alternators do not have a pulley installed, so you may have to switch the pulley from the old unit to the new/rebuilt

one. When buying an alternator, find out the shop's policy regarding pulleys; some shops will perform this service free of charge.

7   Installation is the reverse of removal. Tighten the mounting bolts to the torque listed in this Chapter's Specifications.

8   Install the drivebelt (see Chapter 1).

9   Check the charging voltage to verify proper operation of the alternator (see Section 9).

11   Starting system - general information and precautions

The starter motor assembly is a permanent magnet, planetary gear drive starter motor. The starter motor assembly is serviced as a complete unit. If any component of the starter motor fails, including the solenoid, the entire assembly must be replaced.

The sole function of the starting system is to turn over the engine quickly enough to allow it to start. The starting system consists of the battery, starter motor assembly and the wiring connecting the components.

When the ignition key is turned to the START position, the starter solenoid is actuated through the starter control circuit. The starter solenoid then connects the battery to the starter motor. The battery supplies the electrical energy to the starter motor, which does the actual work of

cranking the engine.

Always observe the following precautions when working on the starting system:

a) *Excessive cranking of the starter motor can overheat it and cause serious damage. Never operate the starter motor for more than 15 seconds at a time without pausing to allow it to cool for at least two minutes.*

b) *The starter is connected directly to the battery and could arc or cause a fire if mishandled, overloaded or shorted.*

c) *Always detach the cable from the negative terminal of the battery before working on the starting system.*

12   Starter motor and circuit - check

▶ **Refer to illustration 12.4**

1   If a malfunction occurs in the starting circuit, do not immediately assume that the starter is causing the problem. First, check the following items:

   Make sure the battery cable clamps, where they connect to the battery, are clean and tight.
   Check the condition of the battery cables (see Section 4). Replace any defective battery cables with new parts.
   Test the condition of the battery (see Section 3). If it does not pass all the tests, replace it with a new battery.
   Check the starter motor wiring and connections.
   Check the starter motor mounting bolts for tightness.
   Check the related fuses in the engine compartment fuse box (see Chapter 12). If they're blown, determine the cause and repair the circuit.
   Check the ignition switch circuit for correct operation (see Chapter 12).
   Check the starter relay (located in the underhood electrical center) for proper operation (see Chapter 12).
   Check the operation of the Park/Neutral position switch (see Chapter 7). These systems must operate correctly to provide battery voltage to the starter relay.

2   If the starter does not activate when the ignition switch is turned to the start position, check for battery voltage to the starter solenoid. This will determine if the solenoid is receiving the correct voltage from the starter relay. Install a 12-volt test light or a voltmeter to the starter solenoid terminal. While an assistant turns the ignition switch to the start position, observe the test light or voltmeter. The test light should shine brightly or battery voltage should be indicated on the voltmeter.

If voltage is not available to the starter solenoid, refer to the wiring diagrams in Chapter 12 and check the fuses, ignition switch, starter relay and related wiring in series with the starting system. If voltage is available but there is no movement from the starter motor, remove the starter from the engine (see Section 13) and bench test the starter (see Step 4).

3   If the starter turns over slowly, check the starter cranking voltage and the current draw from the battery. This test must be performed with

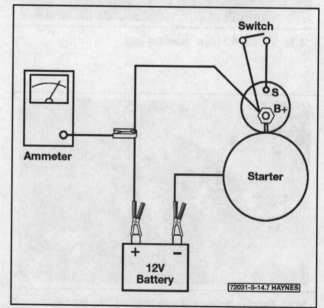

12.4 Starter motor bench testing details

the starter assembly on the engine. Crank the engine over (for 10 seconds or less) and observe the battery voltage. It should not drop below 8.5 volts. Also, observe the current draw using an amp meter. Typically a starter amperage draw should not exceed 350 amps. If the starter motor amperage draw is excessive, have it tested by a dealer service department or other qualified repair shop. There are several conditions that may affect the starter cranking potential. The battery must be in good condition and the battery cold-cranking rating must not be underrated for the particular application. Be sure to check the battery specifications carefully. The battery terminals and cables must be clean and not corroded. Also, in cases of extreme cold temperatures, make sure the battery and/or engine block is warmed before performing the tests.

4   If the starter is receiving voltage but does not activate, remove and check the starter motor assembly on the bench. Most likely the

starter motor or solenoid is defective. In some rare cases, the engine may be seized so be sure to try and rotate the crankshaft pulley before proceeding. With the starter assembly mounted in a vise on the bench, install one jumper cable from the positive terminal of a test battery to the B+ terminal on the starter. Install another jumper cable from the negative terminal of the battery to the body of the starter (see illustration). Install a starter switch and apply battery voltage to the solenoid S terminal (for 10 seconds or less) and observe the solenoid plunger, shift lever and overrunning clutch extend and rotate the pinion drive. If the pinion drive extends but does not rotate, the solenoid is operating but the starter motor is defective. If there is no movement but the solenoid clicks, the solenoid and/or the starter motor is defective. If the solenoid plunger extends and rotates the pinion drive, the starter assembly is operating properly.

13 Starter motor - removal and installation

SIX-CYLINDER MODELS

▶ **Refer to illustrations 13.3 and 13.4**

1   Disconnect the cable from the negative battery terminal.
2   Loosen the left front wheel lug nuts, then raise the front of the vehicle and support it securely on jackstands. Remove the left front wheel.
3   Disconnect the electrical connections at the starter (see illustration).
4   Remove the starter nut (top) and bolt (bottom) then remove the starter through the fenderwell (see illustration).
5   Installation is the reverse of removal. Tighten the starter mounting fasteners to the torque listed in this Chapter's Specifications.
6   Install the wheel and lug nuts. Lower the vehicle and tighten the lug nuts to the torque listed in the Chapter 1 Specifications.

V8 MODELS

▶ **Refer to illustrations 13.9, 13.11, 13.12 and 13.14**

7   Disconnect the cable from the negative battery terminal.
8   Raise the vehicle and support it securely on jackstands.
9   Detach any brackets from the rear steering gear crossmember,

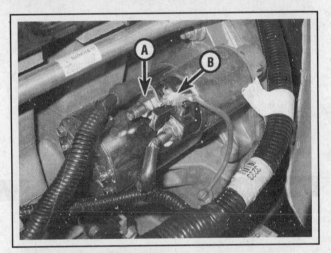

13.3 Remove the nuts and disconnect the battery cable (A) and the solenoid terminal (B) from the starter motor (this photo was taken from above, with the intake manifold removed for clarity; you'll be working through the fenderwell)

then remove it (see illustration) or, remove the catalytic converter (see Chapter 6) for clearance as necessary.

➡**Note: It should not be necessary to remove both components.**

13.4 Remove the starter mounting nut and bolt

13.9 The location for the rear steering gear crossmember (A) and the bottom fasteners (B) (the horizontal fasteners are hidden from view)

13.11 Remove the transmission bellhousing cover bolt (arrow)

13.12 Remove the starter mounting bolts (arrows)

13.14 Remove the nuts and disconnect the battery cable (A) and the solenoid terminal (B) from the starter motor

10 Remove the engine splash shield.

11 Remove the starter solenoid shield and the transmission bell housing bolt (see illustration).

12 Remove the starter mounting bolts (see illustration).

13 Carefully lower the starter with the terminals facing toward the front of the vehicle.

14 Disconnect the wires from the terminals on the starter solenoid (see illustration) and remove the starter from the vehicle.

15 Installation is the reverse of removal.

Specifications

General

Battery voltage	
Engine off	12.0 to 12.6 volts
Engine running	13.5 to 14.7 volts
Alternator output	150 amps

Torque specifications   Ft-lbs (unless otherwise indicated)

➡**Note: One foot-pound (ft-lb) of torque is equivalent to 12 inch-pounds (in-lbs) of torque. Torque values below approximately 15 ft-lbs are expressed in inch-pounds, since most foot-pound torque wrenches are not accurate at these smaller values.**

Alternator mounting bolts	37
Starter mounting bolt/nut	37
Ignition coil bolts	89 in-lbs

6

EMISSIONS AND ENGINE CONTROL SYSTEMS

1 General information

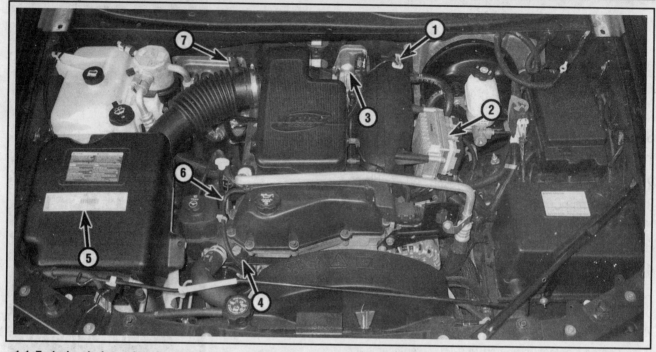

1.1 Typical emission and engine control system components (six-cylinder model shown)

1 *Manifold Absolute Pressure (MAP) sensor*
2 *Powertrain Control Module (PCM)*
3 *Throttle body*
4 *Camshaft Position (CMP) sensor*

5 *Vehicle Emissions Control Information (VECI) label*
6 *Camshaft Position Actuator Solenoid*
7 *Intake Air Temperature (IAT) sensor*

♦ **Refer to illustrations 1.1 and 1.6**

To prevent pollution of the atmosphere from incompletely burned and evaporating gases, and to maintain good driveability and fuel economy, a number of emission control systems are incorporated (see illustrations). They include the:

Electronic engine control system
Crankcase ventilation system
Exhaust gas recirculation system
Evaporative emissions control system
Secondary air injection system
Catalytic converter

All of these systems are linked, directly or indirectly, to the emission control system.

The Sections in this Chapter include general descriptions, checking procedures within the scope of the home mechanic (when possible) and component replacement procedures for each of the systems listed above.

Before assuming that an emissions control system is malfunctioning, check the fuel and ignition systems carefully. The diagnosis of some emission control devices requires specialized tools, equipment and training. If checking and servicing become too difficult or if a procedure is beyond your ability, consult a dealer service department or other properly equipped repair facility. Remember, the most frequent cause of emissions problems is simply a loose or broken vacuum hose or wire, so always check the hose and wiring connections first.

This doesn't mean, however, that emission control systems are particularly difficult to maintain and repair. You can quickly and easily perform many checks and do most of the regular maintenance at home

with common tune-up and hand tools.

➡**Note: Because of a Federally mandated warranty which covers the emission control system components, check with your dealer about warranty coverage before working on any emissions-related systems. Once the warranty has expired, you may wish to perform some of the component checks and/or replacement procedures in this Chapter to say money.**

Pay close attention to any special precautions outlined in this Chapter. It should be noted that the illustrations of the various systems may not exactly match the system installed on the vehicle you're working

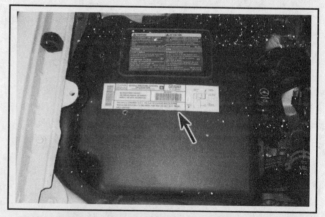

1.6 The Vehicle Emission Control Information (VECI) label is located in the engine compartment and contains information on the emission devices on your vehicle, vacuum line routing, etc.

on because of changes made by the manufacturer during production or from year-to-year.

A Vehicle Emissions Control Information (VECI) label is located in the engine compartment (see illustration). This label contains impor-tant emissions specifications and adjustment information, as well as a vacuum hose schematic with emissions components identified. When servicing the engine or emissions systems, the VECI label in your par-ticular vehicle should always be checked for up-to-date information.

2   On-Board Diagnostic (OBD) system and trouble codes

DIAGNOSTIC TOOL INFORMATION

▶ **Refer to illustrations 2.1 and 2.2**

1   A digital multimeter is necessary for checking fuel injection and emission related components (see illustration). A digital volt-ohmmeter is preferred over the older style analog multimeter for several reasons. The analog multimeter cannot display the volts, ohms or amps mea-surement in hundredths and thousandths increments. When working with electronic circuits which are often very low voltage, this accurate reading is most important. Another good reason for the digital multim-eter is the high impedance circuit. The digital multimeter is equipped with a high resistance internal circuitry (10 million ohms). Because a voltmeter is hooked up in parallel with the circuit when testing, it is vital that none of the voltage being measured should be allowed to travel the parallel path set up by the meter itself. This dilemma does not show itself when measuring large amounts of voltage (9 to 12 volt circuits) but if you are measuring a low voltage circuit such as the oxygen sen-sor signal voltage, a fraction of a volt may be a significant amount when diagnosing a problem. However, there are several exceptions where using an analog voltmeter may be necessary to test certain sensors.

2   Hand-held scanners are the most powerful and versatile tools for analyzing engine management systems used on later model vehicles (see illustration). Each brand scan tool must be examined carefully to match the year, make and model of the vehicle you are working on. Often, interchangeable cartridges are available to access the particular manufacturer (Ford, GM, Chrysler, etc.). Some manufacturers will specify by continent (Asia, Europe, USA, etc.).

3   With the arrival of the Federally mandated emission control system (OBD-II), a specially designed scanner has been developed. Several took manufacturers have released OBD-II scan tools for the home mechanic. Ask the parts salesman at a local auto parts store for additional information concerning availability and cost.

ON-BOARD DIAGNOSTIC SYSTEM GENERAL DESCRIPTION

4   All models described in this manual are equipped with the sec-ond generation On-Board Diagnostic (OBD-II) system. The system con-sists of an onboard computer, known as the Powertrain Control Module (PCM), information sensors and output actuators.

5   The information sensors monitor various functions of the engine and send data to the PCM. Based on the data and the information programmed into the computer's memory, the PCM generates output signals to control various engine functions via control relays, solenoids and other output actuators. The PCM is specifically calibrated to opti-mize the emissions, fuel economy and driveability of the vehicle.

6   Because of a Federally mandated warranty which covers the emis-sions system components and because any owner-induced damage to the PCM, the sensors and/or the control devices may void the warranty, it isn't a good idea to attempt diagnosis or replacement of the system com-ponents while the vehicle is under warranty. Take the vehicle to a dealer service department if the PCM or a system component malfunctions.

INFORMATION SENSORS

7   **Accelerator pedal position (APP) sensor** - The APP sensor is mounted on the accelerator pedal assembly. The APP consists of two individual position sensors within one housing. There are two separate signal, low reference, and 5-volt reference circuits. Position sensor 1 voltage increases as the accelerator pedal is depressed. Position sensor 2 voltage decreases as the accelerator pedal is depressed. This sensor along with several others are needed for the Throttle Actuator Control System operation.

8   **Camshaft Position (CMP) sensor** - The Camshaft Position sensor provides information on camshaft position. The PCM uses this

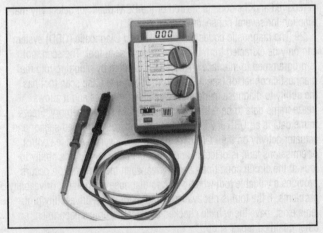

2.1 Digital multimeters can be used for testing all types of circuits; because of their high impedance, they are much more accurate than analog meters for measuring low-voltage computer circuits

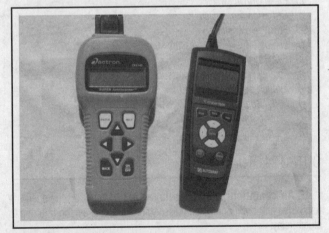

2.2 Scanners like these from Actron and AutoXray are powerful diagnostic aids - they can tell you just about anything you want to know about your engine management system

information, along with the crankshaft position sensor information, to control fuel injection synchronization.

9 **Crankshaft Position (CKP) sensor** - The Crankshaft Position sensor senses crankshaft position (TDC) during each engine revolution. The PCM uses this information to control ignition timing and for misfire detection.

10 **Engine Coolant Temperature (ECT) sensor** - The Engine Coolant Temperature sensor monitors engine coolant temperature. The PCM uses this information to control fuel injection duration and ignition timing.

11 **Intake Air Temperature (IAT) sensor** - The Intake Air Temperature sensor monitors the temperature of the air entering the intake manifold. The PCM uses this information to control fuel injection duration.

12 **Knock Sensor (KS)** - The Knock Sensor is a piezoelectric element that detects the sound of engine detonation, or "pinging." The PCM uses the input signal from the knock sensor to recognize detonation and retard spark advance to avoid engine damage.

13 **Manifold Absolute Pressure (MAP) sensor** - The Manifold Absolute Pressure sensor monitors intake manifold pressure and ambient barometric pressure. The PCM uses this input signal to determine engine load and adjust fuel injection duration accordingly.

14 **Mass Airflow (MAF) sensor** - The Mass Airflow Sensor measures the amount of air passing through the sensor body and ultimately entering the engine. The PCM uses this information to control fuel delivery.

15 **Oxygen (O2) sensor** - The oxygen sensors generate a voltage signal that varies with the varying oxygen content of the exhaust gas. The PCM uses this information to determine if the fuel system is running rich or lean and make adjustments accordingly.

16 **Throttle Position Sensor (TPS)** - The Throttle Position Sensor senses throttle movement and position. This signal enables the PCM to determine when the throttle is closed, in a cruise position, or wide open. The PCM uses this information to control fuel delivery and ignition timing. Note that the TPS on this vehicle is an integral part of the throttle body and must be replaced as a unit.

17 **Vehicle Speed Sensor (VSS)** - The Vehicle Speed Sensor provides information to the PCM to indicate vehicle speed.

18 **Miscellaneous PCM inputs** - In addition to the various sensors, the PCM monitors various switches and circuits to determine vehicle operating conditions. The switches and circuits include:

a) *Air conditioning system*
b) *Battery voltage*
c) *Brake On/Off switch*
d) *Cruise control system*
e) *EGR valve position*
f) *Engine oil level and pressure*
g) *EVAP system*
h) *Fuel level and fuel tank pressure*
i) *Ignition switch*
j) *Park/Neutral Position (PNP) switch*
k) *Sensor signal and ground circuits*
l) *Transmission controls*

OUTPUT ACTUATORS

19 **Air conditioning clutch relay** - The PCM controls the operation of the air conditioning compressor clutch with the air conditioning clutch relay.

20 **Camshaft Position Actuator System** - The PCM pulses voltage to the cam position actuator solenoid to control the exhaust camshaft timing as required for optimal engine operation.

21 **Service Engine Soon light** - The PCM will illuminate the Service Engine Soon light if a malfunction in the electronic engine control system occurs.

22 **Engine cooling fan relay** - The engine cooling fan is controlled by the PCM according to information received from the Engine Coolant Temperature sensor.

23 **EVAP canister purge and vent valve solenoids** - The evaporative emission canister purge and vent valve solenoids are operated by the PCM to purge the fuel vapor canister and route fuel vapor to the intake manifold for combustion.

24 **Secondary Air Injection (AIR) pump and shut-off valve solenoid** - On 2004 and later models, the PCM operates a secondary air injection pump and shut-off valve solenoid to direct fresh air into the exhaust stream. This lowers emission levels under certain operating conditions.

25 **Fuel injectors** - The PCM opens the fuel injectors individually in firing order sequence. The PCM also controls the time the injector is held open (pulse width). The pulse width of the injector (measured in milliseconds) determines the amount of fuel delivered. For more information on the fuel delivery system and the fuel injectors, including injector replacement, refer to Chapter 4.

26 **Fuel pump relay** - The fuel pump relay is activated by the PCM with the ignition switch in the Start or Run position. When the ignition switch is turned on, the relay is activated to supply initial line pressure to the system. For more information on fuel pump check and replacement, refer to Chapter 4.

27 **Ignition coils/control module** - The PCM controls ignition timing through the ignition coils/control module depending on the engine operation conditions. Refer to Chapter 5 for more information on the ignition coil(s) or ignition control module.

OBTAINING DIAGNOSTIC TROUBLE CODES

♦ **Refer to illustration 2.29**

➡**Note: The diagnostic trouble codes on all models can only be extracted from the Powertrain Control Module (PCM) using a specialized scan tool. Have the vehicle diagnosed by a dealer service department or other qualified automotive repair facility if the proper scan tool is not available.**

28 The PCM will illuminate the SERVICE ENGINE SOON light (also known as the Malfunction Indicator Lamp) on the dash if it recognizes a fault in the system. The light will remain illuminated until the problem is repaired and the code is cleared or the PCM does not detect any malfunction for several consecutive drive cycles.

29 The diagnostic codes for the On-Board Diagnostic (OBD) system can only be extracted from the PCM using a scan tool. The scan tool is programmed to interface with the OBD system by plugging into the diagnostic connector (see illustration). When used, the scan tool has the ability to diagnose in-depth driveability problems and it allows freeze frame data to be retrieved from the PCM stored memory. Freeze frame data is an OBD-II PCM feature that records all related sensor and actuator activity on the PCM data stream whenever an engine control or emissions fault is detected and a trouble code is set. This ability to look at the circuit conditions and values when the malfunction occurs provides a valuable tool when trying to diagnose intermittent driveability problems. If the tool is not available and intermittent driveability problems exist, have the vehicle checked at a dealer service department or other qualified repair shop.

CLEARING DIAGNOSTIC TROUBLE CODES

30 After the system has been repaired, the codes must be cleared

from the PCM memory. The preferred method is with a scan tool, but the codes can be cleared by disconnecting the battery power from the PCM for a minimum of thirty seconds. Battery power can be disconnected from the PCM by removing the PCM fuse, disconnecting the PCM power connector near the positive battery terminal (if equipped) or by disconnecting the negative battery cable from the battery. Always clear the codes from the PCM before starting the engine after a new electronic emission control component is installed onto the engine. The PCM stores the operating parameters of each sensor. The PCM may set a trouble code if a new sensor is allowed to operate before the parameters from the old sensor have been erased.

DIAGNOSTIC TROUBLE CODE IDENTIFICATION

31 The accompanying list of diagnostic trouble codes is a compilation of all the codes that may be encountered using a generic scan tool. Additional trouble codes may be obtainable with the use of the

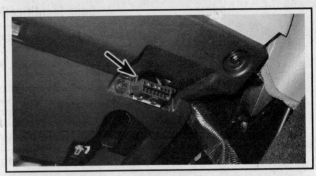

2.29 The diagnostic connector is typically located under the instrument panel

manufacturer specific scan tool. Not all codes pertain to all models and not all codes will illuminate the Service Engine Soon light when set. All models require a scan tool to access the diagnostic trouble codes.

Code	Code Identification
P0013	Camshaft actuator solenoid circuit fault
P0014	Camshaft phase angle error
P0105	MAP sensor voltage is not within the predicted range
P0107	Manifold absolute pressure sensor circuit, low input
P0108	Manifold absolute pressure sensor circuit, high input
P0112	Intake air temperature circuit, low input
P0113	Intake air temperature circuit, high input
P0117	Engine coolant temperature circuit, low input
P0118	Engine coolant temperature circuit, high input
P0122	Throttle position sensor circuit, low input
P0123	Throttle position sensor circuit, high input
P0125	Insufficient coolant temperature for closed loop fuel control
PO128	Insufficient ambient temperature (ECT)
P0130	Oxygen sensor loop status parameter is open
P0131	Oxygen sensor circuit, low voltage (pre-converter sensor, left bank)
P0132	Oxygen sensor circuit, high voltage (pre-converter sensor, left bank)
P0133	Oxygen sensor circuit, slow response (pre-converter sensor, left bank)
P0134	Oxygen sensor circuit - no activity detected (pre-converter sensor, left bank)
P0135	Oxygen sensor heater circuit malfunction (pre-converter sensor, left bank)
P0137	Oxygen sensor circuit, low voltage (post-converter sensor, left bank)
P0138	Oxygen sensor circuit, high voltage (post-converter sensor, left bank)
P0140	Oxygen sensor circuit - no activity detected (post-converter sensor, left bank)
P0141	Oxygen sensor heater circuit malfunction (post-converter sensor, left bank)
P0171	System too lean, left bank

Code	Code Identification
P0172	System too rich, left bank
P0175	System too rich, right bank
P0201 through P0208	Cylinder specific injector control circuit fault
P0220	Throttle Position Sensor 2 circuit
P0222	Throttle Position Sensor 2 circuit low voltage
P0223	Throttle Position Sensor 2 circuit high voltage
P0230	Fuel pump relay control circuit
P0300	Engine misfire detected
P0301 through P0308	Cylinder specific misfire detected
P0324	Knock sensor module performance
P0325	Knock sensor circuit Bank 1
P0326	Knock sensor diagnostic circuit fault
P0327	Knock sensor circuit, low output (front knock sensor)
P0328	Knock sensor 1 circuit high voltage
P0330	Knock sensor circuit Bank 2
P0332	Knock sensor circuit, low output (rear knock sensor on six-cylinder, Bank 2 on V8)
P0333	Knock sensor circuit high voltage Bank 2
P0335	Crankshaft position sensor circuit malfunction
P0336	Crankshaft position sensor circuit, range or performance problem
P0340	Camshaft position sensor circuit
P0341	Camshaft position sensor circuit, range or performance problem
P0351	Ignition coil control circuit (Cylinder #1)
P0352	Ignition coil control circuit (Cylinder #2)
P0353	Ignition coil control circuit (Cylinder #3)
P0354	Ignition coil control circuit (Cylinder #4)
P0355	Ignition coil control circuit (Cylinder #5)
P0356	Ignition coil control circuit (Cylinder #6)
P0357	Ignition coil control circuit (Cylinder #7)
P0358	Ignition coil control circuit (Cylinder #8)
P0411	Secondary Air Injection System incorrect air flow detected
P0412	Secondary Air Injection solenoid control circuit
P0418	Secondary Air Injection pump control circuit
P0420	Catalyst system efficiency below threshold, left bank
P0430	Catalyst system efficiency below threshold bank 2
P0440	Evaporative emission control system malfunction
P0442	Evaporative emission control system, small leak detected

Code	Code Identification
P0446	Evaporative emission control system, vent system performance
P0449	Evaporative emission control system, vent control circuit fault
P0452	Evaporative emission control system, pressure sensor low input
P0453	Evaporative emission control system, pressure sensor high input
P0455	Evaporative Emission System large leak detected
P0480	Cooling fan relay control circuit did not change state
P0483	Cooling fan speed error
P0493	Cooling fan speed error
P0495	Cooling fan speed high
P0502	Vehicle speed sensor circuit low output
P0503	Vehicle speed sensor signal intermittent
P0506	Idle control system, rpm lower than expected
P0507	Idle control system, rpm higher than expected
P0526	Loss of cooling fan speed signal
P0556	Brake Booster Pressure Sensor performance
P0557	Brake Booster Pressure Sensor circuit low voltage
P0558	Brake Booster Pressure Sensor circuit high voltage
P0562	System voltage low
P0563	System voltage high
P0601	Powertrain Control Module, memory error
P0602	Powertrain Control module, programming error
P0603	Powertrain Control Module, memory reset error
P0604	Powertrain Control Module, memory error (RAM)
P0605	Powertrain Control Module, memory error (ROM)
P0606	Control Module internal performance
P0607	Control Module performance
P0615	Starter relay control circuit
P0621	Generator L terminal circuit
P0622	Generator F terminal circuit
P0705	Transmission range sensor (Park/Neutral position switch), circuit malfunction
P0711	Transmission fluid temperature sensor circuit out-of-range
P0712	Transmission fluid temperature sensor circuit low input
P0713	Transmission fluid temperature sensor circuit high input
P0719	Torque converter clutch brake switch circuit low
P0724	Torque converter clutch brake switch circuit high
P0740	Torque converter clutch enable solenoid circuit

Code	Code Identification
P0741	Torque converter clutch system stuck off
P0742	Torque converter clutch system stuck on
P0748	Pressure control solenoid valve circuit
P0751	1-2 shift solenoid performance
P0753	1-2 shift solenoid circuit
P0756	2-3 shift solenoid performance
P0758	2-3 shift solenoid circuit
P0785	3-2 shift solenoid circuit
P1101	Intake air flow system performance
P1120	Throttle position sensor 1 low voltage
P1133	Oxygen sensor insufficient switching (pre-converter sensor)
P1134	Oxygen sensor transition time ratio (pre-converter sensor)
P1137	Oxygen sensor low voltage (post-converter sensor)
P1138	Oxygen sensor high voltage (post-converter sensor)
P1171	System lean during acceleration
P1220	Throttle position sensor out of range
P1221	Throttle position sensor, discrepancy between two sensors
P1258	Engine coolant overtemperature protection mode active
P1271	Excessive voltage difference between Accelerator Pedal Position (APP) sensor 1 and 2
P1275	Accelerator pedal position sensor, voltage too low or too high
P1280	Accelerator pedal position sensor, disagreement between sensors 1 and 2
P1336	Crankshaft position sensor system variation not learned
P1345	Crankshaft position sensor/Camshaft position sensor correlation
P1380	Electronic brake control module rough road sensing error
P1381	No serial data from electronic brake control module
P1441	EVAP system flow during non-purge
P1481	Loss of cooling fan speed signal
P1482	Incorrect voltage at cooling fan clutch circuit
P1484	Cooling fan RPM error
P1512	Predicted and actual throttle position error
P1514	MAF sensor, predicted airflow different than detected
P1515	TPS, difference between actual and detected throttle position
P1516	TPS, sensor out of range
P1621	PCM memory performance
P1630	Vehicle theft deterent controller (excessive time in password learn mode)
P1631	Theft deterent password incorrect
P1633	Ignition 0 voltage not present while ignition 1 voltage is present

Code	Code Identification
P1635	5-volt reference circuit
P1637	Alternator L terminal circuit
P1638	Alternator field duty cycle fault
P1639	5-volt reference circuit
P1682	Ignition 1 voltage less than 10 volts
P1810	Transmission pressure switch assembly malfunction
P1860	Torque converter clutch pulse width modulator solenoid circuit
P1870	Transmission slipping
P2430	Secondary air injection system pressure sensor circuit
P2431	Secondary air injection system pressure sensor A circuit range/performance
P2432	Secondary air injection system pressure sensor A circuit low
P2433	Secondary air injection system pressure sensor A circuit high
P2440	Secondary air injection system valve stuck open
P2444	Secondary air injection system pump stuck on
U0100 through U2199	These codes are related to communication between electronic modules. Diagnosis and repairs should be performed by an automotive service professional.

3 Powertrain Control Module (PCM) (2002 through 2004 models) or Engine Control Module (ECM) (2005 and later models) - removal and installation

SIX-CYLINDER MODELS

▶ Refer to illustrations 3.3 and 3.4

※※ CAUTION:

Avoid static electricity damage to the Powertrain Control Module (PCM) by grounding yourself to the body of the vehicle before touching the PCM and using a special anti-static pad to store the PCM on, once it is removed.

➡Note 1: Whenever the PCM is replaced with a new unit the PCM must be reprogrammed with special equipment. A crankshaft position sensor variation relearn procedure and a vehicle anti-theft system password relearn procedure must be per-

formed, as well. The following procedure pertains to removal and installation of the original PCM only. If the PCM must be replaced with a new unit, take the vehicle to a dealership service department or other properly equipped repair shop.

➡Note 2: Whenever the battery is disconnected, stored operating parameters may be lost from the PCM causing the engine to run rough for a period of time while the PCM relearns the information.

1 Disconnect the cable from the negative battery terminal.
2 Clean any debris from around the PCM connectors.
3 Unscrew the bolts and carefully disconnect the electrical connectors from the PCM (see illustration).
4 Unscrew the PCM mounting bolts and nuts and remove the PCM (see illustration).
5 Installation is the reverse of removal.

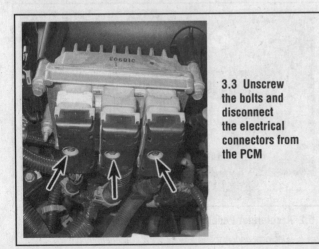

3.3 Unscrew the bolts and disconnect the electrical connectors from the PCM

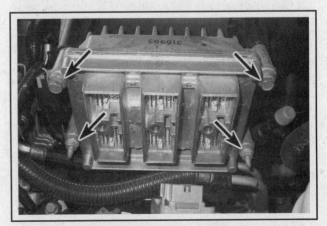

3.4 Remove the four PCM mounting fasteners

3.7 Remove the ECM cover

3.8 Detach the latch (arrow) and remove the ECM from the mounting bracket

3.9 Loosen the retaining bolts and disconnect the electrical connector from the ECM

V8 MODELS (2002 THROUGH 2004)

▶ **Refer to illustrations 3.7, 3.8 and 3.9**

6 Disconnect the cable from the negative battery terminal.

7 Remove the cover from the PCM (see illustration).

8 Detach the PCM retainer latch (see illustration) and release the mounting tabs from the PCM. Remove the PCM from the bracket.

9 Loosen the bolts and carefully disconnect the electrical connections from the PCM (see illustration). Remove the PCM from the vehicle.

10 Installation is the reverse of removal.

V8 MODELS (2005 AND LATER)

11 Disconnect the cable from the negative battery terminal.

12 Disconnect the cooling fan electrical connector (for additional clearance).

13 Remove the cover from the ECM.

14 Clean all debris from around the electrical connectors with compressed air.

15 Disconnect the bank of three electrical connectors from the ECM.

16 Detach the ECM retainer latches, tilt the top of the ECM away from the bracket and remove the ECM.

17 Installation is the reverse of removal.

4 Throttle Position Sensor (TPS) - replacement

1 The Throttle Position Sensor (TPS) is a variable potentiometer connected to the end of the throttle shaft inside the throttle body. By monitoring the output voltage from the TPS, the PCM can determine fuel delivery based on throttle valve angle.

➡ **Note: The TPS sensor works with the Throttle Actuator Control system (TAC) and the Accelerator Pedal Position (APP) sensor. The latter is actually two sensors in one housing. When there is** a difference between the actual throttle position and the position sensed by the TPS, codes are set.

REPLACEMENT

2 The Throttle Position Sensor is part of the throttle body and must be replaced as a unit. Refer to Chapter 4 for the throttle body replacement procedure.

5 Accelerator Pedal Position sensor (APP) - replacement

1 The Accelerator Pedal Position sensor (APP) contains two separate sensors that send an opposing voltage signal to the PCM. The PCM uses this voltage to calculate the throttle position requested by the vehicle driver. The APP sensor is one of the three major components of the Throttle Actuator Control (TAC) system, the other two major components being the throttle body and the PCM. This vehicle uses no throttle cable; instead, the PCM utilizes inputs from the driver and engine to determine the correct throttle opening at the throttle body.

REPLACEMENT

▶ **Refer to illustration 5.2**

2 Disconnect the APP sensor electrical connector (see illustration).

3 Remove the APP sensor mounting bolts and remove the sensor.

4 Installation is the reverse of removal.

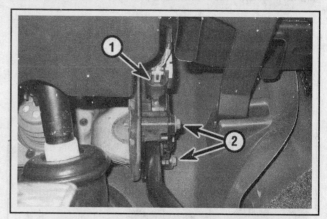

5.2 Accelerator Pedal Position (APP) sensor details

1 Electrical connector   *2 Mounting bolts*

6   Manifold Absolute Pressure (MAP) sensor - replacement

1   The Manifold Absolute Pressure (MAP) sensor monitors the intake manifold pressure changes resulting from changes in engine load and speed and converts the information into a voltage output. The PCM receives information as a varying voltage signal from closed throttle (high vacuum) to wide open throttle (low vacuum). The PCM uses the MAP sensor to control fuel delivery and ignition timing.

REPLACEMENT

▶ **Refer to illustrations 6.2, 6.3a and 6.3b.**

2   On six-cylinder models, disconnect the MAP electrical connector (see illustration). Squeeze the sensor retainer inward then pull straight up and remove it.

3   On V8 models, disconnect the MAP electrical connector (see illustration). Detach the retaining clips and withdraw the MAP sensor from the upper intake manifold (see illustration). Replace the MAP sensor seal in the upper intake manifold.

4   Installation is the reverse of removal.

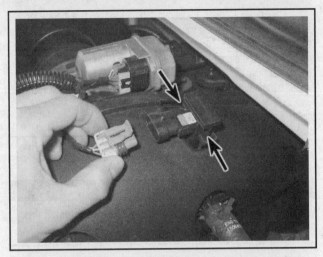

6.2 Unplug the MAP sensor electrical connector, then squeeze the retainer tabs, remove the retainer, then pull the sensor straight up and out of the manifold

6.3a MAP sensor location on the upper intake manifold

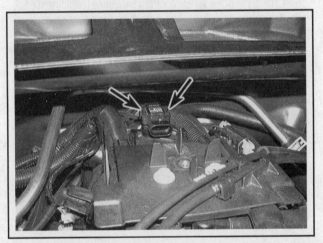

6.3b Detach the clips (arrows) and remove the MAP sensor from the upper intake manifold

7   Intake Air Temperature (IAT) sensor - replacement

1   The Intake Air Temperature (IAT) sensor is a thermistor (a resistor which varies the value of its resistance in accordance with temperature changes). The change in the resistance values will directly affect the voltage signal from the sensor to the PCM. As the sensor temperature INCREASES, the resistance values will DECREASE. As the sensor temperature DECREASES, the resistance values will INCREASE.

REPLACEMENT

▶ **Refer to illustration 7.2**

2   Disconnect the IAT sensor electrical connector (see illustration).
3   Twist and pull the sensor out from the air intake duct.
4   Installation is the reverse of removal.

7.2 Intake Air Temperature (IAT) sensor location

8 Engine Coolant Temperature (ECT) sensor - replacement

1 The Engine Coolant Temperature (ECT) sensor is a thermistor (a resistor which varies the value of its resistance in accordance with temperature changes). The change in the resistance values will directly affect the voltage signal from the sensor to the PCM. As the sensor temperature INCREASES, the resistance values will DECREASE. As the sensor temperature DECREASES, the resistance values will INCREASE.

REPLACEMENT

▶ **Refer to illustrations 8.5a and 8.5b**

✳✳ WARNING:

Wait until the engine is completely cool before beginning this procedure.

2 Drain the cooling system (see Chapter 1).
3 Disconnect the electrical connector from the sensor harness.
4 On six-cylinder engines, remove the alternator (see Chapter 5).
5 Carefully unscrew the sensor from the engine (see illustrations).
6 If the new sensor doesn't have a sealing compound on its threads, wrap the threads with Teflon sealing tape to prevent leakage.
7 Installation is the reverse of removal. Refill the cooling system by following the procedure described in Chapter 1.

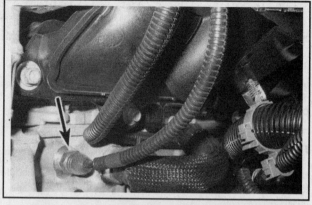

8.5a On six-cylinder engines, the Engine Coolant Temperature (ECT) sensor is threaded into the engine block

8.5b On V8 engines, the ECT sensor is at the front of the left cylinder head, above the Number One spark plug

9 Crankshaft Position (CKP) sensor - replacement

➡Note: Whenever the crankshaft sensor is replaced, the crankshaft pulley is removed and installed, the crankshaft is replaced and/or the engine removed from the vehicle, the PCM must be reprogrammed using special equipment. A crankshaft sensor variation relearn procedure must be performed using a special TECH 2 scan tool. Have the PCM reprogrammed by a dealer service department or other qualified automotive repair facility.

1 The Crankshaft Position (CKP) sensor provides the PCM with a crankshaft position signal. The PCM uses the signal to determine the spark sequence (firing order) for each cylinder. The PCM also uses the signal to precisely control ignition timing and calculate engine speed (RPM). The signal is used by the Onboard Diagnostic system for misfire detection. The crankshaft position sensor is triggered by slots cut into a reluctor ring on the crankshaft. The sensor tip is positioned approximately 0.050 inch from the reluctor ring. As the notches pass the sensor the magnetic field is altered, producing a pulsating voltage. The ignition system will not operate if the PCM does not receive a crankshaft position sensor input.

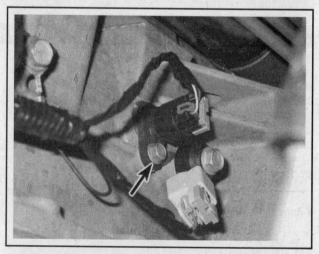

9.5 Remove the mounting bolt (arrow) and withdraw the crankshaft position sensor

REPLACEMENT

▶ **Refer to illustrations 9.5 and 9.6**

➡**Note: Anytime a crankshaft position sensor is disturbed, a Crankshaft Position Sensor variation learning procedure should be performed or a false misfire diagnostic trouble code may be set. If, after replacing the sensor a false diagnostic trouble code is set, take the vehicle to a dealership service department or other properly equipped repair shop for the procedure.**

2   Disconnect the cable from the negative battery terminal.

3   Raise the vehicle and support it securely on jackstands.

4   Disconnect the electrical connector from the sensor.

5   On six-cylinder models, remove the crankshaft position sensor mounting bolt and remove the sensor (see illustration).

6   On V8 models, remove the crankshaft position sensor mounting bolt and remove the sensor (see illustration).

7   Installation is the reverse of removal.

9.6 Remove the mounting bolt (arrow) and withdraw the crankshaft position sensor from the crankcase (starter removed for clarity)

10 Camshaft Position (CMP) sensor - replacement

1   The Camshaft Position sensor is very similar in operation to the crankshaft position sensor. The camshaft position sensor, in conjunction with the crankshaft position sensor, determines the timing for the fuel injection on each cylinder.

REPLACEMENT

Six-cylinder models

▶ **Refer to illustration 10.2**

2   Disconnect the electrical connector from the sensor (see illustration).

3   Remove the camshaft position sensor mounting bolt and withdraw the sensor from the cylinder head.

4   Installation is the reverse of removal.

V8 models

▶ **Refer to illustration 10.5**

5   Disconnect the electrical connector from the sensor (see illustration).

6   Remove the camshaft position sensor mounting bolt and withdraw the sensor from the engine block.

7   Installation is the reverse of removal.

10.2 Unplug the electrical connector from the Camshaft Position (CMP) sensor, then unscrew the bolt and remove the CMP sensor

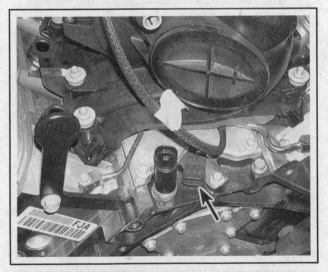

10.5 Camshaft position sensor location on engine block

11 Oxygen sensor - replacement

➡**Note: All models are equipped with two oxygen sensors; one pre-converter oxygen sensor and one post-converter oxygen sensor.**

1   An oxygen sensor, in effect, measures the oxygen remaining in the exhaust gas after the combustion process. The left over oxygen in the exhaust reacts with the elements inside the oxygen sensor to produce a voltage output that varies from 0.1 volt (high oxygen, lean mixture) to 0.9 volt (low oxygen, rich mixture). The pre-converter oxygen sensor is mounted in the exhaust system before the catalytic converter. The PCM monitors the varying voltage signal from the pre-converter oxygen sensor continuously to determine the required fuel injector pulse width, controlling the engine air/fuel ratio. A mixture ratio of 14.7 parts air to 1 part fuel is the ideal ratio for gasoline fuel to minimize exhaust emissions, as well as the best combination of fuel economy and engine performance. Based on oxygen sensor signals, the PCM tries to maintain this air/fuel ratio of 14.7:1 at all times.

2   The post-converter oxygen sensor (mounted in the exhaust system after the catalytic converter) has no effect on PCM control of the air/fuel ratio. However, the post-converter sensor operates in the same way, and the PCM uses the post-converter signal to monitor the efficiency of the catalytic converter. A post-converter oxygen sensor will produce a slower fluctuating voltage signal that reflects the lower oxygen content in the post-catalyst exhaust.

3   An oxygen sensor produces no voltage when it is below its normal operating temperature of about 600-degrees F. During this warm-up period, the PCM operates in an open-loop fuel control mode. It does not use the oxygen sensor signal as a feedback indication of residual oxygen in the exhaust. Instead, the PCM controls fuel metering based on the inputs of other sensors and its own programs. All oxygen sensors are equipped with a heating element, powered by fused ignition voltage, to heat the oxygen sensor to operating range as quickly as possible.

4   Proper operation of an oxygen sensor depends on four conditions:

a) *Electrical - The low voltages generated by the sensor require good, clean connections which should be checked whenever a sensor problem is suspected or indicated.*

b) *Outside air supply - The sensor needs air circulation to the internal portion of the sensor. Whenever the sensor is installed, make sure the air passages are not restricted.*

c) *Proper operating temperature - The PCM will not react to the sensor signal until the sensor reaches approximately 600-degrees F. This factor must be considered when evaluating the performance of the sensor.*

d) *Unleaded fuel - Unleaded fuel is essential for proper operation of the sensor.*

5   The PCM can detect several different oxygen sensor problems and set diagnostic trouble codes to indicate the specific fault (see Section 2). When an oxygen sensor fault occurs, the PCM will disregard the oxygen sensor signal voltage and revert to open-loop fuel control as described previously.

REPLACEMENT

▶ **Refer to illustrations 11.9a and 11.9b**

6   The exhaust pipe contracts when cool, and the oxygen sensor may be hard to loosen when the engine is cold. To make sensor removal easier, start and run the engine for a minute or two; then shut it off. Be careful not to burn yourself during the following procedure. Also observe these guidelines when replacing an oxygen sensor.

a) *The sensor has a permanently attached pigtail and electrical connector which should not be removed from the sensor. Damage or removal of the pigtail or electrical connector can harm operation of the sensor.*

b) *Keep grease, dirt and other contaminants away from the electrical connector and the louvered end of the sensor.*

c) *Do not use cleaning solvents of any kind on the oxygen sensor.*

d) *Do not drop or roughly handle the sensor.*

e) *Do not attempt to repair any oxygen sensor wire, if the wire is damaged the sensor must be replaced.*

7   If replacing the post-converter oxygen sensor, raise the vehicle and place it securely on jackstands.

8   Pre catalytic converter sensor can be replaced with out raising the vehicle.

9   Disconnect the electrical connector from the sensor (see illustrations).

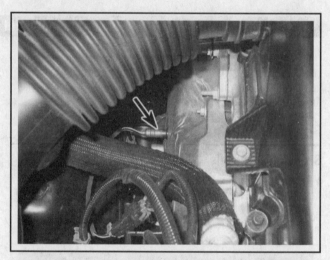

11.9a Location of the engine monitoring (pre-catalyst) oxygen sensor

11.9b Location of the catalyst monitoring (post-catalyst) oxygen sensor

10 Using a suitable wrench or specialized oxygen sensor socket, unscrew the sensor from the exhaust pipe.

11 Anti-seize compound must be used on the threads of the sensor to aid future removal. The threads of most new sensors will be coated with this compound. If not, be sure to apply anti-seize compound before installing the sensor.

12 Install the sensor and tighten it securely.

13 Reconnect the electrical connector to the sensor and lower the vehicle.

12 Knock sensor - replacement

1 The knock sensors detect abnormal vibration (spark knock or pinging) in the engine. The knock control system is designed to reduce spark knock during periods of heavy detonation. This allows the engine to use maximum spark advance to improve driveability. Knock sensors produce an AC output voltage which increases with the severity of the knock. The signal is fed into the PCM and the timing is retarded to compensate for the severe detonation. The 4.2L six-cylinder engine uses two knock sensors sensor; number 1 is toward the front of the engine, and sensor 2 is toward the rear of the engine. In some instances the unnecessary use of premium or high octane fuel can affect the knock sensor system and may set false codes.

REPLACEMENT

Six-cylinder models

▶ Refer to illustrations 12.4a and 12.4b

✻ WARNING:

The engine must be completely cool before beginning this procedure.

2 Disconnect the cable from the negative battery terminal.

3 Raise the vehicle and place it securely on jackstands.

4 Disconnect the knock sensor electrical connector (see illustrations).

5 Remove the knock sensor bolt and sensor.

6 Installation is the reverse of removal. Tighten the sensor mounting bolt to 18 ft-lbs.

V8 models (2002 through 2004)

▶ Refer to illustration 12.10

7 Disconnect the cable from the negative battery cable.

8 Remove the intake manifold (see Chapter 2B).

9 Detach the grommets from the valley cover, pull the grommets up and disconnect the electrical connector from the main harness

10 Remove the knock sensors from the engine block (see illustration).

11 Installation is the reverse of removal.

V8 models (2005 and later)

12 Disconnect the cable from the negative battery cable.

13 Raise the vehicle and support it securely on jackstands.

14 Disconnect the electrical connector from the knock sensor.

15 Detach the mounting bolt and remove the knock sensor from the right side of the cylinder block.

16 Repeat Steps 14 and 15 for the knock sensor on the left side of the cylinder block.

17 Installation is the reverse of removal.

12.4a The front knock sensor is located on the left side of the engine block, just behind the air conditioning compressor

12.4b The rear knock sensor is located on the left rear of the engine block, below the starter

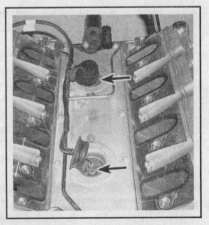

12.10 Knock sensor locations in the cylinder block

13 Vehicle Speed Sensor (VSS) - replacement

1 The Vehicle Speed Sensor (VSS) is a permanent magnet generator mounted on the transmission. The sensor is triggered by a toothed rotor on the transmission output shaft. As the output shaft rotates, the sensor produces an AC voltage, the frequency of which is proportional to vehicle speed. The PCM uses the sensor input signal for several different engine, transmission and radio control functions. The VSS signal also drives the speedometer on the instrument panel. A defective VSS can cause various driveability and transmission problems.

REPLACEMENT

▶ **Refer to illustration 13.3**

2 Raise the vehicle and support it securely on jackstands.
3 Disconnect the electrical connector from the VSS (see illustration).
4 Remove mounting bolt and withdraw the VSS from the transmission case.
5 Replace the sensor O-ring and lubricate it with clean transmission fluid.
6 Installation is the reverse of removal.

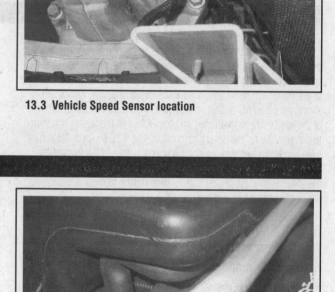

13.3 Vehicle Speed Sensor location

14 Crankcase ventilation system

▶ **Refer to illustration 14.2**

1 When the engine is running, a certain amount of the gasses produced during combustion escape past the piston rings into the crankcase as blow-by gasses. The crankcase ventilation system is designed to reduce the resulting hydrocarbon emissions (HC) by routing the gasses and vapors from the crankcase into the intake manifold and combustion chambers, where they are consumed during engine operation.
2 All models use a fixed-orifice (PCV) system. The main component of the Positive Crankcase Ventilation (PCV) system is the PCV pipe (see illustration). Fresh air flows from the air intake duct through a vent tube into the engine. Crankcase vapors are drawn from the crankcase by the PCV pipe. Other than checking to see that the pipe is attached and has no cracks or leaks there is no other service or maintenance required.

14.2 Crankcase ventilation pipe

15 Evaporative emissions control (EVAP) system

1 The fuel evaporative emissions control (EVAP) system absorbs fuel vapors from the fuel tank and, during engine operation, releases them into the engine intake system where they mix with the incoming air/fuel mixture. The main components of the evaporative emissions system are the canister (filled with activated charcoal to absorb fuel vapors), the purge valve, the vent valve, the fuel tank pressure sensor, the fuel tank and the vapor and purge lines.
2 After passing through a check valve, fuel tank vapor is carried through the vapor hose to the charcoal canister. The activated charcoal in the canister absorbs and stores the vapors. When a programmed set of conditions are met (engine running, warmed to a pre-set temperature, etc.), the PCM opens the purge valve and the vent valve. Fuel vapors from the canister are then drawn through the purge hose by intake manifold vacuum into the intake manifold and combustion chamber where they are consumed during normal engine operation.
3 The PCM regulates the rate of vapor flow from the canister to the

intake manifold by controlling the duty cycle of the EVAP purge valve control solenoid. During cold running conditions and hot start time delay, the PCM does not energize the solenoid. After the engine has warmed up to the correct operating temperature, the PCM purges the vapors into the intake manifold according to the running conditions of the engine. The PCM will cycle (ON then OFF) the purge valve control solenoid about 5 to 10 times per second. The flow rate will be controlled by the pulse width, or length of time, the solenoid is allowed to be energized.
4 The system performs a self-diagnostic check when the engine is started cold. When the programmed conditions are met, the PCM opens the EVAP canister purge valve, leaving the vent valve closed. This action allows the engine to draw a vacuum on the entire EVAP system. Once the proper vacuum level is reached, the PCM closes the purge valve, sealing the system. The PCM then monitors the fuel tank pressure sensor voltage and sets a diagnostic code if a leak is detected.

15.10 The EVAP canister is located near the fuel tank

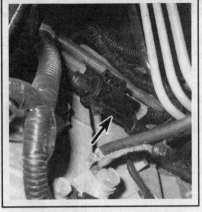

15.13 The EVAP purge valve/control solenoid is located on the left side of the engine block

15.19 EVAP vent valve/control solenoid location

5   The fuel tank pressure sensor operation is similar to the MAP sensor. The PCM supplies a 5-volt reference voltage and ground circuit to the sensor. The sensor returns a signal voltage to the PCM which varies according to the air pressure inside the fuel tank. When the air pressure inside the tank is equal to the outside air pressure (as with the fuel filler cap removed), the sensor output voltage is approximately 1.5 volts. With 14 in-Hg vacuum inside the tank the sensor output voltage is 4.5 volts.

➡**Note: The evaporative control system, like all emission control systems, is protected by a Federally-mandated warranty (5 years or 50,000 miles at the time this manual was written).**

COMPONENT REPLACEMENT

6   All EVAP system hoses are equipped with quick-connect fittings. Before disconnecting a fitting, clean around the fitting and twist the fitting back-and-forth to loosen the seal. To disconnect a large hose fitting, squeeze the retainer tabs together and pull the fitting off the pipe. To disconnect a small hose fitting, push the locking tab in and pull the fitting off the pipe.

EVAP CANISTER

▶ **Refer to illustration 15.10**

7   The EVAP canister is attached to a bracket near the fuel tank.
8   Raise the vehicle and support it securely on jackstands.
9   Remove the fuel tank shield if equipped.
10 Disconnect the hoses from the canister (see illustration).
11 Remove the bracket mounting bolt and remove the canister.
12 Installation is the reverse of removal.

PURGE VALVE

▶ **Refer to illustration 15.13**

13 The purge valve is mounted on the left side of the engine on a bracket above the starter (see illustrations).
14 Disconnect the electrical connector.
15 Depress the locking tab and remove the hose from the purge valve.
16 Remove the mounting nuts/bolt.
17 Remove the purge valve.
18 Installation is the reverse of removal.

VENT VALVE

▶ **Refer to illustration 15.19**

19 The vent valve is mounted on a bracket near the fuel tank (see illustration).
20 Raise the vehicle and support it securely on jackstands.
21 Disconnect the electrical connector.
22 Remove the hose from the vent valve (see Step 9).
23 Release the retainers and remove the vent valve from the bracket.
24 Installation is the reverse of removal.

FUEL TANK PRESSURE SENSOR

▶ **Refer to illustration 15.25**

25 The fuel tank pressure sensor is located on the fuel pump module (see illustration).
26 Remove the fuel tank (see Chapter 4).
27 Disconnect the electrical connector from the fuel tank pressure sensor.
28 Release the retaining clip and remove the sensor from the top of the fuel pump module.
29 Installation is the reverse of removal.

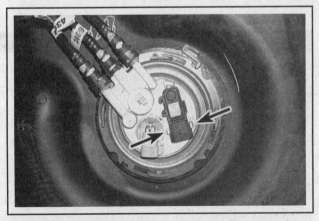

15.25 Fuel tank pressure sensor location - squeeze the sides of the retaining clip to free it

16 Camshaft position sensor solenoid (six-cylinder models) - replacement

1   The camshaft position actuator solenoid is sent a pulse-width modulated 12-volt signal from the PCM. The signal on-off time determines the amount of engine oil that flows through the Cam Phaser advance or retard passage. The Cam Phaser is attached to the exhaust camshaft and hydraulically advances or retards the camshaft from 0 degrees to -25 degrees. This continuous phasing of the exhaust camshaft results in a wider torque range and eliminates the need for an EGR valve.

REPLACEMENT

▶ **Refer to illustration 16.4**

2   Remove the drivebelt (see Chapter 1).

3   Remove the power steering pump (see Chapter 10).

4   Disconnect the electrical connector from the camshaft position actuator solenoid (see illustration).

5   Remove the retaining bolt, then twist and pull the solenoid to remove it.

6   Clean any debris from the camshaft position actuator solenoid hole.

7   Installation is the reverse of removal.

16.4 The camshaft position actuator solenoid valve is located at the right front corner of the cylinder head

17 Catalytic converter

➡ **Note: Because of a Federally mandated warranty which covers emissions-related components such as the catalytic converter, check with a dealer service department before replacing the converter at your own expense.**

1   The catalytic converter is an emission control device added to the exhaust system to reduce pollutants from the exhaust gas stream. A three-way (reduction) catalyst design is used. The catalytic coating on the three-way catalyst contains platinum and rhodium, which lowers the levels of oxides of nitrogen (NOx) as well as hydrocarbons (HC) and carbon monoxide (CO).

2   The test equipment for a catalytic converter is expensive and highly sophisticated. If you suspect that the converter on your vehicle is malfunctioning, take it to a dealer or authorized emissions inspection facility for diagnosis and repair.

REPLACEMENT

➡ **Note: Refer to the exhaust system servicing section in Chapter 4 for additional information.**

3   Raise the vehicle and support it securely on jackstands.

4   Remove the bolts and detach the catalytic converter header pipe from the exhaust manifold.

5   Remove the catalytic converter-to-exhaust pipe flange bolts and separate the exhaust pipe from the catalytic converter. Support the exhaust pipe.

6   Remove the catalytic converter and pipe assembly.

7   Clean the carbon deposits from the mounting flanges.

8   Installation is the reverse of removal.

18 Secondary Air Injection (AIR) system

1   Some 2004 and later models are equipped with a Secondary Air Injection (AIR) system. This system is used to reduce tailpipe emissions during initial engine start-up. The system is controlled by the vehicle's Powertrain Control Module (PCM). When activated, the system directs fresh air from the air cleaner housing to the exhaust manifold resulting in accelerated catalyst operation. Airflow is generated by an electric air pump mounted on the frame rail and controlled by the PCM, relays, a

solenoid actuated shut-off valve and various hoses and pipes.

2   Basic checks of this system include checking the related fuses, relays and hoses. A failure in this system will result in a diagnostic trouble code(s) (DTC) set by the PCM (refer to Section 2 for more information regarding trouble codes). A scan tool is required to thoroughly check the system, and service by a dealer service department or other qualified repair shop is usually necessary.

Section

7A

AUTOMATIC
TRANSMISSION

1 General information

All vehicles covered by this manual come equipped with a four-speed automatic transmission. Information on the automatic transmission is included in this Part of Chapter 7.

The models covered by this manual use the 4L60-E, the 4L65-E or the E/4L70-E electronic automatic 4-speed transmissions. These transmissions are equipped with a torque converter clutch (TCC) that engages in fourth gear, and in third gear when the overdrive switch is turned off. The TCC provides a direct connection between the engine and the drive wheels for improved efficiency and economy. The TCC consists of a solenoid controlled by the Powertrain Control Module (PCM) that locks the converter in third or fourth when the vehicle is cruising on level ground and the engine is fully warmed up. Some

models are also equipped with an auxiliary transmission cooler that is mounted in front of the radiator and air conditioning condenser.

Due to the complexity of the automatic transmission and the need for specialized equipment to perform most service operations, this Chapter contains only general diagnosis, routine maintenance, adjustment and removal and installation procedures.

If the transmission requires major repair work, it should be left to a dealer service department or an automotive or transmission repair shop. Once properly diagnosed you can, however, remove and install the transmission yourself and save the expense, even if the repair work is done by a transmission shop.

2 Diagnosis - general

➡Note: Automatic transmission malfunctions may be caused by five general conditions: poor engine performance, improper adjustments, hydraulic malfunctions, mechanical malfunctions or malfunctions in the Powertrain Control Module or its signal network. Diagnosis of these problems should always begin with a check of the easily repaired items: fluid level and condition (see Chapter 1), and shift cable adjustment (see Section 3). Next, perform a road test to determine if the problem has been corrected or if more diagnosis is necessary. Because the transmission relies on many sensors in the engine control system, and since the transmission shift points are controlled by the Powertrain Control Module, you'll also want to check to see if any trouble codes have been stored in the PCM (see Chapter 6 for a list of trouble codes and how to extract them). If the problem persists after the preliminary tests and corrections are completed, additional diagnosis should be done by a dealer service department or transmission repair shop. Refer to the "Troubleshooting" Section at the front of this manual for transmission problem diagnosis.

PRELIMINARY CHECKS

1 Drive the vehicle to warm the transmission to normal operating temperature.

2 Check the fluid level as described in Chapter 1:

a) If the fluid level is unusually low, add enough fluid to bring the level within the designated area of the dipstick, then check for external leaks.

b) If the fluid level is abnormally high, drain off the excess, then check the drained fluid for contamination by coolant. The presence of engine coolant in the automatic transmission fluid indicates that a failure has occurred in the internal radiator walls that separate the coolant from the transmission fluid (see Chapter 3).

c) If the fluid is foaming, drain it and refill the transmission, then check for coolant in the fluid or a high fluid level.

3 Check the engine idle speed.

➡Note: If the engine is malfunctioning, do not proceed with the preliminary checks until it has been repaired and runs normally.

4 Inspect the shift control cable (see Section 3). Make sure that it's properly adjusted and that it operates smoothly.

5 Check the Park/Neutral Position (PNP) switch adjustment (see Section 5).

FLUID LEAK DIAGNOSIS

6 Most fluid leaks are easy to locate visually. Repair usually consists of replacing a seal or gasket. If a leak is difficult to find, the following procedure may help.

7 Identify the fluid. Make sure it's transmission fluid and not engine oil or brake fluid (automatic transmission fluid is a deep red color).

8 Try to pinpoint the source of the leak. Drive the vehicle several miles, then park it over a large sheet of cardboard. After a minute or two, you should be able to locate the leak by determining the source of the fluid dripping onto the cardboard.

9 Make a careful visual inspection of the suspected component and the area immediately around it. Pay particular attention to gasket mating surfaces. A mirror is often helpful for finding leaks in areas that are hard to see.

10 If the leak still cannot be found, clean the suspected area thoroughly with a degreaser or solvent, then dry it.

11 Drive the vehicle for several miles at normal operating temperature and varying speeds. After driving the vehicle, visually inspect the suspected component again.

12 Once the leak has been located, the cause must be determined before it can be properly repaired. If a gasket is replaced but the sealing flange is bent, the new gasket will not stop the leak. The bent flange must be straightened.

13 Before attempting to repair a leak, check to make sure that the following conditions are corrected or they may cause another leak.

➡Note: Some of the following conditions cannot be fixed without highly specialized tools and expertise. Such problems must be referred to a transmission shop or a dealer service department.

Gasket leaks

14 Check the pan periodically. Make sure the bolts are tight, no bolts are missing, the gasket is in good condition and the pan is flat (dents in the pan may indicate damage to the valve body inside).

15 If the pan gasket is leaking, the fluid level or the fluid pressure may be too high, the vent may be plugged, the pan bolts may be too tight, the pan sealing flange may be warped, the sealing surface of the transmission housing may be damaged, the gasket may be damaged or the transmission casting may be cracked or porous. If sealant instead of gasket material has been used to form a seal between the pan and the transmission housing, it may be the wrong sealant.

Seal leaks

16 If a transmission seal is leaking, the fluid level or pressure may be too high, the vent may be plugged, the seal bore may be damaged, the seal itself may be damaged or improperly installed, the surface of the shaft protruding through the seal may be damaged or a loose bearing may be causing excessive shaft movement.

17 Make sure the dipstick tube seal is in good condition and the tube is properly seated. Periodically check the area around the speedometer gear or vehicle speed sensor for leakage. If transmission fluid is evident, check the O-ring for damage. Also inspect the driveshaft oil seal for leakage.

Case leaks

18 If the case itself appears to be leaking, the casting is porous and will have to be repaired or replaced.

19 Make sure the oil cooler hose fittings are tight and in good condition. The transmission oil cooler lines on these models are equipped with quick connect fittings - always inspect the O-rings if a leak is suspected.

Fluid comes out vent pipe or fill tube

20 If this condition occurs, the transmission is overfilled, there is coolant in the fluid, the case is porous, the dipstick is incorrect, the vent is plugged or the drain back holes are plugged.

3 Shift cable - removal, installation and adjustment

REMOVAL

▶ **Refer to illustrations 3.4, 3.5, 3.6 and 3.8**

1 Disconnect the cable from the negative terminal of the battery.

2 Place the transmission in PARK and apply the parking brake.

3 Block the rear wheels so the vehicle will not accidentally roll in either direction.

4 Carefully pry the shift cable from the ballstud on the transmission shift lever (see illustration).

5 Remove the clip and disengage the shift cable from the cable bracket on the transmission (see illustration). Disengage the cable from the retainer on the underside of the floor board. If you're working on a 4WD model, disengage the cable from the retainers on the transfer case.

6 Trace the cable to the cable grommet (the point at which it goes through the floor board). Push the grommet up and out of its hole in the floorpan (see illustration).

7 Remove the console (see Chapter 11). Remove the floor mat and carpet from the driver's side floor.

3.4 Disconnect the shift cable from the shift lever at the transmission

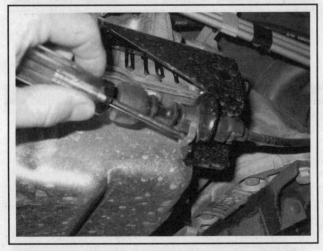

3.5 Remove the retaining clip and detach the shift cable from the bracket

3.6 Push the shift cable grommet up, out of the floorpan

3.8 Carefully pry the shift cable off the shift lever in the passenger compartment

8   Pry the shift cable ball socket from the shift lever ball pivot and detach the cable from the shift lever (see illustration).

9   Trace the cable to the cable grommet. Pull the cable up through the hole in the floor to remove it.

3.12a Lift the latch and slide the secondary lock back in the direction of the arrow . . .

INSTALLATION AND ADJUSTMENT

▸ **Refer to illustrations 3.12a and 3.12b**

10   Installation of the cable is the reverse of removal with the following exceptions:

11   Make sure the driver's shift lever and the transmission shift lever are in the Park position. If you're in doubt about the position of the transmission shift lever, rotate it fully clockwise.

12   Pull up the locking tab on the secondary lock cover and slide the cover off the primary lock (see illustration). Squeeze the tabs of the primary lock to free it, then pull the primary lock upward (see illustration). When this happens, the cable's spring tension will cause it to lengthen, so the cable end extends past the ballstud on the transmission shift lever.

13   Push the cable end back just far enough to align with the ballstud, then snap it onto the ballstud.

➡**Note: If you accidentally push the cable end too far, let it go so the spring tension can push it past the ballstud again, then push the cable end back to align with the ballstud. The cable end must be pushed back into position in one movement.**

14   Once the cable is attached to the lever, push the primary lock down until its tabs lock it, then slide the secondary lock over the primary lock.

15   Make sure the transmission shifts properly into each gear range.

3.12b . . . then squeeze the tabs and pull the primary lock out

4   Park/Lock system - description and component replacement

DESCRIPTION

1   The Park/Lock system prevents the shift lever from being moved out of Park unless the brake pedal is depressed simultaneously. It also prevents the ignition key from being removed from the ignition switch unless the shift lever is in the Park position. When the car is started, a solenoid is energized, locking the shift lever in Park; when the brake pedal is depressed, the solenoid is de-energized, unlocking the shift lever so that it can be moved into some other gear.

2   The system has a manual override that allows the transmission to be shifted out of park in the event of an electrical failure. To use the override, remove the shift lever trim boot (see Chapter 11). Locate the override lever, on the upper right side of the shift lever bracket, and move it toward the front of the vehicle.

SHIFT LOCK CONTROL SOLENOID REPLACEMENT

3   Remove the floor console (see Chapter 11).

4   Disconnect the electrical connector from the solenoid.

5   Free the manual release lever from its pivot bore and remove it.

6   Remove the solenoid mounting screws and take the solenoid off.

7   Installation is the reverse of removal.

5 Park/Neutral Position (PNP) switch/back-up light switch - description, replacement and adjustment

DESCRIPTION

▶ **Refer to illustration 5.1**

1   The Park/Neutral Position switch is part of the transmission range switch, which is mounted on the side of the transmission over the transmission manual shaft (see illustration). The switch is an information sensor for the Powertrain Control Module (PCM). Among its functions are those normally handled by a conventional Park/Neutral switch: it prevents the engine from starting in any gear other than park or Neutral, and closes the circuit for the back-up lights when the shift lever is moved to Reverse.

ADJUSTMENT

2   Verify that the engine will start only in Park or Neutral. If it starts in any other gear, it will be necessary to readjust the switch.

3   To adjust the switch, loosen the switch mounting bolts and turn it slightly one way or the other until the engine now only starts in Park or Neutral. Then tighten the mounting bolts.

REPLACEMENT

▶ **Refer to illustrations 5.9 and 5.11**

4   Disconnect the cable from the negative terminal of the battery.
5   Apply the parking brake and put the shift lever in Neutral.
6   Locate the Park/Neutral Position (PNP) switch which is mounted on the transmission at the manual lever (see illustration 5.1).
7   Disconnect the shift cable from the manual lever.
8   Disconnect the electrical connectors from the PNP switch.
9   Remove the manual lever retaining nut and remove the manual lever (see illustration).

➡ **Note: Be careful not to move the manual lever from the Neutral position while doing this. If the lever moves, insert the manual lever back on the shift shaft loosely and reposition the lever in the Neutral position before removing the PNP switch (see illustration 5.1).**

10 Remove the switch retaining bolts and detach the switch from the transmission (see illustration 5.9).
11 If you're installing a new switch, align the slots on the switch (where the shaft is inserted) with the notch on the switch body (see illustration). Then install the switch onto the shaft.
12 If you're installing the old switch, simply align the flats of the manual shaft with the flats of the Park/Neutral Position switch and install the switch.
13 Install the switch mounting bolts and tighten them to the torque listed in this Chapter's Specifications.
14 Install the manual lever, tightening the nut to the torque listed in this Chapter's Specifications.
15 Attach the shift cable and reconnect the electrical connectors.
16 The remainder of installation is the reverse of removal.

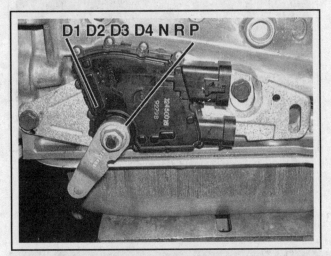

5.1 Transmission manual lever position details

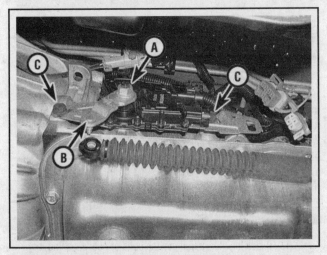

5.9 Remove the manual lever retaining nut (A), the manual lever (B) and the switch mounting bolts (C)

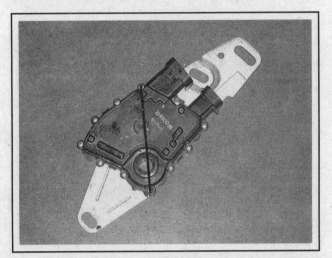

5.11 Before installing the PNP switch, align the tabs on the switch with the notch in the switch body - this is the Neutral position

6 Extension housing oil seal (2WD) - replacement

▶ **Refer to illustrations 6.4 and 6.5**

1   Oil leaks frequently occur due to wear of the extension housing oil seal. Replacement of this seal is relatively easy, since it can be performed without removing the transmission from the vehicle.

2   The extension housing oil seal is located at the extreme rear of the transmission, where the driveshaft is attached. If leakage at the seal is suspected, raise the vehicle and support it securely on jackstands. If the seal is leaking, transmission lubricant will be built up on the front of the driveshaft and may be dripping from the rear of the transmission.

3   Remove the driveshaft (see Chapter 8).

4   Using a seal removal tool or a large screwdriver, carefully pry the oil seal out of the rear of the transmission (see illustration). Do not damage the splines on the transmission output shaft.

5   Using a seal driver, a large section of pipe or a very large deep socket as a drift, install the new oil seal (see illustration). Drive it into the bore squarely and make sure it's completely seated.

6   Lubricate the splines of the transmission output shaft and the outside of the driveshaft yoke with lightweight grease, then install the driveshaft (see Chapter 8). Be careful not to damage the lip of the new seal.

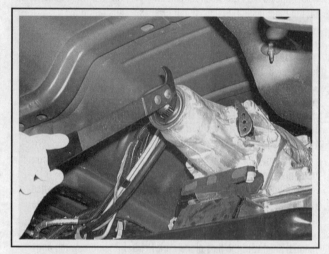

6.4 Carefully pry the old seal out of the extension housing - don't damage the splines on the output shaft

6.5 Drive the new seal into place with a seal driver or a large socket and hammer

7 Transmission mount - check and replacement

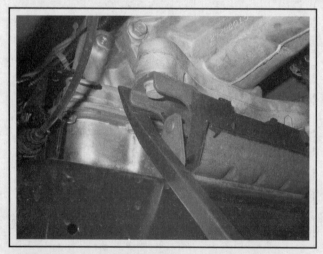

7.2 To check the transmission mount, insert a large screwdriver or prybar between the crossmember and the transmission and try to pry the transmission up - it should move very little

CHECK

▶ **Refer to illustration 7.2**

1   Raise the vehicle and support it securely on jackstands.

2   Insert a large screwdriver or prybar into the space between the transmission extension housing and the crossmember and try to pry the transmission up slightly (see illustration).

3   The transmission should not move much at all - if the mount is cracked or torn, replace it.

REPLACEMENT

▶ **Refer to illustrations 7.4a and 7.4b**

4   To replace the mount, remove the bolts or nuts attaching the

7.4a Transmission mount-to-crossmember bolts

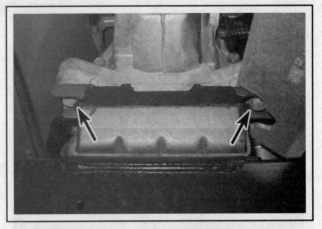

7.4b Transmission mount-to-transmission bolts

mount to the crossmember and the transmission (see illustrations).

5   Raise the transmission slightly with a jack and remove the mount.

6   Installation is the reverse of the removal procedure. Be sure to tighten all nuts and bolts securely.

8   Transmission control module (TCM) (2005 and later models) - replacement

➡Note 1: 4.2L six-cylinder models are not equipped with a TCM. These models incorporate the engine controls and the transmission controls into one module, the Powertrain Control Module (PCM). Refer to Chapter 6 for information and replacement procedures on the PCM.

➡Note 2: Whenever the TCM is replaced with a new unit, the TCM must be reprogrammed using special equipment. The following procedure refers to the removal and installation of the original TCM only. If the TCM requires replacement with a new unit, take the vehicle to a dealer service department or other properly equipped repair shop.

➡Note 3: The Transmission Control Module (TCM) is an electrostatic discharge-sensitive electronic device, meaning a static electricity discharge from your body could possibly damage it. Be sure to properly ground yourself and the TCM before handling it. Avoid touching the electrical terminals of the TCM.

1   Disconnect the cable from the negative terminal of the battery.
2   Disconnect the cooling fan electrical connector (see Chapter 3).
3   Remove the Electronic Control Module (ECM) cover (see Chapter 6).
4   Disconnect the Transmission Control Module (TCM) connector.
5   Release the TCM bracket retainer.
6   Tilt the TCM away from the TCM bracket and separate the module from the bracket housing.
7   Installation is the reverse of the removal.

9   Automatic transmission - removal and installation

REMOVAL

▶ **Refer to illustrations 9.13, 9.15, 9.17a, 9.17b and 9.18**

❊❊ CAUTION:

The transmission and torque converter must be removed as a single assembly. If you try to leave the torque converter attached to the driveplate, the converter driveplate, pump bushing and oil seal will be damaged. The driveplate is not designed to support the load, so none of the weight of the transmission should be allowed to rest on the plate during removal.

1   Disconnect the cable from the negative terminal of the battery.
2   Raise the vehicle and support it securely on jackstands. Remove the skid plate and skid plate crossmember, if equipped.
3   Drain the transmission fluid (see Chapter 1).
4   Detach the fluid filler tube from the right side of the engine.

5   Remove all exhaust components which interfere with transmission removal (see Chapter 4). Remove the EVAP canister from its mounting bracket inside the left frame rail and move it out of the way without disconnecting the hoses. Also remove the fuel tank heat shield.
6   Remove the rear driveshaft (see Chapter 8).
7   Support the engine with a jack. Use a block of wood under the oil pan to spread the load.
8   Support the transmission with a jack - preferably a jack made for this purpose (available at most tool rental yards). Safety chains will help steady the transmission on the jack.
9   Remove the nuts securing the transmission mount to the crossmember (see illustration 7.4a). Then raise the transmission slightly and remove the crossmember.
10 Lower the engine and transmission so you can reach the top and sides of the transmission.
11 On 4WD models, remove the transfer case (see Chapter 7B).
12 Disconnect the shift cable from the manual lever (see Section 3).
13 Remove the transmission heat shield (if equipped) and discon-

9.13 Disconnect the vent hose (arrow) from the transmission

9.15 Pry off the inspection plug and mark the relationship between the torque converter and the driveplate

nect the vent hose (see illustration).

14 Working on the left side of the transmission, disconnect the Park/Neutral position switch electrical connector (see Section 5) and main

9.17a Disconnect the transmission cooler lines at the transmission . . .

electrical connector. Also free the transmission wiring harness from any retainers. Unbolt the fuel line support bracket from the left side of the transmission.

15 Remove the inspection plug at the bottom of the bellhousing and mark the relationship of the torque converter to the driveplate so they can be installed in the same position (see illustration).

16 Remove the torque converter-to-driveplate bolts. Turn the crankshaft for access to each bolt. Turn the crankshaft in a clockwise direction only (as viewed from the front).

17 Disconnect the transmission cooler lines from the right side of the transmission and the engine (see illustrations). To disconnect the lines from the transmission, simply unsnap the plastic collar from the quick-connect fitting, then pry off the quick-connect fitting retaining clip and remove the lines. Plug the ends of the lines to prevent fluid from leaking out after you disconnect them. Always be sure to inspect the O-rings on the cooler lines before reinstallation.

18 Secure the transmission to the jack with a safety chain, then remove the bolts securing the transmission to the engine (see illustration). A long extension and a U-joint socket will greatly simplify this step.

➡Note: The upper bolts are easier to remove after the transmission has been lowered (see the next Step).

9.17b . . . and at the engine

9.18 Remove the bellhousing bolts (lower left side shown)

19 Lower the engine and transmission slightly and remove the fill/dipstick tube bracket bolt and pull the tube out of the transmission. Don't lose the tube seal (it can be reused if it's still in good shape).

20 Clamp a pair of locking pliers on the bellhousing case through the lower inspection hole. Clamp the pliers just in front of the torque converter, behind the driveplate. The pliers will prevent the torque converter from falling out while you're removing the transmission. Move the transmission to the rear to disengage it from the engine block dowel pins and make sure the torque converter is detached from the driveplate. Lower the transmission with the jack.

INSTALLATION

21 Prior to installation, make sure the torque converter is securely engaged in the pump. If you've removed the converter, apply a small amount of transmission fluid on the torque converter rear hub, where the transmission front seal rides. Install the torque converter onto the front input shaft of the transmission while rotating the converter back and forth. It should engage into the transmission front pump in stages. To make sure the converter is fully engaged, lay a straightedge across the transmission-to-engine mating surface and make sure the converter lugs are at least 3/4-inch below the straightedge. Reinstall the locking pliers to hold the converter in this position.

22 With the transmission secured to the jack, raise it into position.

23 Turn the torque converter to line up the holes with the holes in the driveplate. The marks on the torque converter and driveplate made in Step 15 must line up.

24 Move the transmission forward carefully until the dowel pins and the torque converter are engaged. Make sure the transmission mates with the engine with no gap. If there's a gap, make sure there are no wires or other objects pinched between the engine and transmission and also make sure the torque converter is completely engaged in the transmission front pump. Try to rotate the converter - if it doesn't rotate easily, it's probably not fully engaged in the pump. If necessary, lower the transmission and install the converter fully.

25 Install the transmission dipstick tube and seal into the transmission housing, then install the transmission-to-engine bolts and tighten them securely. As you're tightening the bolts, make sure that the engine and transmission mate completely at all points. If not, find out why. Never try to force the engine and transmission together with the bolts or you'll break the transmission case!

26 Raise the rear of the transmission and install the transmission crossmember.

27 Remove the jacks supporting the transmission and the engine.

28 Install the torque converter-to-driveplate bolts. Tighten them to the torque listed in this Chapter's Specifications.

➡**Note: Install all of the bolts before tightening any of them.**

29 Install new retaining rings onto the quick-connect fittings.

➡**Note: Don't push the retaining rings onto the fittings. Instead, hook one of the ends of the clip into a slot in the fitting, then rotate the other end of the ring into the other slot. If the retaining ring isn't installed like this, it may become spread-out and won't be able to retain the cooler lines securely.**

Connect the transmission fluid cooler lines to the fittings, making sure they click into place, then push the plastic caps onto the fittings.

30 Plug in the transmission electrical connectors and install the heat shield.

31 Connect the shift cable (see Section 3).

32 Install the torque converter inspection cover.

33 Install the transfer case, if removed (see Chapter 7C).

34 Install the driveshaft(s) (see Chapter 8).

35 Adjust the shift cable (see Section 3).

36 Install any exhaust system components that were removed or disconnected (see Chapter 4).

37 Remove the jackstands and lower the vehicle.

38 Fill the transmission with the specified fluid (see Chapter 1), run the engine and check for fluid leaks.

Specifications

General

Transmission fluid type	See Chapter 1

Torque specifications   Ft-lbs (unless otherwise indicated)

➡ Note: One foot-pound (ft-lb) of torque is equivalent to 12 inch-pounds (in-lbs) of torque. Torque values below approximately 15 ft-lbs are expressed in inch-pounds, since most foot-pound torque wrenches are not accurate at these smaller values.

Front crossmember bolts	37
Control arm bracket-to-frame bolts	177
Manual lever nut	18
Park/Neutral Position switch bolts	18
Transmission fluid pan bolts	See Chapter 1
Transmission heat shield bolts	156 in-lbs
Torque converter-to-driveplate bolts	44
Transmission-to-engine block bolts	37
Transmission mount bolts	18

7B

TRANSFER CASE

Section

1 General information

Four-wheel drive (4WD) models are equipped with a transfer case mounted on the rear of the transmission. Drive is transmitted from the engine, through the transmission and the transfer case, to the front and rear axles by driveshafts.

The vehicles covered by this manual are equipped with one of the following transfer cases: Electric shift models are equipped with a New Venture Gear NVG 226 transfer case. The electric shift transfer case has five gear selections, 2WD High, 4WD High, 4WD Low, Neutral and automatic four wheel drive (A4WD).

Also available is the NVG 126, a one-speed automatic transfer case. This transfer case is always engaged and provides automatic four wheel drive.

We don't recommend trying to rebuild any of these transfer cases at home. They're difficult to overhaul without special tools, and rebuilt units are available for less than it would cost to rebuild your own. However, there are a number of components that you can check, adjust and/or replace - and those are the items covered in this Chapter.

SELECTABLE FOUR-WHEEL DRIVE (S4WD) SYSTEM

The Selectable Four-wheel Drive (S4WD) system allows the driver four ranges (2WD High, 4WD High, 4WD Low or Neutral) with an additional (fifth) 4WD option, called automatic four-wheel-drive (A4WD). Shifting is accomplished electronically.

When any range is selected at a switch on the dash, the transfer case shift control module receives a voltage signal commanding it to energize the transfer case shift motor, thus rotating the sector shaft (clockwise or counterclockwise) and shifting the transfer case into the appropriate gear. After the transfer case is positioned in the appropri-ate gear, the transmission control module will send a signal to engage the front axle. The transfer case encoder is mounted to the shift motor and is used to relay sector shaft position back to the transfer case shift control module. The transfer case also incorporates a motor lock to assure that the transfer case remains in the current gear position. When the A4WD button is depressed the motor lock remains in adaptive mode so it can be applied or released as the transfer case shift control module determines whether the vehicle should be placed in 2WD or 4WD.

The automatic four-wheel-drive (A4WD) places the transfer case in 4WD High, but varies the engagement of the transfer case internal clutch under varying road conditions. When the transfer case shift control module receives rotating wheel slip information from speed sensors mounted at the front and rear output shafts of the transfer case, the shift control module will engage the shift control motor to compress the clutch, which delivers torque to the front output shaft. When the shift control module receives information that wheel rotation is the same at both axles, it will send a signal to the shift control motor to release the clutch, shifting the transfer case back into 2WD.

A handy feature of the NVG 226 transfer case is that it has a Neutral position. In this position, the transmission and transfer case are not forced to rotate when the vehicle is being towed, saving wear and tear on these components.

AUTOMATIC FOUR-WHEEL DRIVE (A4WD) SYSTEM

The Automatic Four-wheel Drive (A4WD) system is incorporated in the NGV126 transfer case. It works in the same way as the A4WD setting of the NVG 226 transfer case, but is always engaged and is the only setting available.

2 Transfer case control switch (electric-shift models) - replacement

1   Disconnect the cable from the negative terminal of the battery.

2   If you're working on a Chevy TrailBlazer, remove the instrument cluster bezel (see Chapter 11).

3   If you're working on a GMC Envoy or Olds Bravada, remove the floor console and the instrument panel center trim panel (see Chapter 11).

4   Pull out the retaining tabs and remove the transfer case control switch from the instrument panel.

5   Disconnect the electrical connector from the rear of the switch and remove the switch from the vehicle.

6   Installation is the reverse of removal.

3 Transfer case shift motor (electric-shift models) - replacement

1   Make sure the shift motor is in the 2-HI position. Raise the vehicle and place it securely on jackstands.

2   Remove the stone shields from below the transfer case and fuel tank.

3   Remove the front driveshaft (see Chapter 8).

4   Disconnect the shift motor electrical connector.

5   Detach the retaining bolts and remove the electric shift motor and encoder assembly.

6   Inspect the rubber gasket for tears and cracks and replace it if necessary. If the gasket is good it can be reused.

7   Position the gasket and the shift motor in place on the transfer case and install the bolts. Tighten the shift motor retaining bolts to the torque listed in this Chapter's Specifications.

8   Installation is the reverse of removal.

4   Transfer case speed sensors - check and replacement

There are three speed sensors on the transfer case. The first speed sensor is located at the front output shaft and the second sensor is located on the rear output shaft. The third speed sensor is the Vehicle Speed Sensor which sends inputs to the Powertrain Control Module (PCM) and is also located at the rear output shaft. All three of these sensors are a variable reluctance type sensor that produces an AC volt-age signal; as speed increases the AC voltage and the number of pulses increase proportionally with the rotation of the sensor. The procedure for checking and replacement of the transfer case output shaft speed sensors is essentially the same as the procedure for the Vehicle Speed Sensor. Refer to the *Vehicle Speed Sensor check and replacement* Section in Chapter 6.

5   Transfer case control module (electric-shift models) - replacement

1   The transfer case control module is located under the left side of the instrument panel.

2   Disconnect the cable from the negative terminal of the battery.

2002 THROUGH 2005 MODELS

3   Remove the access panel at the driver's end of the instrument panel (see Chapter 11).

4   Remove the knee bolster (see Chapter 11).

5   Remove the lower left sound insulator panel (see Chapter 11).

6   Remove the left-side heating, ventilation and air conditioning vent.

7   Disconnect the electrical connectors from the transfer case control module.

8   Lift the module bracket and the transfer case control module from the dash area.

9   Installation is the reverse of removal.

2006 AND LATER MODELS

10   Remove the access panel at the driver's end of the instrument panel (see Chapter 11).

11   Remove the lower left sound insulator panel (see Chapter 11).

12   Disconnect the electrical connectors from the transfer case control module.

13   Lift the module bracket and the transfer case control module from the dash area.

14   Installation is the reverse of removal.

➡️**Note: Installation will be easier if you connect the connector to the module and install the mounting bracket on the module, then install the module together with the bracket.**

6   Oil seal - replacement

➡️**Note: This procedure applies to both the front and rear output shaft seals.**

1   Raise the vehicle and support it securely on jackstands.

2   If you're replacing the front seal, remove the front driveshaft; if you're replacing the rear seal, remove the rear driveshaft (see Chapter 8).

3   If you're replacing the front seal, slide the dust shield off the output shaft. Tap around the seal with a screwdriver to loosen it in its bore, then pry it out.

4   To remove the rear output shaft seal, simply pry the seal out with a screwdriver or a seal removal tool. Don't damage the seal bore.

5   Lubricate the new seal lips with.petroleum jelly.

6   Drive the seal into place with a seal driver or a large socket. The outside diameter of the socket should be slightly smaller than the outside diameter of the seal. If you replaced the front seal, install the dust shield back onto the output shaft.

7   The remainder of installation is the reverse of removal.

7   Transfer case - removal and installation

1   Disconnect the cable from the negative terminal of the battery.

2   Raise the vehicle and support it securely on jackstands.

3   Remove the stone shields (if equipped).

4   Drain the transfer case lubricant (see Chapter 1).

5   Remove the front and rear driveshafts (see Chapter 8).

6   Disconnect all electrical connectors and detach the vent hose from the top of the transfer case.

7   Free the wiring harnesses and fuel lines from the retainers on the transfer case.

8   Remove any transmission-to-transfer case support braces. Raise the transmission enough to remove the transmission mount (see Chapter 7A), then support the transmission on a jack or jackstands.

9   Support the transfer case with a jack - preferably a special jack made for this purpose. Safety chains will help steady the transfer case on the jack.

10   Remove the adapter-to-transfer case nuts. Don't lose the washers.

11   Make a final check that all wires and hoses have been disconnected from the transfer case, then move the transfer case and jack toward the rear of the vehicle until the transfer case is clear of the transmission. Keep the transfer case level as this is done. Once the input shaft is clear, lower the transfer case and remove it from under the vehicle.

12   Inspect the transfer case gasket. If it's damaged, replace it with a new one. Don't use silicone sealant as a substitute for the gasket.

13   Installation is the reverse of removal. Be sure to tighten the transmission-to-transfer case nuts to the torque listed in this Chapter's Specifications.

8 Transfer case overhaul - general information

Overhauling a transfer case is a difficult job for the do-it-yourselfer. It involves the disassembly and reassembly of many small parts. Numerous clearances must be precisely measured and, if necessary, changed with select-fit spacers and snap-rings. As a result, if transfer case problems arise, it can be removed and installed by a competent do-it-yourselfer, but overhaul should be left to a transmission repair shop. Rebuilt transfer cases may be available - check with your dealer parts department and auto parts stores. At any rate, the time and money involved in an overhaul is almost sure to exceed the cost of a rebuilt unit.

Nevertheless, it's not impossible for an inexperienced mechanic to rebuild a transfer case if the special tools are available and the job is done in a deliberate step-by-step manner so nothing is overlooked.

The tools necessary for an overhaul include internal and external snap-ring pliers, a bearing puller, a slide hammer, a set of pin punches, a dial indicator and possibly a hydraulic press. In addition, a large, sturdy workbench and a vise or transmission stand will be required.

During disassembly of the transfer case, make careful notes of how each piece comes off, where it fits in relation to other pieces and what holds it in place. Note how parts are installed when you remove them; this will make it much easier to get the transfer case back together.

Before taking the transfer case apart for repair, it will help if you have some idea what area of the transfer case is malfunctioning. Certain problems can be closely tied to specific areas in the transfer case, which can make component examination and replacement easier. Refer to the *Troubleshooting* Section at the front of this manual for information regarding possible sources of trouble.

Torque specifications   Ft-lbs (unless otherwise indicated)

➡ **Note: One foot-pound (ft-lb) of torque is equivalent to 12 inch-pounds (in-lbs) of torque. Torque values below approximately 15 ft-lbs are expressed in inch-pounds, since most foot-pound torque wrenches are not accurate at these smaller values.**

Shift motor mounting bolts	144 in-lbs
Transfer case-to-transmission bolts	35
Transfer case speed sensors	156 in-lbs
Control arm bracket-to-frame bolts	177
Steering gear crossmember mounting bolts (front and rear)	37

Section

Reference to other Chapters

1 General information

The information in this Chapter deals with the components from the transmission (and transfer case, if equipped) to the wheels. For the purposes of this Chapter, these components are grouped into two categories: driveshaft and axles. Separate Sections within this Chapter offer general descriptions and checking procedures for components in both of the two groups.

Since nearly all the procedures covered in this Chapter involve working under the vehicle, make sure it's securely supported on sturdy jackstands or on a hoist where the vehicle can be easily raised and lowered.

2 Driveshaft and universal joints - general information and inspection

♦ **Refer to illustration 2.1**

GENERAL INFORMATION

1   A driveshaft is a tube that transmits power between the transmission (or transfer case on 4WD models) and the differential. Universal joints are located at either end of the rear driveshaft and at the front end of the front driveshaft (see illustration).

2   The rear driveshaft employs a splined yoke at the front, which slips into the extension housing of the transmission or transfer case. This arrangement allows the driveshaft to slide back-and-forth during vehicle operation to compensate for changes in length due to suspension movement. An oil seal prevents leakage of fluid at this point and keeps dirt from entering the transmission or transfer case. If leakage is evident at the front of the driveshaft, replace the oil seal (see Chapter 7, Part A).

3   On all models, the driveshaft assembly requires very little service. The universal joints are lubricated for life and must be replaced if problems develop. The driveshaft must be removed from the vehicle for this procedure.

4   Since the driveshaft is a balanced unit, it's important that no undercoating, mud, etc. be allowed to stay on it. When the vehicle is raised for service it's a good idea to clean the driveshaft and inspect it for any obvious damage. Also, make sure the small weights used to originally balance the driveshaft are in place and securely attached. Whenever the driveshaft is removed it must be reinstalled in the same relative position to preserve the balance.

5   Problems with the driveshaft are usually indicated by a noise or vibration while driving the vehicle. A road test should verify if the problem is the driveshaft or another vehicle component. Refer to the *Troubleshooting* Section at the front of this manual. If you suspect trouble, inspect the driveline.

INSPECTION

6   Raise the rear of the vehicle and support it securely on jackstands. Block the front wheels to keep the vehicle from rolling off the stands.

7   Crawl under the vehicle and visually inspect the driveshaft. Look for any dents or cracks in the tubing. If any are found, the driveshaft must be replaced.

8   Check for oil leakage at the front and rear of the driveshaft. Leakage where the driveshaft enters the transmission or transfer case indicates a defective transmission/transfer case seal (see Chapter 7). Leakage where the driveshaft meets the differential indicates a defective pinion seal (see Section 9).

9   While under the vehicle, have an assistant rotate a rear wheel so the driveshaft will rotate. As it does, make sure the universal joints are operating properly without binding, noise or looseness.

10 The universal joint can also be checked with the driveshaft motionless, by gripping your hands on either side of the joint and attempting to twist the joint. Any movement at all in the joint is a sign of considerable wear. Lifting up on the shaft will also indicate movement in the universal joints.

11 Finally, check the driveshaft mounting bolts at the ends to make sure they're tight.

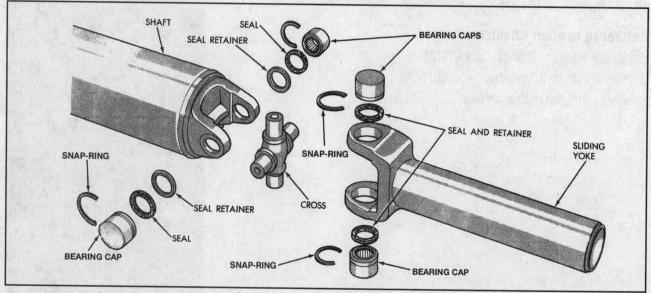

2.1 An exploded view of a typical U-joint

12 On 4WD models, the above driveshaft checks should be repeated on the front driveshaft, as well. In addition, check for leakage around the sleeve yoke, indicating failure of the yoke seal.

13 Check for leakage where the driveshafts connect to the transfer case and front differential. Leakage indicates worn oil seals.

14 At the same time, check for looseness in the joints of the front driveaxles. Also check for grease or oil leakage from around the driveaxles by inspecting the rubber boots and both ends of each axle. Oil leakage around the axle flanges indicates a defective axleshaft oil seal. Grease leakage at the CV joint boots means a damaged rubber boot. For servicing of these components, see the appropriate Sections.

3   Driveshaft(s) - removal and installation

REAR DRIVESHAFT

▶ **Refer to illustrations 3.2 and 3.3**

Removal

1   Raise the vehicle and support it securely on jackstands. Place the transmission in Neutral with the parking brake off. Block the front wheels to prevent the vehicle from rolling.

2   Make reference marks on the driveshaft and the pinion flange in line with each other (see illustration). This is to make sure the driveshaft is reinstalled in the same position to preserve the balance.

3   Remove the rear universal joint bolts and straps. Turn the driveshaft (or wheels) as necessary to bring the bolts into the most accessible position. To prevent the driveshaft from turning when you loosen the bolts, insert a large screwdriver through the driveshaft yoke (see illustration).

4   Tape the bearing caps to the spider to prevent the caps from coming off during removal.

5   Lower the rear of the driveshaft. Slide the front of the driveshaft out of the transmission or transfer case.

6   Wrap a plastic bag over the transmission or transfer case housing and hold it in place with a rubber band. This will prevent loss of fluid and protect against contamination while the driveshaft is out.

Installation

7   Remove the plastic bag from the transmission or transfer case and wipe the area clean. Inspect the oil seal carefully. Procedures for replacement of this seal can be found in Chapter 7.

8   Slide the front of the driveshaft into the transmission or transfer case.

9   Raise the rear of the driveshaft into position, checking to be sure the marks are in alignment. If not, turn the rear wheels to match the pinion flange and the driveshaft.

10 Remove the tape securing the bearing caps and install the straps and bolts. Tighten all bolts to the torque listed in this Chapter's Specifications.

FRONT DRIVESHAFT (4WD MODELS)

Removal

11 Raise the front of the vehicle and place it securely on jackstands. Remove the skid plate, if equipped.

12 Remove the rear steering gear crossmember. The rear steering gear crossmember is positioned directly behind the front crossmember, and shares four bolts with it.

13 Remove the four front crossmember-to-rear crossmember mounting bolts.

14 Remove the ten rear crossmember mounting bolts.

15 Remove the left catalytic converter heat shield.

16 Remove the rear steering gear crossmember from the vehicle.

3.2 Mark the relationship of the rear driveshaft to the differential pinion flange

17 Mark the relationship of the driveshaft to the front differential companion flange.

18 Remove the bolts and straps from the differential flange.

19 Push the driveshaft to the rear far enough to separate it from the differential flange, then lower it and pull the shaft out of the transfer case.

Installation

20 Slide the rear of the driveshaft into the splines in the transfer case output shaft. The retaining ring will give an audible click when it engages.

21 Attach the front end of the shaft to the differential companion flange (be sure to line up the marks), install the straps and bolts and tighten all of the bolts to the torque listed in this Chapter's Specifications.

22 Install the rear steering gear crossmember. Torque the bolts to the Specifications listed in this Chapter.

23 Install the skid plate (if equipped).

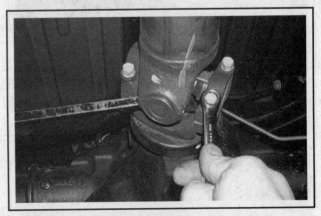

3.3 Insert a screwdriver through the driveshaft yoke to prevent the shaft from turning when you loosen the bolts

4 Universal joints - replacement

➡**Note: Always purchase a universal joint service kit for your model vehicle before beginning this procedure. Also, read through the entire procedure before beginning work.**

1 Remove the driveshaft (see Section 3).

OUTER SNAP-RING TYPE

▶ **Refer to illustrations 4.3, 4.4, 4.5 and 4.6**

2 Place the driveshaft on a bench equipped with a vise.

3 Remove the snap-rings with a small pair of pliers (see illustration).

4 Support the cross (also called a spider) on a short piece of pipe or a large socket and use another socket to press out the cross by closing the vise (see illustration).

5 Press the cross through as far as possible, then grip the bearing cap with pliers and remove it (see illustration).

6 A universal joint repair kit will contain a new cross, seals, bearings, caps and snap-rings (see illustration).

7 Inspect the bearing cap bores in the yokes for wear and damage.

8 If the bearing cap bores in the yoke are so worn that the caps are a loose fit, the driveshaft will have to be replaced with a new one.

9 Make sure the dust seals are properly located on the cross.

10 Using a vise, press one bearing cap into the yoke approximately 1/4-inch.

11 Use chassis grease to hold the needle rollers in place in the caps.

12 Insert the cross into the partially installed bearing cap, taking care not to dislodge the needle rollers.

13 Hold the cross in correct alignment and press both caps into place by slowly and carefully closing the jaws of the vise.

14 Use a socket slightly smaller in diameter than the caps to press them into the yoke. Press in one side, install the snap-ring, then press the other side to shift the cross assembly tight against the installed snap-ring and install the other snap-ring.

15 Repeat the operations for the remaining two bearing caps. Proceed to Step 22.

INJECTED PLASTIC (INNER SNAP-RING) TYPE

▶ **Refer to illustrations 4.16, 4.20 and 4.21**

16 If the joint has been previously rebuilt, remove the snap-rings (bearing retainers) located on the inner part of each bearing cap (see illustration).

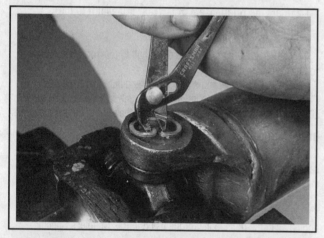

4.3 Use a small pair of pliers to remove the snap-rings from the ends of the universal joint yokes

4.4 To remove the U-joint from the driveshaft, use a vise as a press - the small socket will push the cross bearing cap into the large socket

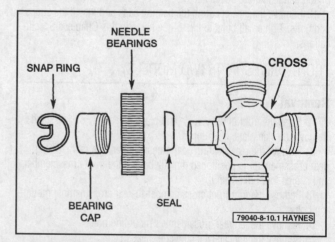

4.5 Locking pliers can be used to remove the bearing caps from the yoke

4.6 Outer snap-ring type U-joint

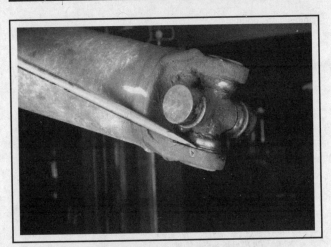

4.16 Remove the inner snap-rings from the U-joint by tapping them off with a screwdriver and hammer

17 If this is the first time the joint is being rebuilt it will not be necessary to remove the snap-rings, since there aren't any; the pressing operation will shear the molded plastic retaining material.

➡**Note: It may be necessary to heat the U-joint over 500-degrees (melting the plastic retaining material) before pressing the U-joint apart.**

18 Press out the bearing caps as described in Steps 4 and 5.

19 Remove the cross and clean all plastic material from the yoke. Use a small punch to remove the plastic from the injection holes.

20 Reassembly is the same as for the outer snap-ring joint described in Steps 9 through 15, except the snap-rings are on the inner part of

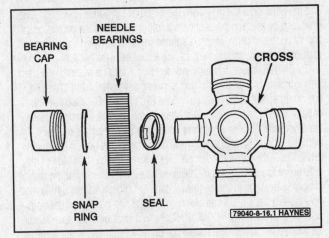

4.20 Inner snap-ring type U-joint

each bearing cap (see illustration).

21 When installing the bearing cap, press it in until the snap-ring can be installed (see illustration).

ALL MODELS

▸ Refer to illustration 4.22

22 If the joint is stiff after assembly, strike the yoke sharply with a hammer (see illustration). This will spring the yoke ears slightly and free up the joint.

4.21 Installing a snap-ring on an inner snap-ring type U-joint

4.22 Strike the yoke sharply with a hammer to "spring" the yoke ears, which will free-up the joint

5   Axles - description and check

DESCRIPTION

1   The rear axle assembly is a hypoid (the centerline of the pinion gear is below the centerline of the ring gear), semi-floating type. When the vehicle goes around a corner, the differential allows the outer rear wheel to turn at a higher speed than the inner wheel. The axleshafts are splined to the differential side gears, so when the vehicle goes around a corner, the inner wheel, which turns more slowly than the outer wheel,

turns its side gear more slowly than the outer wheel turns its side gear. The differential pinion gears roll around the slower side gear, driving the outer side gear - and wheel - more quickly.

2   An optional locking limited-slip rear axle is also available. This differential allows for normal operation until one wheel loses traction. A limited-slip unit is similar in design to a conventional differential, except for the addition of a pair of multi-disc clutch packs which slow the rotation of the differential case when one wheel is on a firm surface

and the other on a slippery one. The difference in wheel rotational speed produced by this condition applies additional force to the pinion gears and through the cone, which is splined to the axleshafts, equalizing the rotation speed of the axleshaft driving the wheel with traction.

3 On 4WD models, a fully independent front axle assembly is used. This consists of a differential and a pair of driveaxles. Each driveaxle has an inner and outer constant velocity (CV) joint. Because the differential - like the transfer case - is offset to the left, the distance between the differential and the right front wheel is greater than the distance from the differential to the left wheel. In order to use two equal-length driveaxles, an extension axleshaft is employed on the right side of the differential to make up the difference. The extension axleshaft passes through a passage in the engine oil pan. The differential on S4WD models employs a shift fork and sleeve to engage and disengage the right axleshaft. This allows the two axleshafts to turn at different speeds when the vehicle is turning. The differential on A4WD models is the same as the S4WD differential, but does not include the shift fork and sleeve.

CHECK

4 Often, a suspected "axle" problem lies elsewhere. Do a thorough check of other possible causes before assuming the axle is the problem.

5 The following noises are those commonly associated with axle

diagnosis procedures:

a) Road noise is often mistaken for mechanical faults. Driving the vehicle on different surfaces will show whether or not the road surface is the cause of the noise. Road noise will remain the same if the vehicle is under power or coasting.

b) Tire noise is sometimes mistaken for mechanical problems. Tires which are worn or low on pressure are particularly susceptible to emitting vibrations and noises. Tire noise will remain about the same during varying driving situations, where axle noise will change during coasting, acceleration, etc.

c) Engine and transmission noise can be deceiving because it will travel along the driveline. To isolate engine and transmission noises, make a note of the engine speed at which the noise is most pronounced. Stop the vehicle and place the transmission in Neutral and run the engine to the same speed. If the noise is the same, the axle is not at fault.

6 Because of the special tools needed, overhauling the differential isn't cost effective for a do-it-yourselfer. The procedures included in this Chapter describe axleshaft removal and installation, axleshaft oil seal replacement, axleshaft bearing replacement and removal of the entire unit for repair or replacement. Any further work should be left to a qualified repair shop.

---

6   Axleshaft (rear) - removal and installation

♦ Refer to illustrations 6.3, 6.4, 6.5a and 6.5b

REMOVAL

1 Loosen the rear wheel lug nuts. Raise the rear of the vehicle, support it securely on jackstands and block the front wheels. Remove the wheel and brake disc (see Chapter 9).

2 Remove the differential cover and allow the lubricant to drain into a container.

3 Remove the lock bolt (see illustration).

4 On models with a conventional differential (non-locking), remove the pinion shaft. On models with a locking differential, withdraw the pinion shaft part way, then rotate the differential until the shaft touches

the case, providing enough clearance for access to the C-locks (see illustration).

5 Have an assistant push in on the outer flanged end of the axleshaft while you remove the C-lock from the groove in the inner end of the shaft (see illustration).

➡Note: On models with a locking differential, use a screwdriver to rotate the C-lock until the open end points in (see illustration).

6 With the C-lock removed, withdraw the axleshaft, taking care not to damage the oil seal (but note that it is a good idea to replace the seal whenever the axleshaft is removed - see Section 7). Some models have a thrust washer in the differential; make sure it doesn't fall out when the axleshaft is removed.

6.3 Remove the pinion shaft lock bolt

6.4 Withdraw the pinion shaft for access to the C-locks (don't turn the axleshafts after the shaft has been pulled out, or the spider gears may become mispositioned)

6.5a Push the axle flange in, then remove the C-lock from the inner end of the axleshaft

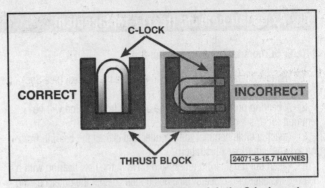

6.5b On models with a locking differential, the C-lock must be positioned as shown before it can be removed

INSTALLATION

7   To install, carefully insert the axleshaft into the housing and seat it securely in the differential.

8   Install the C-lock in the axleshaft groove and pull out on the flange to lock it.

9   Insert the pinion shaft, align the hole in the shaft with the lock bolt hole and install the lock bolt.

➡**Note: Apply a non-hardening, thread-locking compound to the threads of the lock bolt before installing it. Tighten the lock bolt to the torque listed in this Chapter's Specifications.**

10   Check the cover gasket. If it's in good condition it can be re-used. If it isn't, replace it. Install the cover and tighten the bolts to the torque listed in this Chapter's Specifications, then fill the differential with the lubricant specified in Chapter 1.

11   Install the brake disc, caliper mounting bracket and caliper, tightening the fasteners to the torque listed in the Chapter 9 Specifications. Install the wheel and lug nuts, then lower the vehicle. Tighten the lug nuts to the torque listed in the Chapter 1 Specifications.

7   Axleshaft oil seal (rear) - replacement

♦ **Refer to illustrations 7.2 and 7.3**

1   Remove the axleshaft (see Section 6).

2   Pry the oil seal out of the end of the axle housing (see illustration).

3   Apply a film of multi-purpose grease to the oil seal recess and

tap the new seal evenly into place with a hammer and seal installation tool (see illustration), large socket or piece of pipe so the lips are facing in and the metal face is visible from the end of the axle housing. When correctly installed, the face of the oil seal should be flush with the end of the axle housing.

4   Install the axleshaft (see Section 6).

7.2 Prying out the axleshaft oil seal with a seal removal tool

7.3 Using a seal driver to install the axleshaft oil seal - drive the seal in until it's flush with the bore

8 Axleshaft bearing (rear) - replacement

♦ **Refer to illustrations 8.2, 8.3 and 8.4**

1   Remove the axleshaft (see Section 6) and the oil seal (see Section 7).

2   A bearing puller which grips the bearing from behind will be required for this job (see illustration).

3   Attach a slide hammer to the puller and extract the bearing from the axle housing (see illustration).

4   Clean out the bearing recess and drive in the new bearing with a bearing installer or a piece of pipe positioned against the outer bearing race (see illustration). Make sure the bearing is tapped in to the full depth of the recess.

5   Install a new oil seal (see Section 7), then install the axleshaft (see Section 6).

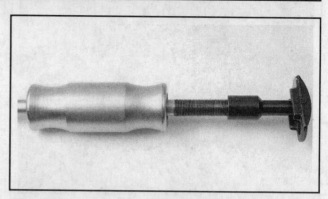

8.2 A typical slide hammer and axleshaft bearing remover attachment

8.3 Removing the axleshaft bearing with a slide hammer

8.4 Use a bearing driver or a large socket to tap the bearing evenly into the axle housing

9 Pinion oil seal - replacement

♦ **Refer to illustrations 9.3, 9.4, 9.5, 9.8 and 9.9**

➡**Note: This procedure applies to the front and rear pinion oil seals.**

1   Loosen the wheel lug nuts. Raise the front (for front differential) or rear (for rear differential) of the vehicle and support it securely on jackstands. Block the opposite set of wheels to keep the vehicle from rolling off the stands. Remove the wheels.

2   Disconnect the driveshaft from the differential pinion flange and fasten it out of the way (see Section 3).

3   Rotate the pinion a few times by hand. Use a beam-type or dial-type inch-pound torque wrench to check the torque required to rotate the pinion (see illustration). Record it for use later.

4   Mark the relationship of the pinion flange to the shaft (see illustration), then count and write down the number of exposed threads on the shaft.

5   A special tool, available at most auto parts stores, can be used to keep the companion flange from moving while the self-locking pinion nut is loosened. A chain wrench can also be used to immobilize the

9.3 Use an inch-pound torque wrench to check the torque required to rotate the pinion shaft

9.4 Before removing the nut, mark the position of the flange to the shaft and count the number of exposed threads

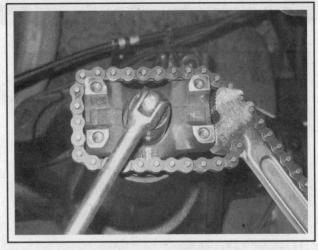

9.5 A chain wrench can be used to hold the pinion flange while removing the nut

flange (see illustration).

6   Remove the pinion nut.

7   Withdraw the flange. It may be necessary to use a two-jaw puller engaged behind the flange to draw it off. Do not attempt to pry or hammer behind the flange or hammer on the end of the pinion shaft.

8   Pry out the old seal and discard it (see illustration).

9   Lubricate the lips of the new seal and fill the space between the seal lips with wheel bearing grease, then tap it evenly into position with a seal installation tool or a large socket (see illustration). Make sure it enters the housing squarely and is tapped in to its full depth.

10 Install the pinion flange, lining up the marks made in Step 4. If necessary, tighten the pinion nut to draw the flange into place. Do not

try to hammer the flange into position.

11 Apply a bead of RTV sealant to the ends of the splines visible in the center of the flange so oil will be sealed in.

12 Install the washer and a new pinion nut. Tighten the nut until the number of threads recorded in Step 4 are exposed.

13 Measure the torque required to rotate the pinion and tighten the nut in small increments (no more than 5 ft-lbs) until it matches the figure recorded in Step 3. To compensate for the drag of the new oil seal, the nut should be tightened a little more until the rotational torque of the pinion exceeds the earlier recording by 5 in-lbs.

14 Reinstall all components removed previously by reversing the removal Steps, tightening all fasteners to their specified torque values.

9.8 Use a seal removal tool or a large screwdriver to remove the pinion seal (be careful not to disturb the pinion while doing this)

9.9 A large socket with a diameter the same as that of the new pinion seal can be used to drive the seal into the differential housing

10 Axle assembly (rear) - removal and installation

REMOVAL

1 Loosen the rear wheel lug nuts, raise the rear of the vehicle and support it securely on jackstands placed under the frame rails. Block the front wheels to keep the vehicle from rolling off the stands. Remove the rear wheels.

2 Position a jack under the rear axle differential housing, then raise it slightly.

3 Disconnect the driveshaft from the rear axle pinion flange (see Section 3). Fasten the driveshaft out of the way with a piece of wire from the underbody.

4 On models with air springs, depressurize the rear suspension (see Chapter 10 Section 14).

5 Disconnect the shock absorbers at their lower mounts.

6 Disconnect the vent hose from the fitting on the axle housing and fasten it out of the way.

7 Disconnect the brake hose from the junction block on the axle housing, then plug the hose to prevent fluid leakage.

8 Remove the brake calipers and discs (see Chapter 9).

9 Disconnect the parking brake cables from the actuating levers and the brackets (see Chapter 9).

10 Remove the stabilizer bar and the rear suspension springs (see Chapter 10).

11 Detach the rear suspension track bar and upper and lower control arms from the axle (see Chapter 10).

12 Lower the jack under the differential, then remove the rear axle assembly from under the vehicle.

INSTALLATION

13 Installation is the reverse of removal. Tighten the U-joint strap bolts to the torque listed in this Chapter's Specifications. Tighten all suspension fasteners to the torque values listed in the Chapter 10 Specifications. Tighten the brake fasteners to the torque values listed in the Chapter 9 Specifications.

14 Bleed the brakes (see Chapter 9).

15 Install the wheels and tighten the lug nuts to the torque listed in the Chapter 1 Specifications.

11 Driveaxles (4WD models) - general information and inspection

1 Power is transmitted from the front differential/axle to the front wheels through a pair of driveaxles. The inner end of the right driveaxle is splined to an axleshaft connected to the right differential side gear; the inner end of the left driveaxle has a short stub shaft and is splined to the left differential side gear. The outer end of each driveaxle has a stub shaft that is splined to the front hub and bearing assembly and locked in place with a large nut.

2 The inner ends of the driveaxles are equipped with sliding constant velocity (CV) joints, which are capable of both angular and axial motion. Each inner CV joint assembly consists of a tripot-type bearing and a housing in which the joint is free to slide in-and-out as the driveaxle moves up-and-down with the wheel.

3 The outer ends of the driveaxles are equipped with "ball-and-cage" type CV joints, which are capable of angular but not axial movement. Each outer CV joint consists of six caged ball bearings running between an inner race and the housing.

4 The boots should be inspected periodically for damage and leaking lubricant. Torn CV joint boots must be replaced immediately or the joints will be damaged. If either boot of a driveaxle is damaged, that driveaxle must be removed in order to replace the boot (see Section 12).

5 Should a boot be damaged, the CV joint can be disassembled and cleaned (see Section 13), but if any parts are damaged, the entire driveaxle assembly must be replaced as a unit.

6 The most common symptom of worn or damaged CV joints, besides lubricant leaks, is a clicking noise in turns, a clunk when accelerating after coasting and vibration at highway speeds. To check for wear in the CV joints and driveaxle shafts, grasp each axle (one at a time) and rotate it in both directions while holding the CV joint housings, feeling for play indicating worn splines or sloppy CV joints. Also check the driveaxle shafts for cracks, dents and distortion.

12 Driveaxle (4WD models) - removal and installation

▶ **Refer to illustrations 12.3 and 12.4**

REMOVAL

1 Loosen the wheel lug nuts, raise the front of the vehicle and support it securely on jackstands. Remove the wheel.

2 Remove the splash shield from under the vehicle (see Chapter 11).

3 Pry off the hub cover (see illustration).

4 Remove and discard the driveaxle/hub nut. To prevent the hub from rotating, brace a large prybar across two of the wheel studs (see illustration), or insert a long punch or screwdriver through the window in the brake caliper and into the disc cooling vanes.

❈❈ WARNING:

The hub nut should not be reused. Install a new hub nut when installing the shaft.

5 Disconnect the wheel speed sensor electrical connector and free the harness from its retainers. Unbolt the brake hose retainer where it

12.3 A hammer and chisel can be used to knock the cover off the hub

12.4 A large prybar can be used to immobilize the hub while loosening the nut, or a screwdriver can be inserted through the window in the brake caliper (arrow) and into the disc cooling vanes

joins the metal brake line at the frame (see Chapter 9).

6   Remove the shock absorber module (see Chapter 10).

7   Remove the steering knuckle (see Chapter 10) and simultaneously pull the driveaxle stub shaft out of the hub.

➡**Note: If the stub shaft sticks in the hub splines, tap on the end of the shaft with a brass punch and a hammer. If that doesn't free the splines, push the driveaxle from the hub with a puller.**

8   Drive the inner end of the driveaxle away from the differential or intermediate shaft with a hammer and brass drift. Place the end of the brass drift against the inner driveaxle joint housing. Apply enough force to disengage the retaining ring on the inner end of the driveaxle from the differential or intermediate shaft. Remove the driveaxle from the differential.

INSTALLATION

9   Installation is the reverse of removal, with the following additions.

10   Before installing the driveaxle, lubricate the splines on the stub shaft with multi-purpose grease.

11   Install a new driveaxle/hub nut and tighten it to the torque value listed in this Chapter's Specifications.

12   Tighten the suspension fasteners to the torque listed in the Chapter 10 Specifications.

13   Tighten the wheel lug nuts to the torque listed in the Chapter 1 Specifications.

13 Driveaxle boot (4WD models) - replacement

➡**Note: If the CV joint boots must be replaced, explore all options before beginning the job. Complete rebuilt driveaxles are available on an exchange basis, which eliminates much time and work. Whichever route you choose to take, check on the cost and availability of parts before disassembling the vehicle.**

1   Remove the driveaxle (see Section 12).

2   Place the driveaxle in a vise lined with rags to avoid damage to the axleshaft. Check the CV joint for excessive play in the radial direction, which indicates worn parts. Check for smooth operation throughout the full range of motion for each CV joint. If a boot is torn, disassemble the joint, clean the components and inspect for damage due to loss of lubrication and possible contamination by foreign matter.

➡**Note: Some models are equipped with a protective cover that clamps around the larger diameter of each boot. Use diagonal cutting pliers to remove the clamps, then slide the cover off for access to the boots.**

INNER CV JOINT

♦ **Refer to illustrations 13.3a through 13.3t**

3   To replace the inner boot, refer to the accompanying illustrations (see illustrations 13.3a through 13.3t).

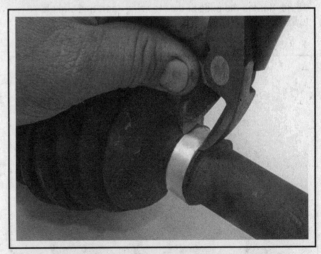

13.3a Cut off the old boot clamps with a pair of diagonal cutting pliers (the smaller diameter clamp is actually a "swage ring;" you may have to use a hand-held grinder to cut through it. When reassembling the joint, use a conventional boot clamp, since special tools are required to swage the ring in place)

13.3b Slide the housing off the spider assembly

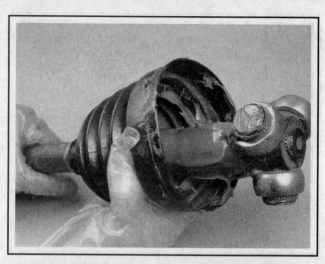

13.3c Slide the boot towards the center of the driveaxle

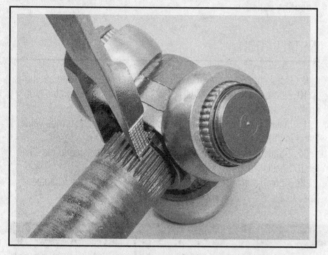

13.3d Spread the ends of the stop ring apart and slide it towards the center of the shaft

13.3e Slide the spider assembly back to expose the retaining ring and pry off the ring

13.3f Carefully tap the spider off the axleshaft with a brass punch (but don't hit it so hard that it flies off, or you'll be picking up needle bearings!)

13.3g When you slide the spider off the driveaxle, hold the bearings in place with your hand; even better, use tape or a cloth wrapped around the spider bearing assembly to retain them

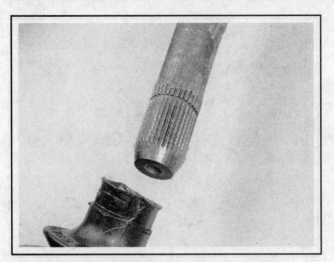

13.3h Slide the boot and the stop ring off the axleshaft

13.3i Clean all of the old grease out of the housing and spider assembly, then remove each bearing, one at time

13.3j Carefully disassemble each section of the spider assembly, clean the needle bearings with solvent and inspect the rollers, spider cross, bearings and housing for scoring, pitting and other signs of abnormal wear

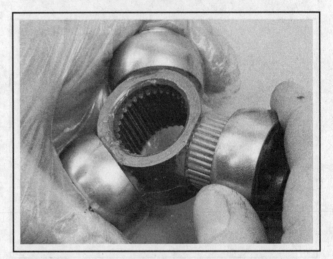

13.3k Apply a coat of CV joint grease to the inner bearing surfaces to hold the needle bearings in place and slide the bearing over them

13.3l Wrap the axleshaft splines with tape to avoid damaging the boot, then slide the small clamp and boot onto the axleshaft

13.3m Slide the spider stop ring onto the axleshaft, past the groove in which it seats

13.3n Install the spider bearing with the recess in the counterbore facing the end of the driveaxle

13.3o Install the spider retaining ring, then slide the spider assembly against it and seat the stop ring in its groove

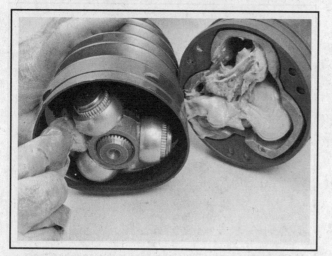

13.3p Pack the housing with half of the grease furnished with the new boot and place the remainder in the boot

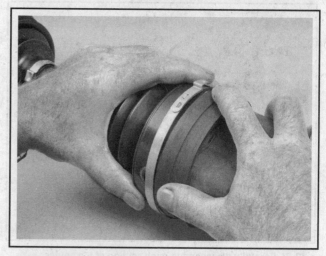

13.3q With the retaining clamps in place (but not tightened), install the tripot housing

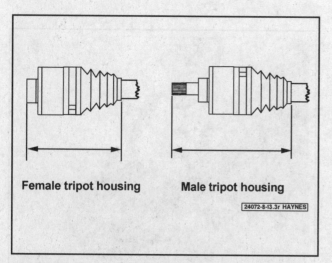

Female tripot housing   Male tripot housing

24072-8-13.3r HAYNES

13.3r Seat the boot in the housing and axle seal grooves, then adjust the length of the joint to the dimension listed in this Chapter's Specifications

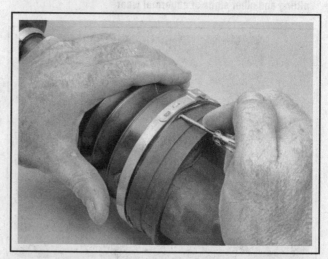

13.3s With the joint set to the proper length, equalize the pressure in the boot by inserting a small screwdriver between the boot and the housing (make sure the boot isn't dimpled, stretched or out of shape) . . .

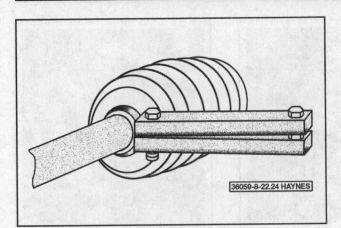

13.3t . . . then secure the boot clamps with a clamp crimping tool (available at auto parts stores)

OUTER CV JOINT

▶ **Refer to illustrations 13.4a through 13.4r**

4   Refer to the accompanying illustrations and perform the outer CV joint boot replacement procedure (see illustrations 13.4a through 13.4r).

13.4b Spread apart the ends of the internal snap-ring, then slide the CV joint off the shaft

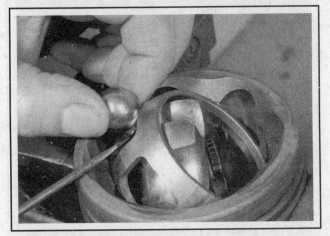

13.4d Pry the balls out of the cage, one at a time

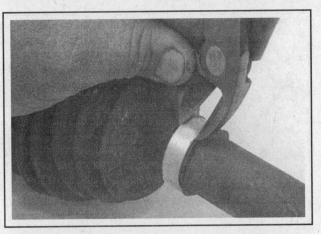

13.4a Cut off the boot retaining clamps with a pair of diagonal cutters (the smaller diameter clamp is actually a "swage ring;" you may have to use a hand-held grinder to cut through it. When reassembling the joint, use a conventional boot clamp, since special tools are required to swage the ring in place)

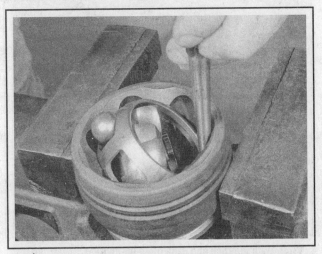

13.4c Press down on the inner race far enough to allow a ball bearing to be removed - if it's difficult to tilt, gently tap the cage and inner race with a brass punch and hammer

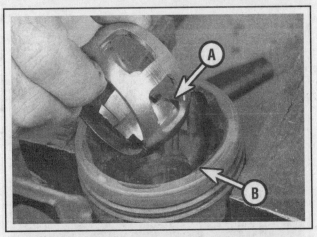

13.4e Tilt the inner race and cage 90-degrees, then align the windows in the cage (A) with the lands of the housing (B) and rotate the inner race and cage up and out of the housing

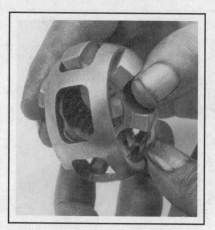

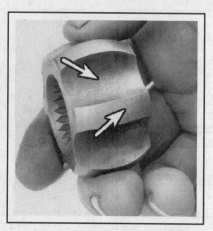

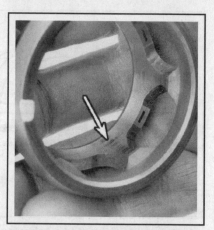

13.4f Align an inner race land with a cage window and rotate the inner race out of the cage

13.4g After cleaning the components with solvent, check the inner race lands and grooves for pitting and score marks

13.4h Check the cage for cracks, pitting and score marks - shiny spots are normal and don't affect operation

13.4i With the race and cage tilted 90-degrees, lower the assembly into the housing

13.4j Rotate the assembly by gently tapping with a hammer and brass punch . . .

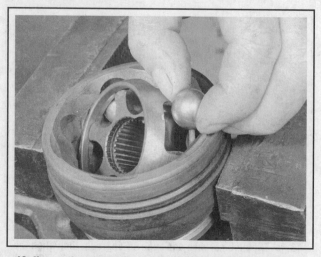

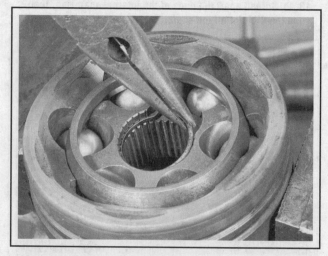

13.4k . . . then press the balls into the cage windows, repeating until all of the balls are installed

13.4l Use needle-nose pliers to lower a new snap-ring into the groove . . .

13.4m . . . then seat it into the groove with snap-ring pliers

13.4n Apply grease through the splined hole, then insert a wooden dowel (with a diameter slightly less than that of the axle) through the splined hole and push down - the dowel will force the grease into the joint - repeat until the bearing is completely packed

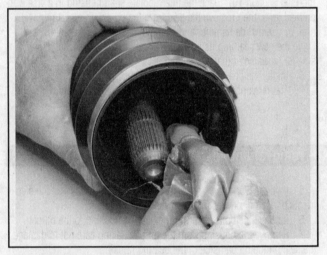

13.4o Install the small clamp and the boot on the driveaxle and apply grease to the inside of the axle boot . . .

13.4p . . . until the level is up to the end of axle

13.4q Position the CV joint assembly on the driveaxle, aligning the splines, then use a soft-face hammer to drive the joint onto the driveaxle until the snap-ring is seated in the groove

13.4r Seat the inner end of the boot in the groove and install the retaining clamp, then do the same on the other end of the boot - tighten boot clamps with the special tool (see illustration 13.3t)

14 Front axle actuator (electric-shift 4WD models) - replacement

1 Raise the front of the vehicle and support it securely on jackstands. Remove the splash shield.

2 Disconnect the electrical connector from the actuator.

3 Remove the actuator mounting bolts and detach the actuator from the intermediate shaft housing.

4 To install the actuator, reverse the removal procedure. Tighten the bolts to the torque listed in this Chapter's Specifications.

15 Intermediate shaft bearing housing oil seals (4WD models) - replacement

1 Loosen the right front wheel lug nuts, raise the vehicle, place it securely on jackstands and remove the right front wheel.

2 Remove the splash shield.

3 Remove the driveaxle from the right side of the vehicle (see Section 12).

4 The outer seal can be replaced with the bearing housing installed on the vehicle. Pry the seal out with a seal removal tool, or use a slide hammer and seal remover adapter to pull the seal. Drive the new seal into its bore with a seal driver or a socket slightly smaller in diameter than the seal.

✳✳ CAUTION:

The seal must be driven in to a depth of 0.35 to 0.43-inch below the bore, or it will be damaged by the intermediate shaft.

5 To replace the seal on the inner (oil pan) side, remove the housing (see Section 16). Place the intermediate shaft housing in a vise with padded jaws, then remove the seal from the bore with a seal removal tool, or use a slide hammer and seal remover adapter to pull the seal. Drive the new seal into its bore with a seal driver or a socket slightly smaller in diameter than the seal.

6 Install the bearing housing (if removed).

7 The remainder of installation is the reverse of the removal steps.

16 Intermediate shaft bearing housing (4WD models) - removal and installation

1 The intermediate shaft bearing housing contains the bearing that supports the right end of the intermediate shaft. On electric-shift 4WD models, it also contains the shifting fork and sleeve that engage and disengage the right front driveaxle.

2 Loosen the wheel lug nuts, raise the vehicle, place it securely on jackstands and remove the right front wheel.

3 Remove the splash shield.

4 Remove the driveaxle from the right side of the vehicle (see Section 12).

5 If you're working on an electric-shift model, disconnect the electrical connector and free the harness from its retainer.

6 Remove the bolts securing the bearing housing to the oil pan.

7 Remove the housing from the oil pan, taking care not to damage the seal on the oil pan side of the bearing housing.

8 Installation is the reverse of the removal steps. Be sure the bearing housing is flush against the oil pan. Tighten the bearing housing mounting bolts to the torque listed in this Chapter's Specifications.

17 Intermediate shaft (4WD models) - removal and installation

1 Loosen the right front wheel lug nuts, raise the vehicle, place it securely on jackstands and remove the right front wheel.

2 Remove the splash shield.

3 Remove the right driveaxle and intermediate shaft bearing housing (see Sections 12 and 16).

4 Thread a slide hammer adapter into the hole in the end of the intermediate shaft. Attach a slide hammer to the adapter.

5 Pull the intermediate shaft out of the differential, taking care not to damage the seal on the opposite side of the oil pan.

6 Make sure the retaining ring is in position on the left end of the intermediate shaft. Insert the intermediate shaft through the oil pan passage and into the differential, taking care not to damage the oil seal. Rotate the shaft as necessary to align its splines with the differential.

7 Install the slide hammer on the shaft, then use the slide hammer to drive the shaft in until its retaining ring locks into place in the differential.

8 The remainder of installation is the reverse of the removal steps.

18 Front differential carrier (4WD models) - removal and installation

1   Disconnect the cable from the negative terminal of the battery.

2   Loosen the front wheel lug nuts, raise the front of the vehicle and support it securely on jackstands.

3   Remove the under-vehicle splash shield. Drain the engine oil and the front differential lubricant (see Chapter 1).

4   Disconnect the front driveshaft from the front differential companion flange (see Section 3). Wrap tape around the bearing caps so they don't fall off. Support the driveshaft with a length of wire or rope so it doesn't hang.

5   Disconnect the ABS wheel speed sensor and free the harness from its retainers. Unbolt the brake hose retainer where it joints the metal line at the frame (see Chapter 9).

6   Disconnect the stabilizer bar links from the stabilizer bar (see Chapter 10).

7   Remove the upper balljoint pinch bolt and separate the steering knuckle from the upper control arm. Be careful not to let the knuckle fall outward, and make sure the brake hose isn't strained.

8   Place a floor jack under the lower control arm, then unscrew the two shock absorber module-to-frame nuts. Lower the jack and detach the shock module from the frame.

9   Drive the inner CV joint out of the differential or off of the intermediate shaft (see Section 12). Have an assistant support the steering knuckle and shock absorber module while this is done.

10 Using wire or rope, support the inner end of the driveaxle to the frame. Also support the steering knuckle and shock module.

11 Repeat Steps 5 through 10 on the other side of the vehicle.

12 Remove the steering gear (see Chapter 10).

13 Remove the intermediate shaft bearing housing and the intermediate shaft (see Sections 16 and 17).

14 Remove the differential carrier mounting bolts. Separate the differential carrier from the oil pan, then tie it to the frame with wire.

15 Remove the oil pan (see Chapter 2A).

16 Place a jack beneath the differential carrier. Carefully untie its support wire, then position it on the jack and lower it to the floor.

17 Installation is the reverse of the removal procedure. Tighten all fasteners to the proper torque values (see the Specifications at the end of this Chapter, Chapter 2A and Chapter 10). Tighten the wheel lug nuts to the torque listed in the Chapter 1 Specifications.

18 Refill the engine with oil and the front differential with the proper lubricant (see Chapter 1).

19 Differential oil seals (front, 4WD models) - replacement

LEFT SIDE SEAL

1   Loosen the wheel lug nuts, raise the vehicle, place it securely on jackstands and remove the wheel. Remove the splash shield from under the front axle.

2   Remove the left driveaxle (see Section 12).

3   Drain the lubricant from the front differential (see Chapter 1).

4   Pry the seal out with a seal remover or pull it out with a slide hammer and adapter.

5   Drive in a new seal, using a seal driver or a socket slightly smaller in diameter than the seal. Lubricate the lips of the seal with multi-purpose grease.

6   Install the axleshaft.

7   Fill the differential with the proper lubricant (see Chapter 1).

8   Install the driveaxle (see Section 12).

9   Install the splash shield.

10 Install the wheel, lower the vehicle and check for proper operation.

RIGHT SIDE SEAL

11 Remove the differential (see Section 18).

12 Drain the lubricant from the front differential (see Chapter 1).

13 Pry the seal out with a seal remover or pull it out with a slide hammer and adapter.

14 Drive in a new seal, using a seal driver or a socket slightly smaller in diameter than the seal. Lubricate the lips of the seal with multi-purpose grease.

15 Refer to Section 18 and install the differential.

Specifications

General

Inner CV joint length (see illustration 13.3r)

Male tripot housing	11 inches
Female tripot housing	9 inches

Torque specifications — Ft-lbs (unless otherwise indicated)

➥**Note: One foot-pound (ft-lb) of torque is equivalent to 12 inch-pounds (in-lbs) of torque. Torque values below approximately 15 ft-lbs are expressed in inch-pounds, since most foot-pound torque wrenches are not accurate at these smaller values.**

Driveshaft

Driveshaft U-joint strap bolts	15
Rear steering gear crossmember mounting bolts	37

Driveaxles (4WD models)

Driveaxle/hub nut	103

Rear axle

Pinion shaft lock bolt	27
Differential cover bolts	
8.0 inch axle	20
8.6 inch axle	18

Front axle (4WD models)

Intermediate shaft bearing housing bolts	35
Differential housing-to-oil pan bolts	63
Shift actuator bolts (electric shift model)	53 inch-lbs

Section

Reference to other Chapters

9

BRAKES

1 General information

GENERAL

The vehicles covered by this manual are equipped with hydrauli-cally operated front and rear disc brake systems. Both the front and rear brakes are self adjusting (disc brakes automatically compensate for pad wear).

HYDRAULIC SYSTEM

The hydraulic system consists of two separate circuits. The master cylinder has separate reservoirs for the two circuits, and, in the event of a leak or failure in one hydraulic circuit, the other circuit will remain operative and a warning indicator will light up on the instrument panel when a substantial amount of brake fluid is lost, showing that a failure has occurred.

POWER BRAKE BOOSTER

The power brake booster uses engine manifold vacuum to provide assistance to the brakes. It is mounted on the firewall in the engine compartment, directly behind the master cylinder.

PARKING BRAKE

The parking brake operates the rear brakes only, through cable actuation. It's activated by a lever mounted in the center console. The parking brake cables actuate a pair of parking brake shoes mounted inside of the drum (hub) portion of each rear brake disc.

SERVICE

After completing any operation involving disassembly of any part of the brake system, always test drive the vehicle to check for proper braking performance before resuming normal driving. When testing the brakes, perform the tests on a clean, dry, flat surface. Conditions other than these can lead to inaccurate test results.

Test the brakes at various speeds with both light and heavy pedal pressure. The vehicle should stop evenly without pulling to one side or the other.

Tires, vehicle load and wheel alignment are factors which also affect braking performance.

> ### ❊ WARNING:
>
> **Never, under any circumstances, rely on a jack to support the vehicle while working on it. Whenever any of the suspension or steering fasteners are loosened or removed they must be inspected and, if necessary, replaced with new ones of the same part number or of original equipment quality and design. Torque specifications must be followed for proper reassembly and component retention. Never attempt to heat or straighten any suspension or steering components. Instead, replace any bent or damaged part with a new one.**

2 Anti-lock Brake System (ABS) - general information

▶ **Refer to illustration 2.3**

Anti-lock Brake Systems (ABS) maintain vehicle maneuverability, directional stability, and optimum deceleration under severe braking conditions on most road surfaces. They do so by monitoring the rota-tional speed of the wheels and controlling the brake line pressure to the wheels during braking. This prevents the wheels from locking up on slippery roads or during hard braking.

The ABS system on these vehicles is a three-sensor system; each front wheel is equipped with its own sensor, and the rear wheels share a sensor (mounted in the extension housing of the transmission on 2WD models and in the transfer case on 4WD models). This means that the brake line pressure to the front wheels can be controlled individually, but the two rear brakes are controlled together.

ELECTRO-HYDRAULIC CONTROL UNIT (EHCU)

The Electro-Hydraulic Control Unit (EHCU), mounted on the left-side frame rail, controls hydraulic pressure to the brake calipers by modulating hydraulic pressure to prevent wheel lock-up (see illustra-tion). It is made up of the Brake Pressure Modulator Valve (BPMV) and the Electronic Brake Control Module (EBCM). Basically, the BPMV bleeds off pressure in a brake line when the Electronic Brake Control Module (EBCM) detects an abnormal deceleration in the speed of a wheel (via a wheel speed sensor signal). When the speed of the wheel is restored to normal, the modulator once again allows full pressure to the brake. This cycle is repeated as many times as necessary, which results in a pulsing of the brake pedal.

➡ **Note: The EHCU can't increase brake line pressure above that which is generated by the master cylinder, and it can't apply the brakes by itself.**

In addition to sensing and processing information received from the brake switch and wheel speed sensors to control the hydraulic line pressure and avoid wheel lock up, the EBCM also continually monitors the system and stores fault codes which indicate specific problems.

2.3 The ABS Electro-Hydraulic Control Unit (EHCU) is located along the left frame rail, underneath the driver

WHEEL SPEED SENSORS

Each front wheel is equipped with a speed sensor, which is mounted on each front hub and wheel bearing assembly. A toothed sensor ring is integral with the bearing; if it becomes damaged, the entire hub/wheel bearing assembly must be replaced. If the actual sensor which bolts to the hub and bearing assembly malfunctions, it can be replaced separately. The sensors are neither adjustable nor rebuildable.

Rear wheel speed is monitored by the Vehicle Speed Sensor (VSS), which is located in the extension housing on 2WD models and the transfer case on 4WD models. For more information on the VSS, see Chapter 6.

A wheel speed sensor measures wheel speed by monitoring the rotation of a toothed ring. As the teeth of the ring move through the magnetic field of the sensor, an AC voltage signal is generated. This signal frequency increases or decreases in proportion to the speed of the wheel. The EBCM monitors these signals for changes in wheel speed; if it detects the sudden deceleration of a wheel, i.e. wheel lockup, the EBCM activates the ABS system.

WARNING LIGHTS

The ABS system has self-diagnostic capabilities. Each time the vehicle is started, the EBCM runs a self-test. There are two warning lights on the instrument panel, a red BRAKE light and an amber ABS light, each with their own functions. During starting, these lights should come on briefly then go out. If the red BRAKE light stays on, it indicates a problem with the main braking system, such as low fluid level detected or the parking brake is still on. If the light stays on after the parking brake is released, check the brake fluid level in the master cylinder reservoir (see Chapter 1).

The amber ABS light indicates a problem with the ABS system, not the main or basic brake system. If the light stays on, it indicates that there is a problem with the ABS system, but the main system is still working. Take the vehicle to a dealer service department or other qualified repair shop for diagnosis and repair.

CHECKS

Although a special electronic tester is necessary to properly diagnose the system, the home mechanic can perform a few preliminary checks before taking the vehicle to a dealer service department or other repair shop which is equipped with this tester:

a) Check the fuses.
b) Check the electrical connectors at the EBCM and the hydraulic modulator/motor pack.
c) Follow the wiring harness to the speed sensors and brake light switch and make sure all connections are secure and the wiring isn't damaged.
d) Make sure the brake lines, calipers and wheel cylinders are in good condition.

If the above preliminary checks don't rectify the problem, the vehicle should be diagnosed by a dealer service department or other qualified repair shop.

---

3   Disc brake pads - replacement

▶ Refer to illustrations 3.5a through 3.5l

> ❋❋ **WARNING:**
>
> **Disc brake pads must be replaced on both front or both rear wheels at the same time - never replace the pads on only one wheel. Also, the dust created by the brake system is harmful to your health. Never blow it out with compressed air and don't inhale any of it. An approved filtering mask should be worn when working on the brakes. Do not, under any circumstances, use petroleum-based solvents to clean brake parts. Use brake system cleaner only!**

➡ **Note: This procedure applies to the front and rear brake pads.**

1   Remove the cap from the brake fluid reservoir. Remove about two-thirds of the fluid from the reservoir, then reinstall the cap.

> ❋❋ **CAUTION:**
>
> **Brake fluid will damage paint. If any fluid is spilled, wash it off immediately with plenty of clean, cold water.**

2   Loosen the front or rear wheel lug nuts, raise the front or rear of the vehicle and support it securely on jackstands. Block the wheels at the opposite end.

3   Remove the wheels. Work on one brake assembly at a time, using the assembled brake for reference if necessary.

4   Inspect the brake disc carefully as outlined in Section 5. If

3.5a Before disassembling the brake, wash it thoroughly with brake system cleaner and allow it to dry - position a drain pan under the brake to catch the residue - DO NOT use compressed air to blow off brake dust!

machining is necessary, follow the information in that Section to remove the disc.

5   Follow the accompanying photo sequence for the actual pad replacement procedure (see illustrations). Be sure to stay in order and read the caption under each illustration.

3.5b To make room for the new pads, use a C-clamp to depress the piston(s) into the caliper before removing the caliper and pads - do this a little at a time, keeping an eye on the fluid level in the master cylinder to make sure it doesn't overflow

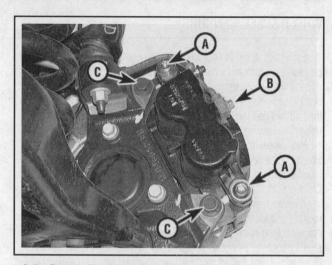

3.5c Front caliper mounting details

A   Caliper mounting bolts
B   Brake hose inlet fitting bolt
C   Caliper mounting bracket bolts

3.5d If you're replacing the front brake pads, remove the lower mounting bolt and pivot the caliper up, supporting it in this position. If you're replacing the rear pads, hold the upper caliper slide pin with an open-end wrench, remove the upper mounting bolt with another wrench, then pivot the caliper down for access to the brake pads

6   When reinstalling the caliper, be sure to tighten the mounting bolts to the torque listed in this Chapter's Specifications. Tighten the wheel lug nuts to the torque listed in the Chapter 1 Specifications.

7   After the job has been completed, firmly depress the brake pedal a few times to bring the pads into contact with the disc. Check the level of the brake fluid, adding some if necessary (see Chapter 1). Check the operation of the brakes carefully before placing the vehicle into normal service.

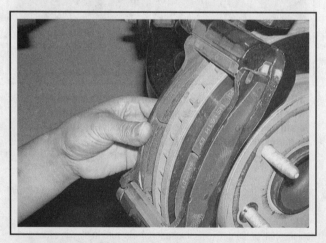

3.5e Remove the inner brake pad

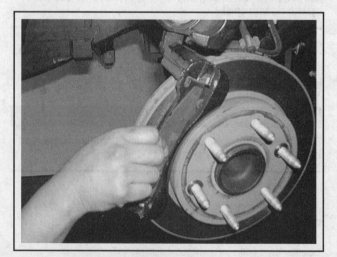

3.5f Remove the outer brake pad

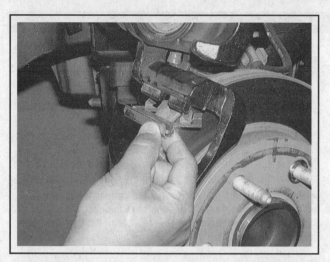

3.5g Remove the upper and lower pad retainers from the caliper mounting bracket; if they are cracked or distorted, replace them

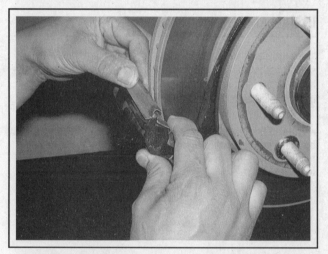

3.5i Install the upper and lower pad retainers on the caliper mounting bracket

3.5k . . . and the outer brake pad

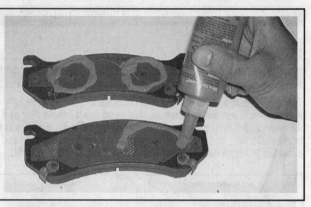

3.5h Apply anti-squeal compound to the back of both pads (let the compound "set up" a few minutes before installing them)

3.5j Install the inner brake pad . . .

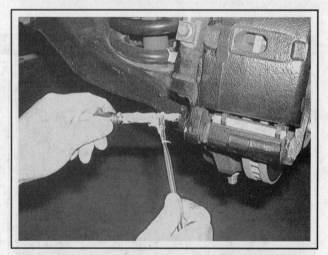

3.5l If you're replacing the front pads, inspect the caliper mounting bolt for scoring and corrosion, then lubricate it with high-temperature brake grease (if it was dry, pivot the caliper up again, slide the upper mounting bolt out of the bracket and lubricate it, too). If you're replacing the rear pads, check the condition of the slide pin and the rubber boot, then lubricate the pin with high-temperature brake grease (if it was dry, do the same thing to the lower slide pin)

4   Brake caliper - removal and installation

♦ Refer to illustration 4.2

✳✳ WARNING:

The dust created by the brake system is harmful to your health. Never blow it out with compressed air and don't inhale any of it. An approved filtering mask should be worn when working on the brakes. Do not, under any circumstances, use petroleum-based solvents to clean brake parts. Use brake system cleaner only!

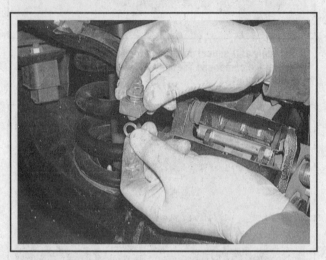

4.2 There is a sealing washer on either side of the brake hose inlet fitting; be sure to replace these with new ones when reconnecting the hose

REMOVAL

1   Loosen the front or rear wheel lug nuts, raise the front or rear of the vehicle and place it securely on jackstands. Block the wheels at the opposite end. Remove the front or rear wheel.

2   Remove the inlet fitting bolt and disconnect the brake hose from the caliper. Discard the old sealing washers (see illustration). Plug the brake hose immediately to keep contaminants and air out of the brake system and to prevent losing any more brake fluid than is necessary.

→Note: If you are simply removing the caliper for access to other components, leave the brake hose connected and suspend the caliper with a length of wire - don't let it hang by the hose (see illustration 5.2).

3   Remove the caliper mounting bolts and detach the caliper from the mounting bracket. When removing a rear caliper, hold the slide pins with an open-end wrench to prevent them from turning when the mounting bolts are unscrewed (see illustration 3.5e).

INSTALLATION

4   Installation is the reverse of removal. Don't forget to use new sealing washers on each side of the brake hose inlet fitting and be sure to tighten the fitting bolt and the caliper mounting bolts to the torque listed in this Chapter's Specifications.

5   Bleed the brake system (see Section 8).

→Note: If the brake hose was not disconnected, bleeding won't be required. Make sure there are no leaks from the hose connections. Test the brakes carefully before returning the vehicle to normal service.

5   Brake disc - inspection, removal and installation

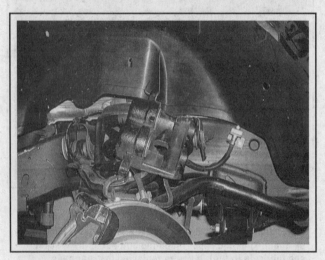

5.2 Hang the caliper out of the way with a piece of wire - don't let it hang by the brake hose!

INSPECTION

♦ Refer to illustrations 5.2, 5.3, 5.4a, 5.4b, 5.5a and 5.5b

1   Loosen the wheel lug nuts, raise the vehicle and support it securely on jackstands. Remove the wheel and install the lug nuts to hold the disc in place.

→Note: If the lug nuts don't contact the disc when screwed on all the way, install washers under them.

2   Remove the brake caliper. It isn't necessary to disconnect the brake hose. After removing the caliper bolts, suspend the caliper out of the way with a piece of wire (see illustration).

3   Visually inspect the disc surface for score marks and other damage. Light scratches and shallow grooves are normal after use and may not always be detrimental to brake operation, but deep scoring requires disc removal and refinishing by an automotive machine shop. Be sure to check both sides of the disc (see illustration). If pulsating has been noticed during application of the brakes, suspect disc runout.

5.3 The brake pads on this vehicle were obviously neglected, as they wore down completely and cut deep grooves into the disc - wear this severe means the disc must be replaced

5.4a To check disc runout, mount a dial indicator as shown and rotate the disc

4   To check disc runout, place a dial indicator at a point about 1/2-inch from the outer edge of the disc (see illustration). Set the indicator to zero and turn the disc. The indicator reading should not exceed the specified allowable runout limit. If it does, the disc should be refinished by an automotive machine shop.

→Note: When replacing the brake pads, it's a good idea to resurface the discs regardless of the dial indicator reading, as this will impart a smooth finish and ensure a perfectly flat surface, eliminating any brake pedal pulsation or other undesirable symptoms related to questionable discs. At the very least, if you elect not to have the discs resurfaced, remove the glaze from the surface with emery cloth or sandpaper, using a swirling motion (see illustration).

5   It's absolutely critical that the disc not be machined to a thickness under the specified minimum thickness. The minimum wear (or discard) thickness is cast into the underside of the front discs (see illustration) and on the outside of rear discs. The disc thickness can be checked with a micrometer (see illustration).

5.4b Using a swirling motion, remove the glaze from the disc with sandpaper or emery cloth

5.5a The minimum thickness is cast into the disc

5.5b Use a micrometer to measure disc thickness

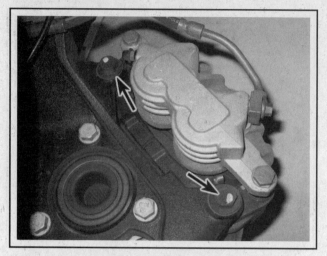

5.6a Caliper mounting bracket bolts - front

5.6b Caliper mounting bracket bolts - rear

REMOVAL

▶ **Refer to illustrations 5.6a, 5.6b and 5.7**

6   Remove the two caliper mounting bracket bolts and detach the mounting bracket (see illustrations).

7   Remove the lug nuts which you installed to hold the disc in place and slide the disc off the hub. If pressed-metal retaining clips are present on any of the wheel studs, cut them off (see illustration). (When reinstalling the disc it isn't necessary to reinstall these clips.)

INSTALLATION

8   Place the disc in position over the threaded studs.

9   Install the mounting bracket and tighten the bolts to the torque listed in this Chapter's Specifications. Install the brake pads.

10 Install the caliper onto the mounting bracket, tightening the bolts to the torque listed in this Chapter's Specifications.

11 Install the wheel and lug nuts. Lower the vehicle and tighten the lug nuts to the torque listed in the Chapter 1 Specifications. Depress the brake pedal a few times to bring the brake pads into contact with the

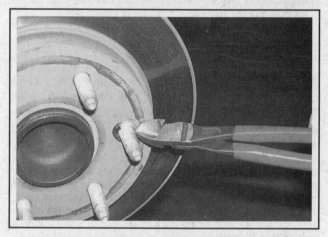

5.7 Cut off and discard the disc retaining washers, if present (it isn't necessary to reinstall them)

disc. Bleeding won't be necessary unless the brake hose was disconnected from the caliper. Check the operation of the brakes carefully before driving the vehicle.

---

6   Master cylinder - removal, installation and reservoir/O-ring replacement

REMOVAL

▶ **Refer to illustration 6.2**

1   Disconnect the cable from the negative terminal of the battery.

2   Unplug the electrical connector for the fluid level warning switch (see illustration).

3   Remove as much fluid as possible from the reservoir with a suction gun, large syringe or a poultry baster.

✳ WARNING:

If a poultry baster is used, never again use it for the preparation of food.

4   Place rags under the fittings and prepare caps or plastic bags to cover the ends of the lines once they're disconnected.

✳ CAUTION:

Brake fluid will damage paint. Cover all body parts and be careful not to spill fluid during this procedure.

Loosen the fittings at the ends of the brake lines where they enter the master cylinder. To prevent rounding off the flats, use a flare-nut wrench, which wraps around the fitting hex.

5   Pull the brake lines away from the master cylinder and plug the ends to prevent contamination.

6   Remove the nuts attaching the master cylinder to the power

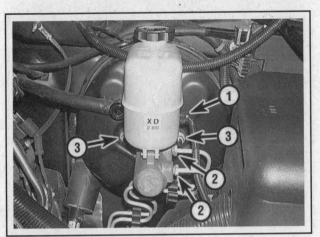

6.2 Master cylinder mounting details

1 *Electrical connector for fluid level sensor*
2 *Brake line fittings*
3 *Mounting nuts*

booster (see illustration 6.2). Pull the master cylinder off the studs to remove it. Again, be careful not to spill the fluid as this is done.

INSTALLATION

▶ **Refer to illustrations 6.8 and 6.16**

7 Bench bleed the new master cylinder before installing it. Mount the master cylinder in a vise, with the jaws of the vise clamping on the mounting flange.

8 Attach a pair of master cylinder bleeder tubes to the outlet ports of the master cylinder (see illustration).

9 Fill the reservoir with brake fluid of the recommended type (see Chapter 1).

10 Slowly push the pistons into the master cylinder (a large Phillips screwdriver can be used for this) - air will be expelled from the pressure chambers and into the reservoir. Because the tubes are submerged in fluid, air can't be drawn back into the master cylinder when you release the pistons.

11 Repeat the procedure until no more air bubbles are present.

12 Remove the bleed tubes, one at a time, and install plugs in the open ports to prevent fluid leakage and air from entering. Install the reservoir cap.

13 Install the master cylinder over the studs on the power brake booster and tighten the attaching nuts only finger tight at this time. Don't forget to use a new gasket.

14 Thread the brake line fittings into the master cylinder. Since the master cylinder is still a bit loose, it can be moved slightly so the fittings thread in easily. Don't strip the threads as the fittings are tightened.

15 Tighten the mounting nuts to the torque listed in this Chapter's Specifications. Tighten the brake line fittings securely.

16 Fill the master cylinder reservoir with fluid, then bleed the lines at the master cylinder, followed by bleeding the remainder of the brake system (see Section 8). To bleed the lines at the master cylinder, have an assistant depress the brake pedal and hold it down. Loosen the fitting to allow air and fluid to escape (see illustration). Tighten the fitting, then allow your assistant to return the pedal to its rest position. Repeat this procedure on both fittings until the fluid is free of air bubbles, then bleed the rest of the system. Check the operation of the brake system carefully before driving the vehicle.

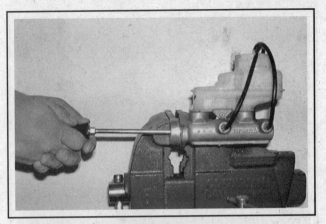

6.8 The best way to bleed air from the master cylinder before installing it on the vehicle is with a pair of bleeder tubes that direct brake fluid into the reservoir during bleeding

❋❋ WARNING:

If you do not have a firm brake pedal at the end of the bleeding procedure, or have any doubts as to the effectiveness of the brake system, DO NOT drive the vehicle. Have it towed to a dealer service department or other qualified repair shop for diagnosis.

RESERVOIR/O-RING REPLACEMENT

▶ **Refer to illustrations 6.19 and 6.21**

➡ **Note: The brake fluid reservoir can be replaced separately from the master cylinder body if it becomes damaged. If there is leakage between the reservoir and the master cylinder body, the O-rings on the reservoir can be replaced.**

17 Remove as much fluid as possible from the reservoir with a suction gun, large syringe or a poultry baster.

❋❋ WARNING:

If a poultry baster is used, never again use it for the preparation of food.

6.16 Have an assistant depress the brake pedal and hold it down, then loosen the fitting nut, allowing air and fluid to escape; repeat this procedure on both fittings until the fluid is clear of air bubbles

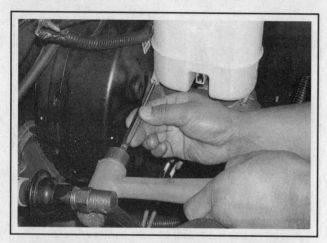

6.19 Driving out the roll pins that retain the master cylinder fluid reservoir

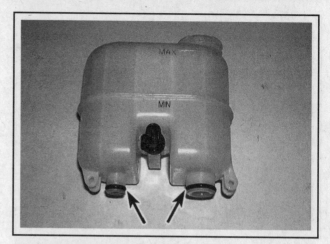

6.21 The reservoir O-rings can be replaced if they are leaking

18 Place rags under the master cylinder to absorb any fluid that may spill out once the reservoir is detached from the master cylinder.

❊❊ CAUTION:

Brake fluid will damage paint. Cover all body parts and be careful not to spill fluid during this procedure.

19 Using a hammer and a small punch, drive out the roll pins that retain the reservoir to the master cylinder (see illustration).

20 Pull the reservoir out of the master cylinder body.

21 If you are simply replacing the O-rings, carefully pry the old O-rings off and install new ones (see illustration).

22 Lubricate the reservoir O-rings with clean brake fluid, then press the reservoir into place on the master cylinder body and secure it with new roll pins.

23 Refill the reservoir with the recommended brake fluid (see Chapter 1) and check for leaks.

24 Bleed the master cylinder (see illustration 6.16).

---

7   Brake hoses and lines - inspection and replacement

INSPECTION

1 About every six months, with the vehicle raised and supported securely on jackstands, the rubber hoses which connect the steel brake lines with the front and rear brake assemblies should be inspected for cracks, chafing of the outer cover, leaks, blisters and other damage. These are important and vulnerable parts of the brake system and inspection should be complete. A light and mirror will be helpful for a thorough check. If a hose exhibits any of the above conditions, replace it with a new one.

REPLACEMENT

Front flexible brake hoses

◗ Refer to illustrations 7.3 and 7.4

2 Loosen the wheel lug nuts, raise the vehicle and support it securely on jackstands. Remove the wheel.

3 At the bracket, unscrew the brake line fitting from the hose (see illustration). Use a flare-nut wrench to prevent rounding off the corners of the fitting nut, and hold the hose end with a wrench to prevent twist-

7.3 Using a flare-nut wrench, unscrew the threaded fitting on the brake line . . .

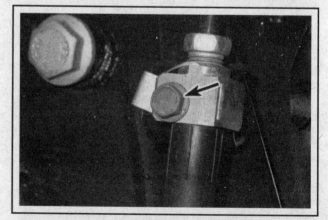

7.4 . . . then remove the bolt and detach the hose from the bracket

7.11 At the end of the brake hose, unscrew the line fitting with a flare-nut wrench . . .

7.12 . . . then unbolt the fitting from the chassis

ing the frame bracket.

4   Remove the bolt from the bracket, then detach the hose from the bracket (see illustration).

5   At the caliper end of the hose, remove the inlet fitting bolt, then separate the hose from the caliper. Note that there are two copper sealing washers on either side of the inlet fitting (see illustration 4.2) - they should be replaced with new ones during installation.

6   To install the hose, connect the fitting to the caliper with the inlet fitting bolt and new sealing washers. Tighten the inlet fitting bolt to the torque listed in this Chapter's Specifications.

7   Route the hose into its original location, making sure it isn't twisted. Tighten the hose bracket bolt securely. Connect the brake line fitting, starting the threads by hand. Tighten the fitting securely.

8   Bleed the caliper (see Section 8).

9   Install the wheel and lug nuts, lower the vehicle and tighten the lug nuts to the torque listed in the Chapter 1 Specifications.

Rear flexible brake hose

▶ **Refer to illustrations 7.11 and 7.12**

10   Raise the rear of the vehicle and support it securely on jackstands. Block the front wheels to prevent the vehicle from rolling.

11   At the bracket, unscrew the brake line fitting from the hose (see illustration). Use a flare-nut wrench to prevent rounding off the corners of the fitting nut, and hold the hose end with a wrench to prevent twisting the frame bracket.

12   Remove the bolt from the bracket, then detach the hose from the bracket (see illustration).

13   At the caliper end of the hose, remove the inlet fitting bolt, then separate the hose from the caliper. Note that there are two copper sealing washers on either side of the inlet fitting (see illustration 4.2) - they should be replaced with new ones during installation.

14   To install the hose, connect the fitting to the caliper with the inlet fitting bolt and new sealing washers. Tighten the inlet fitting bolt to the torque listed in this Chapter's Specifications.

15   Route the hose into its original location, making sure it isn't twisted. Tighten the hose bracket bolt securely. Connect the brake line fitting, starting the threads by hand. Tighten the fitting securely.

16   Bleed the caliper (see Section 8).

17   Install the wheel and lug nuts, lower the vehicle and tighten the lug nuts to the torque listed in the Chapter 1 Specifications.

Metal brake lines

18   When replacing brake lines, be sure to use the correct parts. Don't use copper tubing for any brake system components. Purchase steel brake lines from a dealer or auto parts store.

19   Prefabricated brake line, with the tube ends already flared and fittings installed, is available at auto parts stores and dealer parts departments. These lines must be bent to the proper shapes using a tubing bender.

20   When installing the new line, make sure it's securely supported in the brackets and has plenty of clearance between moving or hot components. Make sure there's at least 1/4-inch of clearance between parallel brake lines.

21   After installation, check the master cylinder fluid level and add fluid as necessary. Bleed the brake system (see Section 8) and test the brakes carefully before driving the vehicle in traffic.

---

8   Brake hydraulic system - bleeding

▶ **Refer to illustration 8.8**

❋❋ WARNING:

Wear eye protection when bleeding the brake system. If the fluid comes in contact with your eyes, immediately rinse them with water and seek medical attention.

➡**Note: Bleeding the hydraulic system is necessary to remove any air that manages to find its way into the system when it's been opened during removal and installation of a hose, line, caliper or master cylinder.**

1   You'll probably have to bleed the system at all four brakes if air has entered it due to low fluid level, or if the brake lines have been disconnected at the master cylinder.

2 If a brake line was disconnected only at a wheel, then only that caliper must be bled.

3 If a brake line is disconnected at a fitting located between the master cylinder and any of the brakes, that part of the system served by the disconnected line must be bled.

4 Remove any residual vacuum from the power brake booster by applying the brake several times with the engine off.

5 Remove the master cylinder reservoir cap and fill the reservoir with brake fluid. Reinstall the cap.

➡**Note: Check the fluid level often during the bleeding operation and add fluid as necessary to prevent the fluid level from falling low enough to allow air bubbles into the master cylinder.**

6 Have an assistant on hand, as well as a supply of new brake fluid, a clear container partially filled with clean brake fluid, a length of clear tubing to fit over the bleeder valve and a wrench to open and close the bleeder valve.

7 Beginning at the right rear wheel, loosen the bleeder valve slightly, then tighten it to a point where it's snug but can still be loos-

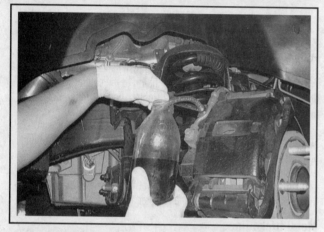

8.8 When bleeding the brakes, a hose is connected to the bleed screw at the caliper and then submerged in brake fluid - air will be seen as bubbles in the tube and container (all air must be expelled before moving to the next wheel)

ened quickly and easily.

8 Place one end of the tubing over the bleeder valve and submerge the other end in brake fluid in the container (see illustration).

9 Have the assistant depress the brake pedal slowly and hold it in the depressed position.

10 While the pedal is held down, open the bleeder valve just enough to allow a flow of fluid to leave the valve. Watch for air bubbles to exit the submerged end of the tube. When the fluid flow slows after a couple of seconds, close the valve and have your assistant release the pedal.

11 Repeat Steps 9 and 10 until no more air is seen leaving the tube, then tighten the bleeder valve and proceed to the left rear wheel, the right front wheel and the left front wheel, in that order, and perform the same procedure. Be sure to check the fluid in the master cylinder reservoir frequently.

12 Never use old brake fluid. It contains moisture which can cause the fluid to boil, rendering the brake system inoperative.

13 Refill the master cylinder with fluid at the end of the operation.

14 Check the operation of the brakes. The pedal should feel solid when depressed, with no sponginess. If necessary, repeat the entire process.

15 Before driving the vehicle, sit in the driver's seat and:

a) *Take your foot off the brake pedal*

b) *Start the engine and let it run for a minimum of 10 seconds. Watch the amber ABS light on the dash.*

c) *If the light comes on and does not turn off after 10 seconds, have the vehicle towed to a dealer service department or other qualified repair shop. A scan tool will have to be used to diagnose the ABS system.*

d) *If the ABS light goes off after three seconds or so, turn off the ignition.*

e) *Repeat paragraphs a) through d) one more time. If the amber ABS light turns off, test drive the vehicle in an isolated area before returning the vehicle to normal service.*

✳✳ **WARNING:**

Do not operate the vehicle if you're in doubt about the effectiveness of the brake system.

9 Power brake booster - check, removal and installation

▸ **Refer to illustrations 9.6, 9.9 and 9.10**

✳✳ **WARNING:**

These models have airbags. Always disable the airbag system before working in the vicinity of any airbag system component to avoid the possibility of accidental deployment of the airbag(s), which could cause personal injury (see Chapter 12).

CHECK

Operating check

1 Depress the pedal and start the engine. If the pedal goes down slightly, operation is normal.

2 Depress the brake pedal several times with the engine running and make sure that there is no change in the pedal reserve distance.

Airtightness check

3 Start the engine and turn it off after one or two minutes. Depress the brake pedal several times slowly. If the pedal goes down farther the first time but gradually rises after the second or third depression, the booster is airtight.

4 Depress the brake pedal while the engine is running, then stop the engine with the pedal depressed. If there is no change in the pedal reserve travel after holding the pedal for 30 seconds, the booster is airtight.

REMOVAL

5 Disable the airbag system (see Chapter 12). Disconnect the cable from the negative terminal of the battery.

6 Detach the vacuum hose from the booster (see illustration).

7 Remove the master cylinder without detaching the brake lines.

9.6 Pull the vacuum hose fitting straight out of the grommet in the booster

9.9 Pry off the clip retaining the brake light switch and the booster pushrod to the pin on the brake pedal

Pull it forward and position it aside. Be careful not to bend or kink the brake lines.

8 Remove the left side under-dash panel.

9 Remove the pushrod retaining clip (see illustration) and slip the brake light switch and the pushrod off the pin.

10 Remove the four nuts holding the brake booster to the firewall (see illustration).

11 Slide the booster straight out from the firewall until the studs clear the holes and pull the booster and gasket from the engine compartment.

INSTALLATION

12 Installation is the reverse of removal. Be sure to use a new gasket, and tighten the booster mounting nuts and the master cylinder mounting nuts to the torque values listed in this Chapter's Specifications.

9.10 Unscrew the booster mounting nuts

10 Brake pedal travel - check

1 The brake pedal is not adjustable, but the travel should be checked if the pedal seems low. You'll need a tape measure, yardstick or ruler for this procedure.

2 Depress the pedal a few times to deplete the reserve in the power brake booster.

3 Measure the position of the pedal at rest. You can either measure from the floor to the pedal or from the pedal to the steering wheel.

Record your reading.

4 Now, depress the pedal (exerting approximately 100 lbs. of force) and measure how far the pedal has traveled. Compare your findings with the measurement listed in this Chapter's Specifications.

5 If the pedal travel is excessive, check for air in the system (bleed the brakes - see Section 8). A failed seal in the master cylinder could also cause excessive pedal travel.

11 Parking brake - adjustment

The parking brake cable is self-adjusting, but if the parking brake pedal travel is excessive or won't hold the vehicle on an incline, the parking brake shoes may need to be adjusted or replaced (see Section 13).

12 Parking brake lever and cables - replacement

LEVER

♦ **Refer to illustrations 12.4, 12.5, 12.7 and 12.10**

1 Disconnect the cable from the negative terminal of the battery.

2 Remove the floor console (see Chapter 11).

3 Block the wheels so the vehicle won't roll and place the parking brake lever in its fully released position.

4 From underneath the vehicle, pull the equalizer toward the rear of the vehicle to expose the inner parking brake cable. Clamp the exposed cable with padded locking pliers to hold the cable extended, which will relieve tension on the rear cables (see illustration).

✳✳ CAUTION:

Don't nick or cut the plastic anti-corrosion coating on the cable.

5 Inside the vehicle, use a screwdriver to rotate the self-adjuster clip into the lock position (see illustration).

6 Under the vehicle, remove the locking pliers from the cable.

7 Inside the vehicle, lift the parking brake lever partway, but stop before the self-adjuster clip touches the mounting bracket tab. Lift the latch, then raise the parking brake lever all the way.

8 Inside the vehicle, disconnect the electrical connector for the parking brake warning light switch.

9 Under the vehicle, free the parking brake cables from the equalizer.

10 Unscrew the mounting nuts, then lift the lever off its mounting studs (see illustration).

11 Install the lever in the vehicle and tighten its mounting nuts securely. Connect the electrical connector for the parking brake switch.

12 Reconnect the cables to the equalizer.

13 Inside the vehicle, lower the parking brake lever all the way, then raise it. Pull the lever boot up to expose the multiplier lever at the front of the parking brake lever, then raise and lower it three times. This will re-enable the automatic adjuster.

14 Pull and release the parking brake lever three times to adjust the cables, then reposition the lever boot.

15 Check the operation of the parking brake before driving the vehicle.

12.4 Pad a pair of locking pliers to protect the cable, then clamp them on the cable to hold it extended

12.5 Use a screwdriver to place the self-adjuster in the lock position

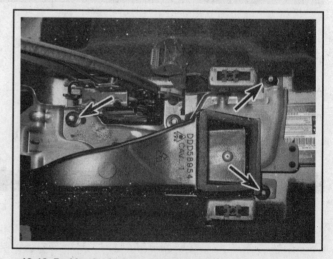

12.7 Lift the latch and raise the lever all the way

12.10 Parking brake lever mounting nuts

12.21 Remove the nuts from the cable retainer studs

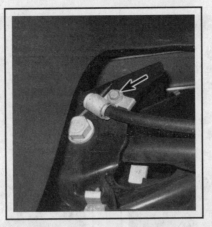

12.22 Remove the nuts securing the cable to the frame bracket

12.23 Compress the prongs, pull the cable out of the bracket and slip the cable through the bracket slot

CABLES

▶ **Refer to illustrations 12.21, 12.22 and 12.23**

16 Disconnect the cable from the negative terminal of the battery. Release the parking brake.

17 Perform Steps 2 through 7 to disengage the automatic cable adjuster.

18 Remove the rear driveshaft from the vehicle (see Chapter 8).

19 Free the parking brake cables from the equalizer, then from the cable bracket.

20 Place a jack beneath the fuel tank to support it. Use a block of wood on top of the jack to protect the tank. Remove the fuel tank plate and rear support bracket (see Chapter 4). Lower the tank approximately four inches (just enough to expose the cable retaining nut and stud on the vehicle floor above the fuel tank).

21 Remove the nuts and slip the cables off the retainer studs on the vehicle floor (see illustration).

22 Remove the bolts and disengage the cables from the brackets on the frame (see illustration).

23 Squeeze the locking tabs that retain each cable in its bracket at the rear wheel. Pull the cable housing out of the bracket, compress the spring and slip the cable through the bracket slot (see illustration).

24 Disengage the cable from the actuator at the rear wheel.

25 Pass the cable through the frame toward the center of the vehicle, then remove it from the vehicle.

26 Start installation by passing the cable(s) over the fuel tank, then through the frame from the center of the vehicle toward the outside. The remainder of installation is the reverse of the removal steps.

27 Activate the automatic adjuster and adjust the cable as described in Steps 13 through 15.

13 Parking brake shoes - replacement

▶ **Refer to illustrations 13.3, 13.4 and 13.6**

❊❊ WARNING:

The dust created by the brake system is harmful to your health. Never blow it out with compressed air and don't inhale any of it. An approved filtering mask should be worn when working on the brakes. Do not, under any circumstances, use petroleum-based solvents to clean brake parts. Use brake system cleaner only!

1 Loosen the rear wheel lug nuts, raise the rear of the vehicle and support it securely on jackstands. Release the parking brake. Block the front wheels to prevent the vehicle from rolling, then remove the rear wheels.

2 Remove the brake caliper (see Section 4), mounting bracket and the brake disc (see Section 5). Deactivate the parking brake adjuster as described in Section 12 to provide some slack in the cables.

3 Wash the brake assembly with brake system cleaner. Slide the shoe downward until it clears the retaining clip (see illustration), then slide the shoe up and off of the actuator.

13.3 Slide the parking brake shoe downward, out of the clip

13.4 Lift one end of the parking brake shoe over the axle flange, then "wind" the rest of the shoe over the flange

13.6 Make sure the ends of the shoe seat in the adjuster screw slot (A) and the tappet slot (B); C is the adjuster screw star wheel

4   Lift one end of the shoe over the axle flange, then work the shoe over the flange and remove it (see illustration).

5   Before installing the new shoe, turn the adjuster screw star wheel in, then make sure the slots in the adjusting screw and the tappet are parallel with the backing plate.

6   To install the shoe, reverse the removal procedure. Slide the shoe under the retaining clip, then make sure the ends of the shoe seat properly in the slots in the adjuster screw and tappet (see illustration).

7   When installing the new shoe and lining assembly, turn the

adjuster screw until the shoe lining just drags on the braking surface inside the disc. Then remove the disc and back-off the adjuster screw until the shoe lining doesn't drag when the disc is installed and turned. The actual clearance between the lining surface of the shoe and the braking surface inside the disc should be 0.026-inch.

8   Installation is otherwise the reverse of the removal procedure. Be sure to tighten the caliper bracket bolts and the caliper mounting bolts to the torque listed in this Chapter's Specifications, and the wheel lug nuts to the torque listed in the Chapter 1 Specifications.

14 Brake light switch - check and replacement

▶ **Refer to illustration 14.1**

CHECK

➡**Note: The brake light switch on these vehicles is not adjustable. If it doesn't work as described below, replace it.**

1   The brake light switch (see illustration) is located on the side of the brake pedal and is retained by the same clip that retains the booster pushrod. The switch activates the brake lights at the rear of the vehicle when the pedal is depressed. To gain access to the switch, remove the left-side under-dash panel and the heater/air conditioning duct.

2   If the brake lights are inoperative, check the fuse first (see Chapter 12).

3   If the fuse is good, check for voltage to the switch on the feed wire (refer to the wiring diagrams at the end of this manual for the proper color wire to check). If no voltage is present, repair the wire between the switch and the fuse box.

4   If voltage is present, depress the brake pedal and check for voltage at the output wire terminal (again, refer to the wiring diagrams). If

14.1 The brake light switch is mounted on the side of the brake pedal arm

no voltage is present, replace the switch.

5   If voltage is present, check for power on the brake light wires at the tail light housings (with the brake pedal depressed). If voltage is not present, repair the circuit between the switch and the brake lights.

6   If voltage is present, check for a bad ground; using a jumper wire connected to a good ground, probe the ground wire terminal at the tail light connector. If the brake lights go on, repair the ground circuit (follow the ground wire from the tail light housing).

7   Keep in mind that the brake light bulbs could be burned out, but the likelihood of all the bulbs being burned out is very slim.

REPLACEMENT

8   Remove left-side under-dash panel and the heater/air conditioning duct, if not already done.

9   Unplug the electrical connector from the switch.

10 Remove the clip that retains the switch and pushrod to the pin on the brake pedal arm (see illustration 9.9) and slip the brake light switch off the pin.

11 To install the new switch, reverse the removal procedure. Make sure the retaining clip is properly installed.

Specifications

General

Brake fluid type	See Chapter 1
Brake pedal travel (maximum)	2.4 inches

Disc brakes

Minimum pad thickness	See Chapter 1
Brake disc minimum thickness	Cast into disc
Maximum disc runout	0.002 inch
Maximum disc thickness variation	0.001 inch

Torque specifications   Ft-lbs (unless otherwise indicated)

➡Note: One foot-pound (ft-lb) of torque is equivalent to 12 inch-pounds (in-lbs) of torque. Torque values below approximately 15 ft-lbs are expressed in inch-pounds, since most foot-pound torque wrenches are not accurate at these smaller values.

Brake booster mounting nuts	30
Brake caliper	
Caliper mounting guide pin bolts	
2002 and 2003	
Front	86
Rear	23
2004 and later	
Front	31
Rear	23
Caliper mounting bracket bolts	
2002 through 2005	
Front	110
Rear	147
2006 and later	
Front	118
Rear	148
Brake hose-to-caliper inlet fitting bolt	33
Brake hose-to-bracket bolt	18
Master cylinder-to-brake booster retaining nuts	27
Parking brake backing plate bolts	100
Parking brake cable mounting nuts	151 inch-lbs
Wheel speed sensor (front) mounting screw	144 inch-lbs
Wheel lug nuts	See Chapter 1

Notes

Section

Reference to other Chapters

10

SUSPENSION AND STEERING SYSTEMS

1 General information

♦ **Refer to illustrations 1.1 and 1.2**

FRONT SUSPENSION

The front suspension (see illustration) is fully independent. Each wheel is connected to the frame by a steering knuckle, upper and lower balljoints and upper and lower control arms. Shock absorber/coil spring assemblies (called shock absorber modules) are used on all models. A stabilizer bar connected to the frame and to the two lower control arms reduces body roll during cornering.

REAR SUSPENSION

The rear suspension is a five-link design, using coil springs, upper and lower control arms, a lateral link (track bar), two shock absorbers and a stabilizer bar (see illustration).

STEERING SYSTEM

The steering system consists of a rack-and-pinion steering gear and two adjustable tie-rods. Power assist is standard. The steering damper, if equipped, is attached to a bracket on the frame and to the relay rod.

RIDE CONTROL SYSTEMS

A rear air suspension is available as an option. Air springs, used in place of the standard coil springs, are automatically adjusted by an on-board compressor to keep the rear of the vehicle at the proper ride height according to the weight of the payload in the vehicle.

PRECAUTIONS

Frequently, when working on the suspension or steering system

1.1 Front suspension and steering components

1 Upper control arm	5 Lower balljoint	9 Steering gear boot
2 Stabilizer bar clamp	6 Shock absorber yoke	10 Shock absorber/coil spring module
3 Stabilizer bar	7 Tie-rod end	11 Lower control arm
4 Stabilizer bar link	8 Steering gear	12 Steering knuckle

components, you may come across fasteners which seem impossible to loosen. These fasteners on the underside of the vehicle are continually subjected to water, road grime, mud, etc., and can become rusted or "frozen," making them extremely difficult to remove. In order to unscrew these stubborn fasteners without damaging them (or other components), be sure to use lots of penetrating oil and allow it to soak in for a while. Using a wire brush to clean exposed threads will also ease removal of the nut or bolt and prevent damage to the threads. Sometimes a sharp blow with a hammer and punch is effective in breaking the bond between a nut and bolt threads, but care must be taken to prevent the punch from slipping off the fastener and ruining the threads. Heating the stuck fastener and surrounding area with a torch sometimes helps too, but isn't recommended because of the obvious dangers associated with fire. Long breaker bars and extension, or "cheater," pipes will increase leverage, but never use an extension pipe on a ratchet - the ratcheting mechanism could be damaged. Sometimes, turning the nut or bolt in the tightening (clockwise) direction first will help to break it loose. Fasteners that require drastic measures to unscrew should always be

replaced with new ones.

Since most of the procedures that are dealt with in this Chapter involve jacking up the vehicle and working underneath it, a good pair of jackstands will be needed. A hydraulic floor jack is the preferred type of jack to lift the vehicle, and it can also be used to support certain components during various operations.

❋❋ WARNING:

Never, under any circumstances, rely on a jack to support the vehicle while working on it. Also, whenever any of the suspension or steering fasteners are loosened or removed they must be inspected and, if necessary, replaced with new ones of the same part number or of original equipment quality and design. Torque specifications must be followed for proper reassembly and component retention. Never attempt to heat or straighten suspension or steering components. Instead, replace bent or damaged parts with new ones.

1.2 Rear suspension components

1	Track bar	4	Stabilizer bar link
2	Coil spring	5	Stabilizer bar
3	Shock absorber	6	Rear axle
7	Trailing arm (lower; upper arm not visible)		

2 Shock absorber module (front) - removal and installation

◆ **Refer to illustrations 2.1, 2.4a and 2.4b**

1 Open the hood and remove the shock module upper nuts (see illustration).

2 Loosen the front wheel lug nuts. Raise the front of the vehicle and support it securely on jackstands, then remove the wheel.

3 Support the outer end of the lower control arm with a floor jack (the shock absorber module serves as the down-stop for the suspension). The jack must remain in this position throughout the entire procedure.

4 Remove the nut that secures the shock absorber yoke to the control arm, then pull the yoke off the control arm stud with a two-jaw puller (see illustrations).

5 Lower the shock module clear of the vehicle and take it out.

6 Install the shock module in the vehicle with its upper studs in the upper mounting holes and slip the yoke onto the control arm stud.

7 Tighten the upper mounting nuts, then the lower nut, to the torques listed in this Chapter's Specifications.

8 Install the wheels and lug nuts, lower the vehicle and tighten the lug nuts to the torque listed in the Chapter 1 Specifications.

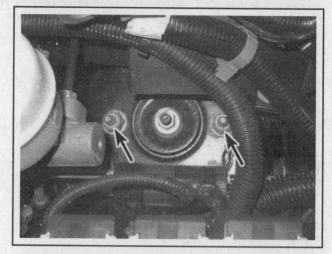

2.1 Loosen the nuts that secure the upper end of the shock module to the body

2.4a Unscrew the shock absorber yoke-to-control arm nut . . .

2.4b . . . and pull the yoke off the stud with a small puller

3 Shock absorber or coil spring (front) - replacement

◆ **Refer to illustrations 3.3, 3.4, 3.5, 3.6a and 3.6b**

1 Remove the shock module from the vehicle (see Section 2).

2 Check the shock absorber for leaking fluid, dents, cracks or other obvious damage. Check the coil spring for chips, cracks, or damage to the coating which could cause premature failure. Inspect the spring seats for hardness or general deterioration. Before disassembling your shock module to replace individual components, check on the availability of parts and the price of a complete rebuilt unit.

❊❊ **WARNING:**

Disassembling a shock absorber/coil spring assembly is potentially dangerous and utmost attention must be directed to the job, or serious injury may result. Use only a high-quality spring compressor and carefully follow the manufacturer's instructions furnished with the tool. After compressing the coil spring, set it aside in a safe, isolated area.

3 Remove the pinch bolt that secures the yoke to the shock module (see illustration). Tap a chisel or screwdriver into the gap to open the yoke slightly. Take the yoke off of the shock absorber.

4 Following the tool manufacturer's instructions, install the spring compressor (which can be obtained at most auto parts stores or equipment rental yards on a daily rental basis) on the spring and compress it sufficiently to relieve all pressure from the shock absorber (see illustration).

3.3 Remove the nut and remove the pinch bolt from the yoke, then spread the yoke slightly with a chisel or large screwdriver inserted into the gap

3.4 Install a spring compressor on the shock module

✳✳ CAUTION:

Don't damage the anti-corrosion coating on the spring when tightening the compressor.

5   Unscrew the nut from the top of the shock absorber (see illustration).

6   Remove the upper mounting plate, spring and lower mounting plate (see illustrations).

7   Reassemble the shock module by reversing the disassembly procedure. Thread the nut onto the upper end of the shock absorber and tighten it to the torque listed in this Chapter's Specifications.

8   Release the spring compressor tension and remove it from the spring.

9   Install the yoke on the bottom of the shock module. Install the pinch bolt and nut and tighten them to the torque listed in this Chapter's Specifications.

10   Install the shock module in the vehicle (see Section 2).

3.5 With the spring compressed, unscrew the nut from the top of the shock module (prevent the shaft from turning by inserting a hex bit into the end of the shaft)

3.6a Remove the upper mounting plate, noting how it fits in the spring end . . .

3.6b . . . then remove the spring from the lower mounting plate, again noting how the spring end fits in the plate

4 Stabilizer bar and bushings (front) - removal and installation

▶ **Refer to illustrations 4.2 and 4.3**

1   Raise the vehicle and support it securely on jackstands.
2   Remove the nuts from the links and remove the links (see illustration).

❊❊ CAUTION:

Don't pry the links off the studs or the link boots may be damaged.

4.2 Unscrew the stabilizer link nuts and separate the links from the stabilizer bar

➡ **Note: Be sure to keep the parts for the left and right sides separate.**

3   Remove the stabilizer bar clamp bolts (see illustration).
4   Remove the stabilizer bar.
5   Remove the rubber bushings, noting which way the slits are facing.
6   Inspect all parts for wear and damage.
7   Installation is otherwise the reverse of removal. Be sure to tighten all fasteners to the torques listed in this Chapter's Specifications.

4.3 Remove the clamp bolts and take the stabilizer bar off the vehicle

5 Upper control arm - removal and installation

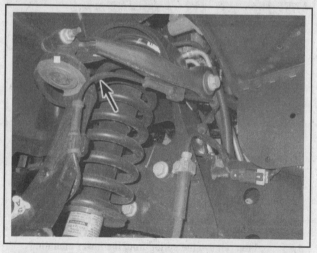

5.2 Detach the speed sensor harness from the control arm

▶ **Refer to illustrations 5.2, 5.3, 5.4 and 5.5**

REMOVAL

1   Loosen the wheel lug nuts, raise the front of the vehicle and support it securely on jackstands. Remove the wheel. Position a floor jack under the lower control arm in the area underneath the balljoint. Raise the jack slightly to take the spring pressure off the upper control arm.

❊❊ WARNING:

The jack must remain in this position throughout the entire procedure.

2   Detach the wheel speed sensor wiring harness from the arm (see illustration).
3   Unscrew the nut from the balljoint pinch bolt and remove the pinch bolt completely (see illustration).

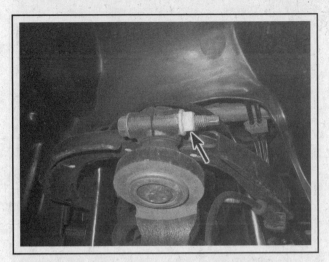

5.3 Unscrew the nut, and remove the balljoint pinch bolt

5.4 Tap a chisel into the gap in the control arm to spread it slightly

4   Disconnect the upper control arm from the steering knuckle. If it's stuck, tap a chisel into the gap in the control arm to spread it slightly (see illustration).

5   Unscrew the upper control arm pivot bolts, and remove the control arm (see illustration).

INSTALLATION

6   Installation is the reverse of the removal steps. Tighten the control arm pivot bolts and balljoint pinch bolt and nut to the torque listed in this Chapter's Specifications. Tighten the wheel lug nuts to the torque listed in the Chapter 1 Specifications.

7   Have the front end alignment checked and, if necessary, adjusted.

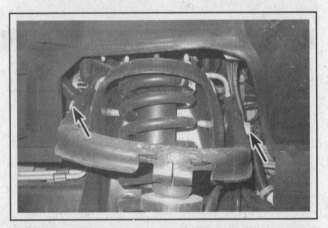

5.5 Unscrew the control arm pivot bolts

6   Lower control arm - removal and installation

▶ Refer to illustrations 6.4 and 6.5

REMOVAL

1   Loosen the wheel lug nuts, raise the vehicle and support it securely on jackstands placed under the frame rails. Remove the wheel.

2   Disconnect the stabilizer bar link from the lower control arm (see Section 4).

3   Detach the shock absorber yoke from the lower control arm (see Section 3).

4   To free the lower control arm balljoint stud from the steering knuckle, loosen the balljoint nut a few turns (don't remove it), install a balljoint remover and break the balljoint loose from the knuckle. Now remove the nut.

➡**Note: If you don't have the proper balljoint removal tool, a "picklefork" type balljoint separator can be used, but keep in mind that this type of tool will probably destroy the balljoint boot (see illustration).**

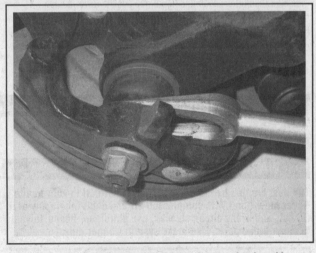

6.4 Separate the lower balljoint from the steering knuckle

5   Remove the lower control arm pivot bolts and nuts, noting which way the bolts are installed (see illustration). Pull the lower control arm from its frame brackets. Slip the balljoint stud out of the steering knuckle and remove the lower control arm from the vehicle.

INSTALLATION

6   Installation is the reverse of removal. Be sure to tighten all fasteners to the torque values listed in this Chapter's Specifications.

7   Install the wheel and lug nuts. Lower the vehicle and tighten the lug nuts to the torque listed in the Chapter 1 Specifications.

8   Have the front end alignment checked and, if necessary, adjusted.

6.5 Unscrew the lower control arm pivot bolts

7   Balljoints - check and replacement

CHECK

1   Inspect the control arm balljoints for looseness anytime either of them is separated. See if you can turn the ballstud in its socket with your fingers. If the balljoint is loose, or if the ballstud can be turned, replace the balljoint. You can also check the lower balljoints with the suspension assembled as follows.

2   Raise the front of the vehicle and support it securely on jackstands placed under the frame rails. Place a floor jack under the lower control arm and raise it slightly. Don't put the floor jack under the steering knuckle - it must be able to move independently of the control arm for this check.

3   Check for looseness in the front wheel bearings (see Chapter 1).

4   Set up a dial indicator with its plunger against the lower edge of the tire.

5   Grasp the bottom of the tire and "rock" the tire in-and-out. The dial indicator should indicate no more than 0.080-inch deflection. If the indicated reading exceeds this figure, replace the lower balljoint.

6   If you're working on a 4WD model, set up a dial indicator to measure vertical movement of the wheel. Insert a pry bar between the lower control arm and the wheel bearing outer race.

✳ CAUTION:

Don't pry against the driveaxle boot or it will be damaged.

Pry them apart and note the reading on the dial indicator. Some movement is okay, but if it exceeds 0.125-inch, replace the balljoint.

REPLACEMENT

7   If you're replacing the lower balljoint, remove the lower control arm (see Section 6). If you're replacing the upper balljoint, remove the steering knuckle (see Section 10).

8   Take the control arm or steering knuckle to an automotive machine shop or other qualified repair facility to have the old balljoint pressed out and the new one pressed in.

9   Install the control arm or steering knuckle (see Section 5 or 10).

10   Have the front end alignment checked and, if necessary, adjusted.

8   Hub and bearing assembly (front) - removal and installation

▶ **Refer to illustrations 8.4 and 8.5**

✳ WARNING:

The dust created by the brake system is harmful to your health. Never blow it out with compressed air and don't inhale any of it. Do not, under any circumstances, use petroleum-based solvents to clean brake parts. Use brake system cleaner only.

➡**Note: The hub and bearing assembly is sealed-for-life. If worn or damaged, it must be replaced as a unit.**

REMOVAL

1   Loosen the front wheel lug nuts, raise the vehicle and support it securely on jackstands. Remove the wheel.

2   If you're working on a 4WD model, remove the hub cover, then unscrew the driveaxle/hub nut with a socket and large breaker bar (see Chapter 8). Brace a large prybar across two of the wheel studs or insert a large screwdriver through the center of the brake caliper and into the disc cooling vanes to prevent the hub from turning as the nut is loosened.

8.4 The ABS wheel speed sensor is retained to the hub by one screw; remove the screw and pull the sensor straight out (don't pry on it)

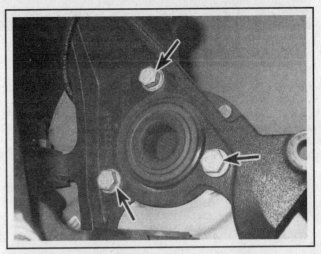

8.5 Remove the bolts that secure the hub and bearing assembly to the knuckle

3   Remove the brake caliper and hang it out of the way with a piece of wire, then remove the caliper mounting bracket (see Chapter 9). Pull the disc off the hub.

4   Remove the wheel speed sensor from the hub (see illustration).

5   Working from the back side of the steering knuckle, remove the hub retaining bolts from the steering knuckle (see illustration). Remove the disc shield.

6   Remove the hub from the steering knuckle. If you're working on a 4WD model, pull the assembly off the driveaxle splines.

✳✳ CAUTION:

Be careful not to pull outward on the driveaxle, as this could separate the inner CV joint components. If the driveaxle splines stick in the hub, attach a two-jaw puller to the hub flange and push the stub axle out of the hub. The hub assembly should come right out of the steering knuckle, but if it doesn't, tap it from side-to-side to free it.

INSTALLATION

7   Clean the mating surfaces on the steering knuckle, bearing flange and knuckle bore.

8   Insert the hub and bearing assembly into the steering knuckle and, on 4WD models, onto the end of the driveaxle.

➡**Note: On 4WD models, lubricate the splines of the driveaxle with multi-purpose grease before installing the hub.**

Position the disc shield and install the bolts, tightening them to the torque listed in this Chapter's Specifications.

9   Insert the ABS wheel speed sensor into its hole in the hub, tightening the bolt to the torque listed in the Chapter 9 Specifications.

10 Install the brake disc, caliper mounting bracket and caliper (see Chapter 9).

11 On 4WD models, install the hub nut and tighten it to the torque listed in the Chapter 8 Specifications. Prevent the axle from turning by inserting a screwdriver through the caliper and into a disc cooling vane. Install the hub cover.

12 Install the wheel, lower the vehicle and tighten the lug nuts to the torque listed in the Chapter 1 Specifications.

9   Wheel studs - replacement

♦ **Refer to illustration 9.3**

➡**Note: This procedure applies to both the front and rear wheel studs.**

1   Loosen the wheel lug nuts, raise the vehicle and support it securely on jackstands. Remove the wheel.

2   Remove the brake disc (see Chapter 9).

3   Push the stud out of the hub flange with a press tool (see illustration).

4   Insert the new stud into the hub flange from the back side and install some flat washers and a lug nut on the stud.

5   Tighten the lug nut until the stud is seated in the flange.

6   Reinstall the disc and caliper (see Chapter 9). Install the wheel and lug nuts. Lower the vehicle and tighten the lug nuts to the torque listed in the Chapter 1 Specifications.

9.3 Use a small press tool such as this to push the stud out of the flange

10 Steering knuckle - removal and installation

1 Loosen the wheel lug nuts, raise the vehicle and support it securely on jackstands. Remove the wheel.

2 If you're working on a 4WD model, remove the hub cover, then unscrew the driveaxle/hub nut with a socket and large breaker bar (see Chapter 8). Brace a large prybar across two of the wheel studs or insert a large screwdriver through the center of the brake caliper and into the disc cooling vanes to prevent the hub from turning as the nut is loosened.

3 Remove the brake caliper and brake disc (see Chapter 9). Hang the caliper out of the way on a piece of wire (don't disconnect the brake hose).

4 Remove the hub and bearing assembly (see Section 8).

5 Remove the disc splash shield from the steering knuckle.

6 Unbolt the brake hose bracket from the top of the steering knuckle.

7 Disconnect the tie-rod end from the steering knuckle (see Section 19).

8 Disconnect the balljoints from the steering knuckle (see Sections 5 and 6).

9 Remove the steering knuckle.

10 Installation is the reverse of removal. Be sure to tighten the balljoint, tie-rod end and hub and bearing assembly fasteners to the torque values listed in this Chapter's Specifications. Tighten the caliper mounting bolts to the torque values listed in the Chapter 9 Specifications. Tighten the driveaxle/hub nut to the torque listed in the Chapter 8 Specifications (4WD models). Tighten the wheel lug nuts to the torque listed in the Chapter 1 Specifications.

11 Shock absorber (rear) - removal and installation

▶ Refer to illustrations 11.3a and 11.3b

1 Raise the rear of the vehicle and support it securely on jackstands placed underneath the frame rails. Block the front wheels so the vehicle doesn't roll off the stands.

➡ Note: It isn't necessary to remove the rear wheels, but doing so will improve access to the shock absorbers.

2 Support the rear axle with a floor jack placed under the axle tube closest to the shock absorber being removed.

3 Remove the shock absorber upper and lower mounting fasteners (see illustrations).

4 Remove the shock absorber.

5 Installation is the reverse of removal. Tighten all fasteners to the torque values listed in this Chapter's Specifications.

11.3a Rear shock absorber upper mounting bolt/nut

11.3b Rear shock absorber lower mounting bolt/nut

12 Stabilizer bar and bushings (rear) - removal and installation

▶ Refer to illustrations 12.2 and 12.4

1 Loosen the rear wheel lug nuts, raise the rear of the vehicle and support it securely on jackstands. Block the front wheels to keep the vehicle from rolling off the stands. Remove the rear wheels.

2 Remove the stabilizer bar link-to-frame nuts/bolts (see illustration).

3 Remove the nuts from the lower ends of the links, then separate the links from the bar.

12.2 Stabilizer bar link nuts

12.4 Remove the clamp bolt from each stabilizer bar and slip the clamp out of the slot

4   Remove the stabilizer bar clamp nuts (see illustration) and remove the stabilizer bar.

5   Inspect the stabilizer bar bushings and link bushings for cracks, tears and other signs of deterioration. Replace as necessary.

6   Installation is the reverse of removal. Be sure to tighten all fasteners to the torque listed in this Chapter's Specifications.

13 Coil spring (rear) - removal and installation

REMOVAL

1   Loosen the rear wheel lug nuts. Raise the rear of the vehicle and support it securely on jackstands placed underneath the frame rails. Block the front wheels to prevent the vehicle from rolling. Remove the rear wheels.

2   Support the rear axle housing with a floor jack placed underneath the differential. Raise the jack slightly.

3   Disconnect the lower ends of the shock absorbers from the axle housing (see Section 11).

4   Slowly lower the floor jack until the coil springs are fully extended, then remove the springs and insulators.

❋❋ CAUTION:

Don't let the upper trailing arms rest on the frame or they may be damaged.

5   Check the condition of the insulators. If they're cracked, hardened or otherwise deteriorated, replace them.

INSTALLATION

6   Place the springs and insulators in position on the axle and raise the axle until the ends of the springs engage properly with their upper mounts (an assistant would be helpful).

7   Continue to raise the axle until the shock absorbers can be connected to the axle housing. Install the bolts and nuts, tightening them to the torque listed in this Chapter's Specifications.

8   Install the wheels and lug nuts. Lower the vehicle and tighten the lug nuts to the torque listed in the Chapter 1 Specifications.

14 Air spring (rear) - removal and installation

REMOVAL

1   Locate the fuse for the air suspension system and remove it (see Chapter 12).

2   Loosen the rear wheel lug nuts. Raise the rear of the vehicle and support it securely on jackstands placed underneath the frame rails. Block the front wheels to prevent the vehicle from rolling. Remove the rear wheels.

3   Support the rear axle housing with a floor jack placed underneath the differential. Position the axle so the distance between the top of the axle tube and the jounce bumper bracket is at the "D" height listed in this Chapter's Specifications. Make sure the axle stays between the "D" height and full jounce for the remainder of this procedure.

❋❋ WARNING:

Wear eye and ear protection while performing this Step.

4   Depressurize the rear suspension. To do this, unbolt the air suspension compressor from the frame rail. Disconnect the air supply lines from the side of the compressor that faces the frame and allow the pressurized air to escape. Reconnect the air lines to the compressor,

then reinstall it on the frame and tighten its mounting bolts to the torque listed in this Chapter's Specifications.

5   Locate the raised boss on the outer edge of the air spring at the top. This indicates the position of the anti-rotation peg. Press down on the anti-rotation peg, turn the air spring counterclockwise and remove it from the upper spring seat.

6   At the top of the air spring, push the air line into its fitting, press down on the retaining collet and pull the air line out of the fitting.

7   Take the air spring off the lower spring seat and remove it.

INSTALLATION

8   Install the air spring on the upper spring seat, aligning the mounting tabs on the air spring with the slots in the spring seat.

❋❋ WARNING:

Be sure the air spring is correctly positioned in its spring seats or the spring may break apart while driving, resulting in loss of control of the vehicle.

9   The remainder of installation is the reverse of the removal steps.

10 Install the wheels and lug nuts. Lower the vehicle and tighten the lug nuts to the torque listed in the Chapter 1 Specifications.

11 Run the engine for one minute to make sure the air suspension system works.

12 Recheck the rear suspension "D" height (see Step 3).

15   Suspension arms (rear) - removal and installation

❋❋ WARNING:

If the vehicle is equipped with air suspension, depressurize the air suspension system before beginning this procedure (see Section 14, Step 4).

TRAILING ARMS

▶ **Refer to illustrations 15.2a and 15.2b**

❋❋ WARNING:

Remove and install only one arm at a time. This will prevent the axle housing from shifting on the jack.

1   Loosen the rear wheel lug nuts. Raise the rear of the vehicle and support it securely on jackstands placed underneath the frame rails. Block the front wheels to prevent the vehicle from rolling. Remove the wheel(s).

2   Support the rear axle with a floor jack. If you're removing an upper arm on a vehicle equipped with air suspension, detach the leveling sensor link from the arm. Remove the nuts, washers and bolts from each end of the trailing arm (see illustrations).

3   Remove the arm. Check the bushings in the arm for cracking, hardness or other signs of deterioration. If the bushings are in need of replacement, check with your local auto parts store or dealer parts department regarding the availability of replacement bushings. If replacement bushings are available, take the arm and the bushings to an automotive machine shop or other qualified repair facility to have the old ones pressed out and the new ones pressed in.

4   Installation is the reverse of removal. Before tightening the bolts/nuts, raise the rear axle with a floor jack to simulate normal ride height, then tighten the fasteners to the torque listed in this Chapter's Specifications.

TRACK BAR

▶ **Refer to illustration 15.6**

5   Raise the rear of the vehicle and support it securely on jackstands placed underneath the frame rails. Block the front wheels to prevent the

15.2a Lower trailing arm mounting bolts/nuts

15.2b Upper trailing arm mounting bolts/nuts

15.6 Track bar mounting bolts/nuts

vehicle from rolling.

6   Remove the nuts/bolts from each end of the bar (see illustration).

7   Remove the bar. Check the bushings in the bar for cracking, hardness or other signs of deterioration. If the bushings are in need of replacement, check with your local auto parts store or dealer parts department regarding the availability of replacement bushings. If replacement bushings are available, take the bar and the bushings to an automotive machine shop or other qualified repair facility to have the old ones pressed out and the new ones pressed in.

8   Installation is the reverse of removal. Before tightening the bolts/nuts, raise the rear axle with a floor jack to simulate normal ride height, then tighten the fasteners to the torque listed in this Chapter's Specifications.

16 Steering wheel - removal and installation

✳✳ WARNING:

These models are equipped with airbags. Always disable the airbag system (see Chapter 12) before working in the vicinity of any airbag system component to avoid the possibility of accidental deployment of the airbag, which could cause personal injury.

REMAL

▶ **Refer to illustrations 16.3a, 16.3b, 16.4, 16.6 and 16.7**

1   Park the vehicle with the wheels pointing straight ahead. Disconnect the cable from the negative terminal of the battery.

2   Refer to Chapter 12 and disable the airbag system.

3   Insert a screwdriver into the hole for the spring clip that retains the airbag module (see illustrations) and push the spring aside to release the pin. Now do the same thing to release the pin on the other side of the steering wheel.

4   Pry up the connector lock and disconnect the yellow electrical connector from the module (see illustration). Set the module aside in a safe, isolated area, with the airbag side of the module facing UP.

16.3a To release the pins that secure the airbag module to the steering wheel, insert a screwdriver into the holes in the back side of the steering wheel . . .

16.3b . . . and pry each spring clip aside to clear the pin (there are two pins; one on each side of the steering wheel) - steering wheel removed for clarity

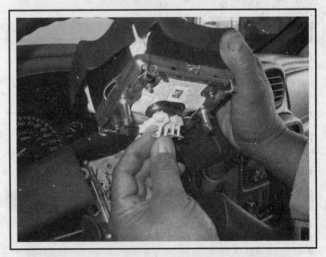

16.4 Pry up the connector lock, then pull the connector out of the airbag module

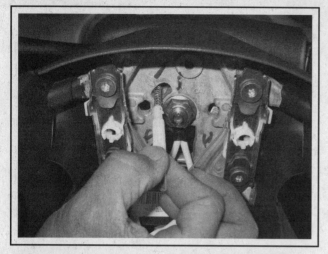

16.6 Remove the horn plunger and disconnect the steering wheel electrical connector

16.7 Check to see if there are alignment marks on the steering wheel and the steering shaft; if there are none, make your own

✻✻ WARNING:

When carrying the airbag module, keep the driver's (trim) side of it away from your body, and when you set it down, make sure the driver's side is facing up.

5   Center the steering wheel.

6   Push the horn plunger all the way in, then rotate it 1/4-turn and remove it from the steering wheel (see illustration). Disconnect the electrical connector for the steering wheel.

7   Remove the steering wheel retaining nut and mark the position of the steering wheel to the shaft, if marks don't already exist or don't line up (see illustration).

8   Use a puller to detach the steering wheel from the shaft.

✻✻ WARNING:

Do not hammer on the shaft or the puller in an attempt to loosen the wheel from the shaft.

9   Lift the steering wheel from the shaft.

✻✻ WARNING:

Don't allow the steering shaft to turn with the steering wheel removed. If the shaft turns, the airbag clockspring will become uncentered, which may cause the wire inside to break when the vehicle is returned to service.

INSTALLATION

▶ Refer to illustrations 16.10a, 16.10b, 16.11 and 16.13

✻✻ WARNING:

The airbag clockspring assembly is a ribbon-like mechanism which allows electrical current to flow to the airbag module regardless of steering wheel position. If the clockspring becomes uncentered, it may break when the vehicle is returned to service.

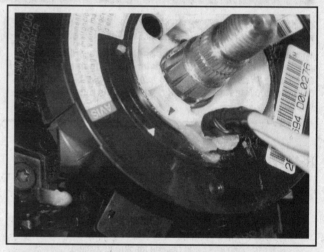

16.10a When the clockspring is centered on models with a spring lock tab, the arrow on the housing will be aligned with the arrow on the hub

16.10b On clocksprings with a centering window, the clockspring is centered when the window (A) appears yellow and the two arrows (B) are aligned

16.11 The clockspring is retained to the steering shaft with a snap-ring

➡Note: It is not necessary to remove the clockspring unless repairs to the steering column are required. The clockspring does not have to be centered unless the center hub of the clockspring was moved while the steering wheel was off or the clockspring was removed from the steering column. Follow the centering procedure if the clockspring was removed and the alignment was changed.

10 Before installing the steering wheel, make sure the airbag clockspring is centered.

➡Note: On the models covered by this manual, two style clocksprings are used; one type has a window on the front face and no spring lock tab on the back. The other type does not have a window but does have a spring lock tab (see illustrations).

11 If the airbag system clockspring is not centered, remove the steering column covers (see Chapter 11). Remove the snap-ring (see illustration) and lift the clockspring off the steering column. You may have to cut a plastic wire-tie securing the clockspring harness to the steering column.

12 If your clockspring has a window on the front and no spring lock tab on the back, hold it face up and turn the hub clockwise until it stops (don't apply excessive force). Now slowly turn the hub counterclockwise at least two turns until the window turns yellow and the arrows on the hub and the housing are in alignment (see illustration 16.10b). Proceed to Step 15.

13 If your clockspring does not have a window on the front, turn it

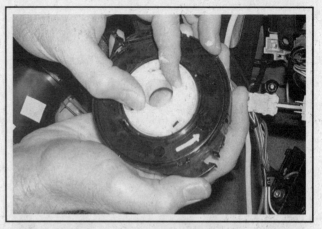

16.13 To center the clockspring on models with a spring lock tab, hold it with its underside facing up, depress the spring lock and rotate the hub in the direction of the arrow until it stops, then turn it in the opposite direction 2-1/2 turns

over and depress the spring lock on the back, then rotate the hub in the direction of the arrow on the housing until it stops (don't apply too much force). Now turn the hub 2-1/2 turns in the opposite direction and release the spring lock tab (see illustration). Proceed to Step 15.

14 If your clockspring has a window on the front and a spring lock tab on the back, depress the spring lock on the back while holding it face up, and turn the hub clockwise until it stops (don't apply excessive force). Now slowly turn the hub counterclockwise at least two turns until the window turns yellow and the arrows on the hub and the housing are in alignment (see illustration 16.10b).

15 Install the clockspring and snap-ring. Secure the wiring harness with a new wire-tie, making sure the harness isn't kinked. Also install the steering column covers.

16 Install the wheel on the steering shaft, aligning the marks.

17 Install the steering wheel nut and tighten it to the torque listed in this Chapter's Specifications.

18 Plug in the horn wire, push down and twist it clockwise to lock it in place.

19 Connect the airbag connector to the back of the airbag module. Make sure the connector lock is securely engaged.

20 Position the airbag module on the steering wheel and push it in until the pins on the module engage with the spring clips.

21 Refer to Chapter 12 for the procedure to enable the airbag system.

17 Steering column - removal and installation

▸ **Refer to illustrations 17.6a, 17.6b, 17.7, 17.8 and 17.9**

❋❋ **WARNING:**

The models covered by this manual are equipped with airbags. Always disable the airbag system when working in the vicinity of airbag system components (see Chapter 12).

REMOVAL

1 Park the vehicle with the wheels pointing straight ahead. Disconnect the cable from the negative terminal of the battery. Disable the airbag system (see Chapter 12).

2 Remove the steering wheel (see Section 17), then turn the ignition key to the LOCK position to prevent the steering shaft from turning.

❋❋ **CAUTION:**

If this is not done, the airbag clockspring could be damaged.

3 Remove the knee bolster and the reinforcement behind it (see Chapter 11).

4 If the vehicle is equipped with a tilt column, pull the tilt lever out of the steering column.

5 Remove the steering column shrouds (see Chapter 11).

6 Disconnect the electrical connectors for the steering column har-

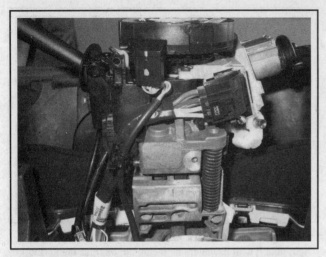

17.6a Disconnect the steering wheel electrical connectors

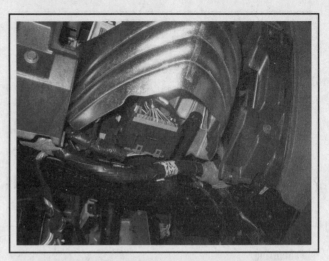

17.6b Disconnect the body harness electrical connector

ness and body harness (see illustrations).

7   Unscrew the screw that secures the left heater duct (see illustration). Position the duct so you can disconnect its temperature sensor, then disconnect the sensor and remove the duct from the vehicle.

8   Remove the shaft coupler nut and remove the bolt securing the steering shaft to the upper intermediate shaft (see illustration).

➡Note: Unscrew the nut, not the bolt. Mark the relationship of the intermediate shaft to the steering column shaft.

9   Remove the steering column mounting nuts (see illustration), lower the column and pull it to the rear, making sure nothing is still connected. Separate the intermediate shaft from the steering shaft and remove the column.

INSTALLATION

➡Note: If a new column is being installed, check to see if a shipping lock pin is present. If so, remove it.

10 Guide the steering column into position, connect the intermediate shaft, then install the mounting nuts, but don't tighten them yet.

11 Install the coupler bolt and nut, then tighten the nut to the torque

listed in this Chapter's Specifications.

12 Tighten the column mounting nuts to the torque listed in this Chapter's Specifications.

13 The remainder of installation is the reverse of removal.

17.7 Remove the mounting screw and the left heater duct

17.8 Upper intermediate shaft-to-steering column shaft bolt and nut; don't attempt to unscrew the bolt, since it has an anti-rotation tang. Unscrew the nut, then pull the bolt out

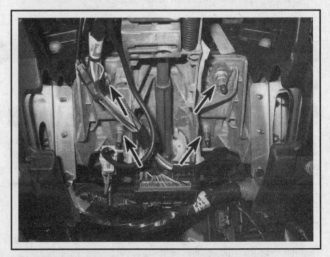

17.9 Remove the steering column mounting nuts

21.6 Rack-and-pinion steering gear mounting nut/bolt (right side shown)

gear and pull the lines out (see illustration). Cap the lines to prevent leakage.

6   Unscrew the mounting nuts, remove the washers and slide the bolts out. Lower the steering gear from the vehicle (see illustration).

7   Installation is the reverse of removal. Be sure to tighten all fasteners to the torque values listed in this Chapter's Specifications and the Chapter 11 Specifications. Tighten the wheel lug nuts to the torque listed in the Chapter 1 Specifications. Check the power steering fluid level and add some, if necessary (see Chapter 1), then bleed the system as described in Section 24.

22   Power steering pump - removal and installation

SIX-CYLINDER MODELS

Removal

▶ **Refer to illustrations 22.3, 22.5 and 22.6**

1   Disconnect the cable from the negative terminal of the battery.

2   Remove the radiator upper fan shroud (see Chapter 3) and the serpentine drivebelt (see Chapter 1).

3   Position a drain pan under the power steering pump. Unscrew the pressure hose fitting from the pump with a flare nut wrench (see illustration). Loosen the clamp and disconnect the power steering cooler hose from the pump. Plug the hoses to prevent contaminants from entering.

4   Free the wiring harness from the retainer on the power steering pump.

5   Remove the pump mounting fasteners (see illustration) and lift the pump from the vehicle, taking care not to spill fluid on the painted surfaces.

6   If necessary, remove the pulley from the pump with a special power steering pump pulley remover (see illustration).

22.3 Detach the power steering pressure line (right arrow) and return hose (left arrow) from the pump

22.5 The power steering pump mounting bolts are accessible through the pulley

22.6 Remove the pulley from the power steering pump with a pulley removal tool

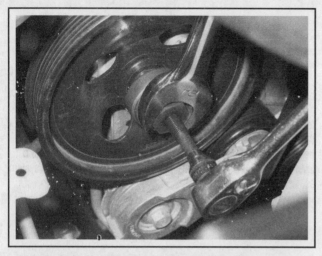

22.7 Press the pulley onto the shaft using a pulley installation tool - don't attempt to drive it on with a hammer or push it on with a traditional press!

22.16 Remove the pulley from the power steering pump with a pulley removal tool

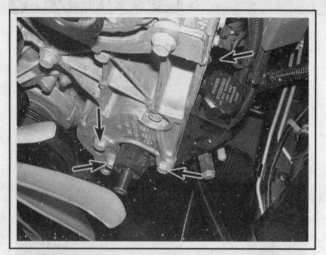

22.17 The power steering pump is secured by four bolts (the bolt on the back of the pump securing the bracket to the engine is not visible in this photo)

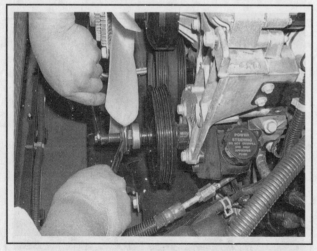

22.20a Press the pulley onto the shaft using a pulley installation tool - don't attempt to drive it on with a hammer or push it on with a traditional press!

Installation

▶ Refer to illustration 22.7

7   Press the pulley onto the shaft using a special pulley installer tool (see illustration). An alternative tool can be fabricated from a long bolt, nut, washer and a socket of the same diameter as the pulley hub. Push the pulley onto the shaft until the front of the hub is flush with the shaft, but no further.

8   Position the pump in the mounting bracket and install the mounting bolts or nuts. Tighten the fasteners to the torque listed in this Chapter's Specifications.

9   Connect the hoses to the pump. Tighten the fittings securely.

10   Install the drivebelt and fan shroud.

11   Fill the power steering reservoir with the recommended fluid (see Chapter 1) and bleed the system following the procedure described in Section 24.

V8 MODELS

Removal

▶ Refer to illustrations 22.16 and 22.17

12   Disconnect the cable from the negative terminal of the battery.

13   Remove the radiator upper fan shroud (see Chapter 3) and serpentine drive belt (see Chapter 1).

14   Remove the Powertrain Control Module (PCM) or Engine Control Module (ECM) (see Chapter 6).

15   Position a pan under the power steering pump. Unscrew the power steering pressure hose fitting from the pump with a flare nut wrench. Loosen the clamp and disconnect the power steering return hose from the pump. Plug the hoses to prevent contamination from entering.

16   Using a special power steering pump pulley remove, remove the pulley from the pump (see illustration).

17   Remove the pump mounting fasteners (see illustration) and lift the pump from the vehicle, taking care not to spill fluid on the painted surfaces.

22.20b An alternative to the special tool can be fabricated from a long bolt with the same thread pitch as the internal threads of the pump shaft, a nut, washer and a socket that's the same diameter as the pulley hub

Installation

▶ **Refer to illustrations 22.20a and 22.20b**

18 Position the pump in the mounting bracket and install the mounting bolts. Tighten the fasteners to the torque listed in this Chapter's Specifications.

19 Connect the hoses to the pump. Tighten the fittings securely.

20 Press the pulley onto the shaft using a special pulley installer tool (see illustrations). An alternative tool can be fabricated from a long bolt, nut, washer and socket of the same diameter as the pulley hub. Push the pulley onto the shaft until the front of the hub is flush with shaft, but no further.

21 Install the drive belt and fan shroud.

22 Fill the power steering reservoir with the recommended fluid (see Chapter 1) and bleed the system (see Section 24).

23 Power steering cooler - removal and installation

▶ **Refer to illustrations 23.2 and 23.3**

1 Remove the radiator air intake baffle.

2 Place a drain pan under the front of the vehicle and disconnect the power steering hoses from the cooler (see illustration). Cap the cooler hoses to keep out contamination.

3 Unbolt the cooler from the radiator support brackets and take it out (see illustration).

4 Installation is the reverse of the removal steps. Tighten the cooler mounting bolts to the torque listed in this Chapter's Specifications.

5 Fill the power steering system with fluid (see Chapter 1), then bleed it (see Section 24).

23.2 Remove the clamps and disconnect the hoses from the power steering cooler

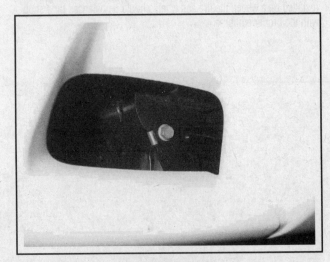

23.3 Remove the cooler mounting bolts

24 Power steering system - bleeding

1   Following any operation in which the power steering fluid lines have been disconnected, the power steering system must be bled to remove all air and obtain proper steering performance.

2   With the front wheels in the straight ahead position, check the power steering fluid level and, if low, add fluid until it reaches the Cold mark on the dipstick.

3   Start the engine and allow it to run at fast idle. Recheck the fluid level and add more if necessary to reach the Cold mark on the dipstick.

4   Bleed the system by turning the wheels from side-to-side, without hitting the stops. This will work the air out of the system. Keep the res-

ervoir full of fluid as this is done.

5   When the air is worked out of the system, return the wheels to the straight ahead position and leave the vehicle running for several more minutes before shutting it off. Recheck the fluid level.

6   Road test the vehicle to be sure the steering system is functioning normally and noise free.

7   Recheck the fluid level to be sure it's up to the Hot mark on the dipstick while the engine is at normal operating temperature. Add fluid if necessary (see Chapter 1).

25 Wheels and tires - general information

▶ **Refer to illustration 25.1**

The vehicles covered by this manual are equipped with metric-size fiberglass or steel belted radial tires (see illustration). Use of other size or type of tires may affect the ride and handling of the vehicle. Don't mix different types of tires, such as radials and bias belted, on the same vehicle as handling may be seriously affected. It's recommended that tires be replaced in pairs on the same axle, but if only one tire is being replaced, be sure it's the same size, structure and tread design as the other.

Because tire pressure has a substantial effect on handling and wear, the pressure on all tires should be checked at least once a month or before any extended trips (see Chapter 1).

Wheels must be replaced if they're bent, dented, leak air, have elongated bolt holes, are heavily rusted, out of vertical symmetry or if the lug nuts won't stay tight. Wheel repairs that use welding or peening are not recommended.

Tire and wheel balance is important to the overall handling, braking and performance of the vehicle. Unbalanced wheels can adversely affect handling and ride characteristics as well as tire life. Whenever a tire is installed on a wheel, the tire and wheel should be balanced by a shop with the proper equipment.

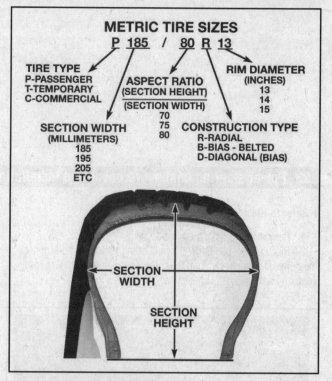

25.1 Metric tire size code

26 Front end alignment - general information

▶ **Refer to illustration 26.1**

A front end alignment (see illustration) refers to the adjustments made to the front wheels so they're in proper angular relationship to the suspension and the ground. Front wheels that are out of proper alignment not only affect steering control, but also increase tire wear.

Getting the proper front wheel alignment is a very exacting process, one in which complicated and expensive machines are necessary to perform the job properly. Because of this, you should have a technician with the proper equipment perform these tasks. We will, however, use this space to give you a basic idea of what is involved with front end alignment so you can better understand the process and deal intelligently with the shop that does the work.

Toe-in is the turning in of the front wheels. The purpose of a toe specification is to ensure parallel rolling of the front wheels. In a vehicle with zero toe-in, the distance between the front edges of the wheels will be the same as the distance between the rear edges of the wheels. The actual amount of toe-in is normally only a fraction of an inch. Toe-in is adjusted by turning the tie-rod in the tie-rod end to lengthen or shorten

the tie-rod. Incorrect toe-in will cause the tires to wear improperly by making them scrub against the road surface.

Camber is the tilting of the front wheels from vertical when viewed from the front of the vehicle. When the wheels tilt out at the top, the camber is said to be positive (+). When the wheels tilt in at the top the camber is negative (-). The amount of tilt is measured in degrees from the vertical and this measurement is called the camber angle. This angle affects the amount of tire tread which contacts the road and compensates for changes in the suspension geometry when the vehicle is cornering or traveling over an undulating surface. Camber is adjusted by loosening the lower control arm adjustment bolts and repositioning the arm on the frame.

Caster is the tilting of the top of the front steering axis from vertical. A tilt toward the rear is positive caster and a tilt toward the front is negative caster. Caster is also adjusted by loosening the lower control arm adjustment bolts and repositioning the arm on the frame.

When making adjustments to the front end alignment, the caster is set first, then the camber, then the toe-in.

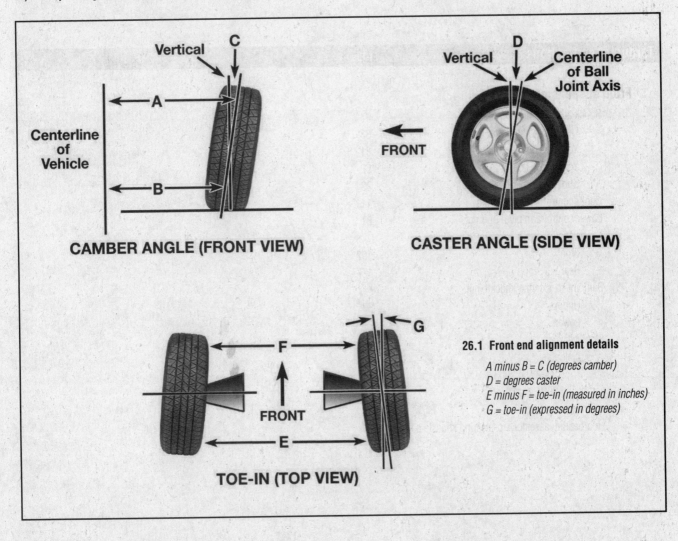

26.1 Front end alignment details

A minus B = C (degrees camber)
D = degrees caster
E minus F = toe-in (measured in inches)
G = toe-in (expressed in degrees)

Specifications

General

Power steering fluid type	See Chapter 1

Rear suspension "D" height (measured between jounce bumper bracket and top of axle tube)

Air suspension

SS models

Permissible	4-11/64 to 4-31/64 inches
Preferred	4-21/64 inches

All other models

Air spring suspension

Permissible	5-11/64 to 5-31/64 inches
Preferred	5-21/64 inches
Side-to-side variation limit	5/16-inch

Coil spring suspension

Permissible	5-7/8 to 6-11/32 inches
Preferred	6-1/8 inches
Side-to-side variation limit	1/2-inch

Torque specifications

Ft-lbs

Front suspension

Shock absorber module	
Upper mounting nuts	33
Yoke-to-control arm nut	81
Yoke pinch bolt	52
Shock absorber retaining nut	33
Upper control arm pivot bolts	111
Lower control arm pivot bolt nuts	81
Lower control arm bracket-to-frame bolts	
Front	192
Rear	177
Balljoint-to-steering knuckle nut	
Upper	30
Lower	81
Stabilizer bar	
Link nuts	
2002 and 2003	74
2004 and later	114
Clamp bolts	41
Hub/bearing assembly-to-steering knuckle bolts	77

Torque specifications   Ft-lbs (unless otherwise indicated)

Rear suspension

Air suspension compressor mounting bolts	18
Shock absorber	
Upper bolt/nut	63
Lower bolt/nut	
2002	52
2003	59
Stabilizer bar	
Link nuts	74
Clamp bolts	55
Trailing arm bolts/nuts	
Upper	97
Lower	74
Track bar bolts/nuts	144

Steering

Steering gear-to-frame bolts/nuts	81
Intermediate shaft pinch bolt	
Upper-to-lower shaft	37
Lower shaft to power steering gear	30
Tie rod end-to-steering knuckle ballstud nut	
2002 and 2003	33
2004 and later	44

Steering column

Steering wheel nut	30
Steering column mounting nuts	20
Shaft coupler bolt	35

Power steering pump

Mounting bolts	18

Power steering cooler

Mounting bolts	15

Wheel lug nuts   See Chapter 1

Notes

Section

11

BODY

1 General information

The vehicles covered by this manual are built with body-on-frame construction. The frame is a hydroformed, ladder-type, consisting of C-shaped center rails welded to boxed front and rear sections, with both welded-in and bolt-in crossmembers.

The body incorporates the cab, back-seat area and cargo compartment in one unitized structure.

Certain components are particularly vulnerable to accident damage and can be unbolted and repaired or replaced. Among these parts are the hood, doors, seats, tailgate, liftgate, bumpers and front fenders.

Only general body maintenance practices and body panel repair procedures within the scope of the do-it-yourselfer are included in this Chapter.

2 Body - maintenance

1   The condition of your vehicle's body is very important, because the resale value depends a great deal on it. It's much more difficult to repair a neglected or damaged body than it is to repair mechanical components. The hidden areas of the body, such as the wheel wells, the frame and the engine compartment, are equally important, although they don't require as frequent attention as the rest of the body.

2   Once a year, or every 12,000 miles, it's a good idea to have the underside of the body steam cleaned. All traces of dirt and oil will be removed and the area can then be inspected carefully for rust, damaged brake lines, frayed electrical wires, damaged cables and other problems. The front suspension components should be greased after completion of this job.

3   At the same time, clean the engine and the engine compartment with a steam cleaner or water-soluble degreaser.

4   The wheel wells should be given close attention, since undercoating can peel away and stones and dirt thrown up by the tires can cause the paint to chip and flake, allowing rust to set in. If rust is found, clean down to the bare metal and apply an anti-rust paint.

5   The body should be washed about once a week. Wet the vehicle thoroughly to soften the dirt, then wash it down with a soft sponge and plenty of clean, soapy water. If the surplus dirt is not washed off very carefully, it can wear down the paint.

6   Spots of tar or asphalt thrown up from the road should be removed with a cloth soaked in tar remover or kerosene lamp oil.

7   Once every six months, wax the body and chrome trim. If a chrome cleaner is used to remove rust from any of the vehicle's plated parts, remember that the cleaner also removes part of the chrome, so use it sparingly.

3 Vinyl trim - maintenance

Don't clean vinyl trim with detergents, caustic soap or petroleum-based cleaners. Plain soap and water works just fine, with a soft brush to clean dirt that may be ingrained. Wash the vinyl as frequently as the rest of the vehicle. After cleaning, application of a high-quality rubber and vinyl protectant will help prevent oxidation and cracks. The protectant can also be applied to weatherstripping, vacuum lines and rubber hoses, which often fail as a result of chemical degradation, and to the tires.

4 Upholstery and carpets - maintenance

1   Every three months remove the floormats and clean the interior of the vehicle (more frequently if necessary). Use a stiff whiskbroom to brush the carpeting and loosen dirt and dust, then vacuum the upholstery and carpets thoroughly, especially along seams and crevices.

2   Dirt and stains can be removed from carpeting with basic household or automotive carpet shampoos available in spray cans. Follow the directions and vacuum again, then use a stiff brush to bring back the "nap" of the carpet.

3   Most interiors have cloth or vinyl upholstery, either of which can be cleaned and maintained with a number of material-specific cleaners or shampoos available in auto supply stores. Follow the directions on the product for usage, and always spot-test any upholstery cleaner on an inconspicuous area (bottom edge of a backseat cushion) to ensure that it doesn't cause a color shift in the material.

4   After cleaning, vinyl upholstery should be treated with a protectant.

➡**Note: Make sure the protectant container indicates the product can be used on seats - some products may make a seat too slippery.**

❋❋ CAUTION:

Do not use protectant on vinyl-covered steering wheels.

5   Leather upholstery requires special care. It should be cleaned regularly with saddlesoap or leather cleaner. Never use alcohol, gasoline, nail polish remover or thinner to clean leather upholstery.

6   After cleaning, regularly treat leather upholstery with a leather conditioner, rubbed in with a soft cotton cloth. Never use car wax on leather upholstery.

7   In areas where the interior of the vehicle is subject to bright sunlight, cover leather seating areas of the seats with a sheet if the vehicle is to be left out for any length of time.

5 Body repair - minor damage

PLASTIC BODY PANELS

The following repair procedures are for minor scratches and gouges. Repair of more serious damage should be left to a dealer service department or qualified auto body shop. Below is a list of the equipment and materials necessary to perform the following repair procedures on plastic body panels.

Wax, grease and silicone removing solvent
Cloth-backed body tape
Sanding discs
Drill motor with three-inch disc holder
Hand sanding block
Rubber squeegees
Sandpaper
Non-porous mixing palette
Wood paddle or putty knife
Curved-tooth body file
Flexible parts repair material

Flexible panels (front and rear bumper trim)

1   Remove the damaged panel, if necessary or desirable. In most cases, repairs can be carried out with the panel installed.

2   Clean the area(s) to be repaired with a wax, grease and silicone removing solvent applied with a water-dampened cloth.

3   If the damage is structural, that is, if it extends through the panel, clean the backside of the panel area to be repaired as well. Wipe dry.

4   Sand the rear surface about 1-1/2 inches beyond the break.

5   Cut two pieces of fiberglass cloth large enough to overlap the break by about 1-1/2 inches. Cut only to the required length.

6   Mix the adhesive from the repair kit according to the instructions included with the kit, and apply a layer of the mixture approximately 1/8-inch thick on the backside of the panel. Overlap the break by at least 1-1/2 inches.

7   Apply one piece of fiberglass cloth to the adhesive and cover the cloth with additional adhesive. Apply a second piece of fiberglass cloth to the adhesive and immediately cover the cloth with additional adhesive in sufficient quantity to fill the weave.

8   Allow the repair to cure for 20 to 30 minutes at 60-degrees to 80-degrees F.

9   If necessary, trim the excess repair material at the edge.

10 Remove all of the paint film over and around the area(s) to be repaired. The repair material should not overlap the painted surface.

11 With a drill motor and a sanding disc (or a rotary file), cut a "V" along the break line approximately 1/2-inch wide. Remove all dust and loose particles from the repair area.

12 Mix and apply the repair material. Apply a light coat first over the damaged area; then continue applying material until it reaches a level slightly higher than the surrounding finish.

13 Cure the mixture for 20 to 30 minutes at 60-degrees to 80-degrees F.

14 Roughly establish the contour of the area being repaired with a body file. If low areas or pits remain, mix and apply additional adhesive.

15 Block sand the damaged area with sandpaper to establish the actual contour of the surrounding surface.

16 If desired, the repaired area can be temporarily protected with several light coats of primer. Because of the special paints and techniques required for flexible body panels, it is recommended that the vehicle be taken to a paint shop for completion of the body repair.

STEEL BODY PANELS

♦ See photo sequence

Repair of minor scratches

17 If the scratch is superficial and does not penetrate to the metal of the body, repair is very simple. Lightly rub the scratched area with a fine rubbing compound to remove loose paint, then use a wax-and-grease remover (available at auto parts stores) to clean the area. Rinse the area with clean water.

18 Apply touch-up paint to the scratch, using a small brush. Continue to apply thin layers of paint until the surface of the paint in the scratch is level with the surrounding paint. Allow the new paint at least two weeks to harden, then blend it into the surrounding paint by rubbing with a very fine rubbing compound. Finally, apply a coat of wax to the scratch area.

19 If the scratch has penetrated the paint and exposed the metal of the body, causing the metal to rust, a different repair technique is required. Remove all loose rust from the bottom of the scratch with a pocketknife, then apply rust inhibiting paint to prevent the formation of rust in the future. Using a rubber or nylon applicator, coat the scratched area with glaze-type filler. If required, the filler can be mixed with thinner to provide a very thin paste, which is ideal for filling narrow scratches. Before the glaze filler in the scratch hardens, wrap a piece of smooth cotton cloth around the tip of a finger. Dip the cloth in thinner and then quickly wipe it along the surface of the scratch. This will ensure that the surface of the filler is slightly hollow. The scratch can now be painted over as described earlier in this Section.

Repair of dents

20 When repairing dents, the first job is to pull the dent out until the affected area is as close as possible to its original shape. There is no point in trying to restore the original shape completely as the metal in the damaged area will have stretched on impact and cannot be restored to its original contours. It is better to bring the level of the dent up to a point that is about 1/8-inch below the level of the surrounding metal. In cases where the dent is very shallow, it is not worth trying to pull it out at all.

21 If the backside of the dent is accessible, it can be hammered out gently from behind using a soft-face hammer. While doing this, hold a block of wood firmly against the opposite side of the metal to absorb the hammer blows and prevent the metal from being stretched.

22 If the dent is in a section of the body which has double layers, or some other factor makes it inaccessible from behind, a different technique is required. Drill several small holes through the metal inside the damaged area, particularly in the deeper sections. Screw long, self-tapping screws into the holes just enough for them to get a good grip in the metal. Now pulling on the protruding heads of the screws with locking pliers can pull out the dent.

23 The next stage of repair is the removal of paint from the damaged area and from an inch or so of the surrounding metal. This is easily done with a wire brush or sanding disk in a drill motor, although it can be done just as effectively by hand with sandpaper. To complete the preparation for filling, score the surface of the bare metal with a screwdriver or the tang of a file or drill small holes in the affected area. This will provide a good grip for the filler material. To complete the repair, see the Section on filling and painting.

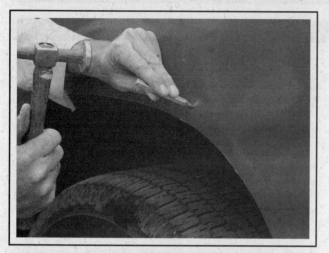

1 If you can't access the backside of the body panel to hammer out the dent, pull it out with a slide-hammer-type dent puller. In the deepest portion of the dent or along the crease line, drill or punch hole(s) at least one inch apart . . .

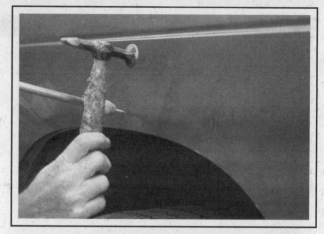

2 . . . then screw the slide-hammer into the hole and operate it. Tap with a hammer near the edge of the dent to help 'pop' the metal back to its original shape. When you're finished, the dent area should be close to its original contour and about 1/8-inch below the surface of the surrounding metal

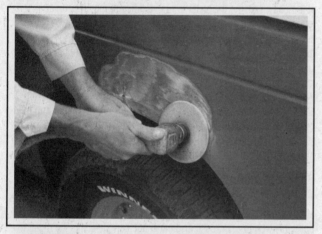

3 Using coarse-grit sandpaper, remove the paint down to the bare metal. Hand sanding works fine, but the disc sander shown here makes the job faster. Use finer (about 320-grit) sandpaper to feather-edge the paint at least one inch around the dent area

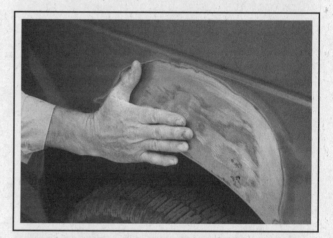

4 When the paint is removed, touch will probably be more helpful than sight for telling if the metal is straight. Hammer down the high spots or raise the low spots as necessary. Clean the repair area with wax/silicone remover

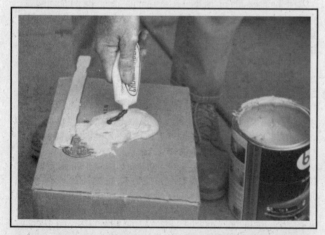

5 Following label instructions, mix up a batch of plastic filler and hardener. The ratio of filler to hardener is critical, and, if you mix it incorrectly, it will either not cure properly or cure too quickly (you won't have time to file and sand it into shape)

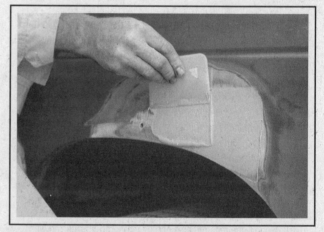

6 Working quickly so the filler doesn't harden, use a plastic applicator to press the body filler firmly into the metal, assuring it bonds completely. Work the filler until it matches the original contour and is slightly above the surrounding metal

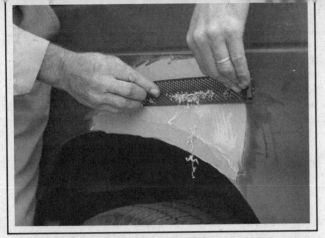

7 Let the filler harden until you can just dent it with your fingernail. Use a body file or Surform tool (shown here) to rough-shape the filler

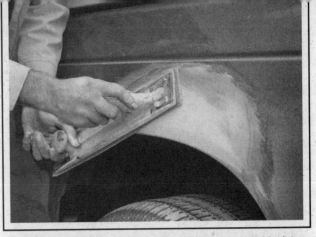

8 Use coarse-grit sandpaper and a sanding board or block to work the filler down until it's smooth and even. Work down to finer grits of sandpaper - always using a board or block - ending up with 360 or 400 grit

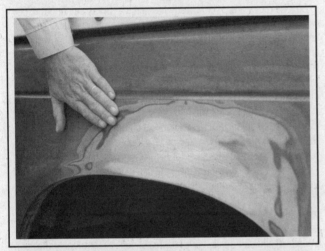

9 You shouldn't be able to feel any ridge at the transition from the filler to the bare metal or from the bare metal to the old paint. As soon as the repair is flat and uniform, remove the dust and mask off the adjacent panels or trim pieces

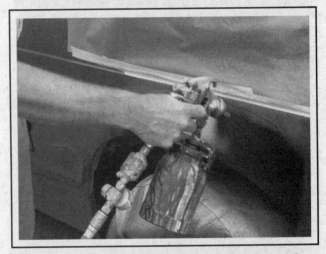

10 Apply several layers of primer to the area. Don't spray the primer on too heavy, so it sags or runs, and make sure each coat is dry before you spray on the next one. A professional-type spray gun is being used here, but aerosol spray primer is available inexpensively from auto parts stores

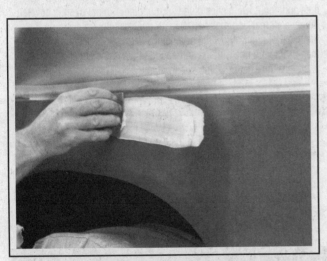

11 The primer will help reveal imperfections or scratches. Fill these with glazing compound. Follow the label instructions and sand it with 360 or 400-grit sandpaper until it's smooth. Repeat the glazing, sanding and respraying until the primer reveals a perfectly smooth surface

12 Finish sand the primer with very fine sandpaper (400 or 600-grit) to remove the primer overspray. Clean the area with water and allow it to dry. Use a tack rag to remove any dust, then apply the finish coat. Don't attempt to rub out or wax the repair area until the paint has dried completely (at least two weeks)

Repair of rust holes or gashes

24 Remove all paint from the affected area and from an inch or so of the surrounding metal using a sanding disk or wire brush mounted in a drill motor. If these are not available, a few sheets of sandpaper will do the job just as effectively.

25 With the paint removed, you will be able to determine the severity of the corrosion and decide whether to replace the whole panel, if possible, or repair the affected area. New body panels are not as expensive as most people think and it is often quicker to install a new panel than to repair large areas of rust.

26 Remove all trim pieces from the affected area except those which will act as a guide to the original shape of the damaged body, such as headlight shells, etc. Using metal snips or a hacksaw blade, remove all loose metal and any other metal that is badly affected by rust. Hammer the edges of the hole in to create a slight depression for the filler material.

27 Wire-brush the affected area to remove the powdery rust from the surface of the metal. If the back of the rusted area is accessible, treat it with rust inhibiting paint.

28 Before filling is done, block the hole in some way. This can be done with sheet metal riveted or screwed into place, or by stuffing the hole with wire mesh.

29 Once the hole is blocked off, the affected area can be filled and painted. See the following subsection on filling and painting.

Filling and painting

30 Many types of body fillers are available, but generally speaking, body repair kits which contain filler paste and a tube of resin hardener are best for this type of repair work. A wide, flexible plastic or nylon applicator will be necessary for imparting a smooth and contoured finish to the surface of the filler material. Mix up a small amount of filler on a clean piece of wood or cardboard (use the hardener sparingly). Follow the manufacturer's instructions on the package, otherwise the filler will set incorrectly.

31 Using the applicator, apply the filler paste to the prepared area. Draw the applicator across the surface of the filler to achieve the desired contour and to level the filler surface. As soon as a contour that approximates the original one is achieved, stop working the paste. If you continue, the paste will begin to stick to the applicator. Continue to add thin layers of paste at 20-minute intervals until the level of the filler is just above the surrounding metal.

32 Once the filler has hardened, the excess can be removed with a body file. From then on, progressively finer grades of sandpaper should be used, starting with a 180-grit paper and finishing with 600-grit wet-or-dry paper. Always wrap the sandpaper around a flat rubber or wooden block, otherwise the surface of the filler will not be completely flat. During the sanding of the filler surface, the wet-or-dry paper should be periodically rinsed in water. This will ensure that a very smooth finish is produced in the final stage.

33 At this point, the repair area should be surrounded by a ring of bare metal, which in turn should be encircled by the finely feathered edge of good paint. Rinse the repair area with clean water until all of the dust produced by the sanding operation is gone.

34 Spray the entire area with a light coat of primer. This will reveal any imperfections in the surface of the filler. Repair the imperfections with fresh filler paste or glaze filler and once more smooth the surface with sandpaper. Repeat this spray-and-repair procedure until you are satisfied that the surface of the filler and the feathered edge of the paint are perfect. Rinse the area with clean water and allow it to dry completely.

35 The repair area is now ready for painting. Spray painting must be carried out in a warm, dry, windless and dust free atmosphere. These conditions can be created if you have access to a large indoor work area, but if you are forced to work in the open, you will have to pick the day very carefully. If you are working indoors, dousing the floor in the work area with water will help settle the dust that would otherwise be in the air. If the repair area is confined to one body panel, mask off the surrounding panels. This will help minimize the effects of a slight mismatch in paint color. Trim pieces such as chrome strips, door handles, etc., will also need to be masked off or removed. Use masking tape and several thickness of newspaper for the masking operations.

36 Before spraying, shake the paint can thoroughly, then spray a test area until the spray painting technique is mastered. Cover the repair area with a thick coat of primer. The thickness should be built up using several thin layers of primer rather than one thick one. Using 600-grit wet-or-dry sandpaper, rub down the surface of the primer until it is very smooth. While doing this, the work area should be thoroughly rinsed with water and the wet-or-dry sandpaper periodically rinsed as well. Allow the primer to dry before spraying additional coats.

37 Spray on the top coat, again building up the thickness by using several thin layers of paint. Begin spraying in the center of the repair area and then, using a circular motion, work out until the whole repair area and about two inches of the surrounding original paint is covered. Remove all masking material 10 to 15 minutes after spraying on the final coat of paint. Allow the new paint at least two weeks to harden, then use a very fine rubbing compound to blend the edges of the new paint into the existing paint. Finally, apply a coat of wax.

6   Body repair - major damage

1   Major damage must be repaired by an auto body shop specifically equipped to perform body and frame repairs. These shops have the specialized equipment required to do the job properly.

2   If the damage is extensive, the body must be checked for proper alignment or the vehicle's handling characteristics may be adversely affected and other components may wear at an accelerated rate.

3   Due to the fact that all of the major body components (hood, fenders, etc.) are separate and replaceable units, any seriously damaged components should be replaced rather than repaired. Sometimes the components can be found in a wrecking yard that specializes in used vehicle components, often at considerable savings over the cost of new parts.

7   Hinges and locks - maintenance

Once every 3000 miles, or every three months, the hinges and latch assemblies on the doors, hood and trunk should be given a few drops of light oil or lock lubricant. The door latch strikers should also be lubricated with a thin coat of grease to reduce wear and ensure free movement. Lubricate the door and trunk locks with spray-on graphite lubricant.

8 Windshield and fixed glass - replacement

Replacement of the windshield and fixed glass requires the use of special fast-setting adhesive/caulk materials and some specialized tools and techniques. These operations should be left to a dealer service department or a shop specializing in glasswork. The fixed glass also includes the quarter windows.

9 Radiator grille - removal and installation

▶ **Refer to illustrations 9.1 and 9.2**

1   Open the hood and remove the plastic panel over the radiator (see illustration).

2   If you're working on a Chevrolet or Oldsmobile model, locate the clips that secure the grille to the headlamp panel (see illustration).

Release the clips with a flat-bladed screwdriver and pull the grille forward off the vehicle.

3   If you're working on a GMC model, locate the clips that secure the top of the grille to the radiator support. Release the clips with a flat-bladed screwdriver and lift the grille out of the vehicle.

4   Installation is the reverse of the removal steps.

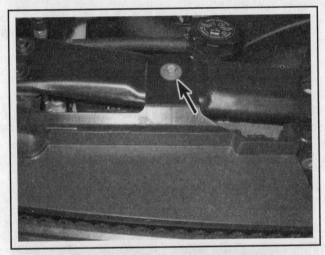

9.1 Remove the screws and lift off the radiator panel

9.2 Release the grille clips with a screwdriver

10 Hood - removal, installation and adjustment

▶ **Refer to illustrations 10.2, 10.10 and 10.11**

➡**Note: The hood is heavy and somewhat awkward to remove and install - at least two people should perform this procedure.**

REMOVAL AND INSTALLATION

1   Use blankets or pads to cover the cowl area of the body and the fenders. This will protect the body and paint as the hood is lifted off.

2   Scribe alignment marks around the hinge flanges to insure proper alignment during installation (paint or a permanent type felt-tip marker also will work for this) (see illustration).

3   Disconnect the electrical connector at the underhood light, and the ground wire lug attached to the rear of the hood.

4   Have an assistant support the weight of the hood. Remove the hinge-to-hood bolts.

5   Lift off the hood.

6   Installation is the reverse of removal.

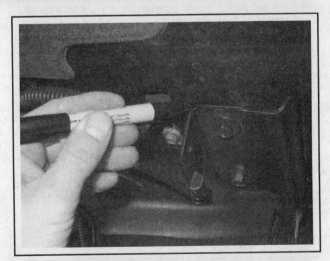

10.2 With the help of an assistant to hold the hood, mark the relationship of the hinges to the hood, remove the bolts and lift the hood off

10.10 Mark the position of the latch for reference, then loosen the latch bolts and move the latch as necessary to adjust the hood-closed position

10.11 Twist the rubber bumpers in-or-out to make fine adjustments to the hood closed height

ADJUSTMENT

7 Fore-and-aft and side-to-side adjustment of the hood is done by moving the hood in relation to the hinge flanges after loosening the bolts.

8 Scribe or trace a line around the entire hinge plate so you can judge the amount of movement.

9 Loosen the nuts and move the hood into correct alignment. Move it only a little at a time. Tighten the hinge nuts and carefully lower the hood to check the alignment.

10 Remove the plastic radiator cover (see Section 9), and adjust the hood latch so the hood closes securely (see illustration).

11 Adjust the hood bumpers on the radiator support so the hood is flush with the fenders when closed (see illustration).

12 The safety catch assembly on the hood itself can also be adjusted fore-and-aft and side-to-side after loosening the bolts.

13 The hood latch assembly, as well as the hinges, should be periodically lubricated with white lithium-base grease to prevent sticking and wear.

11 Hood latch and release cable - removal and installation

✳✳ WARNING:

The models covered by this manual are equipped with Supplemental Restraint Systems (SRS), more commonly known as airbags. Always disable the airbag system before working in the vicinity of any airbag system components to avoid the possibility of accidental deployment of the airbags, which could cause personal injury (see Chapter 12).

LATCH

▶ **Refer to illustration 11.1**

1 Remove the grille (see Section 9). Remove the bolts and detach the latch assembly (see illustration 10.10). Unhook the spring and use pliers to detach the cable end from the latch (see illustration).

2 Installation is the reverse of removal. Adjust the latch so the hood engages securely when closed and the hood bumpers are slightly compressed (see Section 10).

RELEASE CABLE

▶ **Refer to illustrations 11.5a, 11.5b and 11.6**

3 Disconnect the release cable from the hood latch assembly as

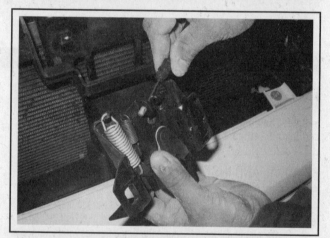

11.1 To disconnect the cable from the hood latch mechanism, pry the cable end out of the latch assembly and use pliers to disengage the cable housing end from its slot in the latch

described in Step 1.

4 Unclip the release cable from the engine wiring harness. Attach a length of wire to the cable to assist with the installation of the new cable.

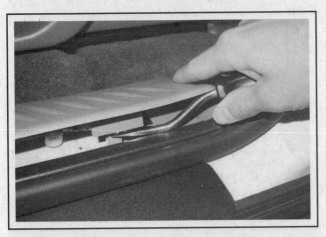

11.5a Firmly grasp the door sill trim and pull it up

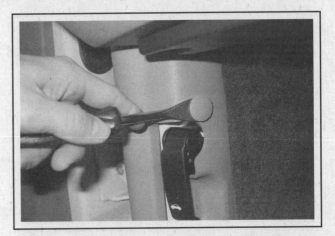

11.5b Pry up the retainer, then pull out the driver's kick panel while guiding the release handle through the opening

5 Working in the passenger compartment, remove the driver's sill panel and kick panel to expose the hood latch release cable and handle (see illustrations).

6 Use pliers to pull the cable housing end from the tab on the handle frame (see illustration).

➡**Note: If the handle assembly itself must be replaced, remove the one mounting bolt and remove the handle from the cowl.**

7 Trace the cable forward to the grommet where the cable goes through the firewall and pry the grommet out of the firewall. Pull the handle and cable rearward into the passenger compartment.

8 Disconnect the guide wire from the old cable and fasten it to the new cable.

9 With the new cable attached to the wire, pull the wire back through the firewall until the new cable reaches the latch assembly. Make sure that the grommet is properly seated on both sides of the hole in the firewall. Push on the grommet with your fingers from the passenger compartment side to seat the grommet in the firewall correctly.

10 The remainder of installation is the reverse of removal.

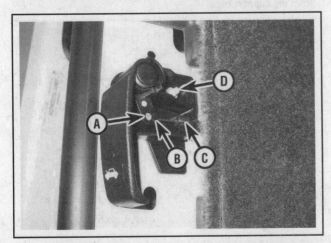

11.6 Work the cable housing end (A) out of the notch (B), then use pliers to twist the housing end (C) out of the bracket - to detach the hood latch release cable handle, remove the retaining nut (D)

12 Bumpers - removal and installation

❊❊ WARNING:

The models covered by this manual are equipped with Supplemental Restraint Systems (SRS), more commonly known as airbags. Always disable the airbag system before working in the vicinity of any airbag system components to avoid the possibility of accidental deployment of the airbags, which could cause personal injury (see Chapter 12).

1 Front and rear bumpers on all models use a plastic fascia panel over a metal impact bar.

FRONT BUMPER

▶ **Refer to illustrations 12.4a, 12.4b, 12.5, 12.9 and 12.11**

2 Disconnect the electrical connectors at the fog lights and cornering lights, if equipped.

3 Refer to Section 9 and remove the radiator grille.

Chevrolet and GMC models

4 Remove the bolts and plastic pushpins that secure the fascia panel to the headlamp panel (see illustrations). Some of these are

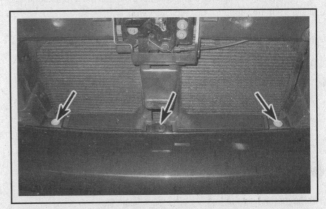

12.4a Remove the bolts and pushpin from the upper side of the panel . . .

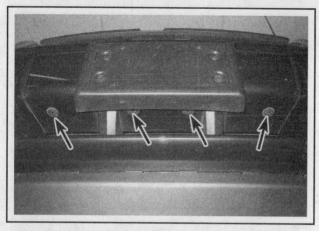

12.4b . . . and from the lower side

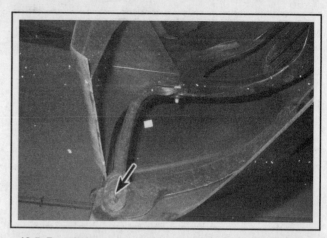

12.5 From below, remove the pushpins to detach the fascia from the support rods

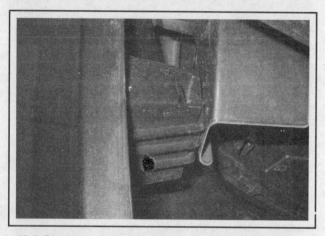

12.9 Disengage the fascia clip at each end of the bumper

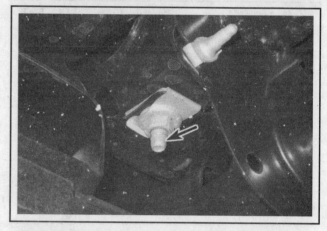

12.11 Remove the bolt on each side and take the impact bar off the vehicle

accessible from above the fascia; the remainder are accessible from below.

5   Working beneath the vehicle, remove the pushpins to detach the fascia from the support rods (see illustration).

Oldsmobile models

6   Remove the bolts that secure the top of the fascia panel to the headlamp panel.

7   Working beneath the vehicle, remove the pushpins to detach the fascia from the support rods (see illustration 12.5).

8   Remove four pushpins that secure the lower edge of the fascia to the air dam.

All models

9   Free the clip on each end of the fascia from the peg on the body (see illustration). Pull the fascia forward off the body.

10   Unbolt the fascia support rods from the bumper impact bar.

11   With an assistant supporting the impact bar, unbolt the impact bar from the frame and take it off (see illustration).

12   Disconnect any wiring harnesses or any other components that would interfere with bumper removal and detach the bumper.

13   Installation is the reverse of removal. Tighten the retaining bolts to the torque listed in this Chapter's Specifications.

REAR BUMPER

▶ **Refer to illustrations 12.15, 12.16, 12.17 and 12.19**

14   Disconnect the back-up lights.

15   Remove the pushpins from the underside of the fascia panel (see illustration).

12.15 Remove the pushpins from the underside of the rear bumper fascia

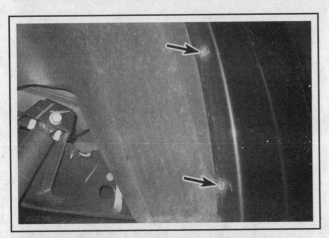

12.16 On each side of the fascia, remove the screws securing it to the wheel well

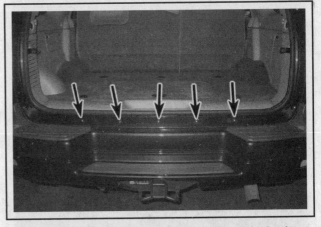

12.17 Remove the bolts along the upper edge of the fascia

16 Remove the screws that secure each end of the fascia panel to the wheel well (see illustration).

17 Unscrew the bolts that secure the upper edge of the fascia to the body, then lift the fascia off (see illustration).

18 If you're going to remove the impact bar, remove the spare tire carrier. Free the wiring harness from the trailer connector receptacle, twist the receptacle counterclockwise and remove it from the body.

19 Remove two of the impact bar retaining bolts from each side of the vehicle (see illustration).

20 With an assistant supporting the impact bar, remove the remaining bolt from each side. Take the impact bar off the vehicle.

21 Installation is the reverse of removal. Tighten the bolts to the torque listed in this Chapter's Specifications.

12.19 Remove the impact bar retaining bolts

13   Front fenders - removal and installation

▶ **Refer to illustrations 13.4a, 13.4b, 13.4c, 13.5, 13.6a, 13.6b, 13.6c, 13.7a and 13.7b**

❊❊ WARNING:

The models covered by this manual are equipped with Supplemental Restraint Systems (SRS), more commonly known as airbags. Always disable the airbag system before working in the vicinity of any airbag system components to avoid the possibility of accidental deployment of the airbags, which could cause personal injury (see Chapter 12).

1 Disconnect the negative cable from the battery. Loosen the wheel lug nuts, raise the vehicle, support it securely on jackstands and remove the front wheel.

2 Refer to Section 9 and remove the radiator grille.

3 Remove the assist step mounting nuts and remove the assist step.

4 Remove the scuff plate and rocker panel molding (see illustrations).

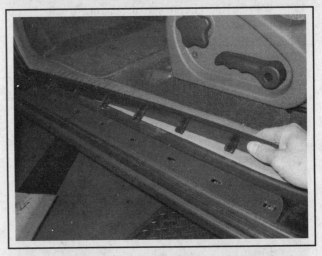

13.4a Lift the scuff plate, working from rear to front, to disengage the clips

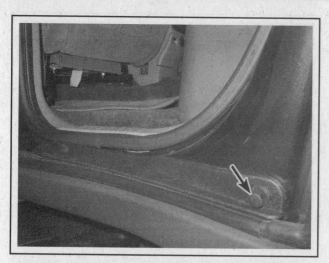

13.4b Remove the rear scuff plate pushpin, then disengage the clips

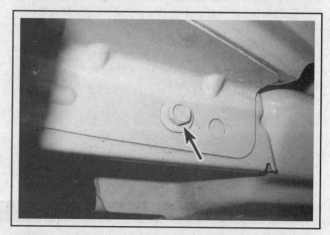

13.5 Remove the bolt and pushpins that secure the inner fender liner

➥**Note: On Trailblazer EXT and Envoy XL models, only the forward molding need be removed.**

5   Pry out the plastic rivets, remove the bolt and remove the inner fenderwell liner (see illustration).

6   From below, remove the fender bolt at the front of the fender opening, the bolt at the lower rear and the bolt securing the fender to the doorjamb (see illustrations).

7   Remove the upper fender mounting bolts (see illustrations).

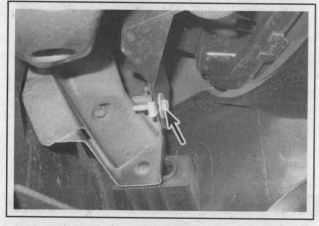

13.6a With the fender liner removed, remove this bolt at the front . . .

13.6b . . . this bolt at the lower rear . . .

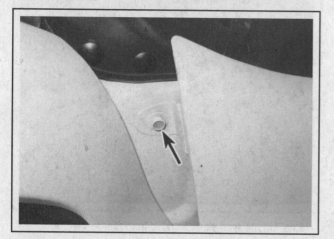

13.6c . . . and the fender-to-door jamb bolt

13.7a Remove the fender-to-radiator support bolt . . .

8   Detach the fender. It's a good idea to have an assistant support the fender while it's being moved away from the vehicle to prevent damage to the surrounding body panels.

9   Installation is the reverse of the removal procedure. Tighten all nuts, bolts and screws securely.

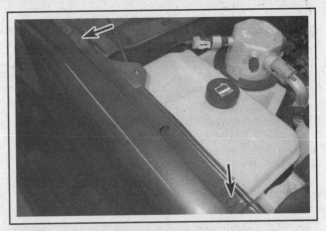

13.7b . . . and the bolts along the top edge of the fender (arrows) (one bolt not shown)

14   Cowl cover - removal and installation

▶ **Refer to illustration 14.3a and 14.3b**

1   Mark the position of the windshield wiper blades on the windshield with a wax marking pencil.

2   Remove the wiper arms (see Chapter 12).

3   Remove the cowl cover nuts and pushpins and disconnect the windshield washer hose. Carefully lift the cowl cover to free the retaining clips and take it off the vehicle (see illustrations).

4   Installation is the reverse of removal. Make sure to align the wiper blades with the marks made during removal.

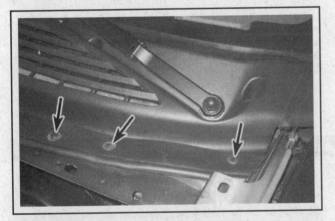

14.3a   Remove the cowl cover fasteners (driver's side shown) . . .

14.3b . . . **and disengage the clips to free the cowl cover**

15   Door trim panel - removal and installation

▶ **Refer to illustrations 15.2 and 15.6**

1   Disconnect the cable from the negative terminal of the battery (see Chapter 1).

2   If you're working on a front door, pry the power switch assembly out of the door panel with a flat-bladed trim tool (see illustration). If you're working on a rear door, remove the power window switch (see Chapter 12).

3   Remove the two door trim panel retaining screws.

4   Pry the panel outward with a flat-bladed trim tool to release the door panel clips from the door.

5   Once all of the clips are disengaged, raise the trim panel up and off the door. Remove the trim panel from the vehicle.

15.2   Pry up the power window switch assembly and disconnect the electrical connectors

6   For access to the inner door, carefully peel back the plastic watershield (see illustration).

7   Prior to installation of the door panel, be sure to reinstall any clips in the panel which may have come out during the removal procedure and remain in the door itself.

8   Place the panel in position on the door and hook its upper edge into the window slot.

9   If you're working on a front door, install the upper rear retaining clip in its hole, then the upper front retaining clip, then the remaining retaining clips. Install the front trim panel bolt, but don't tighten it yet. Install the rear bolt, tighten it securely, then tighten the front bolt.

10 If you're working on a rear door, push the retaining clips into their seated position. Install and tighten the screws, then install the screw trim panel.

11 Install the switch panel (front door) or power window switch (rear door). Connect the negative battery cable.

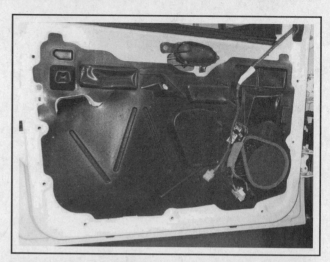

15.6 Peel the water deflector carefully away from the door, taking care not to tear it

16 Doors - removal and installation

1   Remove the door trim panel (see Section 15). Disconnect any electrical connectors and push them through the door opening so they won't interfere with door removal. Leave the wiring harness boot attached to the door but disconnected from the body.

2   Place a jack under the door or have an assistant on hand to support it when the hinge bolts are removed.

➡**Note: If a jack is used, place a rag between it and the door to protect the door's painted surfaces.**

3   Pull the rubber boot from the check strap and unbolt it from the door pillar.

4   Remove the fasteners and carefully lift off the door.

➡**Note: The hinges separate into two halves. Each hinge half is welded to the door or the cowl, and they are not adjustable. If a hinge needs to be replaced, the work should be performed at a body shop.**

5   Installation is the reverse of removal.

17 Door latch, lock cylinder and handles - removal and installation

LATCH

▶ **Refer to illustrations 17.2 and 17.3**

1   Raise the window completely and remove the door trim panel and the rear section of the watershield (see Section 15).

2   Detach the latch rods from the lock cylinder, outside handle and inside handle (see illustration).

3   Remove the three Torx-head mounting screws (it may be necessary to use an impact-type screwdriver to loosen them), then remove the latch from the door (see illustration). If possible, disconnect the rods while the latch is in the door. If not, pull the latch out with the rods attached, then disconnect the rods and electrical connectors.

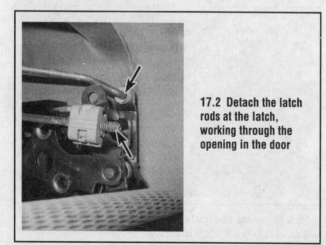

17.2 Detach the latch rods at the latch, working through the opening in the door

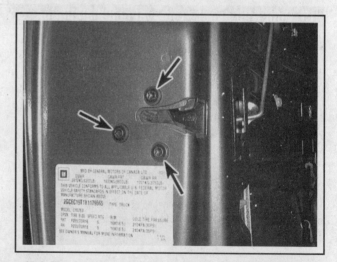

17.3 The door latch is retained by three Torx-head screws

17.5 Disconnect the link and pry off the C-clip, then remove the lock cylinder

4   Installation is the reverse of the removal procedure. Check the door to make sure it latches and unlatches properly.

LOCK CYLINDER

▶ **Refer to illustration 17.5**

5   Remove the outside door handle (see below). Disconnect the link, use a screwdriver to push the key lock cylinder retainer off and withdraw the lock cylinder from the door handle (see illustration).

6   Installation is the reverse of removal.

OUTSIDE HANDLE

7   Disconnect the outside handle link from the handle, remove the mounting nut(s) and detach the handle from the door.

8   Place the handle in position, attach the link and install the nut(s). Tighten the nut(s) securely.

17.11 Remove the inside door handle mounting bolt (left arrow) and slide the handle forward out of the locator cutout (right arrow)

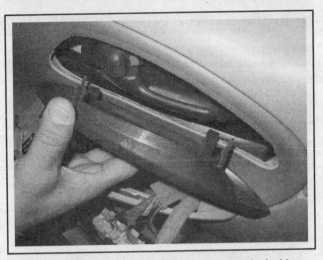

17.10 Carefully disengage the clips and remove the inside door handle trim bezel

INSIDE HANDLE

▶ **Refer to illustrations 17.10 and 17.11**

9   Follow the Steps in Section 15 to remove the door trim panel.

10 Remove the inside handle trim bezel (see illustration).

11 Disconnect the latch rod from the handle assembly, then remove the mounting bolt (see illustration). Slide the handle forward to detach it from the location holes, then take it out of the door.

LATCH STRIKER

▶ **Refer to illustration 17.12**

12 To make minor door adjustments for latch alignment, the bolts on the latch striker (which is mounted opposite the latch) can be loosened and the striker moved slightly (see illustration). Retighten the striker mounting bolts and check for proper latch operation.

➡**Note: The striker can be moved up-and-down, or left-and-right to make adjustments.**

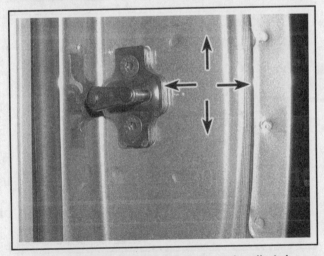

17.12 The latch striker on the door jamb can be adjusted slightly up/down or in/out

18 Door window glass - removal and installation

❋❋ WARNING:

Disconnect the power window switch connector when working inside the driver's door to prevent the window from lowering suddenly and causing injury.

ALL EXCEPT TRAILBLAZER EXT AND ENVOY XL REAR DOORS

▶ **Refer to illustration 18.4**

1   Remove the door trim panel and watershield (see Section 15). Remove the radio speaker from the door (see Chapter 12).
2   Remove the beltline weatherstripping from the door.
3   Lower the glass until the glass track bolts are visible in the door openings. Mark the position of the regulator clamps on the glass with a felt pen.
4   Loosen the regulator clamp bolts to allow the glass to move (see illustration).
5   Lift the glass up and out of the door through the glass opening.
6   To install, lower the glass into the door, slide it into position and tighten the nuts.
7   The remainder of installation is the reverse of removal.

TRAILBLAZER EXT AND ENVOY XL REAR DOORS

8   Remove the door trim panel and watershield (see Section 15).

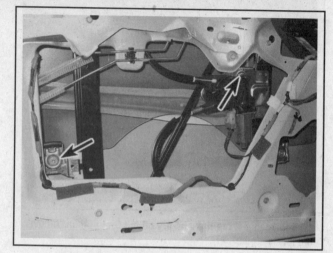

18.4 Loosen the glass clamp bolts

Remove the radio speaker from the door (see Chapter 12).
9   Remove the beltline weatherstripping from the door.
10 Remove the window regulator (see Section 19) and let the window rest in the bottom of the door.
11 Remove the glass channel bolt and take the channel out of the door.
12 Lift the glass up and out of the door through the glass opening.
13 Installation is the reverse of the removal steps.

19 Door window glass regulator - removal and installation

❋❋ CAUTION:

Do not remove the electric motor from the regulator assembly. The motor is available only as an integral unit with a new regulator.

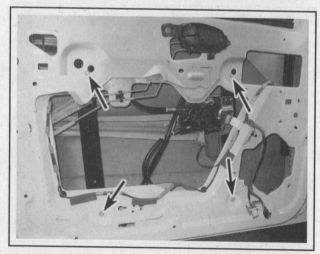

19.4 Door window regulator mounting bolt locations

FRONT DOOR

▶ **Refer to illustration 19.4**

1   Remove the door trim panel, watershield and radio speaker (see Section 15 and Chapter 12).
2   Remove the door window glass (see Section 18).
3   Disconnect the window motor's electrical connector.
4   Loosen the two upper regulator bolts, but don't remove them (see illustration). Remove the three lower bolts, then slide the regulator off of the two upper bolts. Tilt the regulator toward the front of the door and lift it out.
5   Installation is the reverse of removal.

REAR DOOR

All except TrailBlazer EXT and Envoy XL

6   Remove the door trim panel, watershield and radio speaker (see Section 15 and Chapter 12).
7   Remove the door window glass (see Section 18).
8   Disconnect the window motor's electrical connector.
9   Remove the regulator mounting bolts and lift it out of the door.
10 Installation is the reverse of the removal steps.

TrailBlazer EXT and Envoy XL

11 If the window can be moved, lower or raise it halfway.

12 Remove the door trim panel and watershield (see Section 15).

13 Loosen the clamp bolts that secure the glass to the regulator. Slide the glass all the way up, then either have an assistant hold it or secure it with duct tape.

14 Disconnect the window motor's electrical connector.

15 Detach the regulator cable retainer from its bracket on the door. Unscrew the two lower bolts that secure the regulator to the door. If the regulator is working, loosen the upper bolt; if not, remove the bolt completely.

16 Lift the regulator out through the slot in the inner door panel.

17 Installation is the reverse of the removal steps.

20 Mirrors - removal and installation

▶ **Refer to illustrations 20.1, 20.3 and 20.6**

OUTSIDE MIRRORS

1 Remove the door trim panel (see Section 15). Remove the door insulator (see illustration).

2 Detach the mirror wiring harness from the door and disconnect the connector.

3 Remove the nuts and detach the mirror from the door (see illustration).

4 Installation is the reverse of removal.

INSIDE MIRROR

5 If the mirror is equipped with an electrical connector, disconnect it.

6 Remove the setscrew, then slide the mirror up off the support base on the windshield (see illustration).

7 Installation is the reverse of removal.

8 If the support base for the mirror has come off the windshield, it can be reattached with a special mirror adhesive kit available at auto

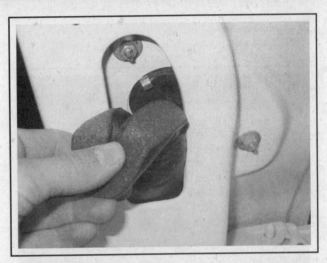

20.1 Remove the door insulator

parts stores. Clean the glass and support base thoroughly and follow the directions on the adhesive package, allowing the base to bond overnight before attaching the mirror.

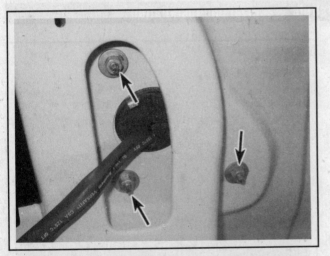

20.3 Remove the three outside mirror mounting nuts; on power models (shown), disconnect the electrical connector

20.6 Using a Torx screwdriver, remove the setscrew and slide the inside mirror from the support base

21 Liftgate and liftgate glass - removal and installation

LIFTGATE

▸ **Refer to illustration 21.4**

✳✳ WARNING:

The liftgate is heavy and awkward to hold. At least two people should perform this procedure.

1 Open the liftgate and support it fully in this position.
2 Disconnect the electrical connectors for the liftgate.
3 Detach the support struts at the liftgate (see Section 22).
4 Remove the liftgate hinge-to-body mounting nuts (see illustration). Remove the bolts while at least one assistant, preferably two, helps you hold the liftgate.
5 Installation is the reverse of the removal procedure.

21.4 Remove the liftgate hinge-to-body mounting nuts

LIFTGATE GLASS

6 Disconnect the electrical connector for the rear window defogger.
7 Open the liftgate and remove the liftgate window struts (see Section 22).
8 Close the liftgate.

✳✳ WARNING:

Don't try to open the liftgate once the hinge pins have been removed.

Remove the C-clips from the hinge pins, then slide the pins out of the hinges (see illustration). With an assistant to help, take the liftgate glass off the vehicle.
9 Installation is the reverse of the removal procedure. Make sure the C-clips snap firmly into place in the grooves in the hinge pins.

21.8 Remove the C-clips and pull out the hinge pins

22 Liftgate panels, lock cylinder, latch and support struts - removal and installation

INTERIOR TRIM PANELS

▸ **Refer to illustrations 22.1a, 22.1b and 22.2**

1 Open the liftgate glass, then remove the plastic pushpins securing the upper trim panel to the liftgate, and the lower trim panel to the liftgate glass latch (see illustrations). Guide the wiring harness out of the slot in the upper trim panel and set the panel aside.
2 Remove the assist strap (see illustration), then remove the plastic fastener on the trim panel (see illustration 22.1b). The upper trim panel must be removed first for access to the lower (larger) liftgate trim panel.
3 Installation is the reverse of the removal procedure.

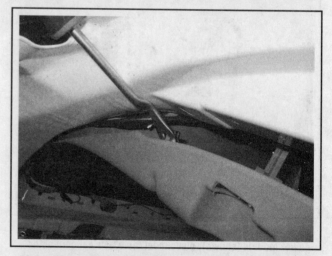

22.1a Disengage the clips, lift the trim panel off and slip the wiring harness out of the slot

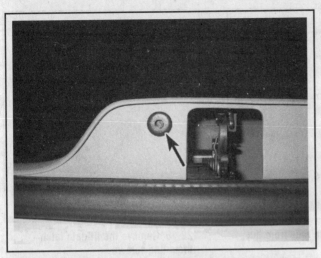

22.1b Remove the pushpin at the liftgate glass latch - push the center pin in the fastener down to remove it

22.2 Remove the Torx screw securing the assist strap in the center of the lower trim panel

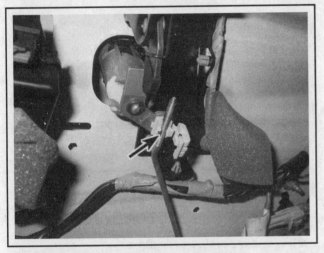

22.5 Detach the latch rod from the tailgate lock cylinder lever . . .

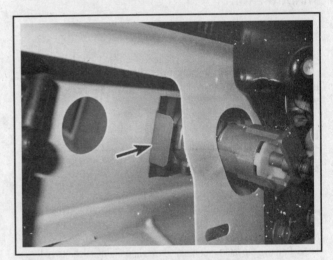

22.6 . . . and remove the lock cylinder C-clip

LOCK CYLINDER

▶ **Refer to illustrations 22.5 and 22.6**

   4 Remove the trim panel from the liftgate (Steps 1 and 2).
   5 Open the clip and detach the latch rod from the lock cylinder lever (see illustration).
   6 Remove the C-clip and take the lock cylinder out of the tailgate (see illustration).
   7 Installation is the reverse of the removal procedure.

WINDOW HANDLE AND STRIKER

▶ **Refer to illustration 22.9**

   8 Open the tailgate window.
   9 Remove the mounting nuts and separate the handle and striker from the glass (see illustration).
   10 Installation is the reverse of the removal procedure. If the window is hard to latch or is loose when latched, add or remove striker shims.

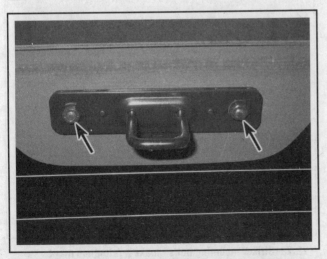

22.9 Remove the nuts securing the tailgate glass striker and handle

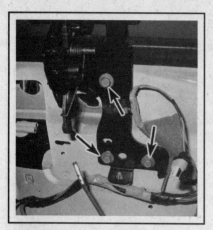

22.12 Remove the tailgate window latch mounting bolts

22.14 Disconnect the rods from the tailgate door latch

22.15 Remove the liftgate latch mounting screws

WINDOW LATCH

▶ **Refer to illustration 22.12**

11 Remove the interior liftgate panels (see Steps 1 and 2).

12 Remove the latch mounting bolts, lift the latch out and disconnect the electrical connector (see illustration). Remove the latch from the vehicle.

DOOR LATCH

▶ **Refer to illustrations 22.14 and 22.15**

13 Remove the liftgate trim panels (see Steps 1 and 2).

14 Detach the outside handle rod from the bellcrank and the bellcrank rod from the latch. Remove the bellcrank mounting screws and detach it from the latch (see illustration).

15 Remove the latch mounting screws and lift the latch out of the door (see illustration). Disconnect the electrical connector, detach the lock cylinder rod from the latch and remove the latch from the vehicle.

16 Installation is the reverse of the removal procedure.

SUPPORT STRUTS

▶ **Refer to illustration 22.18**

17 There are two support struts for the liftgate, and two separate struts to support the glass. Open the liftgate (or liftgate glass) and prop it securely in the full open position.

18 Release the small clip at each end of the strut, then pull the strut from the mounting ball (see illustration).

19 Installation is the reverse of the removal procedure.

LIFTGATE STRIKER

▶ **Refer to illustration 22.22**

20 The closing position of the liftgate can be adjusted slightly by moving the liftgate striker.

21 To access the striker, open the liftgate.

22 Loosen the striker mounting bolts, move the striker slightly, retighten the bolts and check the liftgate closing (see illustration).

22.18 Detach either end of the liftgate support strut by pulling out the retainer clip with a small screwdriver, then pull the strut from the ballstud (liftgate strut shown, liftgate glass strut similar)

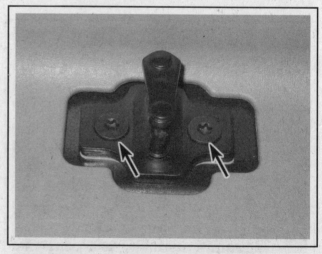

22.22 Striker mounting bolts - make a reference mark around the edges of the striker before repositioning it for adjustment

23 Console - removal and installation

☀ WARNING:

The models covered by this manual are equipped with Supplemental Restraint Systems (SRS), more commonly known as airbags. Always disable the airbag system before working in the vicinity of any airbag system components to avoid the possibility of accidental deployment of the airbags, which could cause personal injury (see Chapter 12).

CENTER CONSOLE

◆ **Refer to illustration 23.2, 23.4 and 23.5**

1   Block the wheels so the vehicle can't roll. It will be necessary to shift out of Park and release the handbrake lever during this procedure.

2   Loosen the setscrew that secures the transmission shift knob (see illustration). Squeeze the sides of the shift lever boot together at the bottom to free the clips, then lift the knob and boot off the shift lever.

3   If you're working on an Oldsmobile model, push the shift handle release button, and at the same time push the shift lock release tab forward and move the shift lever all the way to the rear. Remove the screws and release the clips that secure the console trim plate, then remove the trim plate.

4   On all models, open the console lid and remove the six screws securing the storage bin to the console (see illustration). Lift the bin off.

5   Remove the console mounting screws (see illustration).

6   Lift the parking brake lever all the way.

7   If you're working on an Oldsmobile model, detach the two console-to-instrument panel trim pieces at the front of the console.

8   Lift the console up and back for access to the electrical connectors under the console. Disconnect the connectors, lower the parking brake lever halfway and lift the console out of the vehicle.

9   Installation is the reverse of removal.

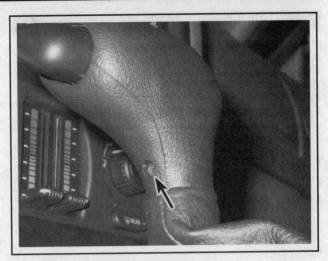

23.2 Remove the shift lever setscrew

OVERHEAD CONSOLE

10 If you're working on a front overhead console, remove the two screws at the rear of the console. Disengage the two tabs at the front, lower the console, disconnect its electrical connectors and remove it from the vehicle.

11 If you're working on a rear overhead console, remove the four screws that secure the console. Lower the console and remove it from the vehicle.

12 Installation is the reverse of the removal steps.

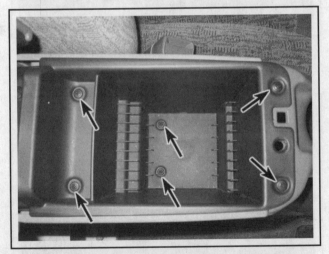

23.4 Remove the screws from inside the storage bin and remove the bin

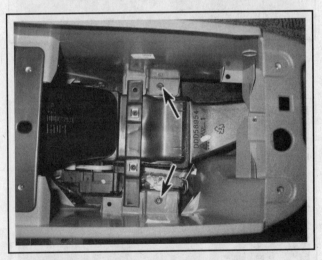

23.5 Remove the console mounting screws

24 Dashboard trim panels - removal and installation

❋❋ WARNING:

The models covered by this manual are equipped with Supplemental Restraint Systems (SRS), more commonly known as airbags. Always disable the airbag system before working in the vicinity of any airbag system components to avoid the possibility of accidental deployment of the airbags, which could cause personal injury (see Chapter 12).

LOWER LEFT SOUND INSULATOR PANEL

▶ **Refer to illustration 24.1**

1   To access components under the left side of the instrument panel, remove the two screws, release the clip and lower the panel (see illustration).

2   Detach the electrical components and wiring harnesses from the upper side of the panel and remove the panel from the vehicle.

LOWER RIGHT SOUND INSULATOR PANEL

▶ **Refer to illustration 24.3**

3   To access components under the right side of the instrument panel, remove the screws, free the electrical connector clip (if equipped) and remove the lower sound panel from the vehicle (see illustration).

CENTER SOUND INSULATOR PANEL (GMC/CHEVROLET MODELS)

▶ **Refer to illustration 24.5**

4   Remove the center console (see Section 23).

5   Remove the insulator panel retaining screws (see illustration), then remove the insulator panel from the instrument panel.

6   Installation is the reverse of the removal steps.

24.1 Remove the screws that secure the lower left sound insulator panel

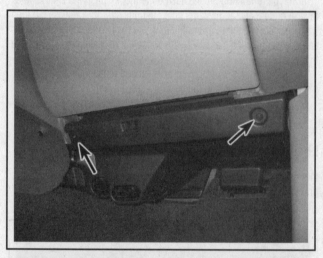

24.3 Remove the screws that secure the lower right sound insulator panel

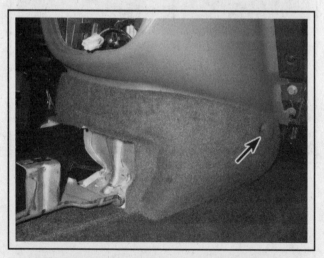

24.5 Remove the screws (right side shown) that secure the lower center dash trim panel

24.9 Knee bolster mounting nut locations

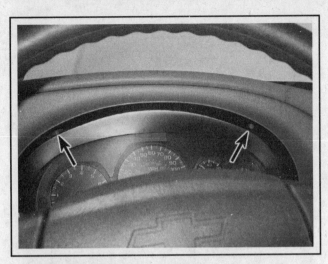

24.18 Instrument cluster bezel screws

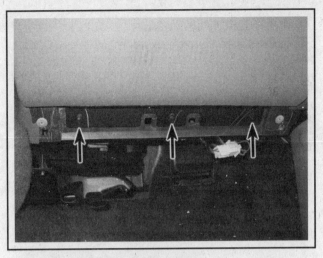

24.21 Glove box door retaining screws

KNEE BOLSTER

▶ **Refer to illustration 24.9**

7   Remove the left sound insulator panel (see Step 1).
8   Remove the screws and free the clips, then remove the bolster trim panel from the dash.
9   If the knee bolster reinforcement panel has to be removed for any reason, remove the four nuts and take down the bolster (see illustration).
10   Installation is the reverse of removal.

LEFT ACCESSORY TRIM PANEL

11   Remove the left insulator panel and knee bolster trim panel.
12   Remove the nuts and free the clips, then remove the panel from the dash.

CENTER ACCESSORY TRIM PANEL (GMC/OLDSMOBILE MODELS)

13   Remove the center console and, if equipped, the center sound insulator panel (see above).

14   Remove two screws at the bottom of the panel, then release the clips, starting at the bottom and working upward. Disconnect the panel electrical connectors and remove it from the vehicle.
15   Installation is the reverse of the removal steps.

INSTRUMENT CLUSTER BEZEL

▶ **Refer to illustration 24.18**

16   On models equipped with tilt steering columns, tilt the steering wheel down as far as possible.
17   Remove the left insulator panel (see above).
18   Remove the bezel screws and take it off (see illustration).
19   Installation is the reverse of the removal steps.

GLOVE BOX

▶ **Refer to illustration 24.21**

20   Remove the lower right insulator panel (see Step 3).
21   Remove three screws along the bottom of the glove compartment and take it out of the dash (see illustration).
22   Installation is the reverse of the removal steps.

25   Steering column covers - removal and installation

▶ **Refer to illustration 25.6**

❈❈ **WARNING:**

The models covered by this manual are equipped with Supplemental Restraint Systems (SRS), more commonly known as airbags. Always disable the airbag system before working in the vicinity of any airbag system components to avoid the possibility of accidental deployment of the airbags, which could cause personal injury (see Chapter 12).

❈❈ **CAUTION:**

Perform this procedure exactly in the order described to prevent damage to the covers.

1   Remove the steering wheel (see Chapter 10). Pull the steering wheel tilt lever off the column.
2   Sitting on the driver's seat, pull down the left side of the closeout (forward) cover, if equipped to disengage the left snap. Don't pull the

cover down any farther than necessary and don't try to remove it at this point.

3 Repeat Step 2 on the right side of the closeout cover to disengage its snap.

4 Working from the left, carefully rotate the forward cover to the right to free the remaining four snaps.

5 If there are two screws in the underside of the lower cover, remove them.

6 Carefully separate the lower cover from the upper cover and remove the lower cover (see illustration).

7 If there's a screw in the top of the upper trim cover, remove it.

8 Take the upper cover and closeout cover off the steering column.

9 Installation is the reverse of removal. If the snaps were damaged during removal, install screws at the snap locations.

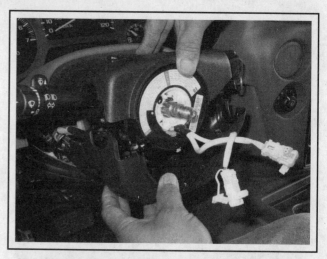

25.6 Separate the lower cover from the upper cover

26 Instrument panel and carrier - removal and installation

❋❋ WARNING:

The models covered by this manual are equipped with Supplemental Restraint Systems (SRS), more commonly known as airbags. Always disable the airbag system before working in the vicinity of any airbag system components to avoid the possibility of accidental deployment of the airbags, which could cause personal injury (see Chapter 12).

➡Note: This procedure is lengthy and difficult, even for an experienced mechanic. Due to the number of electrical connections, fasteners used, and the various safety systems involved, we don't recommend instrument panel removal for the home mechanic.

1 Turn the front wheels to the straight-ahead position and lock the steering column, then disconnect the negative battery cable (see Chapter 1).

2 Disable the airbag system (see Chapter 12).

INSTRUMENT PANEL UPPER TRIM PAD

▶ **Refer to illustrations 26.4 and 26.5**

3 Use a trim tool to remove the windshield post interior trim strips.

4 Carefully pull up the trim clips along the length of the upper trim pad (see illustration).

5 Locate the ambient light sensor in the center of the trim pad. Rotate it 1/4-turn counterclockwise to disengage it from the pad, then lift the pad off the dash (see illustration).

6 Installation is the reverse of the removal steps.

26.4 Carefully pry the upper trim pad from the instrument panel

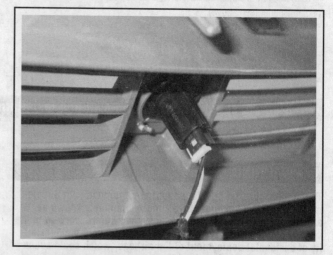

26.5 Twist the ambient light sensor 1/4-turn counterclockwise to free it from the trim pad

26.15 Detach the cover from each end of the instrument panel, then remove the screw underneath

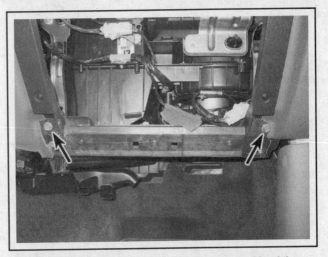

26.16a Remove the screws from the lower right side of the instrument panel . . .

26.16b . . . and the radio recess . . .

26.16c . . . and the instrument cluster recess

INSTRUMENT PANEL

▶ **Refer to illustrations 26.15, 26.16a, 26.16b, 26.16c, 26.17a and 26.17b**

7 Disable the airbag system (see Chapter 12).

8 Remove the instrument panel upper trim pad (see above).

9 Remove the center console (see Section 23).

10 Remove all of the panels described in Section 24. Also remove the instrument cluster (see Chapter 12).

11 Detach the steering column from the dash and lower it (see Chapter 10). If you're planning to remove the instrument panel support structure, remove the steering column completely.

12 Remove the left heater duct (see Chapter 10, illustration 17.7).

13 Remove the radio (see Chapter 12). If the vehicle has upper front speakers, remove them.

14 Remove the heater/AC control module and free its wiring harness from the retainer (see Chapter 3).

15 Remove the access cover from each end of the instrument panel, then remove the screw that secures each end of the instrument panel (see illustration).

16 Remove the lower mounting bolts from the right side of the instrument panel, from in the center of the panel (in the radio recess),

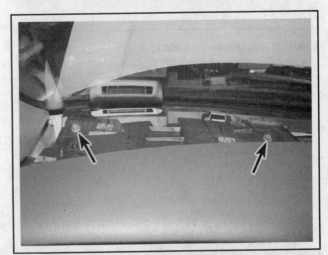

26.17a Remove the bolts from the top of the left end of the instrument panel . . .

and from the instrument cluster recess (see illustrations).

17 Remove the bolts along the top of the instrument panel (see illustrations).

18 Have an assistant help you lift the instrument panel out of the vehicle.

19 Installation is the reverse of removal.

INSTRUMENT PANEL CARRIER

20 The instrument panel carrier is a complicated, unitized structure that supports the steering column, the heating/air conditioning modules and other components. The carrier is removed together with the HVAC assembly containing the evaporator and heater core (see Chapter 3).

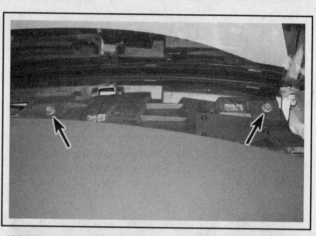

26.17b ... and from the right end, then check to make sure nothing is still connected and carefully remove the instrument panel

27 Seats - removal and installation

※※ WARNING:

The models covered by this manual are equipped with Supplemental Restraint Systems (SRS), more commonly known as airbags. Always disable the airbag system before working in the vicinity of any airbag system components to avoid the possibility of accidental deployment of the airbags, which could cause personal injury (see Chapter 12).

FRONT BUCKET SEAT (ALL MODELS)

1 Remove the trim covers from the mounting fasteners, then unscrew the mounting nuts and bolt. Unplug the electrical connector, disconnect the harness from the frame, then remove the seat.

2ND SEAT

◆ Refer to illustrations 27.3 and 27.4

2 Fold the right-side middle seat forward. Remove the cover from the vehicle communication interface module, then disengage the VCIM retainer and lift it off the bracket. Disconnect the VCIM electrical connectors and place the VCIM out of the way.

3 Raise the seat (see illustration).

4 Remove the mounting nuts (see illustration).

5 Remove the seat assembly as a unit.

➡Note: This is a job for two people.

6 Installation is the reverse of removal.

3RD SEAT

7 Remove the seat mounting nuts. Detach the seat belt anchors from the mounting studs.

8 Remove the mounting bolts. Remove the seat assembly as a unit.

➡Note: This is a job for two people.

9 Installation is the reverse of the removal steps.

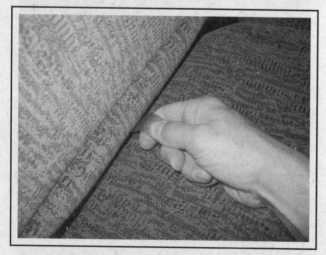

27.3 Pull the strap and raise the seat

27.4 Fold the second seat forward and remove the remaining mounting nuts (arrows)

28 Steering gear crossmember - removal and installation

1   Loosen the wheel lug nuts, raise the front of the vehicle and support it securely on jackstands. Remove the wheels. Support both lower control arms with floor jacks.

2   Remove the splash shield from under the vehicle.

3   Remove the lower control arm bracket-to-frame bolts (see Chapter 10).

4   Unbolt the steering gear front crossmember from the vehicle and remove it.

5   Unbolt the steering gear rear crossmember from the vehicle and remove it.

6   Installation is the reverse of the removal steps. Tighten the control arm bracket bolts to the torque listed in the Chapter 10 Specifications and the steering gear crossmember bolts to the torque listed in this Chapter's Specifications.

Specifications

	Ft-lbs
Front impact bar-to-frame bolts	63
Rear impact bar-to-frame bolts	268
Steering gear crossmember bolts	37

Notes

12

CHASSIS ELECTRICAL SYSTEM

1 General information

⁂ WARNING:

Refer to the Warning and Caution in Chapter 5, Section 1 under "Battery disconnection."

The electrical system is a 12-volt, negative ground type. Power for the lights and all electrical accessories is supplied by a lead/acid-type battery that is charged by the alternator.

This Chapter covers repair and service procedures for the various electrical components not associated with the engine. Information on the battery, alternator, ignition system and starter motor can be found in Chapter 5.

It should be noted that when portions of the electrical system are serviced, the negative cable should be disconnected from the battery to prevent electrical shorts and/or fires.

2 Electrical troubleshooting - general information

◆ **Refer to illustrations 2.5a, 2.5b, 2.6, 2.9 and 2.15**

A typical electrical circuit consists of an electrical component, any switches, relays, motors, fuses, fusible links or circuit breakers related to that component and the wiring and connectors that link the component to both the battery and the chassis. To help you pinpoint an electrical circuit problem, wiring diagrams are included at the end of this Chapter.

Before tackling any troublesome electrical circuit, first study the appropriate wiring diagrams to get a complete understanding of what makes up that individual circuit. Trouble spots, for instance, can often be narrowed down by noting if other components related to the circuit are operating properly. If several components or circuits fail at one time, chances are the problem is in a fuse or ground connection, because several circuits are often routed through the same fuse and ground connections.

Electrical problems usually stem from simple causes, such as loose or corroded connections, a blown fuse, a melted fusible link or a failed relay. Visually inspect the condition of all fuses, wires and connections in a problem circuit before troubleshooting the circuit.

If test equipment and instruments are going to be utilized, use the diagrams to plan ahead of time where you will make the necessary connections in order to accurately pinpoint the trouble spot.

The basic tools needed for electrical troubleshooting include a circuit tester or voltmeter (a 12-volt bulb with a set of test leads can also be used), a continuity tester, which includes a bulb, battery and set of test leads, and a jumper wire, preferably with a circuit breaker incorporated, which can be used to bypass electrical components (see illustrations). Before attempting to locate a problem with test instruments, use the wiring diagram(s) to decide where to make the connections.

VOLTAGE CHECKS

Voltage checks should be performed if a circuit is not functioning properly. Connect one lead of a circuit tester to either the negative battery terminal or a known good ground. Connect the other lead to a connector in the circuit being tested, preferably nearest to the battery or fuse (see illustration). If the bulb of the tester lights, voltage is present, which means that the part of the circuit between the connector and the battery is problem free. Continue checking the rest of the circuit in the

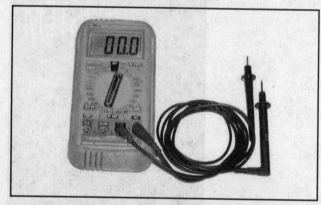

2.5a The most useful tool for electrical troubleshooting is a digital multimeter that can check volts, amps, and test continuity

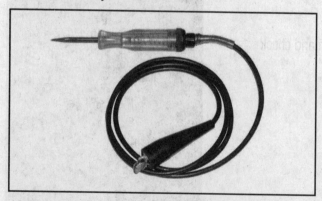

2.5b A test light is a very handy tool for checking voltage

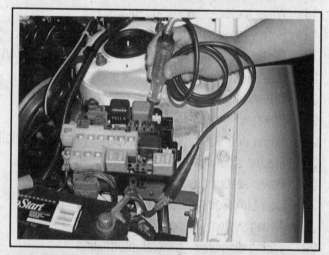

2.6 In use, a basic test light's lead is clipped to a known good ground, then the pointed probe can test connectors, wires or electrical sockets - if the bulb lights, the part being tested has battery voltage

same fashion. When you reach a point at which no voltage is present, the problem lies between that point and the last test point with voltage. Most of the time the problem can be traced to a loose connection.

➡Note: Keep in mind that some circuits receive voltage only when the ignition key is in the Accessory or Run position.

FINDING A SHORT

One method of finding shorts in a circuit is to remove the fuse and connect a test light or voltmeter in place of the fuse terminals. There should be no voltage present in the circuit. Move the wiring harness from side-to-side while watching the test light. If the bulb goes on, there is a short to ground somewhere in that area, probably where the insulation has rubbed through. The same test can be performed on each component in the circuit, even a switch.

GROUND CHECK

Perform a ground test to check whether a component is properly grounded. Disconnect the battery and connect one lead of a continuity tester or multimeter (set to the ohms scale), to a known good ground. Connect the other lead to the wire or ground connection being tested. If the resistance is low (less than 5 ohms), the ground is good. If the bulb on a self-powered test light does not go on, the ground is not good.

CONTINUITY CHECK

A continuity check is done to determine if there are any breaks in a circuit - if it is passing electricity properly. With the circuit off (no power in the circuit), a self-powered continuity tester or multimeter can be used to check the circuit. Connect the test leads to both ends of the circuit (or to the "power" end and a good ground), and if the test light comes on the circuit is passing current properly (see illustration). If the resistance is low (less than 5 ohms), there is continuity; if the reading is 10,000 ohms or higher, there is a break somewhere in the circuit. The same procedure can be used to test a switch, by connecting the continuity tester to the switch terminals. With the switch turned On, the test light should come on (or low resistance should be indicated on a meter).

FINDING AN OPEN CIRCUIT

When diagnosing for possible open circuits, it is often difficult to locate them by sight because the connectors hide oxidation or terminal misalignment. Merely wiggling a connector on a sensor or in the wiring harness may correct the open circuit condition. Remember this when an open circuit is indicated when troubleshooting a circuit. Intermittent problems may also be caused by oxidized or loose connections.

Electrical troubleshooting is simple if you keep in mind that all electrical circuits are basically electricity running from the battery, through the wires, switches, relays, fuses and fusible links to each electrical component (light bulb, motor, etc.) and to ground, from which it is passed back to the battery. Any electrical problem is an interruption in the flow of electricity to and from the battery.

CONNECTORS

Most electrical connections on these vehicles are made with multiwire plastic connectors. The mating halves of many connectors are secured with locking clips molded into the plastic connector shells. The

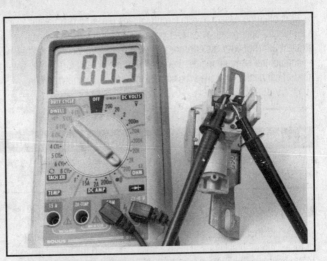

2.9 With a multimeter set to the ohms scale, resistance can be checked across two terminals - when checking for continuity, a low reading indicates continuity, a high reading indicates lack of continuity

mating halves of large connectors, such as some of those under the instrument panel, are held together by a bolt through the center of the connector.

To separate a connector with locking clips, use a small screwdriver to pry the clips apart carefully, then separate the connector halves. Pull only on the shell, never pull on the wiring harness as you may damage the individual wires and terminals inside the connectors. Look at the connector closely before trying to separate the halves. Often the locking clips are engaged in a way that is not immediately clear. Additionally, many connectors have more than one set of clips.

Each pair of connector terminals has a male half and a female half. When you look at the end view of a connector in a diagram, be sure to understand whether the view shows the harness side or the component side of the connector. Connector halves are mirror images of each other, and a terminal shown on the right side end-view of one half will be on the left side end-view of the other half.

2.15 To backprobe a connector, insert a small, sharp probe (such as a straight-pin) into the back of the connector alongside the desired wire until it contacts the metal terminal inside; connect your meter leads to the probes - this allows you to test a functioning circuit

It is often necessary to take circuit voltage measurements with a connector connected. Whenever possible, carefully insert a small straight pin (not your meter probe) into the rear of the connector shell to contact the terminal inside, then clip your meter lead to the pin. This kind of connection is called "backprobing" (see illustration). When inserting a test probe into a terminal, be careful not to distort the terminal opening. Doing so can lead to a poor connection and corrosion at that terminal later. Using the small straight pin instead of a meter probe results in less chance of deforming the terminal connector.

3 Fuses and fusible links - general information

FUSES

▶ **Refer to illustrations 3.1a through 3.1f, 3.3a and 3.3b**

The electrical circuits of the vehicle are protected by a combination of fuses, circuit breakers and fusible links. The main fuse/relay panel is in the engine compartment (see illustrations), while the rear fuse/relay panel is located beneath the left rear seat (see illustrations).

Each of the fuses is designed to protect a specific circuit, and the various circuits are identified on the fuse panel itself.

Several sizes of fuses are employed in the fuse blocks. There are small, medium and large sizes of the same design, all with the same blade terminal design. The medium and large fuses can be removed with your fingers, but the small fuses require the use of pliers or the small plastic fuse-puller tool found in most fuse boxes.

If an electrical component fails, always check the fuse first. The best way to check the fuses is with a test light. Check for power at the exposed terminal tips of each fuse (see illustration). If power is present at one side of the fuse but not the other, the fuse is blown. A blown fuse can also be identified by visually inspecting it (see illustration).

3.1a The main fuse/relay box is in the engine compartment; disengage the locking tabs and remove the outer cover . . .

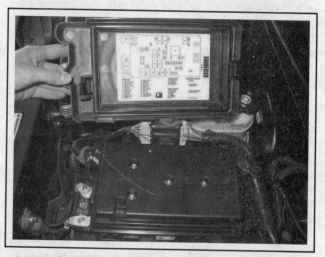

3.1b . . . which has a legend to identify the fuses and relays . . .

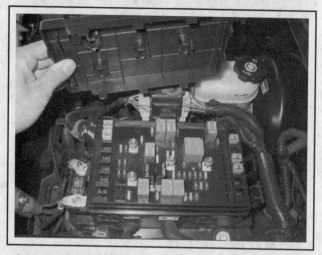

3.1c . . . and the inner cover for access to the fuses and relays

3.1d The interior fuse/relay panel is located beneath the left rear seat; remove the outer cover (which also has a legend to identify the fuses and relays) . . .

3.1e . . . and the inner cover for access . . .

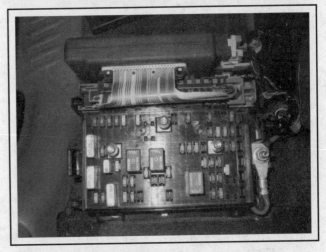

3.1f . . . to the fuses and relays

Be sure to replace blown fuses with the correct type. Fuses (of the same physical size) of different ratings may be physically interchangeable, but only fuses of the proper rating should be used. Replacing a fuse with one of a higher or lower value than specified is not recommended. Each electrical circuit needs a specific amount of protection.

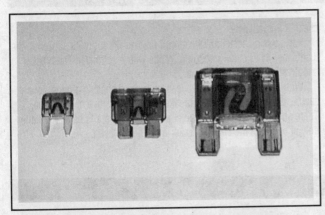

3.3a All three of these fuses are of 30-amp rating, yet are different sizes, at left is a small fuse, the center is a medium, and at right is a large - make sure you get the right amperage and size when purchasing replacement fuses

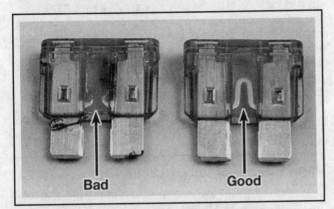

3.3b When a fuse blows, the element between the terminals melts - the fuse on the left is blown, the one on the right is good

The amperage value of each fuse is molded into the top of the fuse body.

If the replacement fuse immediately fails, don't replace it again until the cause of the problem is isolated and corrected. In most cases, this will be a short circuit in the wiring caused by a broken or deteriorated wire.

FUSIBLE LINKS

▶ **Refer to illustrations 3.7 and 3.9**

Some circuits are protected by fusible links. The links are used in circuits that are not ordinarily fused, such as the alternator circuit.

The fusible link for the alternator circuit is located in the wire from the battery to the alternator, and is easily identified (see illustration). The link is a short length of heavy wire that is marked "fusible link" on the outer cover.

To replace a fusible link, first disconnect the negative battery cable.

Although the fusible links appear to be a heavier gauge than the wires they're protecting, the appearance is due to the thick insulation. All fusible links are several wire gauges smaller than the wire they're designed to protect. Fusible links can't be repaired, but a new link of the

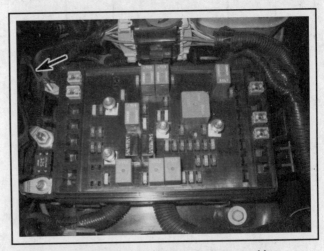

3.7 The cable from the alternator to the battery cable junction terminal is the fusible link

same size wire can be installed. The procedure is as follows:

a) *Cut the damaged fusible link out of the wire just behind the connector.*

b) *Strip the insulation back approximately 1-inch.*

c) *Spread the strands of the exposed wire apart, push them together and twist them in place (see illustration).*

d) *Use rosin core solder and solder the wires together to obtain a good connection.*

e) *Use plenty of electrical tape around the soldered joint. No wires should be exposed.*

f) *Connect the negative battery cable. Test the circuit for proper operation.*

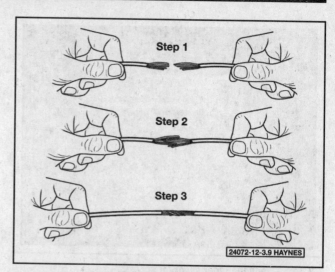

3.9 To repair a fusible link, cut out the damaged section, then join a new section by stripping the wire and twisting it together, as shown here - when securely joined, solder the connections and wrap them with electrical tape

4 Circuit breakers - general information and check

Circuit breakers protect certain circuits, such as the power windows and power seats. Depending on the vehicle's accessories, there may be two 25-amp circuit breakers for the door locks and one 30-amp circuit breaker for the power seats, located in the interior fuse/relay box under the left rear seat.

Because the circuit breakers reset automatically, an electrical overload in a circuit-breaker-protected system will cause the circuit to fail momentarily, then come back on. If the circuit does not come back on,

check it immediately.

For a basic check, pull the circuit breaker up out of its socket on the fuse panel, but just far enough to probe with a voltmeter. The breaker should still contact the sockets.

With the voltmeter negative lead on a good chassis ground, touch each end prong of the circuit breaker with the positive meter probe. There should be battery voltage at each end. If there is battery voltage only at one end, the circuit breaker must be replaced.

5 Relays - general information and testing

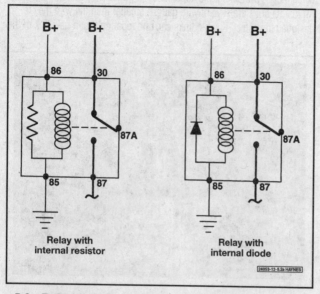

5.2a Typical ISO relay designs, terminal numbering and circuit connections

GENERAL INFORMATION

1 Several electrical accessories in the vehicle, such as the fuel injection system, horns, starter, and fog lamps use relays to transmit the electrical signal to the component. Relays use a low-current circuit (the control circuit) to open and close a high-current circuit (the power circuit). If the relay is defective, that component will not operate properly. Most relays are mounted in the engine compartment and interior fuse/relay boxes (see illustrations 3.1c and 3.1f). If a faulty relay is suspected, it can be removed and tested using the procedure below or by a dealer service department or a repair shop. Defective relays must be replaced as a unit.

TESTING

♦ Refer to illustrations 5.2a and 5.2b

2 Most of the relays used in these vehicles are of a type often called "ISO" relays, which refers to the International Standards Organization. The terminals of ISO relays are numbered to indicate their usual circuit connections and functions. There are two basic layouts of terminals on the relays used in these vehicles (see illustrations).

3   Refer to the wiring diagram for the circuit to determine the proper connections for the relay you're testing. If you can't determine the correct connection from the wiring diagrams, however, you may be able to determine the test connections from the information that follows.

4   Two of the terminals are the relay control circuit and connect to the relay coil. The other relay terminals are the power circuit. When the relay is energized, the coil creates a magnetic field that closes the larger contacts of the power circuit to provide power to the circuit loads.

5   Terminals 85 and 86 are normally the control circuit. If the relay contains a diode, terminal 86 must be connected to battery positive (B+) voltage and terminal 85 to ground. If the relay contains a resistor, terminals 85 and 86 can be connected in either direction with respect to B+ and ground.

6   Terminal 30 is normally connected to the battery voltage (B+) source for the circuit loads. Terminal 87 is connected to the ground side of the circuit, either directly or through a load. If the relay has several alternate terminals for load or ground connections, they usually are numbered 87A, 87B, 87C, and so on.

7   Use an ohmmeter to check continuity through the relay control coil.

a) *Connect the meter according to the polarity shown in the illustration for one check; then reverse the ohmmeter leads and check continuity in the other direction.*

b) *If the relay contains a resistor, resistance should be indicated on the meter, and should be the same value with the ohmmeter in either direction.*

c) *If the relay contains a diode, resistance should be higher with the ohmmeter in the forward polarity direction than with the meter leads reversed.*

d) *If the ohmmeter shows infinite resistance in both directions, replace the relay.*

5.2b Most relays are marked on the outside to easily identify the control circuit and power circuit - this one is of the four-terminal type

8   Remove the relay from the vehicle and use the ohmmeter to check for continuity between the relay power circuit terminals. There should be no continuity between terminal 30 and 87 with the relay de-energized.

9   Connect a fused jumper wire to terminal 86 and the positive battery terminal. Connect another jumper wire between terminal 85 and ground. When the connections are made, the relay should click.

10 With the jumper wires connected, check for continuity between the power circuit terminals. Now, there should be continuity between terminals 30 and 87.

11 If the relay fails any of the above tests, replace it.

6   Turn signal and hazard flashers - check and replacement

▶ **Refer to illustration 6.5**

1   The "combination" flasher, located under the left side of the instrument panel, flashes the turn signals when the turn signal switch is operated, and all four signals when the emergency flasher switch on top of the steering column is On.

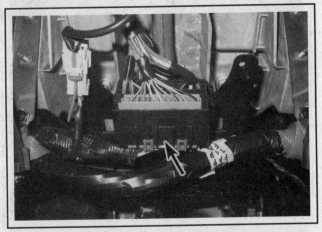

6.5 The turn signal/hazard flasher (hidden above connector) is located beneath the left side of the instrument panel

2   When the flasher unit is functioning properly, an audible click can be heard during its operation. If the turn signal indicator on one side of the vehicle flashes much more rapidly than normal, a faulty turn signal bulb is indicated.

3   If both turn signals fail to blink, the problem may be due to a blown fuse, a faulty flasher unit, a broken switch or a loose or open connection. If a quick check of the fuse box indicates that the turn signal fuse has blown, check the wiring for a short before installing a new fuse.

4   The type of combination flasher unit used on these models has complex internal circuitry, and can't be tested using standard electrical test equipment. Refer to the wiring diagrams at the end of this Chapter and test the circuitry before replacing the flasher with a known-good unit.

5   To remove the flasher, remove the left insulator panel from the instrument panel (see Chapter 11). Reach up under the left end of the instrument panel and pull the flasher out of the wiring harness (see illustration).

➡**Note: It will be easier to access if the driver's knee bolster is removed first (see Chapter 11).**

6   Make sure that the replacement unit is identical to the original. Compare the old one to the new one before installing it.

7   Installation is the reverse of removal.

7   Steering column multi-function switch - replacement

♦ Refer to illustrations 7.4 and 7.5

✳✳ WARNING:

The models covered by this manual are equipped with Supplemental Restraint Systems (SRS), more commonly known as airbags. Always disable the airbag system before working in the vicinity of any airbag system components to avoid the possibility of accidental deployment of the airbags, which could cause personal injury (see Section 28).

1   The multi-function switch is located on the left side of the steering column. It incorporates into one switch the turn signal, headlight dimmer, windshield wiper/washer and, if equipped, cruise control functions.

2   Place the tilt steering wheel in the center position.

3   Remove the steering column trim covers (see Chapter 11).

4   Trace the multi-function switch wires down to the connectors and disconnect them (see illustration).

5   Remove the multi-function switch screws, then detach the switch from the steering column (see illustration).

➡Note: Late models are equipped with steering column switches that use one screw at the face and another located at the top of the switch assembly.

6   Installation is the reverse of removal.

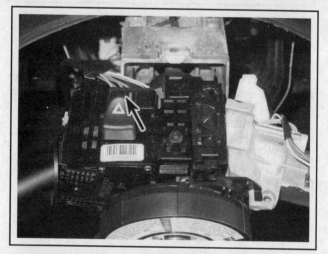

7.4 The two multi-function switch harness connectors are plugged into this larger connector next to the steering column

7.5 Remove the screws to detach the switch

8   Electronic Park lock switch - replacement

♦ Refer to illustration 8.3

✳✳ WARNING:

The models covered by this manual are equipped with Supplemental Restraint Systems (SRS), more commonly known as airbags. Always disable the airbag system before working in the vicinity of any airbag system components to avoid the possibility of accidental deployment of the airbags, which could cause personal injury (see Section 28).

1   Disconnect the battery negative cable.

2   Remove the steering column trim covers (see Chapter 11).

3   Disconnect the electrical connector from the park lock switch and pry it off the lock cylinder case (see illustration).

4   Installation is the reverse of the removal steps.

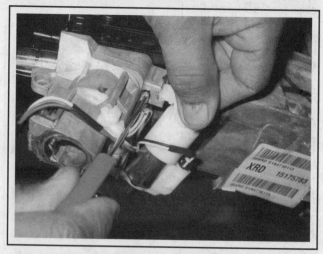

8.3 Use the tip of a small screwdriver to pry the park lock switch from the ignition lock cylinder case

9 Ignition switch and key lock cylinder - replacement

♦ Refer to illustrations 9.3, 9.4, 9.5a, 9.5b and 9.8

❋ WARNING:

The models covered by this manual are equipped with Supplemental Restraint Systems (SRS), more commonly known as airbags. Always disable the airbag system before working in the vicinity of any airbag system components to avoid the possibility of accidental deployment of the airbags, which could cause personal injury (see Section 28).

➡Note: These models are equipped with a Body Control Module (BCM). Several systems are linked to a centralized control module that allows simple and accurate troubleshooting, but only with a professional-grade scan tool. The Body Control Module governs the door locks, the power window switches, the ignition lock and security system, the interior lights, the Daytime Running Lights headlight system, the windshield wipers, the heating/air conditioning system and the power mirrors. In the event of malfunction with this system, have the vehicle diagnosed by a dealership service department or other qualified automotive repair facility.

1 Disconnect the negative battery cable.

2 Remove the steering column covers (see Chapter 11) and the Electronic Park Lock switch (see Section 8).

3 To remove the key lock cylinder, install the key into the lock and rotate it clockwise to the Run position. Push in the retainer pin (see illustration) and pull the key and the lock cylinder from the ignition switch/lock cylinder housing.

4 To remove the ignition switch, slide the theft deterrent control module off the key lock cylinder barrel (see illustration), if equipped.

5 Disconnect the multi-terminal connector and the two single wire connectors (see illustrations).

6 Remove the key lock cylinder (if not removed) (see Steps 1 through 3).

7 Insert a special forked tool into the release tabs on the ignition switch/key lock cylinder housing to release the ignition switch.

➡Note: Use two small screwdrivers if the special tool is not available.

8 Observe the location of the gears on the new ignition switch. Make sure the gears on the new switch are positioned correctly (see illustration) to allow proper alignment with the key lock cylinder housing.

9 Use a screwdriver and insert the tip into the key lock cylinder housing (lock cylinder removed) and rotate the lock cylinder gear counterclockwise until it hits the stop. This is the ignition switch install position.

➡Note: To be able to reach a stop while rotating the lock cylinder housing gear, it is necessary to push and hold in the solenoid for the electric park lock.

10 Insert the ignition switch into the lock cylinder housing. Make sure the tabs align with the slots in the housing.

11 Use a screwdriver and insert the tip into the key lock cylinder housing (lock cylinder removed) and rotate the lock cylinder gear clockwise until it reaches the Start position, then release into the Run position.

12 Install the lock cylinder.

13 The remainder of installation is the reverse of the removal steps.

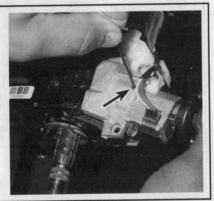

9.3 Push the retaining pin in to unseat the lock cylinder, then withdraw the key and cylinder

9.4 Turn the alarm connector 90-degrees, then disconnect the passkey and alarm connectors

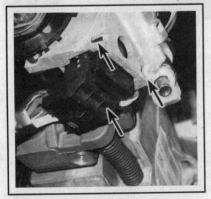

9.5a Remove the electrical portion of the ignition switch (lower arrow)

9.5b Separate the turn signal and multi-function connectors from the bulkhead connector

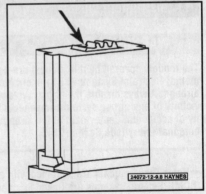

9.8 Make sure the off-set gear is positioned correctly before installing the ignition switch into the key lock

10 Instrument panel switches - replacement

❊❊ WARNING:

The models covered by this manual are equipped with Supplemental Restraint Systems (SRS), more commonly known as airbags. Always disable the airbag system before working in the vicinity of any airbag system components to avoid the possibility of accidental deployment of the airbags, which could cause personal injury (see Section 28).

HEADLIGHT SWITCH

▶ Refer to illustration 10.3

1 Disconnect the negative cable at the battery.
2 Remove the access cover from the left end of the instrument panel (see Chapter 11).
3 Use a small screwdriver to pry the four plastic clips, then pull the headlight switch out of the instrument panel through the access hole (see illustration).
4 Disconnect the electrical connectors on the back of the switch.
5 Installation is the reverse of removal.

10.3 Pry the two clips on each side (left clips shown) with a small screwdriver to remove the headlight switch

ON/OFF SWITCHES

▶ Refer to illustration 10.7

6 Depending on the options of the vehicle, there may be one or more switches on the instrument panel, including transfer case shift control and rear wiper/washer.
7 All of the above-mentioned switches are accessible when the instrument cluster bezel or center trim plate is removed (see Chapter 11). The switches are removed from the bezel or trim plate by prying clips with a small screwdriver and pulling the switch out (see illustration).

❊❊ CAUTION:

Before removing the airbag On/Off switch, disable the airbag system (see Section 28).

8 With simple on/off switches, use an ohmmeter or self-powered continuity tester to check the switch for proper continuity between the terminals. There should be continuity between terminals only when the switch is engaged. If the switch fails the test, replace the switch.

10.7 Remove on/off type switches by depressing the clips and pulling the switch out of the panel

11 Instrument cluster - removal and installation

❊❊ WARNING:

The models covered by this manual are equipped with Supplemental Restraint Systems (SRS), more commonly known as airbags. Always disable the airbag system before working in the vicinity of any airbag system components to avoid the possibility of accidental deployment of the airbags, which could cause personal injury (see Section 28).

➡Note: These models are equipped with a Body Control Module (BCM). Several systems are linked to a centralized control module that allows simple and accurate troubleshooting, but only with a professional-grade scan tool. The Body Control Module governs the door locks, the power window switches, the ignition lock and security system, the interior lights, the Daytime Running Lights headlight system, the windshield wipers, the heating/air conditioning system and the power mirrors. In the event of malfunction with this system, have the vehicle diagnosed by a dealership service department or other qualified automotive repair facility.

1 Disconnect the negative cable from the battery.
2 Remove the lower left sound insulator panel and the knee bolster (see Chapter 11).
3 If you're working on a Chevrolet model, remove the instrument cluster bezel (see Chapter 11). If you're working on a GMC or Oldsmobile model, remove the instrument panel trim plate.
4 Remove the screws securing the cluster to the instrument panel.
5 Pull the cluster forward enough to disconnect the electrical connectors at the back, then pull the cluster out, tilting the bottom out first.
6 Installation is the reverse of removal.

12 Radio and speakers - removal and installation

※※ WARNING:

The models covered by this manual are equipped with Supplemental Restraint Systems (SRS), more commonly known as airbags. Always disable the airbag system before working in the vicinity of any airbag system components to avoid the possibility of accidental deployment of the airbags, which could cause personal injury (see Section 28).

RADIO

▶ **Refer to illustration 12.5**

1 Disconnect the negative battery cable.

2 If you're working on a Chevrolet model, remove the lower center insulator panel from the instrument panel (see Chapter 11).

3 If you're working on an Oldsmobile model, remove the transmission shift lever bezel (see Chapter 11).

12.5 Remove the mounting screws and pull the radio out

4 On all models, remove the accessory trim plate from the instrument panel (see Chapter 11).

5 Remove the mounting screws, pull the radio out of the instrument panel, disconnect the connectors, then remove it from the vehicle (see illustration).

6 Installation is the reverse of removal.

SPEAKERS

▶ **Refer to illustration 12.8**

7 To replace a door speaker remove the door trim panel. To replace a front dash-top speaker, remove the instrument panel upper trim pad (see Chapter 11).

8 Remove the speaker mounting screws (see illustration). Pull the speaker out, disconnect the electrical connector and remove the speaker from the vehicle.

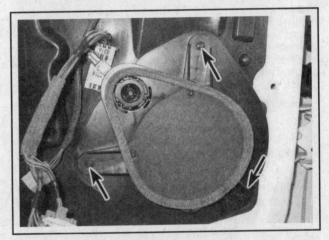

12.8 Remove the speaker mounting screws

13 Antenna - removal and installation

▶ **Refer to illustrations 13.1 and 13.4**

1 Use a small open-end wrench to unscrew the antenna mast (see

illustration). Be very careful - the tool could slip and scratch the body. It's a good idea to surround the base of the antenna with masking tape to prevent scratching.

13.1 Use a small wrench to remove the antenna mast

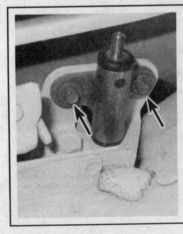

13.4 To remove the antenna base and cable, remove the base mounting screws

2 If the antenna base/cable assembly must be replaced, remove the glove compartment and detach the lower rear portion of the inner fender liner (see Chapter 11).

3 Disconnect the antenna mast cable from the radio cable where they join in a connector under the far right end of the instrument panel. Attach a "fish" wire to the end of the cable. Working inside the inner fender liner, pass the cable and grommet through the hole in the cowl into the fender opening.

4 Under the hood, remove the antenna mast base mounting screws

and pull out the base and its cable (see illustration).

5 Attach the new cable to the fish wire and pull the wire back slowly and carefully into the body, routing it as the original cable had been.

6 If the extension cable (between the antenna base cable and the radio) must be replaced, remove the glove compartment and the passenger's airbag module (see Section 28). Release the cable from the clips along the top of the instrument panel and disconnect it from the radio and antenna base cable.

7 Installation is the reverse of the removal procedure.

14 Headlight bulb - replacement

▶ **Refer to illustrations 14.2a, 14.2b and 14.3**

✳✳ WARNING:

Halogen bulbs are gas-filled and under pressure and may shatter if the surface is scratched or the bulb is dropped. Wear eye protection and handle the bulbs carefully, grasping only the base whenever possible. Don't touch the surface of the bulb with your fingers because the oil from your skin could cause it to overheat and fail prematurely. If you do touch the bulb surface, clean it with rubbing alcohol.

➡**Note: Low and high beam bulbs can be identified by the color of their sockets; low beam bulbs have gray sockets and high beam bulbs have black sockets.**

1 Refer to Section 16 and remove the headlight housing.

2 Remove the access cover from the back of the headlight housing (see illustration). Twist the bulb holder counterclockwise and withdraw the bulb holder and connector from the housing (see illustration).

3 Unplug the electrical connector from the bulb holder (see illustration).

➡**Note: The bulb and holder are not separable.**

Handling the new bulb only by the bulb holder portion, reconnect the electrical connector and insert the new bulb/holder into the housing.

14.2a Remove the access cover from the back of the headlight housing . . .

Twist the holder clockwise to lock it in place, then install the cover.

4 Installation of the housing is the reverse of the removal procedure.

14.2b . . . turn the bulb holder counterclockwise and remove it from the housing . . .

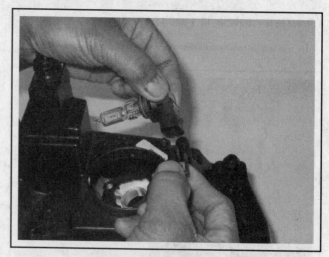

14.3 . . . then unplug the electrical connector

15 Headlights and fog lights - adjustment

❊❊ WARNING:

The headlights must be aimed correctly. If adjusted incorrectly, they could temporarily blind the driver of an oncoming vehicle and cause an accident or seriously reduce your ability to see the road. The headlights should be checked for proper aim every 12 months and any time a new headlight is installed or front-end bodywork is performed. The following procedure is only an interim step to provide temporary adjustment until the headlights can be adjusted by a properly equipped shop.

HEADLIGHTS

◗ Refer to illustrations 15.1 and 15.2

➡Note: It is important that the headlights are aimed correctly. If adjusted incorrectly they could blind the driver of an oncoming vehicle and cause a serious accident or seriously reduce your ability to see the road. The headlights should be checked for proper aim every 12 months and any time a new headlight is installed or front end body work is performed. It should be emphasized that the following procedure is only an interim step that will provide temporary adjustment until the headlights can be adjusted by a properly equipped shop.

1   These models are equipped with composite headlights with adjustment screw, controlling up-and-down movement (see illustration). Left-and-right movement is not adjustable.
2   There are several methods of adjusting the headlights. The simplest method requires a blank wall 25 feet in front of the vehicle and a level floor (see illustration).
3   Position masking tape on the wall in reference to the vehicle centerline and the centerlines of both headlights.
4   Measure the height of the headlight reference marks (in the centers of the headlight lenses) from the ground. Position a horizontal tape line on the wall at the same height as the headlight reference marks.

➡Note: It may be easier to position the tape on the wall with the vehicle parked only a few inches away.

5   Adjustment should be made with the vehicle sitting level, the gas tank half-full and no unusually heavy load in the vehicle.
6   Turn on the low beams. Turn the adjusting screw (see illustration 15.1) to position the high intensity zone so it is two inches below the horizontal line.
7   Have the headlights adjusted by a dealer service department at the earliest opportunity.

FOG LIGHTS

8   Some models have optional fog lights that can be aimed just like headlights. As with the headlights, there are no left-and-right adjustments.
9   Position tape on a wall 25 feet in front of the vehicle (see illustration 15.2). Tape a horizontal line on the wall that represents the height of the fog lamp centers, and another tape line four inches below that line.
10 Using the adjusting screws on the fog lamps (there's one on the back of each lamp, next to the electrical connector), adjust the pattern on the wall so that the top of the fog lamp beam meets the lower line on the wall.

15.1 The headlight adjuster is on the back of the headlight housing

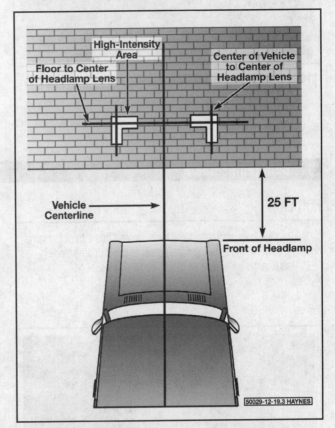

15.2 Headlight adjustment details

16 Headlight housing - removal and installation

▶ **Refer to illustrations 16.2a and 16.2b**

1   Open the hood. If you're working on a Chevrolet model, remove the grille (see Chapter 11).

2   Pull up the headlight housing retaining tabs (see illustration). Remove the park/turn signal bulb socket from the headlight housing (see illustration). If you're working on a Chevrolet or GMC model,

remove the side marker socket as well.

3   Disconnect the electrical connector(s). Take the headlamp housing out of the panel.

4   Installation is the reverse of removal. Align the housing locating pins with the holes in the panel and push the retaining tabs down to lock the housing in place.

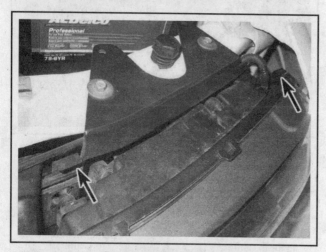

16.2a Pull up on the headlight housing retaining tabs . . .

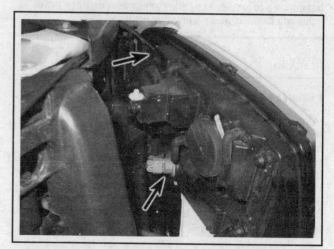

16.2b . . . then remove the housing and detach the bulb holders and electrical connectors (not all are visible in this photo)

17 Bulb replacement

FOG LAMPS

1   Turn the bulb socket counterclockwise and free it from the lamp housing. Remove the bulb from the socket and install a new one.

2   Installation is the reverse of the removal steps.

TURN SIGNAL, PARKING AND SIDE MARKER LIGHTS

▶ **Refer to illustrations 17.4a, 17.4b, 17.4c and 17.4d**

3   Refer to Section 16 and remove the headlight housing.

4   Each bulb is replaced in the same manner. Twist the bulb holder out and pull the bulb straight out of the holder (see illustrations).

5   Installation is the reverse of removal.

17.4a Remove the turn signal socket . . .

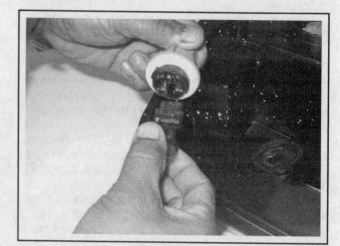

17.4b . . . and pull out the bulb

17.4c Pull out the parking/side marker socket (Chevrolet shown) . . .

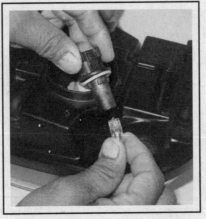

17.4d . . . and pull the bulb straight out of the socket

17.9a Remove the screws . . .

CORNERING LAMPS (GMC AND OLDSMOBILE MODELS)

6   Push the retaining tab in, turn the socket counterclockwise and remove it from the headlamp housing (GMC) or cornering/side marker lamp housing (Oldsmobile). Remove the bulb from the socket.

7   Installation is the reverse of the removal steps.

TAIL/STOP/TURN/BACK-UP LIGHT

▸ **Refer to illustrations 17.9a, 17.9b, 17.10a and 17.10b**

All except GMC back-up lights

8   On all models, these rear lights are all in one housing with the exception of the back-up lights on GMC models.

9   Remove the lamp housing screws and take the lamp housing off the body (see illustrations).

10 Remove the screws that secure the socket assembly, disengage the retaining tabs and remove the socket assembly (see illustrations).

11 Pull the bulb straight out of the socket and push a new one in.

12 Installation is the reverse of the removal steps.

17.9b . . . and take the taillight housing off the vehicle . . .

17.10a . . . then remove the screws (2003 model shown) . . .

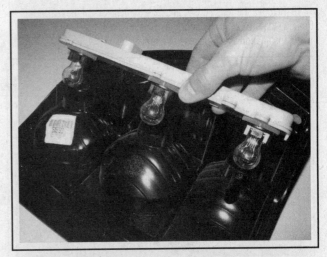

17.10b . . . and take the socket assembly off for access to the bulbs

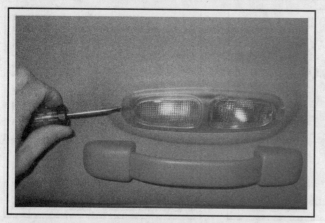

17.26 Pull the dome light down and free the rear retaining tab, then slide it rearward

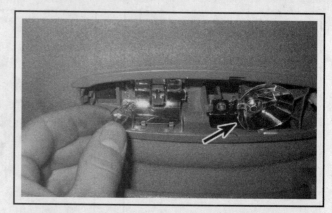

17.27 Pull out the dome light bulb; remove the reflector and reading lamp from the dome light, then remove the bulb from the reading lamp

GMC back-up lights

13 Push the retaining tab in, turn the socket counterclockwise and remove it from the housing. Remove the bulb from the socket.

14 Installation is the reverse of the removal steps.

HIGH-MOUNTED STOP LIGHT

15 Raise the liftgate and remove the two retaining pins at the rear of the headliner to access the electrical connector. Disconnect the connector and remove its grommet.

16 Close the liftgate and open the liftgate window.

> **✳✳ CAUTION:**
>
> **Don't open the liftgate window unless the liftgate is closed.**

17 Remove the stop light mounting screws and remove the stop light from the vehicle.

18 Installation is the reverse of removal.

LICENSE PLATE BULB

19 Remove the lens screws and take the lens out of the rear door. Remove the bulb from the socket and install a new one.

20 Installation is the reverse of removal.

17.31 Lower the trim panel and remove the lamp

INSTRUMENT CLUSTER LIGHTS

21 To gain access to the instrument cluster illumination lights, the instrument cluster will have to be removed (see Section 11). The bulbs can then be removed and replaced from the rear of the cluster, after removing a cover panel. The only bulbs used are for the turn signal indicators, high beam indicator and cruise control indicator. All others are light-emitting diodes (LED). If an LED fails, the instrument cluster must be replaced.

22 Installation is the reverse of removal.

UNDERHOOD LIGHT

23 Open the hood and disconnect the lamp electrical connector.

24 Release the lower tab, pull the lamp out and lower it away from the hood.

25 Installation is the reverse of the removal steps.

INTERIOR LIGHTS

Overhead console dome and reading lights

▶ **Refer to illustrations 17.26 and 17.27**

26 Pull on the sides of the lens for access to the retaining tab at the rear of the lamp. Release the retaining tab with a small screwdriver (see illustration), then lower the lens and pull it rearward to free the front retaining tab.

27 To replace the reading lamp bulb, remove the reflector and bulb from the lamp, then remove the bulb from the reflector (see illustration).

28 To replace the dome lamp bulb, remove it from the socket.

29 Installation is the reverse of removal.

Instrument panel courtesy light

▶ **Refer to illustration 17.31**

30 Remove the left insulator panel (see Chapter 11).

31 Pull out the courtesy lamp and install a new one, then install the insulator panel (see illustration).

Glove compartment light

▶ **Refer to illustration 17.33**

32 Open the glove compartment, release the latch and lower the glove compartment all the way.

33 Remove the trim panel screws (see illustration) and take the trim panel out of the dash, then disconnect the electrical connector for the glove box light.

34 Squeeze the tabs that retain the bulb socket, take the socket out of the trim panel and remove the bulb.

35 Installation is the reverse of the removal steps.

Vanity mirror light

36 Open the vanity mirror cover and carefully pry out the lens. Remove the bulb from the socket.

37 Installation is the reverse of the removal steps.

17.33 Remove the glove compartment trim panel screws

18 Wiper motor - check and replacement

WIPER MOTOR CIRCUIT CHECK

➡**Note 1: These models are equipped with a Body Control Module (BCM). Several systems are linked to a centralized control module that allows simple and accurate troubleshooting, but only with a professional-grade scan tool. The Body Control Module governs the door locks, the power window switches, the ignition lock and security system, the interior lights, the Daytime Running Lights headlight system, the windshield wipers, the heating/air conditioning system and the power mirrors. In the event of malfunction with this system, have the vehicle diagnosed by a dealership service department or other qualified automotive repair facility.**

➡**Note 2: Refer to the wiring diagrams for wire colors and locations in the following checks. When checking for voltage, probe a grounded 12-volt test light to each terminal at a connector until it lights; this verifies voltage (power) at the terminal. If the following checks fail to locate the problem, have the system diagnosed by a dealer service department or other properly equipped repair facility. The BCM is capable of storing trouble codes that can be retrieved with the proper equipment.**

1 If the wipers work slowly, make sure the battery is in good condition and has a strong charge (see Chapter 5). If the battery is in good condition, remove the wiper motor (see below) and operate the wiper arms by hand. Check for binding linkage and pivots. Lubricate or repair the linkage or pivots as necessary. Reinstall the wiper motor. If the wipers still operate slowly, check for loose or corroded connections, especially the ground connection. If all connections look OK, replace the motor.

2 If the wipers fail to operate when activated, check the fuse. If the fuse is OK, connect a jumper wire between the wiper motor's ground terminal and ground, then retest. If the motor works now, repair the ground connection. If the motor still doesn't work, turn the wiper switch to the HI position and check for voltage at the motor.

➡**Note: The cowl cover will have to be removed (see Chapter 11) to access the electrical connector.**

3 If there's voltage at the connector, remove the motor and check it off the vehicle with fused jumper wires from the battery. If the motor now works, check for binding linkage (see Step 1 above). If the motor still doesn't work, replace it. If there's no voltage to the motor, check for voltage at the wiper control relays. If there's voltage at the wiper control relays and no voltage at the wiper motor, have the switch tested. If the

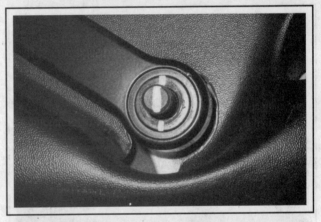

18.7 Remove the nut, mark the wiper arm location and rock the wiper arm to detach it from the shaft - use a small puller if it's stuck

switch is OK, the wiper control relay is probably bad. See Section 5 for relay testing.

4 If the interval (delay) function is inoperative, check the continuity of all the wiring between the switch and wiper control module.

5 If the wipers stop at the position they're in when the switch is turned off (fail to park), check for voltage at the park feed wire of the wiper motor connector when the wiper switch is OFF but the ignition is ON. If no voltage is present, check for an open circuit between the wiper motor and the fuse panel.

REPLACEMENT

Front

▶ **Refer to illustrations 18.7, 18.9a, 18.9b and 18.10**

6 Disconnect the negative cable from the battery (see Chapter 1).

7 Remove the wiper arm nuts, mark the positions of the arms to their shafts, then remove the wiper arms (see illustration).

➡**Note: If the wiper arm is stuck, try rocking it on the shaft. If that doesn't work, use a small puller such as a battery terminal puller.**

8 Remove the cowl grille (see Chapter 11).

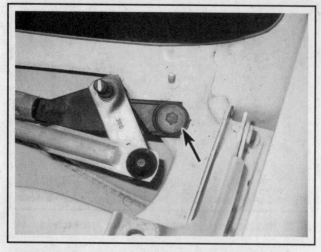

18.9a Remove the wiper linkage mounting bolt from each side (left side shown) . . .

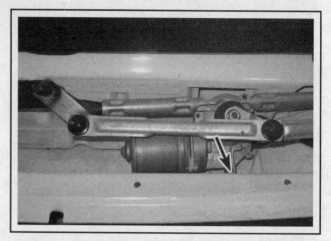

18.9b . . . and from the center (arrow, hidden)

18.10 Remove the nut to separate the wiper motor from the linkage assembly

9 Remove the wiper motor/linkage mounting bolts (see illustrations).

10 Remove the assembly and unbolt the motor from the linkage (see illustration).

11 Installation is the reverse of removal.

Rear

▶ **Refer to illustrations 18.13 and 18.15**

12 Disconnect the negative cable from the battery (see Chapter 1).

13 Mark the positions of the wiper arm on the liftgate glass, then remove the wiper arm cover and nut at the outside of the liftgate, then the bezel (see illustration). Be careful not to scratch the paint on the liftgate.

14 Refer to Chapter 11 and remove the upper and lower liftgate interior trim panels.

15 Disconnect the electrical connector at the rear wiper motor, then remove the two mounting bolts (see illustration).

❋❋ CAUTION:

Support the motor while removing the bolts.

---

16 Installation is the reverse of removal.

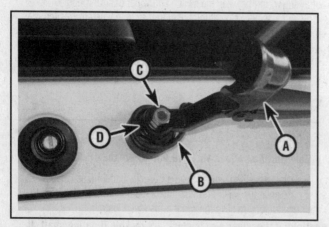

18.13 At the liftgate, lift the cover (A), disconnect the washer hose (B), remove the nut (C), arm and bezel (D)

18.15 Disconnect the electrical connector (upper arrow) at the rear wiper motor, then remove the two mounting bolts (lower arrows)

19 Horn - replacement

▶ **Refer to illustration 19.3**

1   Remove the left (driver's side) headlight housing (see Section 16).

2   Detach the battery vent hose from the battery tray.

3   Disconnect the electrical connector, remove the mounting bolt and detach the horns (see illustration).

4   Installation is the reverse of removal.

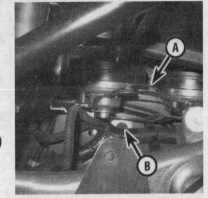

19.3 Follow the wiring harness (A) to the horn connector, then disconnect it and remove the mounting bolt (B)

20 Daytime Running Lights (DRL) - general information

➡**Note: These models are equipped with a Body Control Module (BCM). Several systems are linked to a centralized control module that allows simple and accurate troubleshooting, but only with a professional-grade scan tool. The Body Control Module governs the door locks, the power window switches, the ignition lock and security system, the interior lights, the Daytime Running Lights headlight system, the windshield wipers, the heating/air conditioning system and the power mirrors. In the event of malfunction with this system, have the vehicle diagnosed by** a dealership service department or other qualified automotive repair facility.

The Daytime Running Lights (DRL) system used on all models illuminates the low beam headlights at reduced intensity whenever the ignition is On. The only exception is with the engine running and the shift lever in Park. Once the parking brake is released or the shift lever is moved, the lights will remain on as long as the ignition switch is on.

21 Rear window defogger (SUV models) - check and repair

1   The rear window defogger consists of a number of horizontal heating elements baked onto the inside surface of the glass. Power is supplied through a large fuse from the underhood fuse/relay box in the engine compartment. The heater is controlled by the instrument panel switch.

2   Small breaks in the element can be repaired without removing the rear window.

CHECK

▶ **Refer to illustrations 21.5, 21.6 and 21.8**

3   Turn the ignition switch and defogger switch to the ON position.

4   Using a voltmeter, place the positive probe against the defogger grid positive terminal and the negative probe against the ground terminal. If battery voltage is not indicated, check the fuse, defogger switch, defogger relay and related wiring. If voltage is indicated, but all or part of the defogger doesn't heat, proceed with the following tests.

5   When measuring voltage during the next two tests, wrap a piece of aluminum foil around the tip of the voltmeter positive probe and press the foil against the heating element with your finger (see illustration). Place the negative probe on the defogger grid ground terminal.

6   Check the voltage at the center of each heating element (see illustration). If the voltage is 5 to 6 volts, the element is okay (there is no break). If the voltage is 0 volts, the element is broken between the center of the element and the positive end. If the voltage is 10 to 12 volts

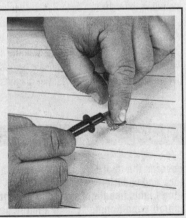

21.5 When measuring the voltage at the rear window defogger grid, wrap a piece of aluminum foil around the positive probe of the voltmeter and press the foil against the wire with your finger

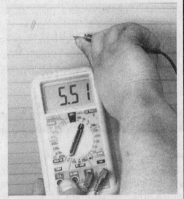

21.6 To determine if a heating element has broken, check the voltage at the center of each element - if the voltage is 6-volts, the element is unbroken

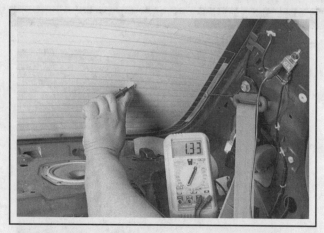

21.8 To find the break, place the voltmeter negative lead against the defogger ground terminal, place the voltmeter positive lead with the foil strip against the heat wire at the positive terminal end and slide it toward the negative terminal end - the point at which the voltmeter deflects from several volts to zero volts is the point at which the wire is broken

the element is broken between the center of the element and the ground side. Check each heating element.

7   If none of the elements are broken, connect the negative probe to a good chassis ground. The voltage reading should stay the same; if it doesn't, the ground connection is bad.

8   To find the break, place the voltmeter negative probe against the defogger ground terminal. Place the voltmeter positive probe with the foil strip against the heating element at the positive side and slide it toward the negative side. The point at which the voltmeter deflects from several volts to zero is the point where the heating element is broken (see illustration).

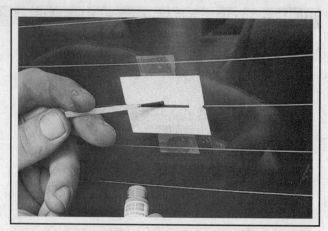

21.14 To use a defogger repair kit, apply masking tape to the inside of the window at the damaged area, then brush on the special conductive coating

REPAIR

▶ **Refer to illustration 21.14**

9   Repair the break in the element using a repair kit specifically for this purpose, such as Dupont paste No. 4817 (or equivalent). The kit includes conductive plastic epoxy.

10 Before repairing a break, turn off the system and allow it to cool for a few minutes.

11 Lightly buff the element area with fine steel wool; then clean it thoroughly with rubbing alcohol.

12 Use masking tape to mask off the area being repaired.

13 Thoroughly mix the epoxy, following the kit instructions.

14 Apply the epoxy material to the slit in the masking tape, overlapping the undamaged area about 3/4-inch on either end (see illustration).

15 Allow the repair to cure for 24 hours before removing the tape and using the system.

22 Cruise control system - description and check

1   The cruise control system maintains vehicle speed with the Powertrain Control Module (PCM), throttle actuator control motor, brake switch, control switches and associated wiring. There is no mechanical connection, such as a vacuum servo or cable. Some features of the system require special testers and diagnostic procedures that are beyond the scope of the home mechanic. Listed below are some general procedures that may be used to locate common problems.

2   Check the fuses (see Section 3).

3   The brake pedal position (BPP) switch (or brake light switch) deactivates the cruise control system. Have an assistant press the brake pedal while you check the brake light operation.

4   If the brake lights do not operate properly, correct the problem and retest the cruise control.

5   Check the wiring between the PCM and throttle actuator motor for opens or shorts and repair as necessary.

6   The cruise control system uses information from the PCM, including the Vehicle Speed Sensor, which is located in the transmission or transfer case. Refer to Chapter 6 for more information on the VSS.

7   Test drive the vehicle to determine if the cruise control is now working. If it isn't, take it to a dealer service department or an automotive electrical specialist for further diagnosis.

23 Power window system - description and check

➡**Note: These models are equipped with a Body Control Module (BCM). Several systems are linked to a centralized control module that allows simple and accurate troubleshooting, but only with a professional-grade scan tool. The Body Control Module** governs the door locks, the power window switches, the ignition lock and security system, the interior lights, the Daytime Running Lights headlight system, the windshield wipers, the heating/air conditioning system and the power mirrors. In the event of malfunction with this system, have the vehicle diagnosed by a dealership service department or other qualified automotive repair facility.

1   The power window system operates electric motors, mounted in the doors, which lower and raise the windows. The system consists of the control switches, the motors, regulators, glass mechanisms and associated wiring.

2   The power windows can be lowered and raised from the master control switch by the driver or by remote switches located at the individual windows. Each window has a separate motor that is reversible. The position of the control switch determines the polarity and therefore the direction of operation.

3   The circuit is protected by a fuse and a circuit breaker. Each motor is also equipped with an internal circuit breaker; this prevents one stuck window from disabling the whole system.

4   The power window system will only operate when the ignition switch is ON. In addition, many models have a window lockout switch at the master control switch which, when activated, disables the switches at the rear windows and, sometimes, the switch at the passenger's window also. Always check these items before troubleshooting a window problem.

5   These procedures are general in nature, so if you can't find the problem using them, take the vehicle to a dealer service department or other properly equipped repair facility.

6   If the power windows won't operate, always check the fuse and circuit breaker first.

7   If only the rear windows are inoperative, or if the windows only operate from the master control switch, check the rear window lockout switch for continuity in the unlocked position. Replace it if it doesn't have continuity.

8   Check the wiring between the switches and fuse panel for continuity. Repair the wiring, if necessary.

9   If only one window is inoperative from the master control switch, try the other control switch at the window.

➡Note: This doesn't apply to the driver's door window.

10 If the same window works from one switch, but not the other, check the switch for continuity.

11 If the switch tests OK, check for a short or open in the circuit between the affected switch and the window motor.

12 If one window is inoperative from both switches, remove the switch panel from the affected door. Check for voltage at the switch and at the motor (refer to Chapter 11 for door panel removal) while the switch is operated.

13 If voltage is reaching the motor, disconnect the glass from the regulator (see Chapter 11). Move the window up and down by hand while checking for binding and damage. Also check for binding and damage to the regulator. If the regulator is not damaged and the window moves up and down smoothly, replace the motor. If there's binding or damage, lubricate, repair or replace parts, as necessary.

14 If voltage isn't reaching the motor, check the wiring in the circuit for continuity between the switches and motors. You'll need to consult the wiring diagram at the end of this Chapter. If the circuit is equipped with a relay, check that the relay is grounded properly and receiving voltage.

15 Test the windows after you are done to confirm proper repairs.

24 Power door lock and keyless entry system - description and check

➡Note: These models are equipped with a Body Control Module (BCM). Several systems are linked to a centralized control module that allows simple and accurate troubleshooting, but only with a professional-grade scan tool. The Body Control Module governs the door locks, the power window switches, the ignition lock and security system, the interior lights, the Daytime Running Lights headlight system, the windshield wipers, the heating/air conditioning system and the power mirrors. In the event of malfunction with this system, have the vehicle diagnosed by a dealership service department or other qualified automotive repair facility.

1   The power door lock system operates the door lock actuators mounted in each door. The system consists of the switches, actuators, Body Control Module (BCM) and associated wiring. Diagnosis can usually be limited to simple checks of the wiring connections and actuators for minor faults that can be easily repaired.

2   Power door lock systems are operated by bi-directional solenoids located in the doors. The lock switches have two operating positions: Lock and Unlock. These switches send a signal to the BCM, which in turn sends a signal to the door lock solenoids.

3   If you are unable to locate the trouble using the following general steps, consult your dealer service department.

4   Always check the circuit protection first. Some vehicles use a combination of circuit breakers and fuses. Refer to the wiring diagrams at the end of this Chapter.

5   Check for voltage at the switches. If no voltage is present, check the wiring between the fuse panel and the switches for shorts and opens.

6   If voltage is present, test the switch for continuity. Replace it if there's not continuity in both switch positions. To remove the switch, use a flat-bladed trim tool to pry out the door/window switch assembly (see Chapter 11).

7   If the switch has continuity, check the wiring between the switch and door lock solenoid.

8   If all but one lock solenoids operate, remove the trim panel from the affected door (see Chapter 11) and check for voltage at the solenoid while the lock switch is operated. One of the wires should have voltage in the Lock position; the other should have voltage in the Unlock position.

9   If the inoperative solenoid is receiving voltage, replace the solenoid.

10 If the inoperative solenoid isn't receiving voltage, check for an open or short in the wire between the lock solenoid and the relay.

➡Note: It's common for wires to break in the portion of the harness between the body and door (opening and closing the door fatigues and eventually breaks the wires).

11 On the models covered by this manual, power door lock system communication goes through the Body Control Module. If the above tests do not pinpoint a problem, take the vehicle to a dealer or qualified shop with the proper scan tool to retrieve trouble codes from the BCM.

KEYLESS ENTRY SYSTEM

12 The keyless entry system consists of a remote control transmitter that sends a coded infrared signal to a receiver, which then operates the doorlock system.

13 Replace the battery when the transmitter doesn't operate the locks at a distance of ten feet. Normal range should be about 30 feet.

14 Use a small screwdriver to carefully separate the case halves.

15 Replace the three-volt, CR2032 lithium battery.

16 Snap the case halves together.

25 Electric side view mirrors - description

➡Note: These models are equipped with a Body Control Module (BCM). Several systems are linked to a centralized control module that allows simple and accurate troubleshooting, but only with a professional-grade scan tool. The Body Control Module governs the door locks, the power window switches, the ignition lock and security system, the interior lights, the Daytime Running Lights headlight system, the windshield wipers, the heating/air conditioning system and the power mirrors. In the event of malfunction with this system, have the vehicle diagnosed by a dealership service department or other qualified automotive repair facility.

1 The electric rear view mirrors use two motors to move the glass; one for up and down adjustments and one for left-right adjustments.

2 The control switch has a selector portion which sends voltage to the left or right side mirror. With the ignition in the ACC position and the engine OFF, roll down the windows and operate the mirror control switch through all functions (left-right and up-down) for both the left and right side mirrors.

3 Listen carefully for the sound of the electric motors running in the mirrors.

4 If the motors can be heard but the mirror glass doesn't move, there's probably a problem with the drive mechanism inside the mirror. Power mirrors have no user-serviceable parts inside - a defective mirror must be replaced as a unit (see Chapter 11).

5 If the mirrors don't operate and no sound comes from the mirrors, check the fuses (see Section 3).

6 If the fuses are OK, remove the mirror control switch. Have the switch continuity checked by a dealer service department or other qualified shop.

7 Check the ground connections.

8 If the mirror still doesn't work, remove the mirror and check the wires at the mirror for voltage.

9 If there's not voltage in each switch position, check the circuit between the mirror and control switch for opens and shorts.

10 If there's voltage, remove the mirror and test it off the vehicle with jumper wires. Replace the mirror if it fails this test.

26 Power seats - description

1 Power seats allow you to adjust the position of the seat with little effort. These models feature a six-way seat that goes forward and backward, up and down and tilts forward and backward. The seats are powered by three reversible motors, mounted in one housing, that are controlled by switches on the side of the seat. Each switch changes the direction of seat travel by reversing polarity to the drive motor.

2 Diagnosis is a simple matter, using the following procedures.

3 Look under the seat for any object which may be preventing the seat from moving.

4 If the seat won't work at all, check the circuit breaker. See Section 4 for circuit breaker testing.

5 With the engine off to reduce the noise level, operate the seat controls in all directions and listen for sound coming from the seat motors.

6 If the motors make noise or don't work, check for voltage at the motors while an assistant operates the switch. With the door open, try the seat switch again. If the dome light dims while trying to operate the seat, this indicates something may be jammed in the seat tracks.

7 If the motor is getting voltage but doesn't run, test it off the vehicle with jumper wires. If it still doesn't work, replace it.

8 If the motor isn't getting voltage, remove the switch and check for voltage. If there's no voltage to the switch, check the wiring between the fuse block and the switch. If there's battery voltage at the switch, check the other terminals for voltage while moving the switch around. If the switch is OK, check for a short or open in the wiring between the switch and motor.

9 Test the completed repairs.

27 Data Link Communication system - description

1 The vehicles covered by this manual have a complex electrical system, encompassing many power accessories, and a number of separate electronic modules.

2 The Powertrain Control Module (PCM) is mainly responsible for engine and transaxle control, but also communicates with other modules around the vehicle through a Data Link Communication system, which sends serial port data very quickly between the various modules. Many of the computer functions involved in the operation of body systems are routed through the Body Control Module (BCM), which communicates with the PCM.

3 Among the modules in the Data Link system besides the BCM and PCM are the Sensing Diagnostic Module (airbag system), the Electronic Brake Control Module and the instrument panel cluster. The BCM further communicates with various body subsystems.

4 All of the modules in the vehicle have associated trouble codes. When other troubleshooting procedures fail to pinpoint the problem, check the wiring diagrams at the end of this Chapter to see if the BCM or PCM are involved in the circuit. If so, bring your vehicle to a dealer with the factory diagnostic tools to extract the trouble codes.

28 Airbag system - general information

▶ **Refer to illustrations 28.1, 28.8 and 28.13**

1   These models are equipped with a Supplemental Restraint System (SRS), more commonly known as airbags, designed to protect the driver and front seat passenger from serious injury in the event of a head-on or frontal collision. Side airbags mounted in the front seat backs are standard equipment, and are designed to deploy only in a side impact of sufficient force. All models have a sensing/diagnostic control unit, located under the rear of the center console (see illustration).

✳✳ WARNING:

If your vehicle is ever involved in a flood, or the interior carpeting is soaked for any reason, disconnect the battery and do not start the vehicle until the airbag system can be checked by your dealer. If the SRS system is subjected to flooding, the airbags could go off upon starting the vehicle, even without an accident taking place.

AIRBAG MODULES

2   The airbag modules consist of a housing incorporating the cushion (airbag) and inflator unit. The inflator assembly is mounted on the back of the housing over a hole through which gas is expelled, inflating the bag almost instantaneously when an electrical signal is sent from the system. The specially wound wire on the driver's side that carries this signal to the driver's module is called a clockspring. The clockspring is a flat, ribbon-like electrically conductive tape that is wound many times so that it can transmit an electrical signal regardless of steering wheel position. Airbag modules are located in the steering wheel, on the passenger side above the glove box, and on some models, at the upper side of each front seat (side-impact airbags).

SENSING/DIAGNOSTIC CONTROL UNIT AND SENSORS

3   The sensing/diagnostic control unit contains an on-board microprocessor which monitors the operation of the system, and also contains a crash sensor. It checks this system every time the vehicle

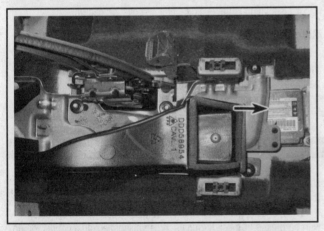

28.1 The airbag control module is located underneath the rear of the center console - do not tamper with the electrical connectors attached to it

is started, causing the "AIRBAG" light to flash seven times then go off, if the system is operating properly. If there is a fault in the system, the light may not come on at all, or the light will go on and continue, either illuminated steadily or blinking, and the unit will store fault codes indicating the nature of the fault.

4   A pair of impact-activated sensors, called the discriminating sensors, are mounted to the underside of the radiator support. The side airbags are triggered by side impact sensors mounted behind the front door panels, attached to the inner door frame.

OPERATION

5   For the airbag(s) to deploy, the discriminating sensors and the impact sensor in the sensing/diagnostic control unit must be activated. When this condition occurs, the circuit to the airbag inflator is closed and the airbag inflates. If the battery is destroyed by the impact, or is too low to power the inflator, a back-up power unit inside the SRS system provides power.

SELF-DIAGNOSIS SYSTEM

6   A self-diagnosis circuit in the SRS unit displays a light on the instrument panel when the ignition switch is turned to the On position. If the system is operating normally, the light should go out after about seven blinks. If the light doesn't come on, or doesn't go out after a short time, or if it comes on while you're driving the vehicle, or if it blinks at any time, there's a malfunction in the SRS system. Have it inspected and repaired as soon as possible. Do not attempt to troubleshoot or service the SRS system yourself. Even a small mistake could cause the SRS system to malfunction when you need it.

SERVICING COMPONENTS NEAR THE SRS SYSTEM

7   Nevertheless, there are times when you need to remove the steering wheel, radio or service other components on or near the dashboard or near other airbag system components. At these times, you'll be working around components and wire harnesses for the SRS system. Do not use electrical test equipment on airbag system wires; it could cause the airbag(s) to deploy. ALWAYS DISABLE THE SRS SYSTEM BEFORE WORKING NEAR THE SRS SYSTEM COMPONENTS OR RELATED WIRING.

DISABLING THE SRS SYSTEM

✳✳ WARNING:

Any time you are working in the vicinity of airbag wiring or components, DISABLE THE SRS SYSTEM.

8   To disable the airbag system, perform the following steps:
   a) *Turn the steering wheel to the straight-ahead position and turn the ignition switch to the Lock position, then remove the key.*
   b) *Remove the airbag fuse located in the interior fuse/relay box at the left end of the instrument panel.*
   c) *Wait at least two minutes for the back up power supply to be depleted before beginning work.*

28.8 Disconnect the passenger airbag connector behind the glove box area

d) *Remove the driver's knee bolster (see Chapter 11) and disconnect the driver's airbag connector at the steering column (see Chapter 10).*

e) *Open and drop the glove box door (see Chapter 11) and disconnect the connector to the passenger airbag (see illustration).*

f) *To disable a side impact airbag, remove the door trim panel on the side to be disabled (see Chapter 11), then disconnect the electrical connector for the side impact sensor.*

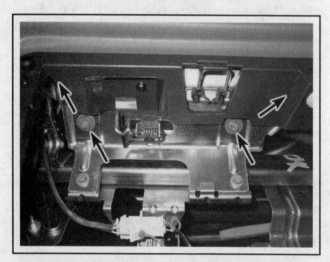

28.13 Remove the passenger airbag module mounting bolts (lower arrows) and nuts (upper arrows, hidden) and lift the module out of the instrument panel

ENABLING THE SYSTEM

9 To enable the airbag system, perform the following steps:

a) *Turn the ignition switch to the Lock position and remove the key.*

b) *Reconnect the passenger and driver's airbag connectors (or the side impact sensor connector), making sure the CPA (Connector Position Assurance) clips are in place so the connectors can't accidentally disengage.*

c) *Reinsert the airbag fuse.*

d) *Turn the ignition switch to the On position. Confirm that the airbag warning light glows for 6 to 8 seconds, then goes out, indicating the system is functioning properly.*

REMOVAL AND INSTALLATION

❋❋ WARNING:

When carrying an airbag module, keep the upholstered (or trim) side of it away from your body, and when you set it down (in an isolated area), have the upholstered (or trim) side facing up.

Driver's side airbag

10 Disable the airbag system (see Step 8). Refer to Chapter 10 for removal and installation of the driver's side airbag.

Passenger side airbag

11 Disable the airbag system (see Step 8).

12 Remove the glove box (see Chapter 11). Remove the access plate from the right end of the dash, then reach through the hole, unbolt the air outlet on the right end of the dash and take it out.

13 Remove the lower mounting bolts and upper nuts (which face forward and are accessed from underneath the instrument panel, on each side of the airbag module) and gently remove the airbag unit from the dashboard (see illustration).

❋❋ CAUTION:

The airbag assembly is heavier than it looks; use both hands when removing it from the dash.

14 Installation is the reverse of the removal procedure.

Side impact airbags

15 The side impact airbags used on some models are mounted in the side of each front seatback. Replacement of these airbags requires partial disassembly of the seat and should be done by a dealer service department or other qualified shop.

29 Wiring diagrams - general information

Since it isn't possible to include all wiring diagrams for every year and model covered by this manual, the following diagrams are those that are typical and most commonly needed.

Prior to troubleshooting any circuits, check the fuse and circuit breakers (if equipped) to make sure they're in good condition. Make sure the battery is properly charged and check the cable connections (see Chapter 1).

When checking a circuit, make sure that all connectors are clean, with no broken or loose terminals. When disconnecting a connector, do not pull on the wires. Pull only on the connector housings themselves.

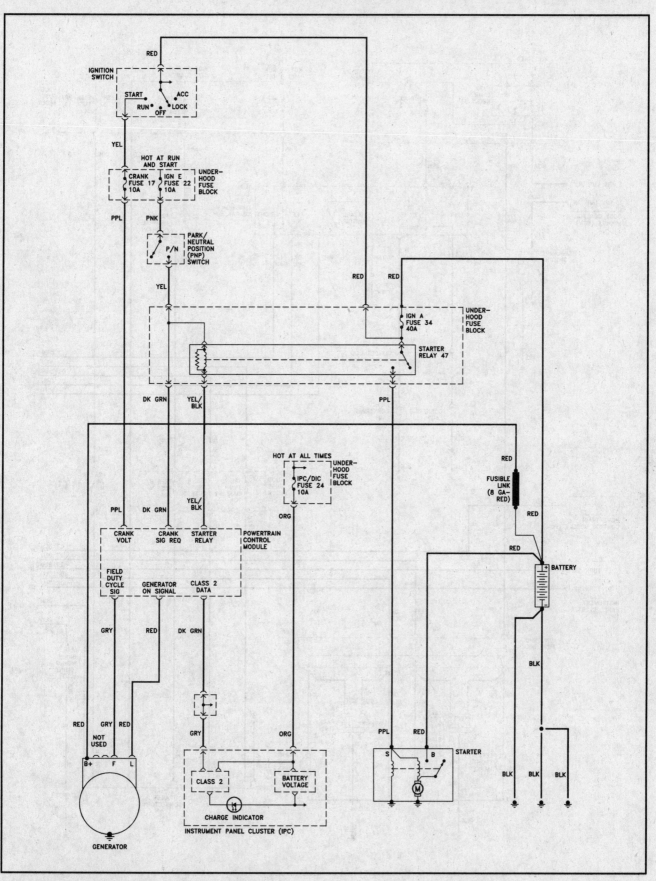

Starting and charging systems

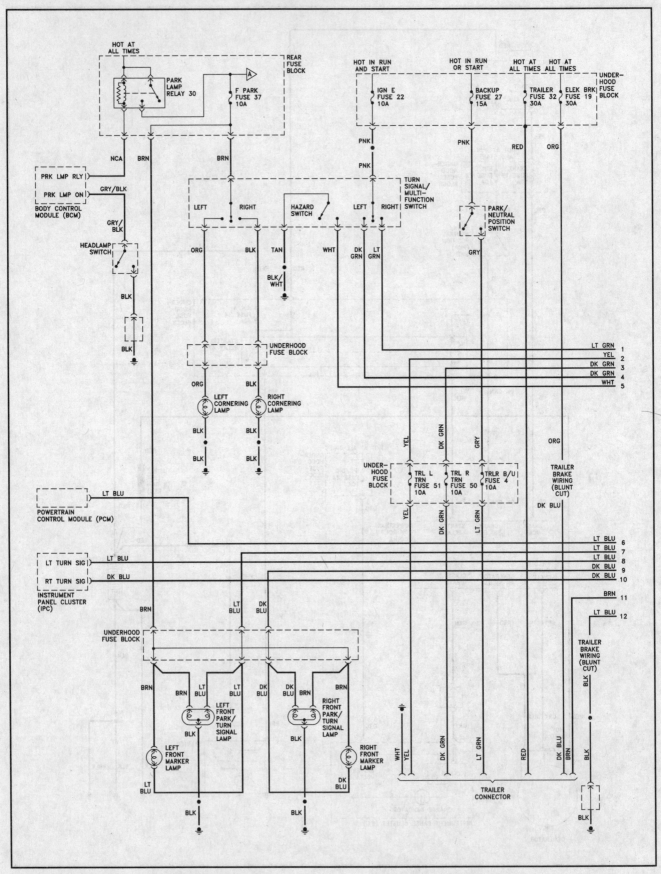

Exterior lighting system - except headlights (1 of 2)

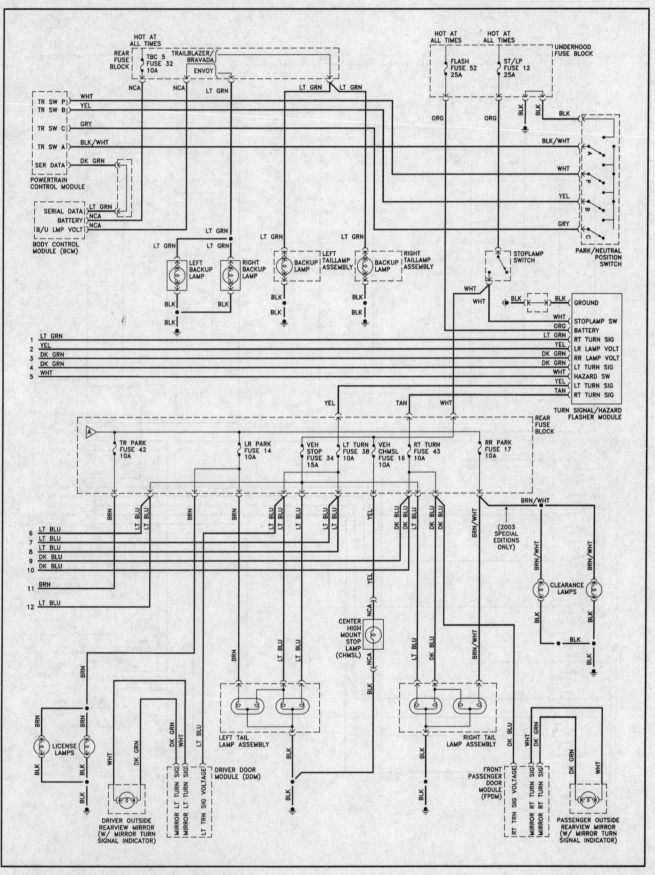

Exterior lighting system - except headlights (2 of 2)

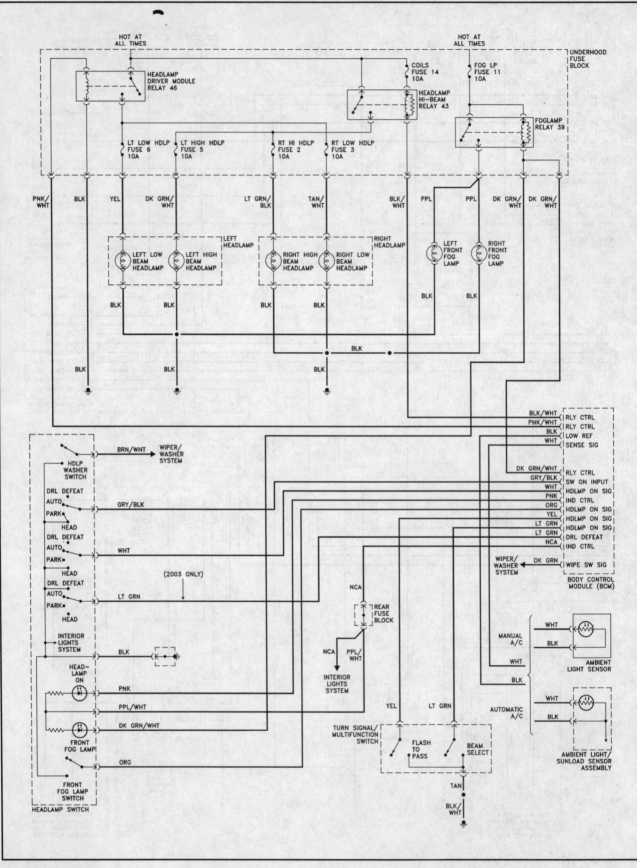

Headlight system

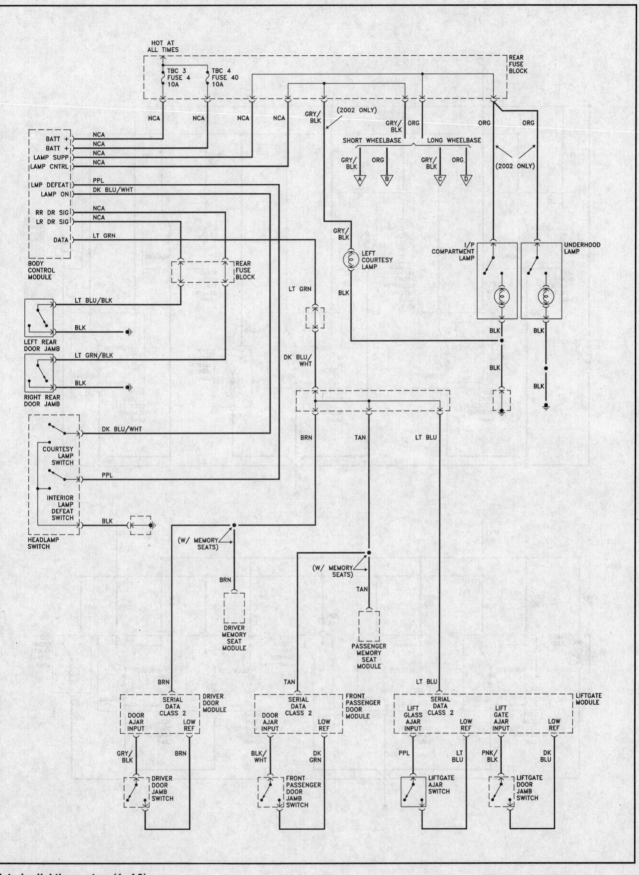

Interior lighting system (1 of 2)

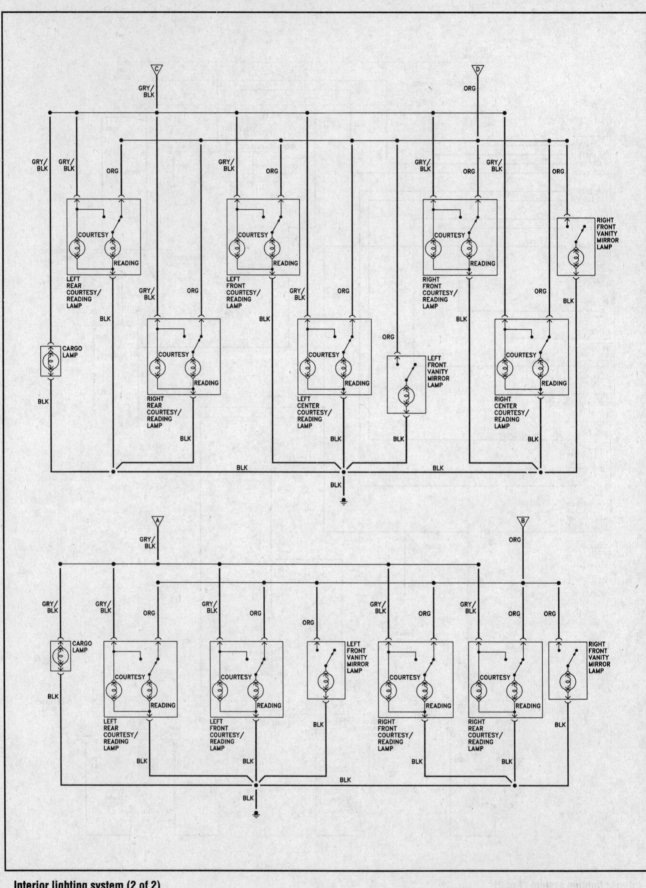

Interior lighting system (2 of 2)

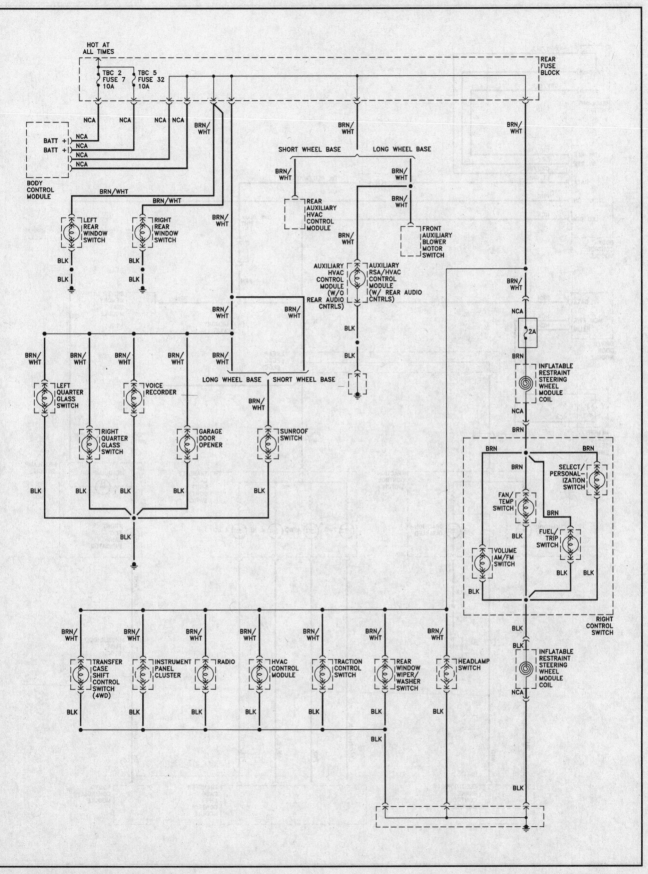

Instrument panel and switch illumination (1 of 2)

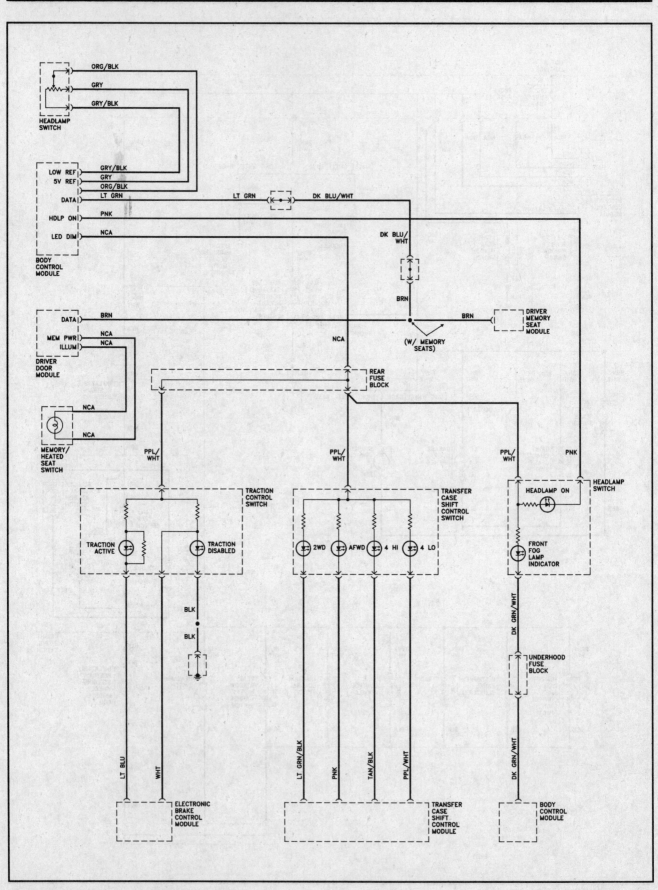

Instrument panel and switch illumination (2 of 2)

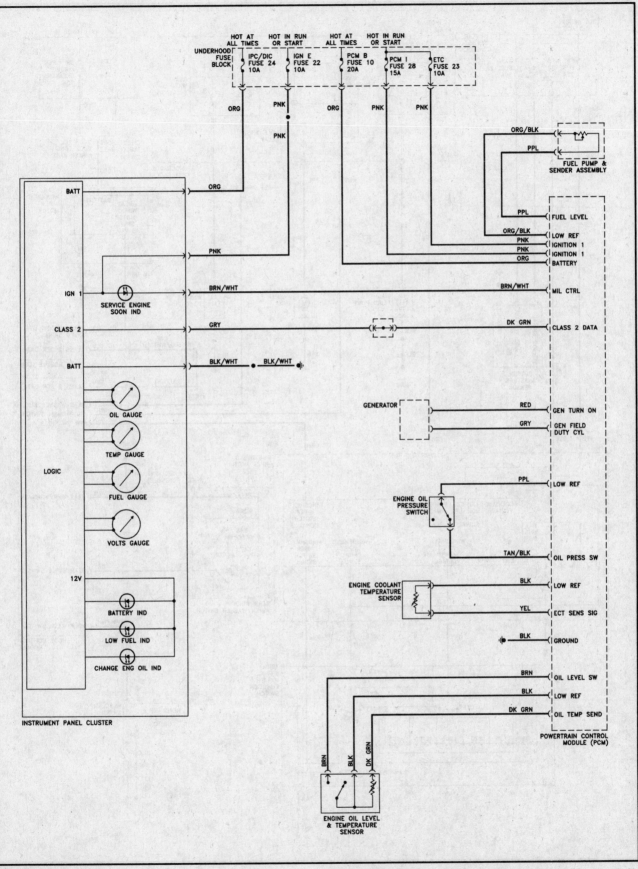

Warning systems

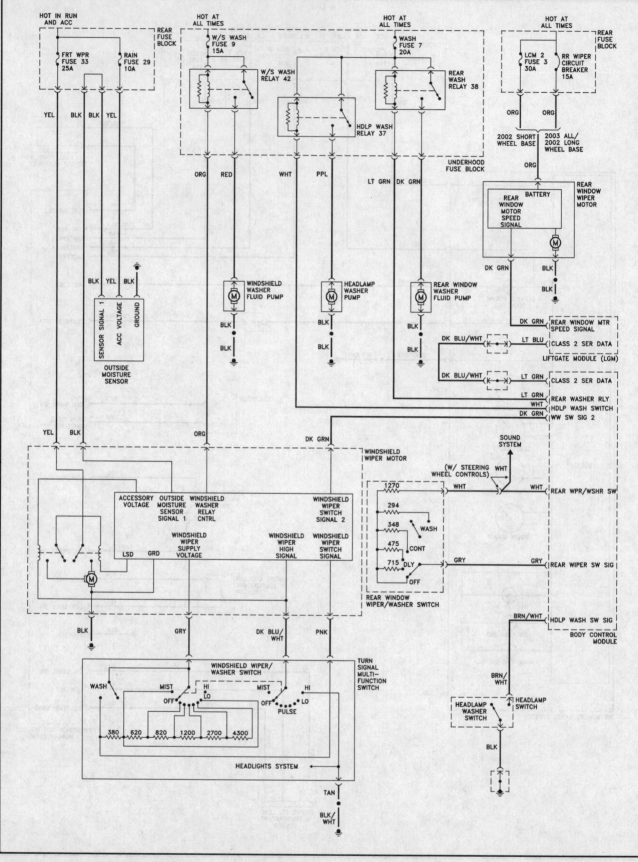

Windshield wiper and washer system

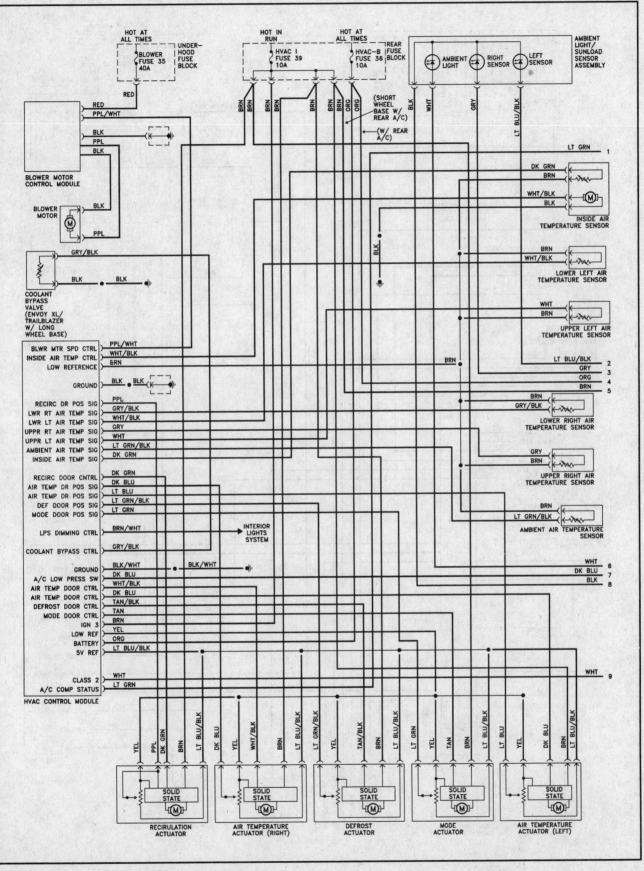

Heating and air conditioning system - automatic (1 of 3)

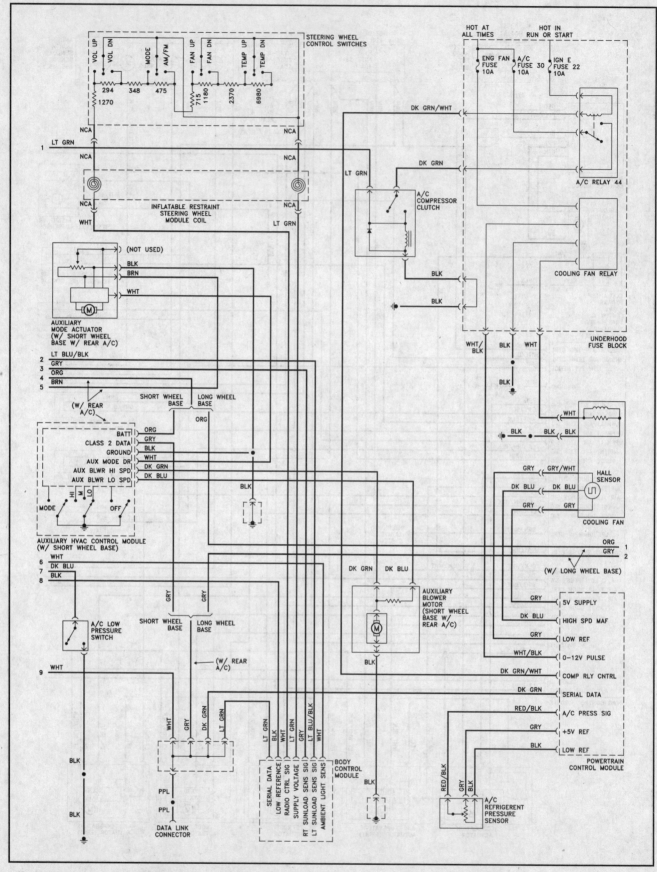

Heating and air conditioning system - automatic (2 of 3)

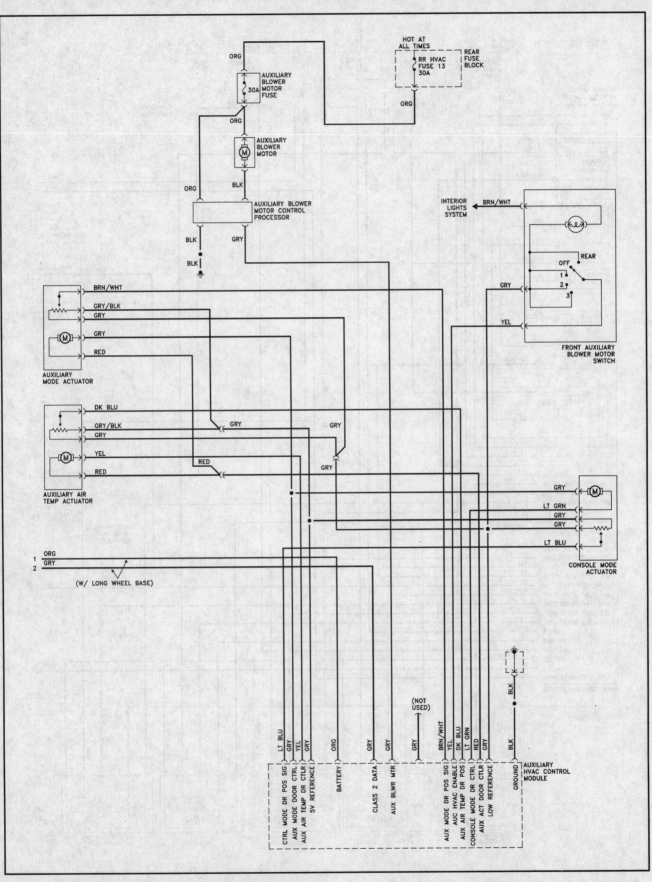

Heating and air conditioning system - automatic (3 of 3)

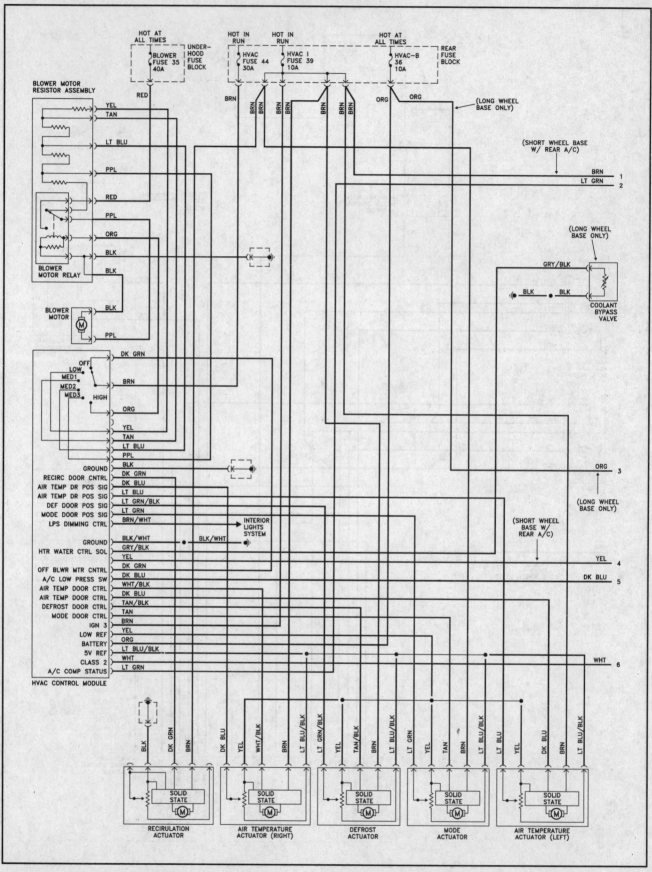

Heating and air conditioning system - manual (1 of 3)

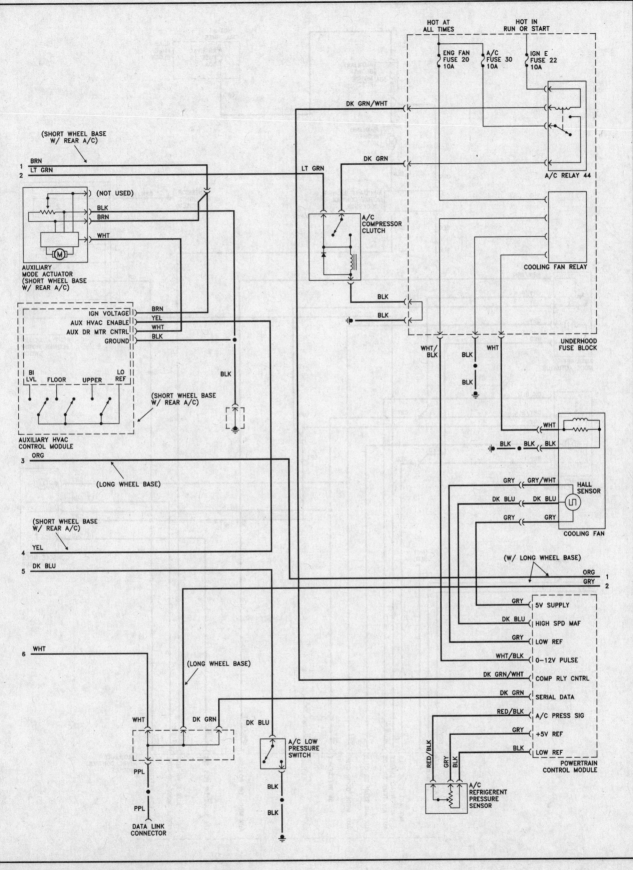

Heating and air conditioning system - manual (2 of 3)

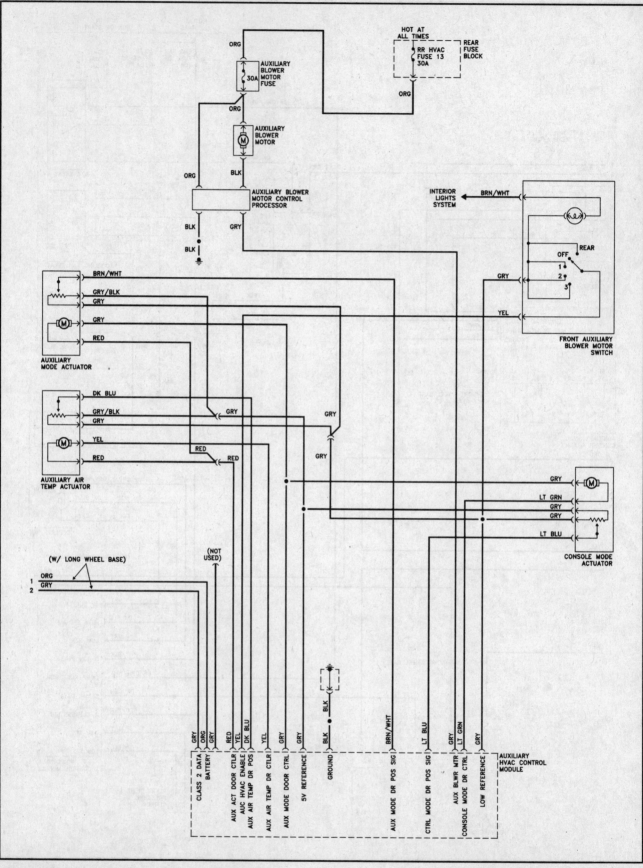

Heating and air conditioning system - manual (3 of 3)

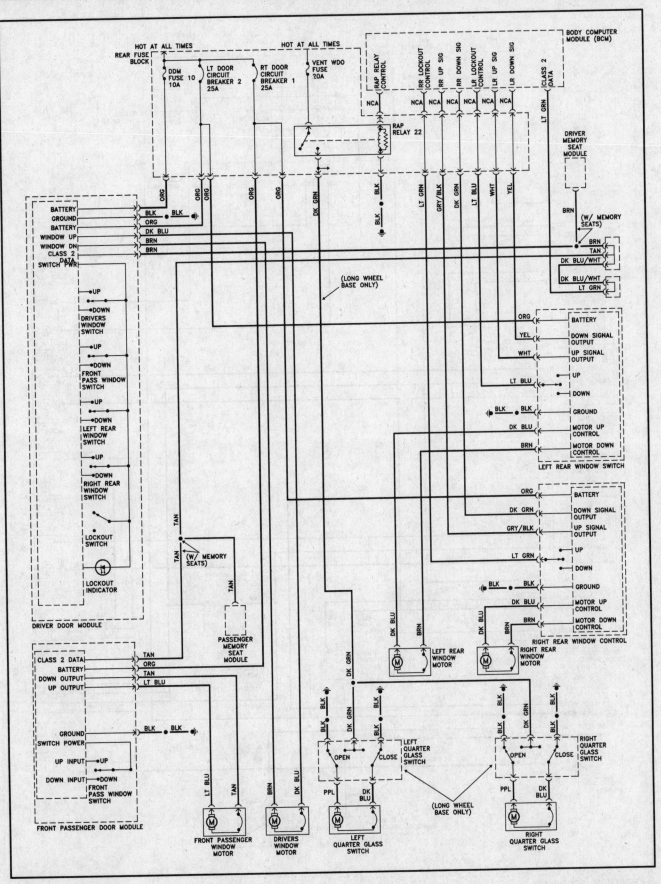

Power window system

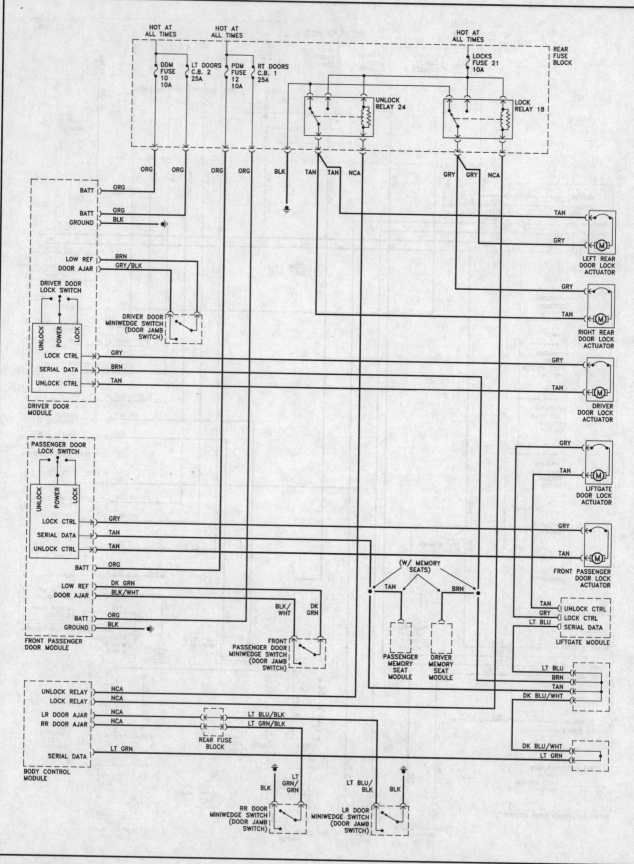

Power door lock system

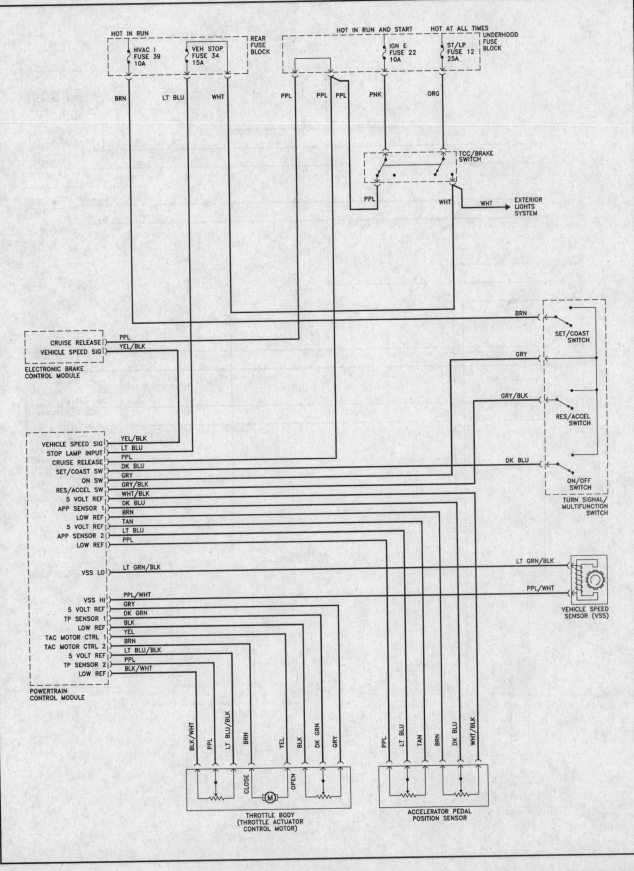

Cruise control system

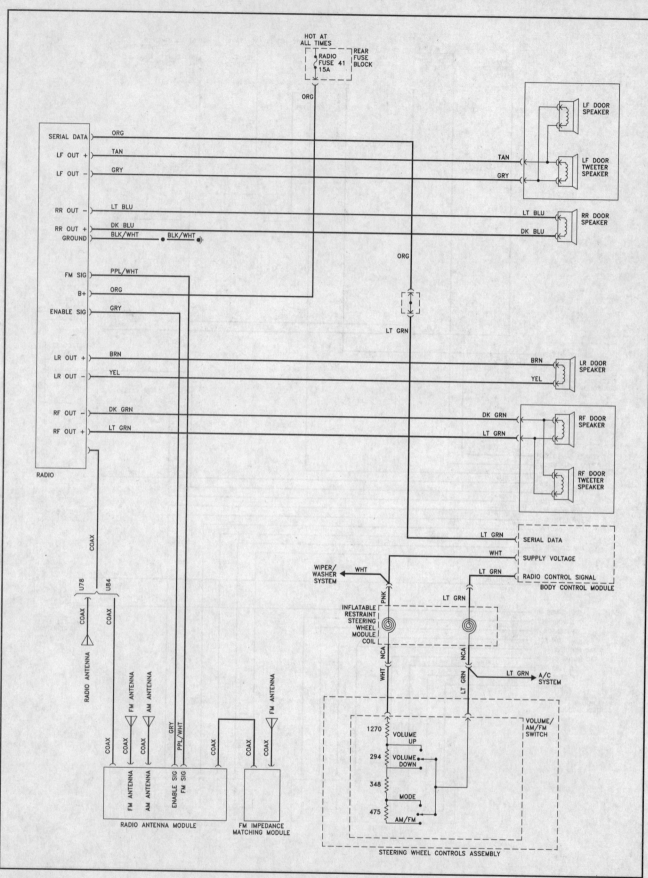

Audio system

GLOSSARY

AIR/FUEL RATIO: The ratio of air-to-gasoline by weight in the fuel mixture drawn into the engine.

AIR INJECTION: One method of reducing harmful exhaust emissions by injecting air into each of the exhaust ports of an engine. The fresh air entering the hot exhaust manifold causes any remaining fuel to be burned before it can exit the tailpipe.

ALTERNATOR: A device used for converting mechanical energy into electrical energy.

AMMETER: An instrument, calibrated in amperes, used to measure the flow of an electrical current in a circuit. Ammeters are always connected in series with the circuit being tested.

AMPERE: The rate of flow of electrical current present when one volt of electrical pressure is applied against one ohm of electrical resistance.

ANALOG COMPUTER: Any microprocessor that uses similar (analogous) electrical signals to make its calculations.

ARMATURE: A laminated, soft iron core wrapped by a wire that converts electrical energy to mechanical energy as in a motor or relay. When rotated in a magnetic field, it changes mechanical energy into electrical energy as in a generator.

ATMOSPHERIC PRESSURE: The pressure on the Earth's surface caused by the weight of the air in the atmosphere. At sea level, this pressure is 14.7 psi at 32°F (101 kPa at 0°C).

ATOMIZATION: The breaking down of a liquid into a fine mist that can be suspended in air.

AXIAL PLAY: Movement parallel to a shaft or bearing bore.

BACKFIRE: The sudden combustion of gases in the intake or exhaust system that results in a loud explosion.

BACKLASH: The clearance or play between two parts, such as meshed gears.

BACKPRESSURE: Restrictions in the exhaust system that slow the exit of exhaust gases from the combustion chamber.

BAKELITE: A heat resistant, plastic insulator material commonly used in printed circuit boards and transistorized components.

BALL BEARING: A bearing made up of hardened inner and outer races between which hardened steel balls roll.

BALLAST RESISTOR: A resistor in the primary ignition circuit that lowers voltage after the engine is started to reduce wear on ignition components.

BEARING: A friction reducing, supportive device usually located between a stationary part and a moving part.

BIMETAL TEMPERATURE SENSOR: Any sensor or switch made of two dissimilar types of metal that bend when heated or cooled due to the different expansion rates of the alloys. These types of sensors usually function as an on/off switch.

BLOWBY: Combustion gases, composed of water vapor and unburned fuel, that leak past the piston rings into the crankcase during normal engine operation. These gases are removed by the PCV system to prevent the buildup of harmful acids in the crankcase.

BRAKE PAD: A brake shoe and lining assembly used with disc brakes.

BRAKE SHOE: The backing for the brake lining. The term is, however, usually applied to the assembly of the brake backing and lining.

BUSHING: A liner, usually removable, for a bearing; an anti-friction liner used in place of a bearing.

CALIPER: A hydraulically activated device in a disc brake system, which is mounted straddling the brake rotor (disc). The caliper contains at least one piston and two brake pads. Hydraulic pressure on the piston(s) forces the pads against the rotor.

CAMSHAFT: A shaft in the engine on which are the lobes (cams) which operate the valves. The camshaft is driven by the crankshaft, via a belt, chain or gears, at one half the crankshaft speed.

CAPACITOR: A device which stores an electrical charge.

CARBON MONOXIDE (CO): A colorless, odorless gas given off as a normal byproduct of combustion. It is poisonous and extremely dangerous in confined areas, building up slowly to toxic levels without warning if adequate ventilation is not available.

CARBURETOR: A device, usually mounted on the intake manifold of an engine, which mixes the air and fuel in the proper proportion to allow even combustion.

CATALYTIC CONVERTER: A device installed in the exhaust system, like a muffler, that converts harmful byproducts of combustion into carbon dioxide and water vapor by means of a heat-producing chemical reaction.

CENTRIFUGAL ADVANCE: A mechanical method of advancing the spark timing by using flyweights in the distributor that react to centrifugal force generated by the distributor shaft rotation.

CHECK VALVE: Any one-way valve installed to permit the flow of air, fuel or vacuum in one direction only.

CHOKE: A device, usually a moveable valve, placed in the intake path of a carburetor to restrict the flow of air.

CIRCUIT: Any unbroken path through which an electrical current can flow. Also used to describe fuel flow in some instances.

CIRCUIT BREAKER: A switch which protects an electrical circuit from overload by opening the circuit when the current flow exceeds a predetermined level. Some circuit breakers must be reset manually, while most reset automatically.

COIL (IGNITION): A transformer in the ignition circuit which steps up the voltage provided to the spark plugs.

COMBINATION MANIFOLD: An assembly which includes both the intake and exhaust manifolds in one casting.

COMBINATION VALVE: A device used in some fuel systems that routes fuel vapors to a charcoal storage canister instead of venting them into the atmosphere. The valve relieves fuel tank pressure and allows fresh air into the tank as the fuel level drops to prevent a vapor lock situation.

COMPRESSION RATIO: The comparison of the total volume of the cylinder and combustion chamber with the piston at BDC and the piston at TDC.

CONDENSER: 1. An electrical device which acts to store an electrical charge, preventing voltage surges. 2. A radiator-like device in the air conditioning system in which refrigerant gas condenses into a liquid, giving off heat.

CONDUCTOR: Any material through which an electrical current can be transmitted easily.

CONTINUITY: Continuous or complete circuit. Can be checked with an ohmmeter.

COUNTERSHAFT: An intermediate shaft which is rotated by a mainshaft and transmits, in turn, that rotation to a working part.

CRANKCASE: The lower part of an engine in which the crankshaft and related parts operate.

CRANKSHAFT: The main driving shaft of an engine which receives reciprocating motion from the pistons and converts it to rotary motion.

CYLINDER: In an engine, the round hole in the engine block in which the piston(s) ride.

CYLINDER BLOCK: The main structural member of an engine in which is found the cylinders, crankshaft and other principal parts.

CYLINDER HEAD: The detachable portion of the engine, usually fastened to the top of the cylinder block and containing all or most of the combustion chambers. On overhead valve engines, it contains the valves and their operating parts. On overhead cam engines, it contains the camshaft as well.

DEAD CENTER: The extreme top or bottom of the piston stroke.

DETONATION: An unwanted explosion of the air/fuel mixture in the combustion chamber caused by excess heat and compression, advanced timing, or an overly lean mixture. Also referred to as "ping".

DIAPHRAGM: A thin, flexible wall separating two cavities, such as in a vacuum advance unit.

DIESELING: A condition in which hot spots in the combustion chamber cause the engine to run on after the key is turned off.

DIFFERENTIAL: A geared assembly which allows the transmission of motion between drive axles, giving one axle the ability to turn faster than the other.

DIODE: An electrical device that will allow current to flow in one direction only.

DISC BRAKE: A hydraulic braking assembly consisting of a brake disc, or rotor, mounted on an axle, and a caliper assembly containing, usually two brake pads which are activated by hydraulic pressure. The pads are forced against the sides of the disc, creating friction which slows the vehicle.

DISTRIBUTOR: A mechanically driven device on an engine which is responsible for electrically firing the spark plug at a predetermined point of the piston stroke.

DOWEL PIN: A pin, inserted in mating holes in two different parts allowing those parts to maintain a fixed relationship.

DRUM BRAKE: A braking system which consists of two brake shoes and one or two wheel cylinders, mounted on a fixed backing plate, and a brake drum, mounted on an axle, which revolves around the assembly.

DWELL: The rate, measured in degrees of shaft rotation, at which an electrical circuit cycles on and off.

ELECTRONIC CONTROL UNIT (ECU): Ignition module, module, amplifier or igniter. See Module for definition.

ELECTRONIC IGNITION: A system in which the timing and firing of the spark plugs is controlled by an electronic control unit, usually called a module. These systems have no points or condenser.

END-PLAY: The measured amount of axial movement in a shaft.

ENGINE: A device that converts heat into mechanical energy.

EXHAUST MANIFOLD: A set of cast passages or pipes which conduct exhaust gases from the engine.

FEELER GAUGE: A blade, usually metal, or precisely predetermined thickness, used to measure the clearance between two parts.

FIRING ORDER: The order in which combustion occurs in the cylinders of an engine. Also the order in which spark is distributed to the plugs by the distributor.

FLOODING: The presence of too much fuel in the intake manifold and combustion chamber which prevents the air/fuel mixture from firing, thereby causing a no-start situation.

FLYWHEEL: A disc shaped part bolted to the rear end of the crankshaft. Around the outer perimeter is affixed the ring gear. The starter drive engages the ring gear, turning the flywheel, which rotates the crankshaft, imparting the initial starting motion to the engine.

FOOT POUND (ft. lbs. or sometimes, ft.lb.): The amount of energy or work needed to raise an item weighing one pound, a distance of one foot.

FUSE: A protective device in a circuit which prevents circuit overload by breaking the circuit when a specific amperage is present. The device is constructed around a strip or wire of a lower amperage rating than the circuit it is designed to protect. When an amperage higher than that stamped on the fuse is present in the circuit, the strip or wire melts, opening the circuit.

GEAR RATIO: The ratio between the number of teeth on meshing gears.

GENERATOR: A device which converts mechanical energy into electrical energy.

HEAT RANGE: The measure of a spark plug's ability to dissipate heat from its firing end. The higher the heat range, the hotter the plug fires.

HUB: The center part of a wheel or gear.

HYDROCARBON (HC): Any chemical compound made up of hydrogen and carbon. A major pollutant formed by the engine as a byproduct of combustion.

HYDROMETER: An instrument used to measure the specific gravity of a solution.

INCH POUND (inch lbs.; sometimes in.lb. or in. lbs.): One twelfth of a foot pound.

INDUCTION: A means of transferring electrical energy in the form of a magnetic field. Principle used in the ignition coil to increase voltage.

INJECTOR: A device which receives metered fuel under relatively low pressure and is activated to inject the fuel into the engine under relatively high pressure at a predetermined time.

INPUT SHAFT: The shaft to which torque is applied, usually carrying the driving gear or gears.

INTAKE MANIFOLD: A casting of passages or pipes used to conduct air or a fuel/air mixture to the cylinders.

JOURNAL: The bearing surface within which a shaft operates.

KEY: A small block usually fitted in a notch between a shaft and a hub to prevent slippage of the two parts.

MANIFOLD: A casting of passages or set of pipes which connect the cylinders to an inlet or outlet source.

MANIFOLD VACUUM: Low pressure in an engine intake manifold formed just below the throttle plates. Manifold vacuum is highest at idle and drops under acceleration.

MASTER CYLINDER: The primary fluid pressurizing device in a hydraulic system. In automotive use, it is found in brake and hydraulic clutch systems and is pedal activated, either directly or, in a power brake system, through the power booster.

MODULE: Electronic control unit, amplifier or igniter of solid state or integrated design which controls the current flow in the ignition primary circuit based on input from the pick-up coil. When the module opens the primary circuit, high secondary voltage is induced in the coil.

NEEDLE BEARING: A bearing which consists of a number (usually a large number) of long, thin rollers.

OHM: (Ω) The unit used to measure the resistance of conductor-to-electrical flow. One ohm is the amount of resistance that limits current flow to one ampere in a circuit with one volt of pressure.

OHMMETER: An instrument used for measuring the resistance, in ohms, in an electrical circuit.

OUTPUT SHAFT: The shaft which transmits torque from a device, such as a transmission.

OVERDRIVE: A gear assembly which produces more shaft revolutions than that transmitted to it.

OVERHEAD CAMSHAFT (OHC): An engine configuration in which the camshaft is mounted on top of the cylinder head and operates the valve either directly or by means of rocker arms.

OVERHEAD VALVE (OHV): An engine configuration in which all of the valves are located in the cylinder head and the camshaft is located in the cylinder block. The camshaft operates the valves via lifters and pushrods.

OXIDES OF NITROGEN (NOx): Chemical compounds of nitrogen produced as a byproduct of combustion. They combine with hydrocarbons to produce smog.

OXYGEN SENSOR: Use with the feedback system to sense the presence of oxygen in the exhaust gas and signal the computer which can reference the voltage signal to an air/fuel ratio.

PINION: The smaller of two meshing gears.

PISTON RING: An open-ended ring with fits into a groove on the outer diameter of the piston. Its chief function is to form a seal between the piston and cylinder wall. Most automotive pistons have three rings: two for compression sealing; one for oil sealing.

PRELOAD: A predetermined load placed on a bearing during assembly or by adjustment.

PRIMARY CIRCUIT: the low voltage side of the ignition system which consists of the ignition switch, ballast resistor or resistance wire, bypass, coil, electronic control unit and pick-up coil as well as the connecting wires and harnesses.

PRESS FIT: The mating of two parts under pressure, due to the inner diameter of one being smaller than the outer diameter of the other, or vice versa; an interference fit.

RACE: The surface on the inner or outer ring of a bearing on which the balls, needles or rollers move.

REGULATOR: A device which maintains the amperage and/or voltage levels of a circuit at predetermined values.

RELAY: A switch which automatically opens and/or closes a circuit.

RESISTANCE: The opposition to the flow of current through a circuit or electrical device, and is measured in ohms. Resistance is equal to the voltage divided by the amperage.

RESISTOR: A device, usually made of wire, which offers a preset amount of resistance in an electrical circuit.

RING GEAR: The name given to a ring-shaped gear attached to a differential case, or affixed to a flywheel or as part of a planetary gear set.

ROLLER BEARING: A bearing made up of hardened inner and outer races between which hardened steel rollers move.

ROTOR: 1. The disc-shaped part of a disc brake assembly, upon which the brake pads bear; also called, brake disc. 2. The device mounted atop the distributor shaft, which passes current to the distributor cap tower contacts.

SECONDARY CIRCUIT: The high voltage side of the ignition system, usually above 20,000 volts. The secondary includes the ignition coil, coil wire, distributor cap and rotor, spark plug wires and spark plugs.

SENDING UNIT: A mechanical, electrical, hydraulic or electro-magnetic device which transmits information to a gauge.

SENSOR: Any device designed to measure engine operating conditions or ambient pressures and temperatures. Usually electronic in nature and designed to send a voltage signal to an on-board computer, some sensors may operate as a simple on/off switch or they may provide a variable voltage signal (like a potentiometer) as conditions or measured parameters change.

SHIM: Spacers of precise, predetermined thickness used between parts to establish a proper working relationship.

SLAVE CYLINDER: In automotive use, a device in the hydraulic clutch system which is activated by hydraulic force, disengaging the clutch.

SOLENOID: A coil used to produce a magnetic field, the effect of which is to produce work.

SPARK PLUG: A device screwed into the combustion chamber of a spark ignition engine. The basic construction is a conductive core inside of a ceramic insulator, mounted in an outer conductive base. An electrical charge from the spark plug wire travels along the conductive core and jumps a preset air gap to a grounding point or points at the end of the conductive base. The resultant spark ignites the fuel/air mixture in the combustion chamber.

SPLINES: Ridges machined or cast onto the outer diameter of a shaft or inner diameter of a bore to enable parts to mate without rotation.

TACHOMETER: A device used to measure the rotary speed of an engine, shaft, gear, etc., usually in rotations per minute.

THERMOSTAT: A valve, located in the cooling system of an engine, which is closed when cold and opens gradually in response to engine heating, controlling the temperature of the coolant and rate of coolant flow.

TOP DEAD CENTER (TDC): The point at which the piston reaches the top of its travel on the compression stroke.

TORQUE: The twisting force applied to an object.

TORQUE CONVERTER: A turbine used to transmit power from a driving member to a driven member via hydraulic action, providing changes in drive ratio and torque. In automotive use, it links the driveplate at the rear of the engine to the automatic transmission.

TRANSDUCER: A device used to change a force into an electrical signal.

TRANSISTOR: A semi-conductor component which can be actuated by a small voltage to perform an electrical switching function.

TUNE-UP: A regular maintenance function, usually associated with the replacement and adjustment of parts and components in the electrical and fuel systems of a vehicle for the purpose of attaining optimum performance.

TURBOCHARGER: An exhaust driven pump which compresses intake air and forces it into the combustion chambers at higher than atmospheric pressures. The increased air pressure allows more fuel to be burned and results in increased horsepower being produced.

VACUUM ADVANCE: A device which advances the ignition timing in response to increased engine vacuum.

VACUUM GAUGE: An instrument used to measure the presence of vacuum in a chamber.

VALVE: A device which control the pressure, direction of flow or rate of flow of a liquid or gas.

VALVE CLEARANCE: The measured gap between the end of the valve stem and the rocker arm, cam lobe or follower that activates the valve.

VISCOSITY: The rating of a liquid's internal resistance to flow.

VOLTMETER: An instrument used for measuring electrical force in units called volts. Voltmeters are always connected parallel with the circuit being tested.

WHEEL CYLINDER: Found in the automotive drum brake assembly, it is a device, actuated by hydraulic pressure, which, through internal pistons, pushes the brake shoes outward against the drums.

A

MASTER INDEX

Notes